THE BLUE GUIDES

Statue of Spring by Pietro Francavilla on the parapet of Ponte Santa Trìnita

BLUE GUIDE

FLORENCE

Alta Macadam

*Street atlas and maps and plans
by John Flower*

A & C Black
London

W W Norton
New York

Fifth edition 1991

Published by A & C Black (Publishers) Limited
35 Bedford Row, London WC1R 4JH

ISBN   0–7136–3385–9

A CIP catalogue record for this book
is available from the British Library

Published in the United States of America by
W W Norton & Company, Inc.
500 Fifth Avenue, New York, NY 10110

Published simultaneously in Canada by
Penguin Books Canada Limited
2801 John Street, Markham, Ontario L3R 1B4

ISBN   0–393–30754–9   USA

Alta Macadam learnt the craft of writing Blue Guides when she
became assistant in 1970 to Stuart Rossiter, distinguished editor of
many Guides in the series. She has lived in Florence since 1973 and,
as author of the Blue Guides to *Northern Italy, Rome, Venice, Sicily,
Florence*, and the forthcoming *Tuscany and Umbria*, she travels
extensively in Italy every year in order to revise new editions of the
books. Combined with work on writing the guides she also spent four
years updating the well-known Italian photo-library of Alinari, and
now works part-time for Harvard University at the Villa I Tatti in
Florence.

Typeset by CRB Typesetting Services, Ely, Cambs.

Reproduced, printed and bound in Great Britain by
BPCC Hazell Books
Aylesbury, Bucks, England
Member of BPCC Ltd.

PREFACE

This edition of 'Blue Guide Florence' has been expanded to include descriptions of many of the lesser known palaces, churches, gardens, oratories, and cloisters, even though not all of them are open regularly to the public. The guide has been written for those with time to visit the city in depth. On days when Florence is particularly crowded with bus loads of tourists or school parties, the serious visitor will wish to seek out the more peaceful parts of the city. The immediate environs, which are a very special feature of Florence, are also described in more detail in this edition: on hot crowded days in the city, a walk in Settignano or up to Bellosguardo, or a visit to one of the Medici villas can be perhaps as rewarding and as important to the understanding of the city as a visit to one of the famous museums. In recent years several new parks have been opened to the public, including Villa il Ventaglio, Villa Strozzi, and an extension of the horticultural gardens, as well as (in summer) the huge Villa Demidoff in Pratolino.

Since the last edition the State Archives, which occupied more than two thirds of the Uffizi building, have been moved, and work is to begin in stages to reorganise the famous picture gallery. Over ambitious projects from the past have, thankfully, been modified including the wise decision to leave the entrance to the gallery through Piazza degli Uffizi and use the alterations already carried out at the back of the building in Via de' Castellani as an exit. The Casa Buonarroti has recently been rearranged, and in 1990 two new rooms were opened in the Bargello, with a delightful display of the Medici collection of medals. Careful work is in progress at the Museo Stibbert where the great collector's original arrangement is being restored. In Fiesole, a remarkable collection of Greek vases (the Antiquarium Costantini) is now on display in a building above new excavations of the Roman city, and the Museo Bandini has been reopened.

Much restoration work proceeds in the city under the excellent guidance of the local restoration office and the Opificio delle Pietre Dure. Not only famous masterpieces such as Duccio's Maestà in the Uffizi, Masaccio's frescoes in the Carmine, and Donatello's statue of Judith have been splendidly restored, but also numerous lesser known works in churches and fresco cycles in cloisters. Michelangelo's statues in the Sagrestia Nuova of San Lorenzo have been beautifully cleaned.

In 1989 it looked as if a huge new urban development was going to be allowed (4 million cubic metres, including tower blocks 50 metres high) on the north-western outskirts of the city on land owned by the Fiat and Fondiaria companies. This 'urban sprawl', so familiar in other large cities, was seen by many people as a threat to the character of the city and a negation of enlightened town planning. A surprise decision taken at the very last minute by the local government stopped the project to the great relief of all those interested in safeguarding the future of this remarkable city. Another positive step was taken in 1988 when a determined member of the local government decided to close the whole of the centre of the city within the ring-road (along the line of the old city walls) to traffic (except for residents). This has been saluted as a major step forward in dealing with pollution and has been an unqualified success, even though the problem of car parking still has to be solved.

However the local government and Italian authorities have been unable to control satisfactorily the work in the very centre of Florence, Piazza Signoria, part of which at the time of writing has been sequestered by the magistrates pending an inquiry to ascertain whether permanent damage has been caused to the appearance of the square. A mandate was received to restore the 18C paving stones and after years of disruptive work (and delays caused by archaeological excavations), and scandals, including the accusation that the original paving stones had been taken up and sold, it is evident that the end result is highly disappointing. It seems incredible that the traditional skill of Florentine stonemasons could not have been called upon to restore in a satisfactory way this historic square.

Ghiberti's Doors of Paradise were removed in 1990 and replaced by casts: it has been declared by all the experts that sculptures can no longer be replaced in the open after restoration because of the damage caused by the polluted air.

The official tourist offices are being reorganised and amalgamated as in the rest of Italy and, despite the effort of a few dedicated individuals in the old Azienda Autonoma, there is at the moment a great lack in the city of informed efficient tourist offices.

In the preparation of the guide the author is particularly grateful to *Magnolia Scudieri* of the local restoration office and Museo di San Marco, who provided much information about recent restorations. For the preparation of the revised text for the Museo Stibbert *Lionello Boccia* was extremely helpful, and *Susanne Probst* kindly accompanied the author on a detailed visit to the museum. At the Opificio delle Pietre Dure *Anna Maria Giusti* took the trouble to provide much information about restoration work in progress. *Lita Medri* was most helpful about the Boboli gardens. At the Azienda Autonoma del Turismo *Fiorella Sica* and *Isa Carapelli Scapigliati* kindly helped check the details in the practical information section of the guide. As in the past, the author is indebted to *Carlo Colella* for his advice about restaurants in Florence. Numerous friends who supplied useful information for the book include *Françoise Chiarini*, *Cristina* and *Marco Lombardi*, *Bruce Boucher*, and *Edward Chaney*.

A NOTE ON BLUE GUIDES

The Blue Guides series began in 1918 when Muirhead Guide-Books Limited published 'Blue Guide London and its Environs'. Finlay and James Muirhead already had extensive experience of guide-book publishing: before the First World War they had been the editors of the English editions of the German Baedekers, and by 1915 they had acquired the copyright of most of the famous 'Red' handbooks from John Murray.

An agreement made with the French publishing house Hachette et Cie in 1917 led to the translation of Muirhead's London Guide, which became the first 'Guide Bleu'—Hachette had previously published the blue-covered 'Guides Joanne'. Subsequently, Hachette's 'Guide Bleu Paris et ses Environs' was adapted and published in London by Muirhead. The collaboration between the two publishing houses continued until 1933.

In 1931 Ernest Benn took over the Blue Guides, appointing Russell Muirhead, Finlay Muirhead's son, editor in 1934. The Muirheads' connection with Blue Guides ended in 1963 when Stuart Rossiter, who had been working on the Guides since 1954, became house editor, revising and compiling several of the books himself.

The Blue Guides are now published by A & C Black, who acquired Ernest Benn in 1984, so continuing the tradition of guide-book publishing which began in 1826 with 'Black's Economical Tourist of Scotland'. The Blue Guide series continues to grow: there are now more than 40 titles in print with revised editions appearing regularly and many new Blue Guides in preparation.

'Blue Guides' is a registered trade mark.

EXPLANATIONS

Type. Smaller type is used for historical and preliminary paragraphs, and (generally speaking) for descriptions in greater detail or of minor importance.

Asterisks indicate points of special interest or excellence.

Heights are given in metres.

Abbreviations. In addition to generally accepted and self-explanatory abbreviations, the following occur in the guide:

Adm. = Admission
APT   = Azienda di Promozione Turistica
C   = century
c   = circa
ENIT = Ente Nazionale Italiano per il Turismo
fest. = *festa*, or festival (i.e. holiday)
fl.   = floruit (flourished)
l.   = lira (pl. lire)
Pl.   = atlas plan
R.   = room(s)
Rte   = Route
tel. = telephone

For glossary see p 40.

References in the text (Pl.1;1) are to the 16-page Atlas at the back of the book, the first figure referring to the page, the second to the square. Ground plan references are given as a bracketed single figure or letter.

CONTENTS

ENVIRONS OF FLORENCE   *Page*

Maps and Plans

THE FLORENTINE RENAISSANCE

by **MARCO CHIARINI**
Director of the Pitti Gallery

The City. Seen from the circle of hills which surrounds the city, Florence gives an impression of completeness of design, its medieval and Renaissance architecture dominated by Brunelleschi's immense terracotta dome 'erta sopra e cieli, ampla da coprire chon sua ombra tucti e popoli toscani' ('Soaring above in the sky, large enough to cover with its shadow all the Tuscan people'), as Leon Battista Alberti described it in his 'Trattato della Pittura' with its celebrated dedication to 'Filippo di Ser Brunellesco'. The city is a perfect whole to which nothing can be added or removed without altering the harmony which it has been given by man over a span of about eight centuries. In perhaps no other city are the intention of man and the design of nature so bound up together. The city is born out of the valley, its monuments enclosed by an amphitheatre of hills. Its architecture has been created by the human mind in imitation of its natural setting, and Brunelleschi cemented this relationship for ever with his great cupola, a poetic masterpiece of engineering.

I advise any visitor, before penetrating the streets and piazze of the city, to take himself 'without the city gates', up onto the circle of hills, so as to perceive the physical unity which embraces the spirit of Florentine art. Probably the most remarkable of all Florentine views is that from the hillside of Bellosguardo, approached by a winding road from which the natural landscape can be seen blending with that of the city. The view from the top of the hill takes in the façades of the most important buildings in an almost unconscious summary of the beauties of Florence, to paraphrase one of the oldest guides to the city. Thousands of modest roofs covered by simple terracotta tiles remind us of the humble but highly skilled craftsmanship which is still an important characteristic of daily life in the city. Above these rise the principal monuments of the city which testify to the presence of exceptional artists, from the Romanesque period onwards, who made Florence the centre to which the art world looked for inspiration and guidance.

The Birth of Florentine Art. The continuity of figurative language which accompanies the evolution of Florentine art is its most distinctive feature—not only in architecture, sculpture, and painting, but also in the decorative arts. This logical development results in a clearly defined style of a consistently high standard. It is as if there were no break in time between the works of the anonymous architects of the Baptistery, Santi Apostoli, and San Miniato al Monte, and the later buildings of Brunelleschi, Michelozzo and Michelangelo: they all represent an unmistakable, uniquely Florentine style. This style is based on forms of such essential simplicity that it lends itself to endless repetitions and variations, without ever becoming stale, reaffirming, on the banks of the Arno, the simple perfection of the civilisation of Athens at the time of Pericles and Phidias.

The orientation of the centre of the city, based on the Roman encampment which preceded it, still follows a plan according to the cardinal points: the religious centre with the Duomo and the political centre with the town hall and its piazza at either end of one axis; and on the other axis the two most important conventual houses, the Dominicans in Santa Maria Novella to the NW, and the Franciscans in Santa Croce to the SE. In these two different worlds some of the most important developments in the artistic history of the city have taken place over the centuries.

The first buildings in Florence to signal the birth of a characteristic style, with a clarity of design based on classical elegance, are the Baptistery, Santi Apostoli, and San Miniato al Monte, built during the eleventh and twelfth centuries. The octagonal Baptistery surmounted by a dome and lantern, clearly takes its inspiration from the centrally planned Pantheon in Rome. It became the prototype for the centralised churches of the Renaissance which were modelled on Brunelleschi's incomplete project for the church of Santa Maria degli Angeli. The green and white marble facing of the Baptistery emphasises the geometric design of the structure, and this relationship between structure and decoration had a fundamental influence on contemporary architecture as well as later buildings, such as the Duomo and the 15C façade of Santa Maria Novella designed by Alberti. The rhythmical arrangement of architectural elements which characterises Florentine Romanesque architecture is applied with particular elegance to the distinctive, luminous façade of San Miniato al Monte. Here the beautiful arches show a study of proportion and an understanding of harmonic rhythms which were later important elements in Brunelleschi's artistic language. The same attempt to find a rhythmic proportion, rescinding the gigantic forms which characterised the architecture of the late Roman Empire, can be seen in the interior of Santi Apostoli where the double line of columns, derived from the basilican form, is surmounted by Romanesque arches in a spatial synthesis which was to find its ultimate refinement in the basilicas of Brunelleschi.

But it was at the end of the thirteenth century, possibly because of the Gothic influence spreading throughout Europe from France, that a series of building and decorative enterprises was started in Florence, which had no equal in any other part of Italy. They not only gave a new face and character to the city, but also determined the beginnings of a new figurative language in art which would eventually become common to other Italian cities. At the end of the 13C the great religious and civic monuments of the city were begun; building continued in the 14C, and, in some cases, such as Santa Maria Novella, was not completed until the 15C. The 13C city was expanding both politically and economically, despite the strife between Guelfs (supporters of the Pope) and Ghibellines (supporters of the Emperor). Thanks to its flourishing commerce and the shrewdness of Florentine businessmen Florence took up a central position in the Tuscan economy. The rich merchants, rather than the aristocracy, now began to come to the forefront of the political scene, and they determined the new plan of the city which was seeing its commerce grow alongside its territorial expansion. The religious orders, too, had their moment of particular importance in the civic and cultural history of the city, and the two convents of Santa Maria Novella and Santa Croce were to become the scene of the great triumphs of Florentine painting. These two 14C buildings offered space for the great families of Florence to build the chapels which would bear their names and be dedicated to their patron saints, and soon rich citizens were competing with each other to have their chapels decorated by the best artists of the day. In the sombre but elegant architecture of these two churches the Gothic style is evident, but it is reinterpreted in the Florentine manner with the accent on perspective and spatial relationships, and on light, which was absent in the great cathedrals of the North. On the white walls of the side aisles and chapels, fresco cycles illustrated some of the important features and stories of religion for the people. The technique of fresco was to play a vital part in Florentine art throughout at least two centuries.

Cimabue and Giotto, on their return from Assisi where they had decorated the transept and nave of the upper church, and had there been influenced by the classical tendencies in the work of the Roman artists involved in the same project, were the creators of a new pictorial language which, according to Vasari, translated painting 'from Greek to Latin'. A memorable event of the time, related by the same historian, was the people's procession in honour of **Cimabue**'s Maestà, painted for the church of Santa Trìnita (now in the Uffizi), around the year 1285, an event which signalled the advent of a new spirituality in pictorial forms, unknown in the Byzantine art which had been predominant until then in Europe. This altarpiece and the one painted at about the same time for the Rucellai chapel in Santa Maria Novella by the Sienese master, **Duccio**, mark the birth of the two important schools of Florentine and Sienese painting, which were to contend for predominance in 14C art.

The Fourteenth Century. The painter who first put the accent on the continuity between classical and medieval art, creating new forms which were clearly a prelude to Humanism and the Renaissance, was **Giotto**, Cimabue's great pupil. Dante Alighieri noted this when he wrote his famous lines:

> Credette Cimabue nella pintura
> Tener lo campo, ed ora ha Giotto il grido,
> Si che la fama di colui è oscura.

(Cimabue thought he held the field/In painting, and now Giotto is the cry,/The other's fame obscured.)

Giotto became the protagonist, not only of Florentine art but of all Italian art of the 14C. Active as a painter, architect, and inspirer of sculptural forms, he embodied the idea of the 'universal' artist which was to culminate in the High Renaissance with Leonardo, Michelangelo, and Raphael. It is significant that some of Giotto's most important works, from his early youth to his full maturity, lie outside Florence: his fame was such that he was called on to work in northern Italy (at Padua his cycle of frescoes for the Scrovegni chapel is considered to be the masterpiece of his mature years), in central Italy, at Rimini, and in the south, in Rome (St Peter's) and Naples. This is an unmistakable sign of the diffusion of his pictorial language, which must have touched all the most important centres of the 14C Italian school. His style was a synthesis of the exalted dramatic qualities of Cimabue (as can be seen by comparing Cimabue's Crucifix now in the Museo dell'Opera di Santa Croce with that by Giotto in the sacristy of Santa Maria Novella) and the classical influence he had encountered in Assisi, and perhaps directly in Rome.

Giotto sought a return in painting to the realism which finds a parallel in the poetry of his friend and admirer, Dante Alighieri. The simplicity of Giotto's style can be seen in the Maestà, a work with origins in the Byzantine tradition, painted for the church of Ognissanti in Florence in the first decade of the 14C (now in the Uffizi). In this work, one of three large paintings to be dedicated to the Madonna in Florence, Giotto affirms a new humanity in the grave but smiling face of the Madonna, and in the upward movement of the figures of the angels and saints which surround her. Here we find the same highly religious but deeply human spirit which pervades the 'Divina Commedia', which was absent from the paintings of the same subject by Cimabue and Duccio thirty years earlier. In Giotto's Maestà the regal, Byzantine qualities of Cimabue and Duccio are softened by contact with a sense of human realities which was to be the leading characteristic of Florentine art from now on, eventually influencing the whole of Italian art. It is difficult to put into words the spirit which pervades Giotto's frescoes in the two chapels (Bardi and Peruzzi) which he decorated in Santa Croce, rediscovered after centuries of critical oblivion by John Ruskin. In these and in Giotto's other Florentine works we see the beginning of a style which was to be continued by his followers, though in a progressively more diluted form, as the Gothic style gained influence during the second half of the 14C.

Giotto's influence was also felt in architecture and sculpture: the early project for the Campanile of the cathedral was entrusted to him and there is evidence of his style in some of the relief panels which decorate the base, although they were probably executed by Andrea Pisano. Giotto's most able follower was **Arnolfo di Cambio**, the architect and sculptor who played a prominent part in the reconstruction of the city under the Republic. The building which was to become the symbol of Florence and its government, the Palazzo dei Priori, today known as Palazzo Vecchio, was entrusted to him. This was the residence of the 'Priori', elected from the rich and powerful city Guilds, whose rule superseded that of the 'Capitano del Popolo' and the 'Podestà', as power gradually shifted from the nobility to the rich merchants and bankers. Begun during the last year of the 13C, the tower was probably completed by 1323, and the rest of the building was enlarged and enriched over the course of the century. As P. Toesca, the Italian art historian, wrote: 'Rappresenta il palazzo dei Priori, non meno della Cattedrale, l'essere della città e dell'arte fiorentina: fermezza e agilità, austerità e finezza; e già vi si esalta quel senso di movimento che è anima di tutte le più grandi creazioni fiorentini' ('Like the cathedral, Palazzo Vecchio represents the essence of the city and of Florentine art: it has a strength and agility, an austerity and finesse which already demonstrates that sense of movement which enlivens all the greatest Florentine works of art') ('Il Trecento', 1951). Two-and-a-half centuries after the building of Palazzo Vecchio, Vasari emphasised its political and social importance when he framed it in a view from the river with the long arcades of his Uffizi building. Its imposing rusticated exterior, lightened by elegant mullioned windows, was to be used during the Renaissance as a model by Brunelleschi and Michelozzo when they designed the first great houses for the rich and powerful families of the city. Arnolfo, who was an engineer (he built a circle of city walls), as well as a sculptor and architect, also designed other buildings in those years of fundamental importance to the face of Florence: the cathedral of Santa Maria del Fiore, built on the site of the older and much smaller Santa Reparata, and very probably also Santa Croce, the Franciscan church which, more than any other, sums up the spatial and structural qualities of Florentine architecture in the late 14C and early 15C. Arnolfo had envisaged an elaborate marble façade for Santa Maria del Fiore, populated with statues and reliefs, but, like the interior, it was left incomplete at his death. The drawings which survive of the façade, and the sculptures preserved in the Museo dell'Opera del Duomo are testimony to the powerful imagery and clarity of form in the work of Arnolfo which place him, as an artist, on a level with Giotto.

We do not know exactly how Arnolfo planned the interior of the cathedral as it was continued after his death in a new spirit, and the architectural framework was put to different use. However Santa Croce, probably based on Arnolfo's designs, seems to preserve his sense of monumental yet lithe clarity in the wide bays between the pilasters of pietra forte and the Gothic arches above them. Santa Croce, although fundamentally Gothic in form and influenced by contemporary architecture north of the Alps, is still characteristically Florentine in its use of light, in the width of its nave, and in the prominence given to the carrying structure in relation to the decorative details in the apse and the side chapels.

Other churches beside Santa Croce underwent alteration and enlargement at this time, including the Badia whose bell tower rises beside the tower of the Bargello and competes with the heavier, more imposing campanile of Santa Maria Novella, and Santa Trìnita and San Remigio, both with overtly Gothic interiors. Meanwhile, alongside Arnolfo's façade of the Duomo rose the Campanile which traditionally bears Giotto's name, even though he only built the first storey. It is an imposing structure framed by corner buttresses. The tower rises without diminishing in volume towards the upper storeys (completed in the second half of the 14C) where the structure is lightened by large Gothic windows. Giotto here repeated the Romanesque style of green and white marble decoration, adding pink marble, a colour scheme which was later copied on the exterior of the Duomo.

The classicism of Giotto and Arnolfo had enormous influence not just in Florence but throughout Italy. Although it was of short duration, it was taken up again in the 15C by Donatello and Masaccio. The various interpretations given to Giotto's art by his immediate followers can be seen in the decoration of Florence's most important churches, Sante Croce and Santa Maria Novella. We must imagine these interiors as they were then, almost completely covered by frescoes depicting religious subjects, arranged in a way which took into account the organic divisions of the wall space determined by the architectural structure. In the Baroncelli Chapel in Santa Croce, **Taddeo Gaddi** rendered his narrative more complex (showing the influence of Giotto's work in Padua), by an insistence on the use of perspective in the painted niches on the lower part of the walls where the liturgical objects give a strong impression of illusionism. In his scenes from the life of Mary, above, the buildings and landscapes are given more satisfying proportions in relation to the figures, even though they lack the coherent strength of the master's hand. **Maso di Banco** produced yet another personal interpretation of Giotto's style in his stories from the life of St Sylvester in the Bardi di Vernio chapel in Santa Croce. He gave a remarkable chromatic emphasis to the plastic qualities of Giotto's painting, as can be seen also in his 'Deposition' for San Remigio (now in the Uffizi; also attributed to 'Giottino'). The delicate works of **Bernardo Daddi**, in particular his small religious paintings and polyptychs, show the influence of the Giottesque school. He approached the dazzling colours of the Sienese school, and the gracefulness that marked his work won him great popularity during his lifetime.

In sculpture, **Andrea Pisano**, though following Giotto's design in the relief panels on the base of the Campanile, moved away from his influence when the bronze doors for the Baptistery were commissioned from him by the Opera del Duomo. The doors, produced between 1330 and 1336, are a masterly piece of metal casting and signal the rebirth of bronze sculpture in which the Florentines were to emulate the art of Ancient Rome. Furthermore, the architecture of these doors was later to serve as a model for the second pair made by Ghiberti during the first quarter of the 15C, the competition for which marked the change from Gothic to Renaissance art. Andrea, in his work on the Campanile begun by Giotto, opened large Gothic niches for statues in the second storey, which found an echo later in the external tabernacles of Orsanmichele, which was already under construction nearby. The sculpture of Andrea Pisano, and even more so that of his son Nino (who, however, worked mostly in Pisa), derived its elegance of style from Gothic forms but at the same time made obvious reference to the powerful plastic qualities to be found in the work of Giotto. This is evident particularly in the solidity of the four prophets sculpted for the niches of the Campanile, and also in his bronze reliefs for the Baptistery doors.

Meanwhile, the commercial and political power of Florence continued to flourish and the conquest of Prato, Pistoia, and San Miniato firmly established the autonomy and sovereignty of the independent Comune. Notwithstanding the great famines of 1346 and then the plague which broke out in 1348, which reduced the populations of Florence and Siena by half, the Florentines did not cease to embellish their city with imposing works of art, including buildings destined for practical use. The church of Orsanmichele, begun in 1337 as a loggia for the storage of grain and only completed in 1404, summarises, especially in its sculptural decoration, more than half a century of Florentine art, and it is witness to the passage from the Gothic to the Renaissance style. **Andrea Orcagna**, one of the most important figures in Florentine art during the second half of the 14C, built for the interior a Gothic tabernacle dedicated to the Madonna in the area which was then enclosed for use as a chapel. This represented a definitive break with the clarity and simplicity of Giotto's style, and the adoption of a flowery, decorative language. This taste for affected elegance and decorative richness later developed into the 'International Gothic' style. It is possible that this radical change in Florentine art owed much to the effects of the plague which caused an accentuation of religious feeling. In what can be seen of the remains of Orcagna's frescoes of the 'Triumph of Death' from the left nave of Santa Croce (now detached and exhibited in the Museo dell'Opera di Santa Croce), the characterisation of the figures achieves a dramatic force that is almost expressionistic. Churches were enriched by more and more decoration, inspired not only by the life of Christ and of the saints, but also by allegories exalting the function of religion and of the saints in daily life. Whilst the simpler style of **Giovanni da Milano**, in his frescoes in the Rinuccini chapel in Santa Croce, looked back to Giotto, and **Giovanni del Biondo** filled churches throughout Florence and her surrounding territories with polyptychs that were easy to understand and bright with colour highlighted with gold, Orcagna and his brothers, **Nardo** and **Jacopo di Cione**, together with **Andrea di Bonaiuto**, evolved a more inspired pictorial language, solemn and allegorical, in its overtly didactic intent.

A large part of Andrea Orcagna's frescoes in Santa Croce was destroyed and those in the choir of Santa Maria Novella were replaced a century later by the frescoes of Ghirlandaio, so that the most important surviving work by Orcagna is probably the triptych in the Strozzi Chapel of Santa Maria Novella. The walls of the chapel were painted by his brother, Nardo, with a rather crowded but picturesque representation of 'The Last Judgement', 'Paradise', and 'Inferno'. The allegorical style of Nardo's work, with its throng of figures, leaves little space for any clarity of concept. This pictorial style was carried still further in the frescoes by Andrea di Bonaiuto in the Chapter House of Santa Maria Novella, known as the Cappellone degli Spagnuoli. The general effect is most impressive; the colours are extremely well-preserved and the decoration is complete in every detail. This is one of the few decorative schemes of the 14C to have reached us intact, complete with its altarpiece, a polyptych by Bernardo Daddi. A particularly interesting element present in these frescoes, which depict the work of the Dominicans for the Church, is the inclusion of a representation of the Duomo, then under construction, showing it complete with its three polygonal tribunes and dome, which would suggest that the E end has already been given this plan by Arnolfo.

Agnolo Gaddi, Taddeo's son, continued in the wake of Orcagna and Bonaiuto. In his cycle dedicated to the Legend of the Cross in the choir of Santa Croce he exhibits an even more narrative style, completely removed from that of Giotto, in which bright colours tend to replace formal structure. Landscapes in pictures of this time show increasingly the influence of the Gothic style, while the individuality of Giotto disappears, and the late-Gothic poetical imagination found in Lorenzo Monaco and Gentile da Fabriano had yet to be developed. Another personality active in Florence at the end of the 14C was **Spinello Aretino** who, with his beautifully preserved frescoes depicting stories of St Benedict in the sacristy of San Miniato al Monte, has left us a work rich in poetry and pictorial values which anticipates the delicacy and elegance to be found in the art of Lorenzo Monaco.

But it was, above all, around the workshops of the Opera del Duomo that the creative energies of the city were concentrated. The Duomo was to be the largest and most important church of Tuscany, more imposing even than the cathedral of Siena which was at that time being enlarged according to very ambitious plans, and which was in fact left unfinished. The chief architect in the second half of the Trecento was **Francesco Talenti**, who had already completed the last three storeys of the Campanile, decorating them with double and triple mullioned windows which unite the styles of his predecessors with Gothic motifs. In fact, as was always the case in Florentine art (in direct contrast to the Sienese school), the Gothic style was classicised. The exterior decoration of the Duomo recalls the Romanesque style with its different coloured marble facing, and the Gothic element is more apparent in the sculptural decoration of the doors and windows on its two flanks. But it is at the E end of the cathedral, with its harmonious rhythm of the architectural elements and volumes, that the originality of the architects is fully revealed. The apsidal structure, with its tribunes, appears almost independent from the nave, and provides a fitting prelude to the cupola which rises abruptly and is only fully revealed from this end of the church. The huge dome, already planned by this time, was to defy construction until the time of Brunelleschi.

In the interior of the Duomo there is the same structural emphasis, the same clarity of conception and spatial amplitude as in Santa Croce, but the nave is higher owing to the use of Gothic vaulting. This Florentine interpretation of Gothic architecture is further emphasised by the use of massive pilasters crowned by capitals designed by Francesco Talenti. These pilasters were copied by Benci di Cione and Simone Talenti in the Loggia della Signoria where the three great round arches and horizontal frieze are motifs derived from the two major ecclesiastical buildings of Florence. It seems that no pictorial decoration was envisaged for the solemn and bare interior of the cathedral, as it was for Santa Maria Novella and Santa Croce; instead, all the decoration was concentrated on the exterior. The carvings and statues in the tympanum above each of the doors, and on the pinnacles and buttresses, repeated the decorative spirit of the Campanile (which was further enriched with statues after the turn of the century).

The building generally considered to be next in importance to the cathedral as regards sculptural decoration is Orsanmichele, where there was a parallel development of Florentine sculpture in the late 14C and 15C, a development which did not have its equal in painting until the advent of Masaccio. The individuality of Florentine art seemed to follow the political vicissitudes of the city where power was increasingly concentrated in the hands of a few families who fought for control of the 'Signoria', always within the limits of the law. The emergence of the Medici family as leaders through their financial supremacy and their ability to govern was accompanied by an extraordinary blossoming of brilliant artists who also made their contribution to the field of humanistic studies, already awakening in Florence. Whereas in the 14C the writings of Dante, Petrarch, and Boccaccio predominated amongst a multitude of followers of the 'dolce stil novo', the 15C saw a series of developments which were to make Florence, as in the days of Giotto and Arnolfo, the artistic centre not only of Italy but of the whole of Europe.

Humanism. Although the Renaissance is usually considered to have begun in 1401, the year of the competition for the second Baptistery doors, it was only very slowly that the new ideas inspired by the Classical world made any headway in Florentine art and literature. These were linked to a new conception of the representation of space for which Brunelleschi was primarily responsible. The times were ripe for this turning point and the first signs of its arrival were to be seen in the cathedral workshop and at Orsanmichele. **Nanni di Banco** demonstrated an evident interest in classical sculpture in the 'Porta della Mandorla' on the left side of the cathedral and in his statues of St Eligius and of the Four Soldier Saints (the 'Quattro Santi Coronati') in two of the Orsanmichele tabernacles. In painting, however, the International Gothic style, which first made its appearance with the work of the Sienese artist **Simone Martini**, became established throughout the first quarter of the 15C with the works of Lorenzo Monaco and Masolino, and the presence in Florence of **Gentile da Fabriano** who, in 1423, painted his 'Adoration of the Magi' (now in the Uffizi) for the Strozzi chapel in Santa Trìnita. For this same chapel Fra Angelico was soon to paint his 'Deposition' (now in the Museum of San Marco), in full Renaissance style.

But it was, above all, Brunelleschi in architecture and Donatello in sculpture who determined the real change in style which was to mark the epoch known, from Vasari onwards, as the 'Renaissance'. By this term is meant the rebirth of the laws of ideal beauty and perfection of the Classical world. **Brunelleschi**'s artistic personality matured slowly, as he became increasingly subject to the influence of Antique models. If we look at the relief (now in the Bargello) executed by him for the competition for the Baptistery doors, we realise that his concepts of space and structure are still Gothic, even if they are seen in the light of a new sense of rationality and realism, consciously in contrast with the superficial linear elegance of the late-Gothic style. In the event, the doors were commissioned from Ghiberti who worked on them throughout the first quarter of the fifteenth century, winning the acclaim of the Florentine people. Brunelleschi had to wait patiently to realise the triumph of his engineering genius in the creation of the cathedral dome, the commission for which he managed to obtain only in 1423. He had already proved his originality as an architect with the building of the Ospedale degli Innocenti and the sacristy of San Lorenzo (known as the 'Old Sacristy' to distinguish it from the later one built by Michelangelo). At this time the Medici began to rebuild San Lorenzo, which was later to become their family mausoleum. Brunelleschi, in fact, became increasingly involved with Giovanni and then with Cosimo de' Medici, the founders of the great power and fortune of the family, which, from then on, was to play a vital role in the political, cultural, and artistic life of the city.

Brunelleschi's style, based on a uniquely personal interpretation of classical forms (columns, capitals, arches, central or basilican plans, all of which he brought back into use), was expressed through a harmonious and well-proportioned use of internal and external space. This was emphasised by his typical use of pietra serena underlining the architectural forms, and alternating with plain white plastered surfaces, apparently inspired by the geometrical quality of Romanesque architecture. But the most important aspect of Brunelleschi's architecture is his use of perspective; it was he who first used regular mathematical proportions in the elevation of his buildings, giving them an appearance of geometrical perfection. The laws which he studied and systematically applied revolutionised architecture which, like all the visual arts, had been dominated especially in the late-Gothic period by an abstract use of form and colour, tending to create a completely transfigured image of reality. Brunelleschi emphasised instead the real, tangible values of representation, indicating to his contemporaries and successors a way forward that was followed for the next five centuries of Western culture.

The Early Renaissance. The impression made by Brunelleschi's buildings (San Lorenzo, Santo Spirito, the Pazzi Chapel, Santa Maria degli Angeli, etc.), rising harmoniously out of the medieval fabric of the old city, was tremendous. For the first time, not only architects, but painters and sculptors as well, realised the possibilities that the use of perspective offered in the representation of reality. **Donatello**, who studied with Brunelleschi the ruins of Ancient Rome, entered with him the intellectual circle under the protection of the Medici. He immediately mastered the idea of perspective and gave its first interpretation in sculpture in the statue and bas-relief which he made for the tabernacle of the armourers' guild for Orsanmichele. In the statue of the young St George, and even more in the 'schiacciato' relief representing the Saint freeing the Princess, he applied Brunelleschi's principles of a unified point of vision and perspective (which were to be so important in the work of the young

Michelangelo). Donatello's style seems rougher and less sophisticated than that of Brunelleschi; in some of his sculptures he seems
to have drawn inspiration from the intense realism found in certain
Etruscan portraits. Indeed Donatello seemed to resuscitate the aesthetic ideals of classical sculpture: his cherubs full of life and energy;
his bronzes, in which he revived for the first time a technique of
sculpture which had not been employed since Antiquity; his use of
very low 'schiacciato' relief which brings to the metal or marble
surface a completely new pictorial quality, using Brunelleschi's
principles of perspective to create an illusion of depth—these were
all innovations which must have had great impact on the younger
generation.

The purpose of the sculptures themselves also changed. They were
no longer works intended simply to decorate public buildings, they
began to stand alone as refined products bought by the rich bour-
geoisie for their palaces, villas, or gardens, buildings which were
now being constructed according to the new principles of Brunelleschi. For their palaces the great families adopted new Renaissance forms. The first notable example was the palace built by
Brunelleschi's pupil, **Michelozzo**, in Via Larga (now Via Cavour) for
Cosimo Il Vecchio. Cosimo appointed Michelozzo as architect having
rejected as too expensive a plan drawn up for him by Brunelleschi.
We can be almost certain, however, that the design was inspired at
least in part by Brunelleschi (although on a simplified scale). Cosimo
also employed Michelozzo on more modest building projects, and he
commissioned from him the convent of San Marco, built in Florence
for the use of the Dominicans of Fiesole, and the villa of Careggi, and
castle of Cafaggiolo.

The third great personality of the Early Renaissance, who com-
pletes the Florentine artistic panorama, was **Masaccio** who effected
the same revolution in painting as Brunelleschi had done in architecture and Donatello in sculpture, despite his death at the early age of
twenty-seven. Although younger than his two colleagues, he was yet
able to impose great changes on the artistic world through the work
he did in collaboration with **Masolino** (a painter who still belonged to
the International Gothic school) in the Brancacci Chapel in the
church of the Carmine. The decorations consisted of a cycle of
frescoes depicting scenes from the life of St Peter, and in the parts
painted by Masaccio we can see a spiritual parallel with the work of
Donatello, especially the Donatello of the 'Prophets' made for the
Campanile. Masaccio's figures are powerful, sculptural and simple,
free of the linear and chromatic grace that had distinguished the
Gothic style. Colour is here used by the painter not to please the eye
but to construct the form, and this he evidently derived from Giotto's
frescoes in Santa Croce (which also provided the young
Michelangelo with the model for his earliest drawings). Masaccio's
figures express the same profound sentiments as those of Giotto, but
within a structure derived from Brunelleschi's use of perspective
which offered greater possibilities of concentration and realism.
Masaccio remained excluded from the protected circle of the Medici
and had to seek work outside Florence during the years which saw
the ascent of the Medici to power. He was already dead when
Cosimo il Vecchio returned, triumphant, to govern Florence after a
year of exile in Padua. The first direct followers of Masaccio,
Donatello, and Brunelleschi, had already appeared, establishing the
predominance of the new language of the Renaissance with the help
of the most powerful family in Florence.

The artists' patrons were still, for the most part, the religious orders, the cathedral workshop, and the 'Signoria'. For these the artists produced the works which unmistakably characterise the Florentine Renaissance. **Luca della Robbia**, who was a follower of Donatello and like him collaborated on the decoration of Brunelleschi's buildings, created a new medium, that of enamelled terracotta, which was to be the speciality of his family workshop until the 16C. Using transparent glazes over red clay which had been simply coloured with white and blue slip, Luca della Robbia was able to achieve effects which were quite unique and which harmonised perfectly with the grey and white of Brunelleschi's buildings. Luca also created purely decorative forms inspired by motifs taken from classical sculpture, such as garlands of flowers, fruit, and leaves which encircle his reliefs, and the coats-of-arms of the Guilds (on Orsanmichele) or noble families, all of which became extremely popular. The rather severe dramatic language of Donatello was now neglected by the younger generation who looked more to his joyful, vigorous works such as the reliefs of the cathedral 'Cantoria', and the Prato pulpit, and the so-called 'Atys-Amorino' made for the Doni, and now in the Bargello (the same family was later to commission works from Michelangelo and Raphael). Donatello's affectionate reliefs of the Madonna anticipate the paintings of the young Raphael. These works were to inspire **Antonio** and **Bernardo Rossellino**, **Desiderio da Settignano**, **Mino da Fiesole**, **Benedetto da Maiano**, and **Agostino di Duccio**, each of whom created his own individual interpretation of Donatello's art. This was also the moment of the revival of portraiture, realistically drawn from life or from death masks. Portraits were used in funerary monuments, for which the Renaissance model was Rossellino's tomb of Leonardo Bruni in Santa Croce.

In painting, Masaccio's work had breached the Gothic tradition, imposing the new laws of perspective in drawing and a rigorous, three-dimensional composition. But some of his followers could not forget the more colourful, lively aspects of the Gothic style, still present in the second decade of the 15C in the elegant work, so full of colour and narrative sense, of **Lorenzo Monaco**. Lorenzo's work brings us to that of **Beato Angelico**, who managed to transform the preciousness of the Gothic style of colouring into a luminosity, derived from his study of natural light, which is innovative even when compared with the work of Masaccio. His great 'Deposition', painted for the Strozzi chapel in Santa Trìnita (now in the Museum of San Marco), as well as the altarpieces he painted for several of the religious houses in Florence (especially the Dominican convent where he took his vows), and the frescoes he painted in the convent of San Marco, place Fra Angelico among the most spiritually rich and talented interpreters of Masaccio's style. Beside him stands another great interpreter of Masaccio's ideas in terms of light and colour, **Domenico Veneziano**, the master of Piero della Francesca, who transmitted the Renaissance style throughout central Italy. In this group of painters may also be included **Filippo Lippi**, a Carmelite friar of indifferent vocation (he eventually left the Order to marry an ex-novice, and their son, Filippino, became a talented follower of his father). Filippo painted a fresco in the cloister of the Carmine directly inspired by Masaccio but with a sense of humour and a closeness to the realities of everyday life which were quite new. In his mature works, notably his frescoes in the choir of Prato cathedral, Lippi was to find a balance between draughtsmanship, colour, and the expression of movement which was to have great importance for his most gifted pupil, Sandro Botticelli.

But the time also seemed ripe for experimentation, even of an extreme kind, as **Paolo Uccello** demonstrated. He was one of the most relentless investigators of the laws of perspective and illusionism in painting. He, too, was connected with the Medici and it was for them that he painted the three paintings of the 'Battle of San Romano', today distributed between the Uffizi, the Louvre, and the National Gallery, London. In the biblical fresco cycle he painted for the Chiostro Verde of Santa Maria Novella, he gives a Renaissance interpretation to this medieval decorative practice. As an historical painter (the 'Battle of San Romano' is one of the first paintings to depict an actual event) he was asked by the 'Signoria' to paint a memorial to John Hawkwood in the cathedral. Hawkwood was an English mercenary who led the Florentine army into battle against the Sienese. A bronze equestrian statue had been planned for his tomb, but this was never carried out because of the expense. Uccello's fresco, on the left wall of the nave, depicts the bronze horse and rider that should have been there, and its greenish colour imitates the patina of bronze. Uccello also painted the cathedral clock and supplied the cartoon for one of the windows in the drum of the dome.

Andrea del Castagno, the youngest of Masaccio's followers, played a similar role to that of Uccello. Primarily a fresco painter, he rigorously applied Brunelleschi's rules of perspective in his great fresco of the Last Supper in the refectory of the convent of Sant' Apollonia, animating it with nervously drawn, grandiose figures in an 'heroic' style, a style which could not fail to impress the young Michelangelo. Similar monumental figures appear in Andrea's frescoes of 'illustrious men and women' painted in a room of the Carducci villa and now in the Uffizi, and in the equestrian painting of Niccolò da Tolentino next to Uccello's John Hawkwood in the cathedral. In all these works, the plastic energy and sculptural feeling of the forms take precedence over the harsh, metallic colour.

Cosimo il Vecchio, after his triumphal return in 1434, increasingly came to be the enlightened 'ruler' of the city, even though he maintained the governmental structures unaltered. His strong personality was evident in all public works and he determined the development of Florentine culture. He surrounded himself with the most talented artists of the day to whom he entrusted important commissions for his family or for the state, and he began to form the rich Medici art collections which were to become celebrated. The houses of wealthy Florentines became more and more luxurious. They were filled with elaborate furniture, gilded and painted (notably 'cassone', or marriage chests): even the beds were often decorated with paintings. The walls were hung with pictures, often of very large dimensions, and sometimes in the form of a roundel (compare the celebrated tondi by Filippo Lippi and Sandro Botticelli), and they were enriched by elaborate carved frames recalling the wreaths of Luca della Robbia, with their flowers and foliage. It seems, indeed, as though there were hardly enough painters available to satisfy the demands of the rich families who competed with each other and with the Medici. Some of the most beautiful palaces of the city were built during these years, such as those designed for the Pazzi and the Antinori by **Giuliano da Maiano**; the Pitti which was probably based on plans by Brunelleschi, and Palazzo Rucellai designed by Leon Battista Alberti, who was also commissioned by Giovanni Rucellai to complete the façade of Santa Maria Novella, and to build the chapel of the Holy Sepulchre in San Pancrazio. The rivalry between families also extended to the various family chapels built and renovated in the most important churches as a testimony to the increasing prosperity of the bourgeois city. One of the finest funerary chapels of this period is that of the Cardinal of Portugal in San Miniato al Monte, which is an exceptional example of collaboration between artists (Rossellino, Pollaiolo, and Baldovinetti).

The arts were codified by **Leon Battista Alberti** who established himself, before Leonardo da Vinci, as a 'universal' artist and theoretician of Renaissance art whose ideas were to become law for anyone wanting to follow the new Renaissance style. The figure of the artist became increasingly more complex; and the researches in the artistic field going on in all three arts were on a theoretical and intellectual level unknown to the medieval world. Artists now tended to work in a number of different fields, and, very often, their careers began in the goldsmiths' workshop because of the ever-increasing demand for precious objects. It is not strange, then, that Pollaiolo and Verrocchio not only produced paintings and sculpture for their patrons, but also armour, crests and jewels for display in parades, festivals, and tournaments, such as that held in 1471 in which Giuliano and Lorenzo de' Medici distinguished themselves.

The stability of the government of Cosimo il Vecchio (who died in 1464) ensured the city's great prosperity, a prosperity founded on commerce. In Florence at this time the principal desire seems to have been to brighten life with all that was most beautiful and precious in art and nature. Even the subject matter of works of art changed and artists increasingly drew inspiration from mythological subjects of antiquity, in the same way as allusions to the classical world abounded in the literature of the time. 'The Procession of the Magi', by Benozzo Gozzoli in the chapel of the Medici palace, is almost a manifesto of this new ideal. Here there are portraits of members of the family, richly dressed and surrounded by pages and courtiers, set against an imaginary landscape. There is little emphasis on the mystical aspect of the event, more on the worldly one, the atmosphere being that of a cavalcade for a tournament or some fairytale procession. But Florence at this time reached the apex of her political importance, and it was in Florence that the meeting of the Council of the Eastern and Western Churches took place in 1439, underlining the socio-political function of the city. The house of the Medici had by now become a royal palace, its rooms decorated with works of art by Paolo Uccello, Filippo Lippi, Benozzo Gozzoli, Pollaiolo and Verrocchio. Cosimo's treasury, with all its marvellous antiques which he passed on to Lorenzo, had its vault decorated with enamelled terracotta tiles by Luca della Robbia (now in the Victoria and Albert Museum).

The 'Crisis' of the 1460s. Around 1460, Florentine art reached a turning point: the **Pollaiolo** brothers sought, above all, new expressive values and imparted a dynamic force to line and form. They were masters at casting bronze, and they imposed on sculpture a new artistic canon based on elegance of line and a swirling, vortical movement and added an expression of force and balance which emulated the art of the Ancient World. **Verrocchio** was also at work at this time, and he was for long favoured by the Medici as a painter and sculptor. He reached a measured perfection and a monumentality even in small-scale works (see, for example, his 'David' in the

Bargello), and marked the advent of a new figurative and aesthetic concept which was to be fully realised by his greatest pupil, Leonardo da Vinci. Verrocchio's high degree of intellectuality is evident in his creation of the tomb destined for the father and uncle of Lorenzo and Giuliano de' Medici in the Old Sacristy of San Lorenzo: the sumptuous sarcophagus, devoid of figure decoration, is framed by a bronze grille of studied simplicity. The importance of Pollaiolo and Verrocchio can also be measured by the role they assumed outside Florence: two Popes' tombs in St Peter's were commissioned from Pollaiolo, and Verrocchio was responsible for the equestrian statue of Colleoni in Venice, a superb sequitor to Donatello's Gattamelata monument in Padua, and directly inspired by the heroic world of Antiquity.

Not even the conspiracy devised by the Pazzi in 1478 against Lorenzo and Giuliano seemed to interrupt this period of incredible creative activity in the artistic life of Florence. Moreover, despite the murder of Giuliano, Lorenzo emerged from the fray even stronger, the absolute ruler of the city, establishing himself as the greatest political and diplomatic genius of the time, besides being something of a poet. He surrounded himself with men of letters, poets, and philosophers, and his 'round table' of Humanists, based at the villa of Careggi, seemed to have brought the culture of Periclean Athens to life in Florence. In the figurative arts the most evident reflection of this was in the mythologies painted by **Sandro Botticelli** which, in their play of line taken from Pollaiolo, carried the rhythmic capacity of drawing to its utmost limit. Botticelli worked mostly for private patrons, and his paintings, even those of religious subjects, reach an almost abstract intellectual level that seems to be in direct antithesis to the world of intensely human images created by Donatello and Masaccio.

Renaissance architecture left little space for the large mural decorations which had been so important a feature of 14C Florentine art. The masters of the new style, although interested in the traditional techniques of their predecessors (with the exception of Botticelli who made only very limited use of this medium), either had to content themselves with a secondary part in the economy of the new architecture or re-use the existing surfaces in older buildings. The latter was often the case, and **Domenico Ghirlandaio** was among the painters who dedicated themselves to fresco painting, reawakening the glories of the 14C. Indeed, he was said to have wanted to cover even the city walls with frescoes! Ghirlandaio typifies, in the best possible way, the bourgeois spirit now increasingly dominant in Florentine society, setting his stories from the past against a background of contemporary Florence. He adapted perfectly the new style to the pre-existing Gothic spaces, and there is no discrepancy in style in the narratives painted by him and his assistants spread over the vast areas available. His works include the stories of the life of St Francis in the Sassetti chapel of Santa Trìnita, and lives of the Virgin and St John the Baptist in the Tornabuoni chapel of Santa Maria Novella; the decoration of the Sala dei Gigli in the Palazzo Vecchio; and a series of vividly coloured altarpieces reminiscent of Flemish painting. He was an accomplished draughtsman and a painter of supreme technical skill, and his easy and pleasing style made him a popular artist in his day.

During these years Florence increasingly became the meeting place of some of the most fundamental tendencies in Italian art. **Pietro Perugino**, the Umbrian artist who taught Raphael, preceded him in leaving some of his greatest works in Florentine churches and private collections. **Filippino Lippi** and **Piero di Cosimo**, who were also active in Florence then, anticipated to a certain extent the restless aspect of Mannerism.

In the field of architecture **Giuliano da Sangallo** built the villa at Poggio a Caiano for Lorenzo il Magnifico, and Santa Maria delle Carceri at Prato, two buildings which reiterated the fundamental teachings of Brunelleschi, though with some original developments. Within the city, new buildings sprang up to embody the wealth and ambitions of the richest families; the Gondi palace by Giuliano da Sangallo, the Guadagni palace by Cronaca, and, above all, Palazzo Strozzi, also by Cronaca. Although he did not complete it, this palace represents the most ambitious and perfect example of a palatial residence of the Renaissance. In sculpture, however, after the death of Pollaiolo and Verrocchio, Sansovino lacked the capacity for innovation. It required the nascent genius of Michelangelo to show that in this field—and not only in this field—art was to take a new direction.

But in the meantime, the genius who, more than anyone else, embodied the Renaissance ideal of the 'universal' artist, **Leonardo da Vinci**, was born in Florence. A pupil of Verrocchio, he was undoubtedly influenced by him in his early works but developed, as he matured, an entirely personal vision which, together with his writings, made him a celebrated figure not only in art but in every field of knowledge. His tireless researches and ingenious engineering, his rare pictorial works, his wanderings throughout Italy, his exile in France, and his unique style which opened new horizons in painting and sculpture (thanks to his anatomical studies), all served to make an almost mythical figure of him. Strange, then, that his genius went unremarked by Lorenzo il Magnifico, who, however, towards the end of his life was increasingly involved with the political problems then troubling Italy. Possibly, Leonardo's subtle and introverted spirit had little appeal to one of Lorenzo's temperament who was drawn instead to the sort of conceptual clarity derived from Platonism, and to the Classicism evident in the sculptural works he had collected over the years in the garden of San Marco.

The artist who embodied Lorenzo's ideals was the very young **Michelangelo Buonarroti**, a pupil of Ghirlandaio and Bertoldo. Legend has it that he came to the notice of Lorenzo when he sculpted the head of a faun in the garden of San Marco. It is certain, however, that the young genius who began his career under the wing of the Medici, represents, more than any other Florentine artist of the time, the aesthetic ideal on which the whole century's art was based; that mythicised vision of the Ancient World which represented absolute perfection, the highest embodiment of human genius. Michelangelo soon established himself as the artist who, more than any other, could offer Florence that continuity in art which summarised the possibilities of so many generations, and that universality so sought after by his predecessors. Sculptor, painter, and architect, poet and philosopher, his solitary personality was recognised for its importance, not only in Florence but throughout Italy and all of Europe. His prodigious working capacity allowed him to develop from his early Florentine works in which he reabsorbed 15C experiences, towards the creation of an artistic idiom, which, although indebted to Masaccio and Luca Signorelli, Donatello and Verrocchio, Brunelleschi and Sangallo, had the capacity of evolving a highly individual style which bridges the centuries to reach the heroic, monumental conception of the art of Imperial Rome.

The early period of this indefatigable artist, which can be defined as 'classical', culminated in his 'David'. At this time certain 15C motifs, such as the use of the tondo in both painting and sculpture, reappear (see, for instance his reliefs for the Pitti and Gaddi, and his painting for the Doni, the married couple whose portraits Raphael was painting at about the same time). Next follows a more complex phase in Michelangelo's art, to which belong works such as his 'St Matthew', and the first 'prisoners' (now in the Louvre) for the tomb of Julius II, in which there are clear signs of the disturbed state of mind of the artist, so sensitive to the difficulties that Florence was undergoing at this period. Dividing his time between Florence and Rome, Michelangelo seemed to reflect in his constantly changing projects an instability that was to become typical of his art and similarly cause him so often to leave his works unfinished.

There is no doubt that with Michelangelo came the break with 15C Humanism, with the serene, joyous style which had characterised the works of the Early Renaissance. Although he still used some of the elements which had distinguished those works, he forged a new style that seemed deliberately to disrupt that balance so carefully sought by his predecessors. An obvious example of this is the construction of the New Sacristy in San Lorenzo, a mausoleum for the Medici family. Here the graceful shapes, reminiscent of Brunelleschi, are reinforced by elements taken from Roman architecture and, above all, by the massive sculptures, conceived as an essential complement to the design. In these figures, as in those of the 'prisoners' (now in the Accademia) for the second project for the tomb of Julius II, Michelangelo eschewed the 15C forms which had occupied him up to then, in favour of dynamic, articulated forms, turning in on themselves, which were to be the model for all the 'serpentine figures' of the Mannerist sculpture of the 16C. In the staircase of the vestibule of the Laurentian Library, the same instability of form is evident, the same desire to break up the centralised perspective which had been Brunelleschi's great innovation, with alternating plays of light and points of view, which were clearly a prelude to the Baroque.

After the demise of the short-lived Florentine Republic, Michelangelo expressed his disillusionment and disapproval of the Medici by leaving Florence for good, leaving behind many of his works incomplete. Nevertheless, it was his example which determined the birth of a new style known as 'Mannerism' in Florence. This style interpreted that aspect of Michelangelo's art which seemed to break away from the classical forms that had been the concern of Florentine artists since Giotto and Arnolfo.

The High Renaissance. Despite the disturbances which troubled Florence after the death of Lorenzo il Magnifico in 1492, the city still remained the centre of some of the most important developments in Italian art between the end of the 15C and the beginning of the 16C. Apart from Michelangelo, who after 1508 was increasingly occupied with commissions from the Pope in Rome, other important artists worked in Florence and created a mature, grandiose language, complex in form and colour, which was to characterise the High Renaissance. With the arrival in the city of the young **Raphael**, who here developed his unique, pure classical style, local artists were influenced towards an evolution of form based primarily on drawing, a medium in which the Florentines excelled. **Fra Bartolomeo** and **Andrea del Sarto** were the two greatest exponents of this trend.

Andrea del Sarto, whom Vasari christened 'the faultless painter', undertook important public works, including altarpieces and frescoes of masterly execution, and created a school of painting which dominated Florentine art in the first half of the 16C. His pupils included **Pontormo** and **Rosso Fiorentino**, who were important for their original interpretation of Mannerism, a style which became increasingly intellectualised and refined, very far removed from the rationalism of the Early Renaissance. In their unique forms and colours, they re-elaborated the teachings of Michelangelo who was still looked to as the supreme master, but in an even more pronounced stylised and almost abstract language.

This period of Mannerism at its most original was soon to come to an end. After the assassination of Duke Alessandro in 1537, a distant cousin, Cosimo de' Medici, took over the government of the city. He brought about rapid changes in its cultural life, as the political ideas of the new Duke prevailed in everything, including the arts. The commissioning of great public works which had characterised the regimes of the Republic and later the Medici 'Signoria' now ceased almost entirely. Even the cathedral workshops fell silent and work on the embellishment of the interior proceeded only sporadically. Artistic manifestations were now almost entirely controlled by the absolute ruler who determined their nature. The face of the city was changed by the talented work of **Giorgio Vasari** and of **Bartolomeo Ammannati**, the two architects to whom the grand-duke entrusted most of the important works of the period. Vasari constructed the new centre of government, the Uffizi, which, with its arcades still inspired by Brunelleschi, frames the view of Palazzo Vecchio on one side and the Arno on the other. He also built (in five months) the Corridor which bears his name to connect the Uffizi with the grand-ducal residence. Ammannati enlarged the palace, which, after its purchase from the Pitti family, became the home of the reigning families of Florence for the next three centuries. The bridge of Santa Trìnita is also the work of Ammannati.

Cosimo continued the tradition of enlivening the city with statuary, but in a way which gave Florence the aspect which it still has today, of a great, open-air museum of sculpture. Piazza della Signoria was peopled by works by the most prestigious sculptors of the day: Ammannati made the fountain of Neptune, assisted by some of the most important protagonists of Mannerism in Florence, such as **Giambologna**, **Vincenzo de' Rossi**, and **Vincenzo Danti**; **Bandinelli** sculpted the 'Hercules and Cacus' which can be seen almost as a challenge to Michelangelo's 'David' nearby; **Benvenuto Cellini** made his beautiful bronze 'Perseus', poised on an exquisite marble base decorated with bronze statuettes; Giambologna sculpted the 'Rape of the Sabines', one of the finest examples of a 'serpentine figure' borrowed from Michelangelo's mature period. The equestrian monuments to Cosimo I (by Giambologna) and to Ferdinando I (by Tacca) are an attempt to recreate the climate of Imperial Rome; they seek to imitate Roman statues rather than works by Donatello or Verrocchio.

Garden architecture was becoming more complicated, enriched as it was with statuary, fountains and artificial grottoes which gave ample opportunity for the full expression of the talent and refinements of Florentine architects and sculptors. Art became, increasingly, the private expression of the Duke, who dictated the fashion and imposed the tastes of his Court on the great families of Florence. Interiors became more and more sumptuous and loaded with decoration. **Bronzino** came to the fore in painting with a very personal form of classicism seen through the formal refinements of Pontormo's Mannerism. His use of gem-like and enamelled colours give his paintings an almost surreal aspect, and his portraits represent the social standing of the sitters rather than their personalities.

The reworking of all the motifs which had characterised 15C Florentine art seemed to find its conclusion in the historical events taking place in the city from the 16C onwards. Ably governed by Cosimo I and his successors, Florence became increasingly a centre of cultural elaboration rather than of original creativity as it had been for three centuries. Even Mannerism, which in its early phase had influenced the whole of European art with its sophisticated style, began to show an irreversible involution, merely repeating the talented inventions of its early protagonists. Court art reflected more and more the private nature of the artist's product, even in fresco— now chiefly used in the decoration of great houses—which had been the glory of Florentine art for three centuries. Once the echoes of Michelangelo's direct influence were spent, Florentine art was no longer capable of formulating its own original language; the city became a provincial centre reflecting pictorial trends from other, more important centres such as Rome, Bologna, and Venice. Basically, Florentine art continued to follow forms which had their roots in the past and especially in the 16C. Even in the so-called Baroque period, architecture, sculpture, and painting reflect the ideas of the great Renaissance tradition, and as late as the 19C, with the enlargement of the city during its brief period as the capital of Italy, there is the same recourse to an eclectic architecture making use of all the styles developed by the great artists of the Renaissance, except when, a little later, mock-Gothic becomes the fashion. But by this time we are dealing with a history of taste rather than the history of the art of a city that has given an unequalled contribution to European civilisation.

HISTORICAL SKETCH

In 2,000,000 BC the site of Florence was as near to the sea as Venice is today. The plain of the Arno was first inhabited in Neolithic times when Italic tribes from the north settled here towards the end of the 10C BC. Although some Etruscan tombs have been found on the plain towards Sesto, there is no evidence of an Etruscan city preceding Florence. The Etruscans preferred to build their stronghold on the hill of Fiesole (5C BC or earlier). The Roman colony of 'Florentia' was founded in 59 BC by Julius Caesar, and the city was built on the Arno where the crossing is narrowest. The river, navigable up to this point, had great importance in the early economic development of the city. The Roman city, which was enlarged in the Augustan era, flourished in the 2C and 3C AD, when it probably contained over 10,000 inhabitants.

By the early 5C the city was already threatened by Ostrogoth invaders. Despite the Byzantine walls erected in 541–544, Totila was able to inflict considerable damage on the city in 552. By the end of the 6C Florence had followed the fate of the rest of central and Northern Italy and was firmly held under Lombard dominion. Charlemagne visited the city in 781 and 786 and the Carolingian circle of walls was set up in 869–896. In the 11C Florence was one of the principal centres of Christianity. The city was favoured by Matilda, Margrave of Tuscany, who saw to the building of a fourth circle of walls in 1078 as a defence against the Emperor Henry IV. Thus the Florentines, who espoused the cause of the Pope, were able to withstand a siege of Imperial troops for ten days. In 1125 the rival town of Fiesole was finally overcome after a fierce battle.

The 'Comune' of Florence came into being in the first decades of the 12C, with a college of officials, a council of some 100 men, and a 'Parlamento' which was called regularly to approve government policy. The Comune protected the business interests of Florentine merchants who had begun to prosper through the cloth trade and money-lending. The fifth line of walls, which now included the Oltrarno, was built in 1172–75. In 1207 the consular regime was replaced, and a 'Podestà' installed who held executive power in the government. The post was traditionally reserved for a foreigner. At this time the first guilds ('Arti') were formed to protect the commercial interests of the merchant and banking community. During the course of the 13C three new bridges were built over the Arno, the Palazzo del Popolo (Bargello) was erected, and the two great mendicant Orders, the Franciscans and Dominicans, came to Florence to found Santa Croce and Santa Maria Novella.

The political life of the 13C was dominated by the long drawn-out struggle between the Guelfs and Ghibellines. This was sparked off by the feuds arising from the murder of one of the Buondelmonti by the Amidei in 1215. The Ghibelline faction, which supported the Emperor, derived its name from Weiblingen, the Castle of the Hohenstaufen, and the Guelfs, who supported the Pope, from the family name ('Welfs') of Otto IV. By the middle of the century Florentine merchants, who travelled as far afield as England and the Near East, were established in a privileged and independent position in trade and commerce. The florin, first minted in silver c 1235, and soon after in gold, was used as the standard gold coin in Europe. The regime of the 'Primo Popolo' (1250–60), supported by the Guelfs, now included the merchant class. The towers of the great noble families in

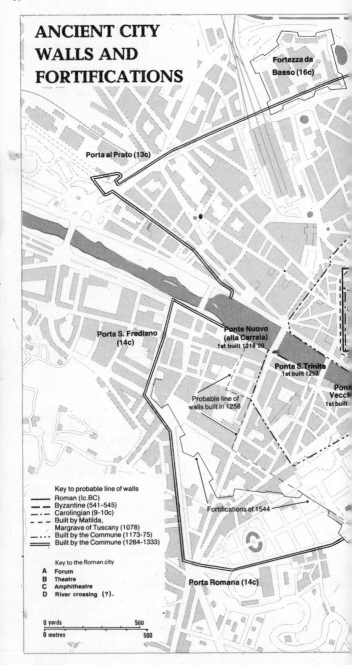

ANCIENT CITY WALLS AND FORTIFICATIONS

Fortezza da Basso (16c)

Porta al Prato (13c)

Porta S. Frediano (14c)

Ponte Nuovo (alla Carraia)
1st built 1218-20

Ponte S.Trinita
1st built 1252

Pon
Vecch
1st built

Probable line of walls built in 1258

Fortifications of 1544

Porta Romana (14c)

Key to probable line of walls
— Roman (Ic.BC)
-- Byzantine (541-545)
-·- Carolingian (9-10c)
--- Built by Matilda, Margrave of Tuscany (1078)
-··- Built by the Commune (1173-75)
═ Built by the Commune (1284-1333)

Key to the Roman city
A Forum
B Theatre
C Amphitheatre
D River crossing (?).

0 yards   500
0 metres   500

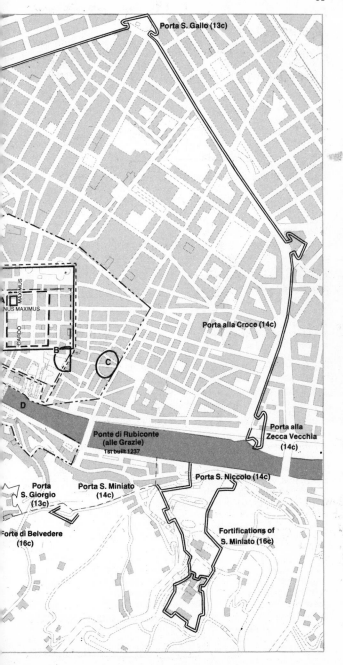

Porta S. Gallo (13c)

DECUMANUS MAXIMUS

CARDO MAXIMUS

A

B

C

Porta alla Croce (14c)

D

Ponte di Rubiconte
(alle Grazie)
1st built 1237

Porta alla
Zecca Vecchia
(14c)

Porta S. Niccolo (14c)

Porta
S. Giorgio
(13c)

Porta S. Miniato
(14c)

Forte di Belvedere
(16c)

Fortifications of
S. Miniato (16c)

1260 Primo Popolo reduce towers
1292 Nobility excluded.
1294 Palazzo Vecchio

Florence were reduced in height by order of the government. The city was victorious in battles against Pisa, Pistoia, and Siena.

In a renewed war against Siena (and the German army led by Manfred) the Florentines were defeated at Montaperti in 1260. However, the city was spared from destruction at the hand of the Ghibellines, through the generosity of their leader, Farinata degli Uberti, a member of one of the oldest noble families of Florence. Count Guido Novello took up residence in the Bargello as 'Podestà' of the Ghibelline government. After continuous struggles between the two factions, the regime of the 'Secondo Popolo' was set up in 1284 by the 'Arti Maggiori' (Greater Guilds). In 1292 Giano della Bella became 'Priore' and through his famous 'ordinamenti di giustizia' the Florentine nobility were excluded from high political office. The last circle of walls was begun in 1284, and the centre of government was moved from the Bargello to Palazzo della Signoria (begun in 1294), the residence of the 'Priori'. By the beginning of the 14C Florence was among the five largest cities in Europe with a population of c 100,000. Her prosperity was based largely on the woollen cloth industry which had accounted for her significant economic growth in the 13C.

The internal struggles within the Guelf party were renewed with the rival factions known as the Neri (Blacks) and Bianchi (Whites), being led respectively by the Cerchi and Donati families. Charles of Valois, called in as a peacemaker by Boniface VIII, favoured the Blacks and sent 600 Whites into exile (1302), among them Dante. In 1342 Walter de Brienne, Duke of Athens, was elected 'Signore' for life and given absolute power, but an insurrection led to his expulsion from the city a year later. The Florentine economy suffered a severe crisis in the 1340s with the bankruptcy of the two most powerful banking families, the Bardi and the Peruzzi (the Mozzi bank had already failed in 1311), partly due to the inability of Edward III of England to repay his debts during the disastrous 100 Years War, and with the Black Death, a catastrophe in which the population was reduced by more than half (and which was to recur seven times between 1350 and 1430). The rising of the Ciompi, or wool-carders, in 1378 under Michele di Lando represented a high point in labour unrest in Florence's chief industry. The demands for recognition and the right to form a guild were met with the creation of three new guilds and direct representation in government for a very brief time. However, in 1382 the 'popolo grasso', united with the Guelf party, succeeded in establishing an oligarchic form of government, and the power of the guilds lost ground in the political life of the city after nearly a century of pre-eminence.

Rule of Wealth The regime of the 'popolo grasso' in which a relatively small group of wealthy middle-class merchant families succeeded in holding power, ruled Florence for 40 years. Every so often the heads of rival families were exiled in order to lessen the risk of power being concentrated in the hands of any one man. Benedetto degli Alberti, one of the wealthiest men in the city, and leader of a moderate faction in the government, was banished in 1387; he was followed into exile by the Strozzi, and finally the Medici. During these turbulent years of warfare against the Visconti in Milan, the government still conducted an ambitious foreign policy. Florence at last gained direct access to the sea when she conquered Pisa in 1406.

At the beginning of the 15C Florence was established as the intellectual and artistic centre of Europe. Cultivated Florentines adopted the civic ideal and the city proclaimed herself heir to Rome.

In the city, 'a misura d'uomo', of human dimension, there was a profound involvement in political life on the part of intellectuals and artists. A new conception of art and learning symbolised the birth of the Renaissance. Chancellors of the republic now included humanist scholars such as Coluccio Salutati, Leonardo Bruni, Poggio Bracciolini, and Carlo Marsuppini.

In 1433 Cosimo de' Medici was exiled for ten years by Rinaldo degli Albizi since his popularity had been growing among the merchant faction in the city, in opposition to the oligarchic regime. But his return just a year later was unanimously acclaimed by the people, and he at once became the first citizen of Florence. His prudent leadership of the city lasted for 30 years. He adhered to the constitutional system of the old regime and managed to dominate the policy of the government abroad as well as at home. He usually avoided holding public office himself, but was careful to keep the support of a wide circle of friends. At the same time he increased the immense wealth of his family banking business which had been founded by his father, Giovanni de' Bicci. In 1439 Cosimo succeeded in having the Council which led to the brief union of the Greek and Roman churches transferred to Florence from Ferrara. The city, now at the height of her prestige in Europe, played host to the emperor John Paleologus, the Patriarch of Constantinople, and Pope Eugenius IV and their huge retinues of courtiers and scholars. Cosimo, perhaps the greatest figure in the history of Florence, symbolised the Renaissance ideal of the 'universal man'; a successful businessman and brilliant politician, he was also patron of the arts and an intellectual (he founded in Florence the first modern libraries in Europe).

On the death of Cosimo il Vecchio, 'Pater Patriae', his son Piero automatically took over his position in the government of the city. Known as 'Piero il Gottoso' because of his ill-health, his brief rule was characterised by his great interest in the arts, and a number of notable monuments of the Renaissance were commissioned by him. His son, Lorenzo, called 'Il Magnifico', was another famous Medici ruler during the Renaissance. His princely 'reign' fostered a revival of learning which lead to the foundation of the Platonic Academy at Careggi, which included among its members Lorenzo's friends Marsilio Ficino, Angelo Poliziano, and Pico della Mirandola. Lorenzo himself was a humanist scholar and poet of considerable standing. In a famous conspiracy in 1478 the Pazzi, old rivals of the Medici, with the help of Pope Sixtus IV, attempted to assassinate Lorenzo. His brother Giuliano was killed, but Lorenzo escaped, with the result that his position in the government of the city was even more secure. Francesco de' Pazzi and the other conspirators were hung from a window of Palazzo Vecchio. In 1489 Lorenzo succeeded in having his son Giovanni (later Pope Leo X) created a cardinal at the tender age of 13, one of his most significant political achievements. However, he was a less able businessman than his grandfather and was unable to save the Medici bank from failure before he died at the age of 44 in 1492.

Lorenzo il Magnifico's eldest son Piero was driven out of the city after his surrender to Charles VIII of France at Sarzana (1494), and the people, under the inspiration of the oratory of the Dominican Girolamo Savonarola, rebelled against the Medici, and a Republican government with a Great Council was formed. Savonarola was burnt at the stake as a heretic (1498) but the republic continued, and in 1502, under Piero Soderini, succeeded in retaking Pisa. After the defeat of Florence in battle by the Spanish army in 1512, Giuliano

34

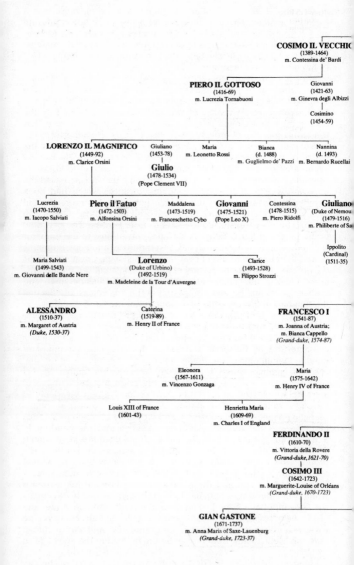

COSIMO IL VECCHIO
(1389-1464)
m. Contessina de' Bardi

Giovanni
(1421-63)
m. Ginevra degli Albizzi

Cosimino
(1454-59)

PIERO IL GOTTOSO
(1416-69)
m. Lucrezia Tornabuoni

LORENZO IL MAGNIFICO
(1449-92)
m. Clarice Orsini

Giuliano
(1453-78)

Giulio
(1478-1534)
(Pope Clement VII)

Maria
m. Leonetto Rossi

Bianca
(d. 1488)
m. Guglielmo de' Pazzi

Nannina
(d. 1493)
m. Bernardo Rucellai

Lucrezia
(1470-1550)
m. Iacopo Salviati

Piero il Fatuo
(1472-1503)
m. Alfonsina Orsini

Maddalena
(1473-1519)
m. Franceschetto Cybo

Giovanni
(1475-1521)
(Pope Leo X)

Contessina
(1478-1515)
m. Piero Ridolfi

Giuliano
(Duke of Nemou.
(1479-1516)
m. Philiberte of Sa

Maria Salviati
(1499-1543)
m. Giovanni delle Bande Nere

Lorenzo
(Duke of Urbino)
(1492-1519)
m. Madeleine de la Tour d'Auvergne

Clarice
(1493-1528)
m. Filippo Strozzi

Ippolito
(Cardinal)
(1511-35)

ALESSANDRO
(1510-37)
m. Margaret of Austria
(Duke, 1530-37)

Caterina
(1519-89)
m. Henry II of France

FRANCESCO I
(1541-87)
m. Joanna of Austria;
m. Bianca Cappello
(Grand-duke, 1574-87)

Eleonora
(1567-1611)
m. Vincenzo Gonzaga

Maria
(1575-1642)
m. Henry IV of France

Louis XIII of France
(1601-43)

Henrietta Maria
(1609-69)
m. Charles I of England

FERDINANDO II
(1610-70)
m. Vittoria della Rovere
(Grand-duke, 1621-70)

COSIMO III
(1642-1723)
m. Marguerite-Louise of Orléans
(Grand-duke, 1670-1723)

GIAN GASTONE
(1671-1737)
m. Anna Maria of Saxe-Lauenburg
(Grand-duke, 1723-37)

THE MEDICI FAMILY

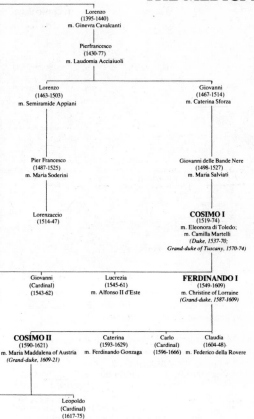

Giovanni di Bicci
(1360-1429)
m. Piccarda Bueri

Lorenzo
(1395-1440)
m. Ginevra Cavalcanti

Pierfrancesco
(1430-77)
m. Laudomia Acciaiuoli

Lorenzo
(1463-1503)
m. Semiramide Appiani

Giovanni
(1467-1514)
m. Caterina Sforza

Pier Francesco
(1487-1525)
m. Maria Soderini

Giovanni delle Bande Nere
(1498-1527)
m. Maria Salviati

Lorenzaccio
(1514-47)

COSIMO I
(1519-74)
m. Eleonora di Toledo;
m. Camilla Martelli
*(Duke, 1537-70;
Grand-duke of Tuscany, 1570-74)*

Giovanni
(Cardinal)
(1543-62)

Lucrezia
(1545-61)
m. Alfonso II d'Este

FERDINANDO I
(1549-1609)
m. Christine of Lorraine
(Grand-duke, 1587-1609)

COSIMO II
(1590-1621)
m. Maria Maddalena of Austria
(Grand-duke, 1609-21)

Caterina
(1593-1629)
m. Ferdinando Gonzaga

Carlo
(Cardinal)
(1596-1666)

Claudia
(1604-48)
m. Federico della Rovere

Leopoldo
(Cardinal)
(1617-75)

Anna Maria
(1667-1743)
m. William, Elector Palatine

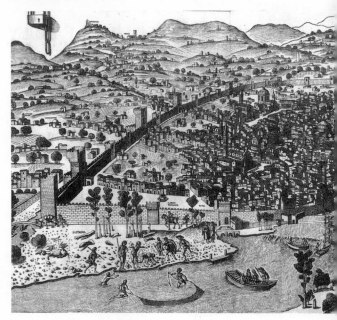

The 'Pianta della Catena', the first known view of the entire city, a woodcut of c 1472 attributed to Francesco Rosselli. (Berlin, Kupferstich Kabinett)

and Giovanni de' Medici returned to the city with the support of the Pope. However, in 1527 when Rome had been sacked by the troops of Charles V, they were again sent into exile. The new Republican government led by Niccolò Capponi lasted only until 1529 when a peace treaty between the Emperor and Pope provided for the reinstatement of the Medici in the government of Florence. The Florentines resisted their return in a last bid for independence but finally succumbed after a famous siege in which not even the new fortifications hastily erected by Michelangelo were able to withstand the united armies of Pope and Emperor. The great-grandson of Lorenzo il Magnifico, Alessandro, was married to the emperor Charles V's daughter Margaret of Parma, and appointed Duke of Florence in 1530.

Alessandro's unpopular rule, in which he was opposed by those who had supported the Republican regime, and by the patricians who saw their power in the government diminished, came to an abrupt end with his murder in 1537 by a cousin, Lorenzaccio. He was succeeded by Cosimo de' Medici, son of the famous condottiere, Giovanni delle Bande Nere. A last attempt by the Republican exiles (led by the rich aristocrat Filippo Strozzi) to abolish the Medici principate ended in their defeat at the battle of Montemurlo. During his long despotic rule, Cosimo I brought the subject cities of Tuscany under Florentine dominion, but his active and enlightened reign assured the independence of the Tuscan State from both Emperor and Pope. In 1570 Cosimo received the title of Grand-Duke of

Tuscany from Pope Pius V and the Medici absolutist principate
continued for another two centuries. Cosimo I commissioned numerous works of art and architecture to embellish the city and glorify his
name, and this patronage was continued by his successors (who also
amassed remarkable private eclectic collections). The Medici grand-
dukes were responsible for the Uffizi collection, which they augmented over the centuries, particularly Ferdinando II and his brother
Cardinal Leopoldo. The last of the Medici, Anna Maria Lodovica,
settled her inheritance on the people of Florence.

Two years before the death of Anna Maria de' Medici in 1737, the
succession of Francesco of Lorraine, afterwards Francis I of Austria,
had been arranged by treaty, and Tuscany became an appendage of
the Austrian Imperial house. The reign of Pietro Leopoldo, grand-
duke in 1765–90, stands out for his remarkable scientific interests
and the agricultural reforms he introduced to Tuscany (it was at this
time that many of the handsome 'case coloniche' were built in the
Tuscan countryside). In 1799 the French expelled the Austrians, and,
after an ephemeral appearance as the Kingdom of Etruria (1801–02),
under the Infante Louis of Bourbon, the grand duchy was conferred
in 1809 upon Elisa Bonaparte Baciocchi, Napoleon's sister. The
Bourbon restoration (1814) brought back the Lorrainers, whose rule,
interrupted by the revolution of 1848, ended in 1859. In March 1860
Tuscany became part of united Italy, and from 1861 to 1875 Florence
was the capital of the Italian kingdom.

Despite the efforts to prevent it by Gerhard Wolf, the wartime
German consul (later made a freeman by grateful Florentines), all the
bridges except the Ponte Vecchio were blown up by the Germans in
the Second World War; the city was occupied by the Allies in August
1944, after considerable although desultory fighting.

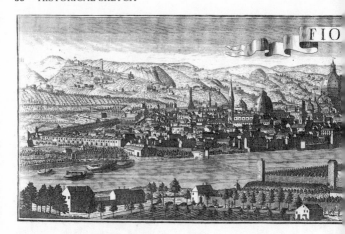

A view of Florence c 1735 from a copper engraving by
F.B. Werner. (Museo di Firenze com'era)

In 1966 the Arno overflowed its banks and severely damaged buildings and works of art. This was treated as an international disaster, and most historical buildings and works of art have now been restored. Reconstruction was necessary, too, of hundreds of houses and artisans' workshops, and it is not clear if sufficient precautions have since been taken to prevent another flood.

Among the many famous names that Florence has contributed to Italian culture the following stand out: the poets *Brunetto Latini* (1212–94), master of Dante, *Guido Cavalcanti* (c 1225–1300), and the great *Dante Alighieri* (1265–1321), whose 'Divina Commedia' established Tuscan as the literary vernacular of Italy. *Petrarch* (1304–74), son of a Florentine father, was a famous poet and the first great humanist. *Boccaccio* was born in Paris in 1312 but lived and died (1375) in Florence. The father of Italian prose, he described Florentine life in his 'Decameron', a brilliant secular work. Other Florentines include: the historians and statesmen *Niccolò Machiavelli* (1469–1527) and *Francesco Guicciardini* (1482–1540); the writers *Giovanni Rucellai* (1403–81), *Benvenuto Cellini* (1500–71), whose memoirs rival his goldsmith's work, *Giorgio Vasari* (born in Arezzo; 1511–74), art historian and author of the 'Lives of the Artists' as well as a painter and architect, and *Bernardo Davanzati* (1529–1606). The explorer *Amerigo Vespucci* (1451–1512) gave his name to America. *Galileo Galilei* (1564–1642) was born in Pisa but lived and died in Florence, and was succeeded by his pupil *Vincenzo Viviani* (1622–1703). Among the multitude of great Florentine artists *Leon Battista Alberti* (1404–72), *Michelangelo Buonarroti* (1475–1564) and *Leonardo da Vinci* (1454–1519) stand out not only for their artistic achievements but also for their writings and 'universal' talents.

Music. The change of style between Jacopo Peri's musical drama 'Dafne', performed in Palazzo Corsi in 1597, and his 'Euridice' composed in 1600 to honour the marriage in Florence of Maria de' Medici to Henri IV of France, is generally held to mark the beginning of opera. The pianoforte was invented in Florence in 1711 by Bartolomeo Cristofori (1655–1731). The composers Jean-Baptiste Lully (1632–87) and Luigi Cherubini (1760–1842) were natives of Florence.

Anglo-American Associations. Florence was one of the principal goals of the 'Grand Tour' and throughout the 18C and 19C was visited by almost every traveller of note. Prince Charles Edward Stuart lived in the city in 1774–85, where he was known to Florentines as the Count of Albany. His wife, the Countess of Albany, entertained Chateaubriand, Shelley, Byron and Von Platen in her 'salon'. Florence Nightingale (1820–1910) was born in Florence. John

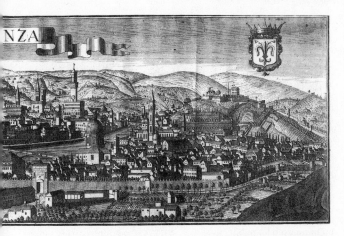

Singer Sargent, R.A. (1856–1925), son of a Boston physician, was likewise a native. Landor had several addresses in the city in 1821–28 before settling at Fiesole; while at the Villa Castiglione (3km beyond Porta San Niccolò) he met Lamartine, entertained Hazlitt, and was drawn by Bewick. He died in Via della Chiesa behind the Carmine. Leigh Hunt lived for a time in Via Magliabechi in 1823–25. Robert and Elizabeth Barrett Browning rented a flat in the Casa Guidi after their marriage in 1846 and lived in Florence until Elizabeth's death in 1861. Mark Twain finished 'Pudd'n-head Wilson' in 1892 at Settignano, and later lived at Quarto in a villa earlier occupied by Jerome Bonaparte. Princess Mary of Teck, later Queen Mary, lived here with her family 'in exile' in 1884–85, mainly at the Villa I Cedri near Bagno a Ripoli.

GLOSSARY

AEDICULE, small opening framed by two columns and a pediment, originally used in classical architecture

ARCHITRAVE, the lowest part of an entablature, the horizontal frame above a door

ARTE (pl. *Arti*), Guild or Corporation (see p 84).

ATTIC, topmost storey of a classical building, hiding the spring of the roof

BADIA, *Abbazia*, Abbey

BALDACCHINO, canopy supported by columns, usually over an altar

BASILICA, originally a Roman building used for public administration; in Christian architecture an aisled church with a clerestory and apse and no transepts

BORGO, a suburb; a street leading away from the centre of a town

BOTTEGA, the studio of an artist; the pupils who worked under his direction

BOZZETTO, sketch, often used to describe a small model for a piece of sculpture

CALDARIUM, room for hot or vapour baths in a Roman bath

CAMPANILE, bell-tower, often detached from the building to which it belongs

CANTORIA, singing-gallery in a church

CAPOMAESTRO, Director of Works

CARTOON, from *cartone*, meaning large sheet of paper. A full-size preparatory drawing for a painting or fresco

CASSONE, a decorated chest, usually a dower chest

CAVEA, the part of a theatre or amphitheatre occupied by the rows of seats

CENACOLO, a scene of the Last Supper (in the refectory of a convent)

CHIAROSCURO, distribution of light and shade, apart from colour, in a painting

CIBORIUM, casket or tabernacle containing the Host

CIPPOLINO, onion marble; greyish marble with streaks of white or green

CIPPUS (pl. *Cippae*), sepulchral monument in the form of an altar

CONTRAPPOSTO, a pose in which the body is twisted. First used in classical statuary, it is characteristic of Michelangelo's sculpture and works by the Mannerist school

CORBEL, a projecting block, usually of stone

CRENELLATIONS, battlements

CUPOLA, dome

DIPTYCH, painting or ivory tablet in two sections

DUOMO, cathedral

EXEDRA, semicircular recess

EX-VOTO, tablet or small painting expressing gratitude to a Saint

FRESCO (in Italian, *affresco*), painting executed on wet plaster. On the wall beneath is sketched the *sinopia*, and the *cartone* (see above) is transferred onto the fresh plaster (*intonaco*) before the fresco is begun either by pricking the outline with small holes over which a powder is dusted, or by means of a stylus which leaves an incised line on the wet plaster. In recent years many frescoes have been detached from the walls on which they were executed

FRIGIDARIUM, room for cold baths in a Roman bath

GRAFFITI, design on a wall made with an iron tool on a prepared surface, the design showing in white. Also used loosely to describe scratched designs or words on walls

GREEK CROSS, cross with the arms of equal length

GRISAILLE, painting in various tones of grey

GROTESQUE, painted or stucco decoration in the style of the ancient Romans (found during the Renaissance in Nero's Golden House in Rome, then underground, hence the name, from 'grotto'). The delicate ornamental decoration usually includes patterns of flowers, sphinxes, birds, human figures, etc., against a light ground

INTARSIA, inlay of wood, marble, or metal

INTRADOS, underside or soffit of an arch

LATIN CROSS, cross with a long vertical arm

LAVABO, hand-basin usually outside a refectory or sacristy

LOGGIA, covered gallery

LUNETTE, semicircular space in a vault or ceiling, or above a door or window, often decorated with a painting or relief

LUNGARNO (pl. *Lungarni*), a road which follows the banks of the Arno

MACIGNO, quartz, used as a building material in Florence

MAESTÀ, Madonna and Child enthroned in majesty

MEDALLION, large medal; loosely, a circular ornament

MONOCHROME, painting or drawing in one colour only

MONOLITH, single stone (usually a column)

NIELLO, black substance used in an engraved design

OCULUS, round window

OPERA (DEL DUOMO), the office in charge of the fabric of a building (i.e. the Cathedral)

OPUS TESSELLATUM, mosaic formed entirely of square tesserae

PALA, large altarpiece

PALAZZO, palace; any dignified and important building

PAX, sacred object used by a priest for the blessing of peace and offered for the kiss of the faithful; usually circular, engraved, enamelled, or painted in a rich gold or silver frame

PENDENTIVE, concave spandrel beneath a dome

PIETÀ, representation of the Virgin mourning the dead Christ (sometimes with other figures)

PIETRE DURE, hard or semi-precious stones, often used in the form of mosaics to decorate cabinets, table-tops, etc.

PIETRA FORTE, fine-grained limey sandstone used as a building material in Florence, and often for the rustication of palace façades

PIETRA SERENA, fine-grained dark grey sandstone, easy to carve. Although generally not sufficiently resistant for the exterior of buildings, it was used to decorate many Renaissance interiors in Florence

PLUTEUS (pl. *plutei*), marble panel, usually decorated; a series of them used to form a parapet to precede the altar of a church

POLYPTYCH, painting or panel in more than three sections

PORTONE, main entrance (large enough for carriages) to a Palazzo or Villa

PREDELLA, small painting or panel, usually in sections, attached below a large altarpiece, illustrating the story of a Saint, the Life of the Virgin, etc.

PRESEPIO, literally, crib or manger. A group of statuary of which the central subject is the Infant Jesus in the manger

PULVIN, cushion stone between the capital and the impost block

PUTTO (pl. *putti*), figure sculpted or painted, usually nude, of a child

QUATREFOIL, four-lobed design

ROOD-SCREEN, a screen below the Rood or Crucifix dividing the nave from the chancel of a church

SCHIACCIATO, term used to describe very low relief in sculpture, where there is an emphasis on the delicate line rather than the depth of the panel

SINOPIA, large sketch for a fresco made on the rough wall in a red earth pigment called sinopia (because it originally came from Sinope on the Black

Sea). By detaching a fresco it is now possible to see the sinopia beneath and detach it also

SPANDREL, surface between two arches in an arcade or the triangular space on either side of an arch

SPORTI, overhang, or projecting upper storey of a building, characteristic of medieval houses in Florence

STELA (Pl. *stelae*), upright stone bearing a monumental inscription

STEMMA, coat-of-arms or heraldic device

STOUP, vessel for Holy Water, usually near the W door of a church

TEPIDARIUM, room for warm baths in a Roman bath

TERM, pedestal or terminal figure in human form, tapering towards the base.

TERRAVERDE, green earth pigment, sometimes used in frescoes

TESSERA, small cube of marble, glass, etc., used in mosaic work

THERMAE, Roman Baths

THOLOS, a circular building

TONDO (pl. *tondi*, round painting or relief

TRANSENNA, open grille or screen, usually of marble, in an early Christian church

TRIPTYCH, painting or tablet in three sections

TROMPE L'OEIL, literally, a deception of the eye. Used to describe illusionist decoration, painted architectural perspectives, etc.

VILLA, country house with its garden

The terms QUATTROCENTO, CINQUECENTO (abbreviated in Italy '400, '500, etc.) refer not to the 14C and 15C, but to the 'fourteen-hundreds' and 'fifteen-hundreds', i.e. the 15C and 16C, etc.

PRACTICAL INFORMATION

Approaches to Florence

The approaches from the North are described in 'Blue Guide Northern Italy'.

Information Offices. General information may be obtained in London from the *Italian State Tourist Office (ENIT, Ente Nazionale Italiano per il Turismo)*, 1 Princes St, W1R 8AY, and in New York from 630 Fifth Avenue, suite 1565, NY 10111, who distribute free an invaluable 'Traveller's Handbook' (revised c every year), a list of hotels in Florence, etc. The official tourist offices throughout Italy are in the process of amalgamation and reorganisation. The local tourist office in Florence is now called the *Azienda di Promozione Turistica* ('*APT*'); the information office is at 16 Via Manzoni (Pl.7;8; open weekdays 8.30–13.30). This supplies useful up-to-date information to visitors. A Hotel Booking Office (*ITA*), who also supply tourist information is open (daily 9–20.30) at the railway station of Santa Maria Novella, and on the motorway approaches to Florence ('Chianti Est' and 'Peretola Sud'), and (in summer) at the Fortezza da Basso car park.

Travel Agents (most of whom belong to the Association of British Travel Agents) sell travel tickets and book accommodation, and also organise inclusive tours and charter trips to Florence. These include: *Citalia*, Marco Polo House, 3–5 Lansdowne Road, Croydon CR9 1LL, tel. 081 686 0677 (agents for the Italian State Railways), *Thomas Cook & Son*, 45 Berkeley St, W1, and other branches, *American Express*, Portland House, Stag Place, London SW1E 5BZ, etc.

Passports or **Visitors' Cards** are necessary for all British travellers entering Italy and must bear the photograph of the holder. American travellers must carry passports. Visitors are stongly advised to carry some means of identity with them at all times when in Italy.

Currency Regulations. Exchange controls have been suspended by the British Government since 1979. There are now no restrictions on the amount of sterling travellers may take out of Great Britain. There are frequent variations in the amount of bank notes which may be taken in or out of Italy; the latest regulations should be checked before departure.

Money. In Italy the monetary unit is the Italian lira (pl. lire). Notes are issued for 1000, 2000, 5000, 10,000, 50,000 and 100,000 lire. Coins are of 5, 10, 20, 50, 100, 200, and 500 lire. The rate of exchange is approximately 2100 lire to the £ and 1300 lire to the US dollar. Travellers' cheques and Eurocheques are the safest way of carrying money while travelling. Certain credit cards are generally accepted. For banking hours, see p 56. Money can also be changed at exchange offices ('Cambio') usually open 7 days a week at Pisa airport and the railway station in Florence, and (usually at a lower rate) at some hotels, restaurants, and shops.

Police Registration is required within three days of entering Italy. For travellers staying at a hotel the management will attend to the formality. The permit lasts three months, but can be extended on application.

Airports. The nearest international airport is at **Pisa**, 85km W of Florence; daily direct flights from London by *British Airways* and *Alitalia*. All services have a monthly excursion fare. Considerable reductions are normally available on scheduled return flights dependent on certain conditions. There is a special reduced fare for full-time students and young people. Charter companies also run services to Pisa from London at low prices, and 'package' holidays, including charter flight and hotel accommodation, are often an advantageous arrangement.—Alitalia also operate a direct flight between Pisa and Frankfurt and Paris, and direct internal services to Rome, Milan, Verona, Palermo, Cagliari, Alghero, and Olbia.

In 1983 a railway station was opened at Pisa airport, with frequent direct TRAIN SERVICES to Florence in 1 hour (via Pisa central and Empoli). There is no longer a coach service between the airport and Florence: there are town buses from the airport to Pisa central station where there are other (slower) train services to Florence. An AIR TERMINAL now operates at Florence Railway Station (on the Platform from which the airport trains depart). Luggage can be checked in here and boarding cards obtained (not later than 20 minutes before the departure of the airport train).

Bologna Airport also has flights from London, Paris, and Frankfurt. It is at Borgo Panicale, 7km NW of the city. Airport bus (No. 91; every half hour) to Piazza Stazione in Bologna, where there are trains (on the main Rome–Milan line) in 60–75 minutes to Florence.

The airport of **Peretola**, a few kilometres N of Florence, is used by small planes for domestic flights (including Milan and Rome) and some flights from Europe (Brussels, Munich, Paris, and Vienna). Bus No. 23C from the Railway Station and Piazza Duomo.

Railway Stations. *Stazione di Santa Maria Novella* (Pl.5;6), very close to the centre of the city. It has a restaurant, a left-luggage office, a bank, and a tourist information office with hotel booking facilities (see above). The station is well served by buses (cf. p 54), and there is a taxi rank on the E side of the building. An underground car park is under construction.—A few local trains, and fast trains to the S depart from *Campo di Marte* station (beyond Pl.7;4).—*Rifredi* station (N of Pl.5;2) is used by local trains, and by the express train (ETR450) between Milan and Rome.

A European Bus Service operates in two days between London and Rome via Florence, daily from June to September, and once or twice a week for the rest of the year. Information in London from the National Express Office at Victoria Coach Station, and in Florence at the SITA office.

Car Parks. The road approaches to Florence are described in 'Blue Guide Northern Italy'. British drivers in Italy will find the speed of the traffic faster than in Britain. Since 1988 the centre of Florence has been closed to private cars (except for those belonging to residents) from 7.30–18.30 (and also at night in summer), except on holidays. The limited traffic zone ('ZTL') includes virtually all the area within the Viali and part of the Oltrarno (from Porta Romana to Ponte Vecchio and Ponte alla Carraia). As a result, public transport functions more efficiently. However, car parking has become increasingly difficult and new car parks are still mostly in the planning stages. At present the only large car park with long-term parking near to the centre of the city is at the Fortezza da Basso (Pl.5;3,4; bus No. 15 to Piazza San Marco, the Duomo, Porta

Romana). Other smaller car parks (with a parking attendant and an hourly tariff) include Piazza di Porta Romana (Pl.8;6), Piazza Libertà (Pl.7;1), Piazza Beccaria (Pl.11;2), and Lungarno della Zecca Vecchia (Pl.11;3). An underground car park is being built in Piazza Stazione. Access is allowed to hotels within the limited traffic zone, but cars can only be parked outside hotels for a maximum of one hour (and must display a card supplied by the hotel). Florence also has a number of garages (Via Nazionale, Via Ghibellina, Borgo Ognissanti, etc., and in some hotels). Valuables should never be left in parked cars. Cars have to be removed once a week when the street is cleaned overnight (otherwise they are towed away; usually to 16 Via Circondaria, Rifredi; Tel. 355231).

Hotels

Florence has numerous hotels all over the city. These are all listed with charges in the annual (free) publication distributed by the official tourist office (APT) of Florence: *'Firenze: Elenco degli Alberghi'*. It is essential to book well in advance in summer and at Easter; to confirm the booking a deposit should be sent. The annual list of hotels in Florence may be obtained in London from the ENIT office, or from the APT in Florence. Reservations may be made on arrival at the ITA office at the railway station.

Every hotel has its fixed charges agreed with the official Tourist Board. In all hotels the service charges are included in the rates. VAT is added at a rate of 9 per cent (14 per cent in 5-star hotels). However the total charge is exhibited on the back of the door of the hotel room. Breakfast (usually disappointing and costly) should be an extra charge and not included in the price of the room. Hotels are now obliged by law (for tax purposes) to issue an official receipt to customers, who should not leave the premises without this document ('ricevuta fiscale'). There are now numerous agencies and hotel representatives in Britain and America who specialise in making hotel reservations (normally for 5-star and 4-star hotels). Florence Promhotels (72 Viale Volta) and Toscana Hotels 80 (9A Viale Gramsci) make hotel reservations in Florence.

In 1986 a new classification of hotels was introduced indicated by 'stars', as in the rest of Europe. At the same time the official categories of 'Pensione' and 'Locanda' were abolished. There are now five official categories of hotels from the luxury 5-star hotels to the most simple 1-star hotels. In the following list, the category has been given. Hotels with more than 100 rooms (100 R) have been indicated. Florence has over 350 hotels and it has been thought necessary to give only a small selection; omission does not imply any derogatory judgement.

Accommodation in Florence and environs

5-STAR HOTELS. **Excelsior** (*1*; Pl.5;7), 3 Piazza Ognissanti (210 R); **Grand Hotel** (*63*; Pl.5;7), 1 Piazza Ognissanti; **Helvetia e Bristol** (*21*; Pl.16;3), 2 Via de' Pescioni; **Regency** (*16*; Pl.7;6), 3 Piazza d'Azeglio; **Savoy** (*2*; Pl.16;4), 7 Piazza della Repubblica (100 R); **Villa Medici** (*3*; Pl.4;6), 42 Via il Prato (100 R), with swimming pool.

4-STAR HOTELS. **Astoria Pullman** (*4*: Pl.16;1), 9 Via del Giglio (100 R); **Berchielli** (*16*; Pl.16;5), 14 Lungarno Acciaiuoli and Piazza del Limbo; **Continental** (*19*; Pl.16;5), 2 Lungarno Acciaiuoli; **Croce di**

Malta (5; Pl.5;7), 7 Via della Scala (100 R); **De la ville** (6; Pl.16;3), Piazza Antinori; **Della Signoria** (20; Pl.16;5), 1 Via delle Terme; **Grand Hotel Baglioni** (7; Pl.5;6), Piazza Unità Italiana (200 R); **Grand Hotel Majestic** (8; Pl.5;6), 1 Via del Melarancio (100 R); **Grand Hotel Minerva** (9; Pl.5;8), 16 Piazza Santa Maria Novella (110 R); **J & J** (23; Pl.7;7), 20 Via di Mezzo; **Kraft** (10; Pl.4;6), 2 Via Solferino; **Londra** (11; Pl.5;5), 16 Via Jacopo da Diacceto (100 R); **Lungarno** (12; Pl.9;2), 14 Borgo San Jacopo; **Monna Lisa** (44; Pl.7;7), 27 Borgo Pinti; **Plaza Hotel Lucchesi** (13; Pl.11;3), 38 Lungarno della Zecca Vecchia (100 R); **Villa Carlotta** (60; Pl.9;7), 3 Via Michele di Lando.

3-STAR HOTELS. **Ambasciatori** (14; Pl.5;5), 3 Via Alamanni (100 R); **Annalena** (35; Pl.9;3), 34 Via Romana; **Aprile** (24; Pl.5;8), 6 Via della Scala; **Ariele** (36; Pl.4;6), 11 Via Magenta; **Balestri** (15; Pl.10;4), 7 Piazza Mentana; **Beacci Tornabuoni** (34; Pl.16;5), 3 Via Tornabuoni; **Bonciani** (17; Pl.5;8), 17 Via Panzani; **Dante** (27; Pl.11;1), 2 Via San Cristofano; **Duomo** (41; Pl.16;2), 1 Piazza Duomo; **Hermitage** (40; Pl.16;5), 1 Vicolo Marzio; **Jennings Riccioli** (22; Pl.10;4), 2 Lungarno delle Grazie; **La Residenza** (42; Pl.16; 3), 8 Via Tornabuoni; **Le Due Fontane** (55; Pl.6; 6), 14 Piazza Santissima Annunziata; **Loggiato dei Serviti** (32; Pl.6;7), 3 Piazza Santissima Annunziata; **Pendini** (45; Pl.16;3), 2 Via Strozzi; **Pitti Palace** (59; Pl.16;7), 2 Via Barbadori; **Porta Rossa** (28; Pl.16;5), 19 Via Porta Rossa; **Quisisana Ponte Vecchio** (46; Pl.16;5), 4 Lungarno Archibusieri; **Rapallo** (29; Pl.6;3), 7 Via Santa Caterina d'Alessandria; **Royal** (30; Pl.6;4), 52 Via delle Ruote; **Silla** (61; Pl.10;4), 5 Via dei Renai; **Villa Azalee** (31; Pl.4;6), 44 Viale Fratelli Rosselli.

2-STAR HOTELS. **Alessandra** (48; Pl.16;5), 17 Borgo Santi Apostoli; **Bellettini** (52; Pl.5;8), 7 Via dei Conti; **Boboli** (53; Pl.9;3), 63 Via Romana; **Bretagna** (37; Pl.9;2), 6 Lungarno Corsini; **Centrale** (38; Pl.5;8), 3 Via dei Conti; **Consigli** (39; Pl.4;8), 50 Lungarno Vespucci; **Delle Nazioni** (26; Pl.5;5), 15 Via Alamanni (130 R); **La Scaletta** (54; Pl.9;4), 13 Via Guicciardini; **Liana** (Pl.7;6), 18 Via Vittorio Alfieri; **Medici** (43; Pl.16;4), 6 Via dei Medici; **Norma** (56; Pl.16;5), 8 Borgo Santi Apostoli; **Rigatti** (47; Pl.16;8), 2 Lungarno Diaz; **Santa Croce** (33; Pl.10;2), 3 Via Bentaccordi; **Villani** (65; Pl.16;4), 11 Via delle Oche.

1-STAR HOTELS. **Antica** (49; Pl.6;8), 27 Via Pandolfini; **Bandini** (50; Pl.9;3), 9 Piazza Santo Spirito; **Brunetta** (Pl.7;7), 5 Borgo Pinti; **Chiazza** (Pl.7;7), 5 Borgo Pinti; **La Fiorentina** (Pl.5;8), 12 Via dei Fossi; **La Locandina** (64; Pl.11;1), 7 Via dei Pepi; **Souvenir** (Pl.6;4), 9 Via XXVII Aprile; and numerous others.

HOTELS OUTSIDE THE CENTRE OF FLORENCE with gardens (and convenient for visitors with cars). *On the S bank of the Arno*: **Grand Hotel Villa Cora** (57; Pl.9;7), 18 Viale Machiavelli, with swimming pool, 5-star; **Torre di Bellosguardo** (65; Pl.8;3,5), 2 Via Roti Michelozzi, with swimming pool, **Park Palace** (62; Pl.9;8), 5 Piazzale Galileo, with swimming pool, both 4-star; **David** (58; Pl.11;6), 1 Viale Michelangelo, 3-star.—*On the N bank of the Arno*: **Ville sull'Arno** (E of Pl.11;4), 1 Lungarno Cristoforo Colombo, with swimming pool, 4-star.—*On the N outskirts of the city*: **Villa Le Rondini** (N of Pl.7;1), 224 Via Bolognese (with swimming pool), 3-star.

HOTELS IN FIESOLE (within easy reach of Florence, and convenient for visitors with cars). All of them have gardens and are in good positions (especially pleasant in summer). *Villa San Michele*, 5-star; *Aurora*, 4-star; *Villa Bonelli, Bencistà, Villa San Girolamo*, all 2-star.

HOTELS IN THE ENVIRONS OF FLORENCE. *Bagno a Ripoli*, **Villa La Massa** (with swimming pool), 5-star; *San Casciano Val di Pesa*, **Antica Posta**, 3-star; *Sesto Fiorentino*, **Park Alexander** (with swimming pool), 3-star; *Artimino*, **Paggeria Medicea**, 4-star; *Reggello*, **Villa Rigacci** (with swimming pool), 76 Via Vaggio, 4-star; also at *Poggio a Caiano, Impruneta*, the *Mugello, Vallombrosa*, etc.

Hostels. The YOUTH HOSTEL of Florence (*Ostello per la Gioventù*) is at 'Villa Camerata', 2 Viale Righi, in a good position in a park at the bottom of the hill of San Domenico (500 beds). Bus No. 17C from the Station and Duomo. The headquarters of the *Italian Youth Hostels Association* (Associazione Italiana Alberghi per la Gioventù) is at Palazzo della Civiltà del Lavoro, 00144 EUR, Rome. A membership card of the AIG or the International Youth Hostel Federation is required for access to Italian Youth Hostels.—Other HOSTELS, some run by religious organisations, are shown in the annual hotel list supplied by the APT. These include the *Centro Ospitalità Santa Monica*, 6 Via Santa Monica, the *Casa di Sette Santi*, 11 Viale dei Mille, *Villa Linda*, 5 Via Poggio Gherardo (Ponte a Mensola), *Oblate dell'Assunzione*, 15 Borgo Pinti.

Camping. A list of camping sites in and around Florence is available from the APT. Full details of all sites in Italy are published annually by the Touring Club Italiano and Federcampeggio in 'Campeggi e Villaggi Turistici in Italia'. The Federazione Italiana del Campeggio have an information office near Florence (Telephone 055/882391), and a booking service (Centro Internazionale Prenotazioni Campeggio-Itcamp travel, Casella Postale 23, 50041, Calenzano).—The main camping site in Florence 'ITALIANI E STRANIERI' is at 80 Viale Michelangelo (Pl.11;5), which takes 320 tents (closed November–March). Another site, 'VILLA CAMERATA', is at 2 Viale Righi in the park of the Youth Hostel at the bottom of the hill of San Domenico.—In Fiesole, 'CAMPING PANORAMICO' in Via Peramonda, Borgunto (see Atlas p 13) is another site in a good position (91 tents; open all year). There are also camping sites in the environs, at *Impruneta*, in the *Mugello, Calenzano*, etc.

Restaurants and Cafés

Restaurants in Italy are called 'Ristoranti' or 'Trattorie'; there is now usually no difference between the two. The least pretentious restaurant almost invariably provides the best value. The menu displayed outside the restaurant indicates the kind of charges the customer should expect. However, many simpler establishments do not offer a menu, and here, although the choice is usually limited the standard of cuisine is often very high.

Prices on the menu generally do not include a cover charge (*coperto*, shown separately on the menu) which is added to the bill. The service charge is now almost always automatically added at the end of the bill. Tipping is therefore not strictly necessary, but a few thousand lire are appreciated. Fish is always the most expensive item on the menu in any restaurant. Lunch is normally around 13.00 and is the main meal of the day, while dinner is around 20.00 or 21.00. Restaurants are now obliged by law (for tax purposes) to issue an official receipt to customers, who should not leave the premises without this document ('rivevuta fiscale'). Many restaurants in Florence close down for part of August (or July). Many restaurants are closed on Mondays.

In the list below a selection of restaurants has been given *grouped according to price range.*

1. Luxury-class, well-known restaurants, with international cuisine

La Capannina di Sante, Piazza Ravenna, Ponte da Verrazzano (beyond Pl.11;4), specialising in fish
Enoteca Pinchiorri, 87 Via Gibellina (Pl.10;2)
Relais Le Jardin, in the Hotel Regency, Piazza d'Azeglio (Pl.7;6)
Helvetia e Bristol, in the Hotel Helvetia e Bristol, 2 Via de' Pescioni (Pl.16;3)

2. First-class elegant restaurants

Al Lume di Candela, 23 Via delle Terme (Pl.16;5)
Cantinetta Antinori, Palazzo Antinori (Pl.16;3)
Cibreo, 118 Via dei Macci (Pl.11;1), with two sections, one more expensive and one simpler and less expensive
Da Noi, 46 Via Fiesolana (Pl.7;7)
Harry's Bar, 22 Lungarno Vespucci (Pl.5;7)
La Loggia, Piazzale Michelangelo (Pl.11;5)
Pepolino, 16 Via Ferrucci (beyond Pl.11;2)
Taverna del Bronzino, Via delle Ruote (Pl.6;4)
Toulà-Olivero, 21 Via delle Terme (Pl.16;5)

3A. First-class restaurants

Celestino, Piazza Santa Felicita (Pl.16;7)
Garga, 18 Via del Moro (Pl.5;8)
La Posta, 20 Via Lamberti (Pl.16;5)
Le Quattro Stagioni, 61 Via Maggio (Pl.9;4)
Mamma Gina, 36 Borgo San Jacopo (Pl.16;7)
Paoli, 12 Via dei Tavolini (Pl.16;4)
San Zanobi, 33 Via San Zanobi (Pl.6;5)
Silvio, 74 Via del Parione (Pl.16;5)
Trattoria del Teatro, 57 Via degli Alfani (Pl.7;7)
Vecchia Cucina, 1 Viale De Amicis (beyond Pl.11;2)

3B. First-class traditional trattorie

Cammillo, 57 Borgo San Jacopo (Pl.16;7)
Cocco Lezzone, 26 Via del Parioncino (Pl.16;5)
Il Francescano, 16 Largo Bargellini (Via San Giuseppe; Pl.11;1)
'Il Troia' (Trattoria Sostanza), 29 Via Porcellana (Pl.5;7)

4. Well-known trattorie

Cafaggi, 33 Via Guelfa (Pl.6;5)
Il Cavallino, Piazza Signoria (with tables outside in summer; Pl.16;6)
Enoteca Pane e Vino, 48 Via Poggio Bracciolini (beyond Pl.11;4)
La Maremmana, 77 Via de' Macci (Pl.11;1)
Latini, 6 Via Palchetti (Pl.5;8)
Mario da Ganino, 4 Piazza Cimatori (Pl.16;6)
Pallottino, 1 Via Isola delle Stinche (Pl.10;2)
Il Profeta, 93 Borgo Ognissanti (Pl.5;7)

5. Simple trattorie of good value

Acquacotta, 51 Via dei Pilastri (Pl.7;7)
Angiolino, 36 Via Santo Spirito (Pl.9;1)
Baldo Vino, 22 Via San Giuseppe (also a pizzeria; Pl.11;1)
Benvenuto, 16 Via Mosca (Pl.16;6)

Borgo Antico, 6 Piazza Santo Spirito (also a pizzeria; with tables outside in summer; Pl.9;3)
Da Ruggero, 89 Via Senese (Pl.8;8)
Diladdarno, 108 Via de' Serragli (Pl.9;3)
Le Mossacce, 55 Via Proconsolo (Pl.16;6)
Le Sorelle, 30 Via San Niccolò (Pl.11;3)
Nella, 19 Via delle Terme (Pl.16;5)
Raddi, 47 Via dell'Ardiglione (Pl.9;3)
Trattoria del Carmine, 18 Piazza del Carmine (with tables outside in summer; Pl.9;1)
   Alessi, 24 (red) Via di Mezzo (Pl.7;7). A club (membership by previous appointment; annual subscription) run by a scholar of Renaissance cuisine who produces excellent traditional Tuscan dishes. Not dressy but suitable for those interested exclusively in a good inexpensive meal (always crowded; when you have finished you are often invited to leave).

6A.   Cheap eating places (usually crowded and often less comfortable than normal trattorie)

La Casalinga, 9 Via Michelozzi (Piazza Santo Spirito; Pl.9;3)
La Taverna, 15 Via Michelozzi (Piazza Santo Spirito; Pl.9;3)
Mario, 2 Via Rosina (lunch only; Pl.16;5)
Nerbone, inside the Mercato Centrale di San Lorenzo (lunch only; Pl.6;5)
Palle d'Oro, 42 Sant'Antonino (Pl.6;5)
Quattro Leoni, Via Toscanella (1 Via Vellutini; Pl.16;7)
Tavola Calda, inside the market of Sant'Ambrogio (lunch only; Pl.11;1)
Trattoria Girrarosto da Pietro (Fratelli Leonessi), 8 Piazza delle Cure (Pl.7;2)

6B.   'Vinai' who sell wine by the glass and good simple food

Vinaio in Via Alfani (No. 70; Pl.6;6)
Vinaio in Via della Chiesa (corner of Via della Caldaia; Pl.9;3)

7.   'Vinai' who sell snacks but have no seating accommodation

Cantina Ristori, 6 Volta di San Piero (Pl.10;2)
Donatello, Via de' Neri (corner of Via de' Benci; Pl.10;2)
Fratellini, 38 Via dei Cimatori (Pl.16;6)
Vinaio, 25 Piazza Castellani (Pl.16;6)
   Egyptian snack bar: *Amon*, 38 Via del Palazzuolo (Pl.5;8)

Pizzas and other good hot snacks are served in a *Pizzeria, Rosticceria,* and *Tavola Calda*. Some of these (in Via Cavour, Via dell'Ariento, the Corso, etc.) have no seating accommodation and sell food to take away or eat on the spot. Tripe, a Florentine speciality, is sold in sandwiches from barrows on the street (at the Arco di San Piero, Via dell'Ariento, Piazza San Frediano, Piazza del Porcellino, Piazza de'Frescobaldi, etc.). *Friggitorie* are small shops where fried snacks (sweet and savoury) are sold (in Via dell'Albero, Via Sant'Antonino, Volta di S. Piero, Borgo Pinti, Via dei Neri, Via Serragli, Piazza dei Ciompi, etc.). Sandwiches ('panini') are made up on request at *Pizzicherie* and *Alimentari* (grocery shops), and *Fornai* (bakeries) often sell individual pizze, cakes, etc.

Vegetarian Restaurants: 30 Via delle Ruote; *Il Santommaso*, 80 Via Romana.

Kosher Restaurant: 3 Via Farini.

Chinese Restaurants include: *Fior di Loto*, 35 Via dei Servi; *Il Mandarino*, 17 Via Condotta; *Peking*, 21 Via del Melarancio.

STUDENTS' CANTEENS ('MENSE') are open at 25 Via San Gallo, Via dei Servi (No. 66), and 51 Viale Morgagni.

Restaurants in the environs of Florence of various categories. Rte 23. **Fiesole:** *Trattoria 'Il Lordo'*, 13 Piazza Mino da Fiesole; *La Romagnola*, Via Gramsci; *Pizzeria di San Domenico*, San Domenico.—**Olmo:** Torre di Buiano, *Casa del Prosciutto, Da Mario.* **Maiano:** *La Graziella* (with tables outside), *Le Cave di Maiano* (with tables outside).—Rte 24. **Settignano** (Ponte a Mensola): *Osvaldo.*— Rte 25. **Arcetri:** *Omero*, 11 Via Pian dei Giullari (with tables outside).—Rte 29. **Serpiolle:** *Strettoio*, 7 Via di Serpiolle. **Cercina:** *Trianon, I Ricchi* (both with tables outside). **Sesto Fiorentino:** *Dulcamara Club*, 2 Via Dante da Castiglione.—Rte 27. **Galluzzo:** *Da Bibe*, 1 Via delle Bagnese, Ponte all'Asse, **Sant'Andrea in Percussina:** *Scopeti.*—**Pozzolatico:** *I Tre Pini*, 134 Via Imprunetana.— Rte 30. **Artimino:** *La Delfina.*—**San Casciano, Val di Pesa:** *Cantinetta del Nonno, Nello.*—**Cerbaia, Val di Pesa:** *La Tenda Rossa.*

Picnic Places. Excellent food for picnics may be purchased from grocery shops, bakeries, cafés, *rosticcerie*, etc. Some of the most pleasant spots in the city to have a picnic include: the Boboli gardens (Pl.9;5,6), Forte di Belvedere (Pl.10;5), the park of Villa Strozzi (Pl.4;7), the Giardino dell'Orticoltura (Pl.7;1), the park of Villa il Ventaglio (beyond Pl.7;2; closed Monday), the park of Villa Stibbert (beyond Pl.6;2), and in the gardens off Viale Machiavelli (Pl.9;7,8). In the immediate environs, particularly beautiful countryside can be found near Fiesole, Maiano, Settignano, and Ponte a Mensola.

Cafés (*Bar*), which are open all day, serve numerous varieties of excellent refreshments which are usually eaten standing up. The cashier should be paid first, and the receipt given to the barman in order to get served. It has become customary to leave a small tip for the barman. If the customer sits at a table the charge is considerably higher (at least double) and he will be given waiter service (and should not pay first). Black coffee (*caffè* or *espresso*) can be ordered diluted (*lungo* or *alto*), with a dash of milk (*macchiato*), with a liquor (*corretto*), or with hot milk (*cappuccino* or *caffè-latte*). In summer cold coffee (*caffè freddo*) and cold coffee and milk (*caffè-latte freddo*) are served.

The best well-known cafés in the city which serve good snacks and all of which have tables (some outside) include: *Rivoire*, Piazza Signoria; *Le Giubbe Rosse, Gilli*, both in Piazza della Repubblica; *Giacosa*, Via Tornabuoni; *San Firenze* Piazza San Firenze; *Il Cafè*, Piazza Pitti.—Cafés without tables, but well-known for their cakes, pastries, and confectionery, include: *Robiglio*, Via dei Servi and Via Tosinghi; *Giurovich*, Viale Don Minzoni; *Procacci*, Via Tornabuoni (famous for truffle sandwiches); *Gambrinus*, Via Brunelleschi; *Sieni*, Via dell'Ariento; *Maioli*, Via Guicciardini; and *Scudieri*, Via Cerretani. The *Pasticceria Alcedo* in Fiesole makes particularly good cakes and pastries.

Among the best ICE-CREAM SHOPS in Florence are: *Vivoli*, 7 Via Isola delle Stinche (near Santa Croce); *Badiani*, 20 Viale dei Mille; *Cavini*, 22 Piazza delle Cure; and *Perchè no?*, 19 Via dei Tavolini.

Food and Wine. As elsewhere in Italy traditional local dishes have become more difficult to find, and Florentine cookery is now similar to that to be found all over the country. The chief speciality of Italian cookery is the *Pasta* served in various forms with different sauces and sprinkled with cheese. A well-known Tuscan soup is *minestrone* made with a variety of vegetables. *Ribollita* or *zuppa di pane* is a thick soup of bread, white beans, cabbage, herbs, etc. In summer, *panzanella* is a tasty dish, made of dry bread, tomatoes, capers, basil, etc. As a main course, *bistecca alla fiorentina* is famous, a large T-bone steak which can be grilled in one piece and served to two or three people. Tripe (*trippa*) is also a traditional Florentine dish, usually cooked in tomato sauce and parmesan cheese. *Baccalà* (salt cod) is an acquired taste; it is boiled or fried *'alla Livornese'* with tomato sauce. Another unusual fish dish is *inzimino,* cuttlefish cooked with vegetables. White beans (*fagioli*) are a favourite Florentine speciality, cooked with sage, in a tomato sauce (*fagioli all'uccelletto*).

Wines. The cheapest wine is always the 'house wine' (*vino della casa*), which varies a great deal, but is normally a drinkable 'vin ordinaire'. The most famous Tuscan wine is *Chianti* (the name is protected by law, and only those wines from a relatively small district which lies between Florence and Siena are entitled to the name 'Chianti Classico'). *Chianti Classico 'Gallo Nero'* (distinguished by a black cock on the bottle) is usually considered the best, but *Chianti 'Putto'* and *Chianti 'Grappolo'* are often just as good. Other wines in Tuscany (where the red table wine is usually of better quality than the white) such as *Vino nobile di Montepulciano, Vernaccia* (white, from San Gimignano), *Aleatico* (a dessert wine from Elba), and *Brunello di Montalcino* (not cheap) are particularly good.

The MENU which follows includes many dishes that are likely to be available in Florentine restaurants:

Antipasti, Hors d'oeuvre

Prosciutto crudo o cotto, Ham, raw or cooked
Prosciutto e melone, Ham (usually raw) and melon
Salame, Salami
Finocchiona, Salami cured with fennel
Crostini, Fresh liver paste served on bread
Salame con funghi e carciofini sott'olio, Salami with mushrooms and artichokes in oil
Tonno, Tunny fish
Salsicce, Dry sausage
Frittata, Omelette
Verdura cruda, Raw vegetables
Carciofi o finocchio in pinzimonio, Raw artichokes or fennel with a dressing
Antipasto misto, Mixed cold hors d'oeuvre
Antipasto di mare, Seafood hors d'oeuvre
Panzanella, A summer salad made with dry bread, tomatoes, capers, basil, onions, etc.
Insalata Russa, Russian salad

Minestre e Pasta, Soups and Pasta

Minestra, zuppa, Thick soup
Brodo, Clear soup
Stracciatella, Broth with beaten egg
Minestrone alla toscana, Tuscan vegetable soup
Taglierini (or *Tagliolini*) *in brodo,* Thin pasta in broth
Spaghetti al sugo or *al ragù,* Spaghetti with a meat sauce
Spaghetti al pomodoro, Spaghetti with a tomato sauce

Penne all'Arrabbiata (or *Strascicata*), Short pasta with a rich spicy sauce
Tagliatelle, Flat spaghetti-like pasta, almost always made with egg
Lasagne, Layers of pasta with meat filling and cheese and tomato sauce
Cannelloni, Rolled pasta 'pancakes' with meat filling and cheese and tomato sauce
Ravioli, Pasta filled with spinach and ricotta cheese (or with minced veal)
Tortellini, Small coils of pasta, filled with a rich stuffing served either in broth or with a sauce
Fettuccine, Ribbon noodles
Spaghetti alla carbonara, Spaghetti with bacon, beaten egg, and black pepper sauce
Spaghetti alla matriciana, Spaghetti with salt pork and tomato sauce
Spaghetti alle vongole, Spaghetti with clams
Agnolotti, Ravioli filled with meat
Pappardelle alla lepre, Pasta with hare sauce
Cappelletti, Form of ravioli often served in broth
Gnocchi, A heavy pasta made from potato, flour, and eggs
Risotto, Rice dish
Risotto di mare, ... with fish
Polenta, Yellow maize flour, usually served with a meat or tomato sauce
Pappa di pomodoro, a thick tomato 'soup' with bread, seasoned with basil, etc.

Pesce, Fish

Zuppa di pesce, Mixed fish usually in a sauce (or soup)
Fritto misto di mare, Mixed fried fish
Fritto di pesce, Fried fish
Pesce arrosto, *Pesce alla griglia*, Roast, grilled fish
Pescespada, Sword-fish
Aragosta, Lobster
Calamari, Squid
Baccalà, Salt cod (*alla Livornese*, fried and cooked in a tomato sauce)
Sarde, Sardines
Coda di Rospo, Angler fish
Dentice, Dentex
Orata, Bream
Triglie, Red mullet
Sgombro, Mackerel
Cefalo, Grey mullet
Anguilla, Eel
Sogliola, Sole
Tonno, Tunny fish
Trota, Trout
Cozze, Mussels
Gamberi, Prawns
Polipi, Octopus
Seppie, Cuttlefish
Acciughe, Anchovies

Pietanze, Entrèes

Bistecca alla fiorentina, T-bone steak, (usually cooked over charcoal)
Vitello, Veal
Manzo, Beef
Agnello, Lamb
Maiale (arrosto), Pork (roast)
Pollo (bollito), Chicken (boiled)
Petto di Pollo, Chicken breasts
Pollo alla cacciatora, Chicken with herbs, and (usually) tomato and pimento sauce
Costoletta alla Bolognese, Veal cutlet with ham, covered with melted cheese
Costolette alla Milanese, Veal cutlets, fried in breadcrumbs
Saltimbocca, Rolled veal with ham
Bocconcini, Rolled veal with cheese
Scaloppine al marsala, Veal escalope cooked in wine
Ossobuco, Stewed shin of veal
Coda alla vaccinara, Oxtail cooked with herbs and wine
Stufato, Stewed meat served in pieces in a sauce

Polpette, Meat balls (often served in a sauce)
Involtini, Thin rolled slices of meat in a sauce
Spezzatino, Veal stew, usually with pimento, tomato, onion, peas, and wine
Cotechino e Zampone, Pig's trotter stuffed with pork and sausages
Stracotto, Beef cooked in a sauce, or in red wine
Trippa, Tripe
Fegato, Calf's liver
Fegatini alla Salvia, Chicken's livers cooked with sage
Tacchino arrosto, Roast turkey
Cervello, Brains
Rognoncini trifolati, Sliced kidneys in a sauce
Animelle, Sweetbreads
Bollito, Stew of various boiled meats
Arista, Pork chop
Rosticciana, Grilled spare ribs
Coniglio, Rabbit
Lepre, Hare
Cinghiale, Wild boar
Piccione, Pigeon

Contorni, Vegetables

Insalata verde, Green salad
Insalata mista Mixed salad
Pomodori, Tomatoes
Funghi, Mushrooms
Spinaci, Spinach
Broccoletti, Tender broccoli
Piselli, Peas
Fagiolini, Beans (French)
Fagioli (all'uccelletto), White beans (in a tomato sauce)
Carciofi, Artichokes
Asparagi, Asparagus
Zucchini, Courgettes
Melanzane, Aubergine
Melanzane alla parmigiana, Aubergine in cheese sauce
Peperoni, Pimentoes
Peperonata, Stewed pimentoes, often with aubergine, onion, tomato, potato, etc.
Finocchi, Fennel
Patatine fritte, Fried potatoes

Dolci, Sweets

Torta, Tart
Monte Bianco, Mont Blanc (with chestnut flavouring)
Saint Honorè, Rich meringue cake
Gelato, Ice cream
Cassata, Ice cream cake
Zuppa Inglese, Trifle
Torta della nonna, Cream flan with almonds
Castagnaccio, Chestnut cake with pine nuts and sultanas
Crostata, Fruit flan
Bongo-Bongo, Chocolate cream éclairs

Frutta, Fruit

Macedonia di frutta, Fruit salad
Fragole (con panna), Strawberries (and cream)
Fragole (al limone), ... with lemon
Fragole (al vino), ... with wine
Fragoline di bosco, Wild strawberries
Mele, Apples
Pere, Pears
Arance, Oranges
Ciliege, Cherries
Pesche, Peaches

Albicocche, Apricots
Uva, Grapes
Fichi, Figs
Melone, Melon
Popone, Water melon

Transport

Buses provide an excellent and fast means of transport in Florence now that the centre of the city has been closed to private traffic. The service is run by ATAF (Information office, 57 (red) Piazza del Duomo, Tel. 580528). Tickets are obtained from machines at bus stops, tobacconists and most bars, or ATAF offices (Piazza del Duomo, the Station, etc.). At present a ticket for unlimited travel on any bus for 70 minutes costs 800 lire; a ticket valid for 120 minutes costs 1000 lire (8 tickets can be purchased together for 6000 lire). Season tickets (30,000 lire) valid for one calendar month (two photographs are necessary), or a season ticket which can be used by more than one person (40,000 lire), can also be purchased at 57 Piazza del Duomo. These can be renewed at tobacconists, bars, etc. A 'biglietto turistico' valid for 24 hours can also be purchased (4000 lire). Tickets must be stamped at an automatic machine on board. Because of one-way streets, return journeys do not always follow the same route as the outward journey. A selection of the more important routes (subject to variation) is given below. An excellent map is now available free at the ATAF office in Piazza del Duomo.

Bus Services

15 Fortezza da Basso (car park)—Piazza Indipendenza—Piazza San Marco—Via Cavour—Via Proconsolo—Ponte alle Grazie—Piazza Pitti—Piazza Santo Spirito—Piazza del Carmine—Viale Petrarca—Porta Romana. The return journey from Porta Romana follows Via Maggio—Ponte Santa Trìnita—Via Tornabuoni—Via Cavour—Piazza San Marco—Piazza Indipendenza—Fortezza da Basso.

1 Piazza Stazione—Via Panzani—Piazza Duomo—Via Cavour—Piazza Libertà—Le Cure, etc.

11 Via Cavour—Piazza Duomo—Via Strozzi—Ponte alla Carraia—Via Serragli—Porta Romana—Poggio Imperiale

17C Cascine—Piazza Stazione—Piazza Duomo—Via Lamarmora—Viale dei Mille—Salvatino (Youth Hostel)

13 red (circular) Piazza Stazione—Ponte alla Vittoria—Viale Raffaello Sanzio—Porta Romana—Viale Michelangelo—Piazzale Michelangelo—Ponte alle Grazie—Via dei Benci—Via dell'Oriuolo—Piazza Duomo—Piazza Stazione

13 black (circular)—as above, but in the opposite direction

38 Porta Romana—Piazzale Galileo—Pian dei Giullari

7 Piazza Stazione—Piazza Duomo—Piazza San Marco—San Domenico—Fiesole

10 Piazza San Marco—Ponte a Mensola—Settignano

28 Piazza Stazione—Via Reginaldo Giuliani—Il Sodo—Castello—Sesto Fiorentino—Calenzano

14C Piazza Duomo—Piazza Stazione—Viale Morgagni—Careggi

25 Piazza San Marco—Piazza Libertà—Via Bolognese—(25A continues to Pratolino)

12 Via Pacinotti—Via Faentina—Ponte alla Badia—Le Caldine—La Querciola

23C Piazza Stazione—Peretola airport

37 Via Fiume—Piazza Santa Maria Novella—Ponte alla Carraia—Porta Romana—Galluzzo—Certosa—Tavarnuzze

31 Piazza Stazione—Piazza Duomo—Lungarno della Zecca Vecchia—Ponte da Verrazzano—Badia a Ripoli—Ponte a Ema—Grassina

32 Piazza Stazione—Piazza Duomo—Lungarno della Zecca Vecchia—Ponte da Verrazzano—Badia a Ripoli—Ponte a Ema—Antella

4 Piazza Stazione—Via Vittorio Emanuele (for Museo Stibbert)

Country Buses. From Florence a wide network of bus services in Tuscany is operated by *Lazzi*, 4 Piazza Stazione (Tel. 215154), *SITA*, 15 Via Santa Caterina da Siena (Tel. 211487), *COPIT*, 22 Piazza Santa Maria Novella (Tel. 215451), and *CAP*, 9 Largo Alinari (Tel. 214637). Details of the main services of interest to the visitor are given in the text of the environs (Rtes 23–30).

Bicycle Hire. In summer the Comune sometimes provides bicycles which can be hired free of charge in Piazza Stazione, Porta Romana, Piazza Piave, Piazza della Libertà, and at the Fortezza da Basso. A Bicycle hire firm ('Ciao e Basta') operates all year round in Via Alamanni (beneath the central railway station).

Taxis (white) are provided with taximeters. They are hired from ranks; there are no cruising taxis. There are ranks at the Station, Piazza Santa Maria Novella, Piazza San Marco, Piazza Santa Trìnita, Piazza del Duomo, Piazza della Signoria, Piazza della Repubblica, Porta Romana, etc. For Radio taxis dial 4390 or 4798. A supplement for night service, and for luggage is charged. Modest tipping is expected.—HORSE CABS are used exclusively by tourists. The fare must be established before starting the journey. In summer, they can usually be hired in Piazza del Duomo and Piazza della Signoria.

Car Hire. The principal car-hire firms have offices at Pisa airport as well as in Florence. *Avis*, 128 Borgo Ognissanti; *Hertz*, 33 Via Maso Finiguerra; *Maggiore*, 11 Via Maso Finiguerra, etc.

Sight-seeing Tours of Florence and environs. Tours of Florence, Pisa, and Siena and San Gimignano are organised by *CIT* (54 Via Cavour), starting at 51 Piazza Stazione (corner of Piazza dell'Unità Italiana), and other travel agents in Florence (see below).—*Agriturist* (3 Piazza San Firenze) usually organise afternoon trips by coach in the Tuscan countryside (in the autumn), and visits to the gardens of Florentine villas, some of them otherwise closed to the public (usually from April–June). These can be booked at any tourist agency in Florence. Information from APT and hotels.

Useful Addresses

Information Offices and Tourist Agents. *APT*, 16 Via Manzoni.—Among the numerous tourist agents in Florence are: *CIT*, 54 Via Cavour, 51 Piazza Stazione; *American Express*, 49r Via Guicciardini; *Wagons-Lits Turismo*, 27 Via del Giglio; *Eyre & Humbert*, 56 Via del Parione; *Universalturismo*, 7 Via Speziali; *CTU Viaggi*, 9 Via San Gallo (also for student travel facilities).

Post Offices are open 8.15–13.40 (Saturday 8.15–12). The head post offices are in 53 Via Pietrapiana (Pl.11;1) and Via Pellicceria (Pl.16;3), with telephone exchanges (always open) and 'Poste Restante' (open 8.15–19.30). A few post Offices are also open in the afternoon (including the one in Viale dei Mille).

Public Offices. For all emergencies, Tel. 113. *Questura* (Central Police Station), 2 Via Zara; *Carabinieri* (flying squad), 48 Borgo Ognissanti (Tel. 112). *Lost-Property Office*, 19 Via Circondaria (Tel. 367943).—HOSPITALS: *Santa Maria Nuova*, 1 Piazza Santa Maria Nuova; *Careggi*, Viale Morgagni; *San Giovanni di Dio*, Via Scandicci, Torregalli, etc. Childrens Hospital: *Meyer*, 14 Via Luca Giordano. For emergency medical service at night and on holidays, Tel. 4976 or 477891. Ambulance service of the Misericordia, Tel. 4976 or 212222. Mobile Coronary Unit, Tel. 214444. Some chemists (*farmacie*) remain open all night and on holidays (including the chemist shop at the main railway station, at No. 7 Via Calzaioli, and at No. 20 Piazza San Giovanni; others are listed in the local newspapers, or Tel. 192).

RAILWAY STATION. Information office, Tel. 278785 (or 110).— *Automobile Club d'Italia* (*ACI*), 36 Viale Amendola. Breakdown service, Tel. 116 (in Florence, Tel. 24861).—*Pisa Airport*, Tel. (050) 28088; *Peretola Airport*, Tel. 318000. *Alitalia*, 10 Lungarno Acciaioli; *British Airways*, 36 Via Vigna Nuova.

Banks (usually open Monday–Friday 8.20–13.30 and for 1 hour in the afternoon, usually about 14.30–15.30; Saturday and holidays closed; early closing on the day preceding a national holiday). *Banca Commerciale Italiana*, 8 Via Strozzi; *Cassa di Risparmio di Firenze*, 4 Via Bufalini; *Banca d'Italia*, 37 Via Oriuolo; *Banca d'America e d'Italia*, 16 Via Strozzi; *Banca C. Steinhauslin & Co.*, 4 Via dei Sassetti; *American Express Company*, 49 Via Giucciardini. Money may also be changed at the bank inside the Railway Station (Monday–Saturday 8.20–18.20 or 19), or at the bank at the Firenze Nord exit of the Autostrada del Sole (Monday–Saturday, 9–13, 14–16).

Consulates. *British Consulate*, 2 Lungarno Corsini (Pl.9;2); *American Consulate*, 38 Lungarno Vespucci (Pl.4;8).

Learned Institutions and Cultural Societies. *British Institute*, 2 Via Tornabuoni (Italian language courses), with an excellent library and reading room at 9 Lungarno Guicciardini. *Institut Français*, 2 Piazza Ognissanti; *German Institute of Art History*, 44 Via Giuseppe Giusti (with excellent art history consulting library open to graduate students); *Dutch Institute*, 5 Viale Torricelli; *Harvard University Center for Italian Renaissance Studies*, Villa I Tatti, 26 Via di Vincigliata, Ponte a Mensola, near Settignano (with a fine arts consulting library open to graduate students); *Fondazione di Studi di Storia dell'Arte Roberto Longhi*, Villa il Tasso, 30 Via Benedetto Fortini; *Centro Linguistico Italiano 'Dante Alighieri'*, 12 Via de' Bardi (Italian language courses); *Centro di Cultura per Stranieri*, Villa Fabbricotti, 64 Via Vittorio Emanuele (courses in Italian language, history of art, etc. attached to the University of Florence); *Istituto Nazionale di Studi sul Rinascimento*, Palazzo Strozzi; *Società Dantesca Italiana*, 1 Via Arte della Lana; *Università Internazionale* *dell'Arte*, Villa il Ventaglio, 24 Via delle Forbici; *Accademia della Crusca*, Villa Medicea di Castello.

Amici dei Musei, 39 Via Alfani, *Italia Nostra*, 9 Viale Gramsci, *Agriturist*, 3 Piazza San Firenze.

Libraries. *Biblioteca Nazionale Centrale*, 1 Piazza Cavalleggeri; *Archivio di Stato*, Viale Giovine Italia (Piazza Beccaria);*Gabinetto Scientifico e Letterario G.B. Vieusseux*, Palazzo Strozzi; *Biblioteca Medicea Laurenziana*, Piazza San Lorenzo; *Biblioteca Riccardiana & Moreniana*, 10 Via Ginori; *Biblioteca Marucelliana*, 43 Via Cavour; *Biblioteche delle Facoltà Universitarie Fiorentine*, 31 Via degli Alfani; *Biblioteca Comunale*, 21 Via Sant'Egidio; and in the French, German, Dutch, and British Institutes.—*Istituto Geografico Militare*, 10 Via Cesare Battisti (a cartography library).

Churches

The opening times of churches vary a great deal but the majority are open from 7.00–12.00. In the afternoons many remain closed until 15.00, 16.00 or even 17.00 and close again at about 18.00; some do not reopen at all in the afternoon. A few churches open for services only. The opening times of the major churches in Florence have been given in the text. The sacristan will usually show closed chapels, crypts, etc., and a small tip should be given. Many pictures and frescoes are difficult to see without lights which are often coin operated (100 lire coins). A torch and a pair of binoculars are especially useful to study fresco cycles, etc. Most churches now ask that sightseers do not enter during a service. Churches in Florence are very often not orientated. In the text the terms N and S refer to the liturgical N (left) and S (right), taking the high altar as at the E end.

Roman Catholic Services. On Sunday and, in the principal churches, often on weekdays, Mass is celebrated up to 12.00 and from 18.00 until 19.00 in the evening. Confessions are heard in English on Sunday at the Duomo, San Lorenzo, San Marco, Santa Trìnita, Santa Croce, Orsanmichele, and San Miniato al Monte.—CHURCH FESTIVALS. On Saints' days mass and vespers with music are celebrated in the churches dedicated to the saints concerned. On the feast of the patron Saint of Florence, San Giovanni (24 June), a local holiday, special services are held. On Easter Day the *Scoppio del Carro* is held in and outside the Duomo (see p 58).

Non-Catholic Churches. *Anglican*, St Mark's, 16 Via Maggio; *American Episcopalian*, St James, 9 Via Bernardo Rucellai; *Lutheran*, 11 Lungarno Torrigiani; *Waldensian*, Via Micheli; *Greek Orthodox*, 76 Viale Mattioli; *Russian Orthodox*, 8 Via Leone X.—*Jewish Synagogue*, 4 Via Farini.

Theatres, Annual Festivals, etc.

Concerts, drama performances, exhibitions, and conferences are organised throughout the year and advertised in the local press and on wall posters (and in 'Florence Today', issued every 2 months and available free from the *APT*, hotels, etc.). An up-to-date list of exhibitions is printed c every 15 days by the *APT*. Tickets for all concerts and drama performances can be obtained at Box Office, Via della Pergola.

Theatres. *La Pergola* (Pl.6;8), 12 Via della Pergola (drama season); *Niccolini*, Via Ricasoli; *Teatro della Compagnia*, 50 Via Cavour; *Teatro Variety*, 47 Via del Madonnone; *Teatro di Rifredi*, 303 Via Vittorio Emanuele; *Oriuolo*, 31 Via dell'Oriuolo; *Teatro Tenda*, Lungarno Aldo Moro; *Teatro Verdi*, 101 Via Ghibellina.—The *Teatro Comunale Metastasio* in Prato has a renowned theatre season from October to April (tickets also available in Florence), and a music festival October–December.

Music. *Teatro Comunale* (Pl.4;6), 16 Corso Italia, symphony concerts and opera. Here is held the MAGGIO MUSICALE, an annual music festival (May–July). However, it has been closed since 1990 for repairs, and concerts are meanwhile held at the Teatro Verdi in Via Ghibellina. The *'Ridotto'* of the Teatro Comunale, a smaller auditorium, was reopened in 1984.—Excellent chamber music concerts given by famous musicians from all over the world are organised by the *'Amici della Musica'* in January–April and October–December at the Pergola Theatre. The *Orchestra Regionale Toscana* holds concerts in the church of Santo Stefano al Ponte. The *Musicus Concentus* and the *Orchestra da Camera Fiorentina* hold chamber music concerts. The Scuola di Musica di Fiesole give concerts at 24 Via delle Fontanelle, San Domenico di Fiesole. Occasional concerts are also held in churches (San Lorenzo, Santa Croce, etc.).—The ESTATE FIESOLANA is an annual festival of music, drama, and films held from the end of June to the end of August. Performances in the Teatro Romano in Fiesole, at the Badia Fiesolana, Santa Croce, the courtyard of Palazzo Pitti, etc.

Exhibitions are held in the Forte di Belvedere, Palazzo Pitti (Sala Bianca), Palazzo Strozzi, Palazzo Medici-Riccardi, Palazzo Vecchio (Sala d'Armi), the Salone delle Reali Poste (Piazzale degli Uffizi), the Accademia di Belle Arti (Piazza San Marco), etc.—The material owned by the Biblioteca Laurenziana and the Gabinetto Disegni e Stampe degli Uffizi is mounted in regular exhibitions of great interest.

Annual festivals and exhibitions. *Scoppio del Carro*, on Easter Day, an annual traditional religious festival held in and outside the Duomo at mid-day. A 'dove' is sent from the high altar through the cathedral to ignite a bonfire of fireworks on a 'carro' led by white oxen outside the W door.—*Festa del Grillo*, on Ascension Day, a large fair in the Cascine where crickets are sold.—On 24 June, St John's Day, the patron saint of Florence, a local holiday is celebrated with fireworks at Piazzale Michelangelo. A 'football' game in 16C costume (*'Calcio in costume'*) is held in three rounds during June usually in Piazza Santa Croce. The teams represent the four 'quartiere' of the city (San Giovanni, Santa Croce, Santa Maria Novella, and Santo Spirito) and the game is played with few rules and considerable violence.—On 25 March, the festival of the Annunziata, a fair is held in Piazza Santissima Annunziata. On 7 September, the eve of the Birth of the Virgin, the *Festa della Rificolona* is celebrated by children carrying colourful paper lanterns through the streets (especially in Piazza Santissima Annunziata and the Lungarni). The name is a corruption of the 'fiera culóna' or 'festa contadina', an ancient traditional festival in which peasants from the surrounding countryside carrying lanterns came to Florence to honour the Virgin at Santissima Annunziata.

An Antiques Fair (the *Mostra Mercato Internazionale dell' Anti-quariato*) is held biennially (next in 1991) in the autumn in Palazzo Strozzi. Numerous annual exhibitions are held at the FORTEZZA DA BASSO, notably *'Pitti-Immagine'*, an international fashion show, and the *'Mostra dell'Artigianato'*, an exhibition of artisans' products from all over the world.—In May, in a garden just below Piazzale Michelangelo, an *Iris festival* is held.

Sport. SWIMMING-POOLS: *Costoli*, Campo di Marte, *Le Pavoniere*, Viale degli Olmi (Cascine), and *Bellariva*, 8 Lungarno Colombo.—TENNIS: Viale Michelangelo, Il Poggetto (Via Michele Mercati), the Cascine, etc.—GOLF COURSE (18 holes) at Ugolino, 12km SE of Florence on the Strada Chiantigiana, beyond Grassina.

Museums, Collections, Monuments and Gardens open to the Public

The table lists the hours of admission to the various museums, galleries, monuments and gardens in Florence at present in force. *Opening times vary and often change without warning;* those given below should therefore be accepted with reserve. An up-to-date list of opening times is always available at the APT offices. Normally all State museums, etc. are closed on the main public holidays: 1 January, Easter Day, 25 April, 1 May, 1st Sunday in June, 15 August, and Christmas Day, but at Easter and Christmas they sometimes have special opening times; ask at the APT. On other holidays (see below) they open only in the morning (9.00–13.00). Almost all State-owned museums and galleries have a standard timetable for the whole year, namely weekdays 9.00–14.00, Sunday and fest. 9.00–13.00, Monday closed. In Florence, an exception has been made for the Galleria degli Uffizi which stays open from 9.00–19.00 Tuesday–Saturday (Sunday 9.00–13.00).

British citizens under the age of 18 or over the age of 60 are entitled to free admission to State-owned museums. The entrance fee for the State museums (marked 'S' in the Museum table) in Florence is between Lire 4000 and Lire 10,000. The Museums owned by the Comune of Florence (marked 'C' in the Museum table) charge between 2000–5000 lire.

For a week in early December (the 'Settimana per i Beni Culturali e Ambientali') some museums are opened specially and there is free entrance to all State owned museums. The Amici dei Musei and the Comune also sometimes arrange for gardens, oratories, churches, palaces, etc. normally closed to the public to be opened for certain periods of the year (information from the APT).

Gardens open to the public. The gardens open regularly to the public, listed in the timetable below are: the Boboli gardens,the Botanical Gardens, Giardino dell'Orticoltura, Villa la Petraia, Villa di Castello, Villa di Poggio a Caiano. Parks open daily to the public include: Villa il Ventaglio, Villa Strozzi, and Villa Stibbert. The park of Villa Demidoff in Pratolino is open on three days a week in summer only. In May the Iris garden below Piazzale Michelangelo is open. Other beautiful gardens privately owned but sometimes accessible (usually included in Agriturist tours; see p 55) include Villa La Pietra and Villa I Tatti. The garden of Villa La Gamberaia in Settignano is open weekdays 8–17 (fee).

HOURS OF ADMISSION TO THE MUSEUMS, COLLECTIONS, MONUMENTS, AND GARDENS OF FLORENCE

NOTES
The opening hours for holidays ('fest.', 'giorni festivi') apply also to Sundays
(S)   Museums owned by the State: Soprintendenza per i Beni Artistici e Storici, 5 Via della Ninna (Tel. 218341); Soprintendenza ai Beni Ambientali e Architettonici, Palazzo Pitti (Tel. 218741); Soprintendenza Archeologica della Toscana, 65 Via della Pergola (Tel. 2478641).
(C)   Museums owned by the Comune of Florence (Ufficio Belle Arti e Musei Comunali, 21 Via Sant'Egidio, Tel. 217305).

General Information

Season. The changeable climate of Florence is conditioned by its position in a small basin enclosed by hills. It can be extremely hot and oppressive in summer. Perhaps the most pleasant months to visit the city are June and October when the temperature is often still quite high. Spring can be unexpectedly wet and cold until well after Easter. The most crowded months are at Easter and July and September. The winter in Florence can be as cold as an English winter.

Plan of Visit. The 30 itineraries in the Guide correspond to at least a month's (leisurely) sight-seeing. For visitors with only a short time at their disposal, the following areas and monuments in the city should not be missed:

1.   The Baptistery, Duomo, and Campanile (including a climb to the top of the cupola), all described in Rte 1, and the Museo dell'Opera del Duomo (Rte 2).

2.   Orsanmichele (Rte 3), Piazza della Signoria (Rte 4), and Palazzo Vecchio (Rte 5).

3.   Galleria degli Uffizi (Rte 6).

4.   Palazzo Pitti (Galleria Palatina) and the Boboli gardens (Rte 8).

5.   Galleria dell'Accademia, and Piazza Santissima Annunziata (Rte 9), and the Museo di San Marco (Rte 10).

6.   Palazzo Medici-Riccardi (the Chapel frescoed by Benozzo Gozzoli), San Lorenzo, Biblioteca Laurenziana, and the Cappelle Medicee (Rte 10).

7.   Santa Maria Novella (and the Spanish Chapel; Rte 11), Santa Trinita, and the exteriors of Palazzo Strozzi and Palazzo Rucellai (Rte 12).

8.   Museo Nazionale del Bargello (Rte 13), Santa Croce (and the Pazzi Chapel), and the Casa Buonarroti (Rte 15).

9.   Santo Spirito and Santa Maria del Carmine (the Brancacci Chapel; Rte 18), and San Miniato al Monte (Rte 20).

10.   Fiesole (Rte 23).

Markets. The main food market in Florence is at *San Lorenzo* (Pl.6;5; open Monday–Saturday, 7–13; also 16.30–19.30 on Saturday except in July and August); another good produce market is at *Sant'Ambrogio* (Pl.11;1; open mornings only). In the streets near both these markets stalls sell clothing, leatherwork, etc. throughout the day (except Monday in winter and Saturday in summer). Another general market (straw, leather, lace, etc.) is *Il Porcellino*, under the Loggia del Mercato Nuovo (Pl. 16;5; open every day in summer; closed Monday and Sunday in winter). A large general market is held every Tuesday morning at *Le Cascine*. The *Mercatino delle Pulci* or 'flea market' ('antiques' and 'junk') is open weekdays in Piazza dei Ciompi. On the last Sunday of every month an 'antique and junk' market is held in and around Piazza dei Ciompi, and on the 2nd Sunday of every month a market of artisans' work etc. is held in Piazza Santo Spirito.

Public Holidays. The main holidays in Italy, when offices, shops, and schools are closed, are as follows: New Year's Day, 25 April (Liberation Day), Easter Monday, 1 May (Labour Day), 15 August (Assumption), 1 November (All Saint's Day), 8 December. (Conception), Christmas Day, and 26 December (St Stephen) and 6 January (Epiphany). In addition the festival of the patron Saint of Florence, St John, is celebrated on 24 June as a local holiday in the city.

Street Numbering. In Florence all private residences have their number written up in blue numbers, and all shops have red numbers, so that there is often the same number in blue and in red in the same street.

Telephones and Postal Information. Stamps are sold at tobacconists (displaying a blue 'T' sign) and post offices (open 8.15–14.00, Monday–Saturday). It is always advisable to post letters at Post Offices or the Railway Station; collection from letterboxes is erratic. There are numerous public telephones all over the city, and in bars and restaurants, etc. These are operated by coins, cards or by metal discs known as 'gettone', which are bought (200 lire each) from tobacconists, bars, some newspaper stands, and post offices (and are considered valid currency). For long-distance calls the telephone exchange at the Post Office in Via Pellicceria is always open. Most cities in Europe can now be dialled direct from Italy.

Newspapers. The Italian newspapers which carry local news of Florence are 'La Repubblica' and 'La Nazione'. Other national newspapers include 'Corriere della Sera', and 'La Stampa'. Foreign newspapers can be purchased at most kiosks.

Working Hours. Government offices usually work weekdays from 8.00–13.30 or 14.00. Shops are open from 8.00 or 9.00–13.00 and 16.00 or 17.00–19.30 or 20.00. Most of the year, food shops are closed on Wednesday afternoon, and other shops (clothes, hardware, hairdressers, etc.), are closed on Monday morning. From mid June to mid September all shops are closed instead on Saturday afternoon. For banking hours, see p 56.

FLORENCE

FLORENCE, in Italian *Firenze*, has been famous for centuries as one of the principal centres of art and learning in Italy. In the later Middle Ages and the early Renaissance it was the intellectual capital of the peninsula, well meriting its designation 'the Italian Athens'. The city remains a treasury of art, not only on account of the priceless collections in its museums and galleries, but also by virtue of its rich endowment of medieval monuments and Renaissance buildings, in which it is rivalled by Rome alone. Today, Florence, with 457,000 inhabitants, is still one of the most beautiful cities in Italy, and the historical centre and the hills in the immediate vicinity have been largely preserved from new buildings. It lies in a delightful position in a small basin enclosed by low hills (which accounts for its changeable climate and high temperatures in summer). It is important as the trading centre for the fertile valleys of Tuscany, and since 1970 has been the capital of the new 'region' of Tuscany. It has for long been favoured as a residence by scholars, artists, and others from abroad. The river Arno, a special feature of the city, is a mountain torrent, subject to sudden floods and droughts.

View of Florence from the cupola of the Duomo

1   The Baptistery and the Duomo

The **Baptistery of San Giovanni** (Pl.16;4; open 13–18; fest. 9.30–12, 14.30–17) is one of the oldest and most revered buildings in the city. Called by Dante his 'bel San Giovanni', it has always held a special place in the history of Florence. The date of its foundation is uncertain; in the Middle Ages it was thought to be a Roman building. Most scholars now consider it to have been built in the 6C or 7C, or even as early as the 4–5C, but anyway not later than 897 when it is first mentioned here. It was reconsecrated in 1059. A Roman palace of the 1C AD has been discovered beneath its foundations. It is an octagonal building of centralised plan derived from Byzantine models, with an exceptionally large dome. The EXTERIOR was entirely encased in white marble from Luni and green marble from Prato in a classical geometrical design in the 11–13C, at the charge of the 'Arte di Calimala', the most important Guild of the medieval city (cf. p 84). The decoration became a prototype for numerous Tuscan Romanesque religious buildings. At the end of the 13C the striped angle pilasters were added, and the semicircular apse was probably replaced at this time by the rectangular 'scarsella' (although some scholars believe this had already been built by the 11C). The cupola was concealed by an unusual white pyramidal roof, probably in the 13C, (and the 12C lantern placed on top). The larger arch which marks the main East entrance faces the Duomo. The two porphyry columns here were brought back as booty by the Florentines who took part in the Pisan war in the Balearic Islands in 1115.

The building is famous for its three sets of gilded bronze doors at its three entrances. The earliest by Andrea Pisano (1336) was followed by those on the N and E sides erected a century later by Lorenzo Ghiberti after a competition held by the 'Arte di Calimala' in which

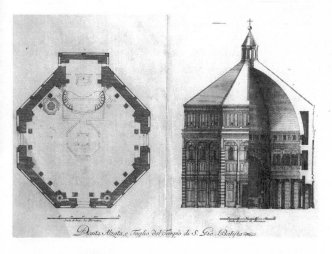

The Baptistery, drawn by C.B. Clemente Nelli and published by Bernardo Sgrilli in 1755. (Museo di Firenze com'era)

his work was preferred to that of many of the greatest artists of the Quattrocento, including Brunelleschi and Jacopo della Quercia. This competition of 1401 is often taken as a convenient point to mark the beginning of the Florentine Renaissance, and it is significant that the Baptistery should have been the monument chosen for adornment. Two trial reliefs for the competition, entered by Brunelleschi and Ghiberti, are preserved in the Bargello (cf. p 164).

The *South Door, by *Andrea Pisano*, was erected in 1336 at the main entrance facing the Duomo. It was moved to its present position in 1424 to make way for Ghiberti's new doors. It has 28 compartments containing reliefs within Gothic quatrefoil frames of the history of St John the Baptist and the theological and cardinal Virtues. The decorations of the bronze frame were added by *Vittorio Ghiberti* (1452–64), son of Lorenzo.—Over the doorway are bronze figures of the Baptist, the Executioner, and Salome, by *Vincenzo Danti* (1571).

The *North Door (1403–24), by *Lorenzo Ghiberti*, is again divided into 28 compartments, and the scenes of the Life of Christ, the Evangelists, and the Doctors of the Church, are contained within Gothic frames copied from the earlier Pisano doors. The chronological sequence of the scenes from the Life of Christ begins on the left-hand door on the 3rd panel from the bottom and continues towards the top, running left to right. The two lower registers depict the Evangelists and Doctors. Ghiberti's self-portrait appears in the 5th head from the top of the left door (middle band); he is wearing an elaborate hat. The beautiful decoration of the frame is also by Ghiberti.—The bronze figures above (1506–11) are St John the Baptist preaching, the Levite, and the Pharisee, by *Francesco Rustici*, from a design by *Leonardo* (mentioned by Vasari).

The **East Door (1425–52) is the most celebrated work of *Lorenzo Ghiberti*, the completion of which took him most of his life. It is said to have been called by Michelangelo the 'Gate of Paradise'. The ten separate panels contain reliefs of scriptural subjects, the design of which probably owes something to Ghiberti's contact with the humanists. The artist was assisted by *Michelozzo, Benozzo Gozzoli*, and others. The pictorial reliefs, no longer restricted to a Gothic frame, depict each episode with great conciseness, and the workmanship of the carving is masterly, with scenes in low relief extending far into the background. The use of perspective here is of great importance, and typical of the new Renaissance concept of art. A copy of the door made from casts taken in 1948 was set up here in 1990 and the original panels will all be exhibited inside the Museo dell'Opera del Duomo after their restoration. So far four panels have been restored and can be seen in the museum (cf. p 81). The gilding has been returned to the surface, with spectacular results. The subjects from above downwards are (left to right): 1. The Creation and Expulsion from Paradise; 2. Cain and Abel; 3. Noah's Sacrifice and Drunkenness; 4. Abraham and the Angels and the Sacrifice of Isaac; 5. Esau and Jacob; 6. Joseph sold and recognised by his Brethren; 7. Moses receiving the Tables of Stone; 8. The Fall of Jericho; 9. Battle with the Philistines; 10. Solomon and the Queen of Sheba. In the framing are 24 very fine statuettes of Prophets and Sibyls, and 24 medallions with portraits of Ghiberti himself (the 4th from the top in the middle row on the left), and his principal contemporaries. The splendid bronze doorframe is by Ghiberti also.—Above the door the sculptural group of the Baptism of Christ, attributed to *Andrea Sansovino* and *Vincenzo Danti*, with an Angel by *Innocenzo Spinazzi* (18C) has been removed and restored, and is to be exhibited in the Museo dell'Opera del Duomo and replaced here by casts.

The harmonious INTERIOR is designed in two orders, of which the lower has huge granite columns from a Roman building, with gilded Corinthian capitals, and the upper, above a cornice, a gallery with divided windows. The walls are in panels of white marble divided by bands of black, in the dichromatic style of the exterior. The beautiful decoration has survived intact. As the floor shows, the centre of the building was occupied until 1576 by a large octagonal font; the Gothic font on the right of the entrance dates from 1371. The oldest part of the splendid mosaic *PAVEMENT (begun 1209) is near the font. The decoration in 'opus tessellatum', which recalls that of San Miniato (see Rte 20), includes geometrical designs, oriental motifs, the signs of the Zodiac, etc. Beside the high altar (13C; recon-structed) is an elaborate paschal candlestick delicately carved by *Agostino di Iacopo* (1320). To the right is the *Tomb of the antipope John XXIII (Baldassarre Cossa, who died in Florence in 1419) by *Donatello* and *Michelozzo*, one of the earliest Renaissance tombs in the city (cleaned in 1986). Apart from the exquisite carving, this monument is especially remarkable for the way it is inserted into a narrow space between two huge Roman columns, and in no way disturbs the architectural harmony of the building. The bronze effigy of the pope is generally attributed to *Donatello* (1424–25). On the left of the apse are two late-Roman sarcophagi adapted as tombs (one showing a wild boar hunt, and the other, the tomb of Bishop Giovanni da Velletri, 1230, with scenes of Roman life).

The *MOSAICS (being restored) in the vault are remarkably well preserved. The earliest (c 1225) are in the 'scarsella' above the altar; they are signed by the monk *'Iacopo'*, a contemporary of St Francis, who was influenced by the Roman or Venetian mosaicists. In the vault, an elaborate wheel with the figures of the Prophets surrounds the Agnus Dei. This is supported by four caryatids kneeling on Corinthian capitals. On either side are the Virgin and St John the Baptist enthroned. On the intrados of the entrance arch is a frieze of Saints, and, on the outer face, half-figures of Saints flank a striking image of the Baptist. The same artist is thought to have begun the main dome, the centre of which is decorated with paleochristian motifs surrounded by a band of angels. Above the apse is the Last Judgement with a huge figure of Christ (8 metres high), attributed to *Coppo di Marcovaldo*. The remaining section of the cupola is divided into four bands: the inner one illustrates the Story of Genesis (beginning on the N side); the 2nd band, the Story of Joseph (the design of some of the scenes has recently been attributed to the *'Maestro della Maddalena'*); the 3rd band, the Story of Christ; and the outer band, the Story of St John the Baptist (some of the early episodes are attributed to *Cimabue*). Work on the mosaics was well advanced by 1271, but probably continued into the 14C. The marble rectangular frames at the base of the dome contain mosaic Saints.

The gallery, and the foundations of the Roman building which formerly stood on this site, may sometimes be visited by scholars with special permission. A medieval cemetery was found between the Baptistery and the Duomo in 1972–73 (since covered over).

The *Duomo (Pl.16;4; open 10–17; fest. 7–12, 14.30–17), the cathe-dral dedicated to the Madonna of Florence, *Santa Maria del Fiore*, fills Piazza del Duomo; a comprehensive view of the huge building is difficult in the confined space. It produces a memorable effect of massive grandeur, especially when seen from its southern flank, lightened by the colour and pattern of its beautiful marble walls (white from Carrara, green from Prato, and red from the Maremma). The famous dome, one of the masterpieces of the Renaissance, rising to the height of the surrounding hills (from which it is nearly always visible), holds sway over the whole city.

History. The palaeochristian church dedicated to the Palestinian saint, Reparata, is thought to have been founded in the 6–7C, or possibly earlier. It was several times reconstructed in the Romanesque period. Considerable remains of this church were found in 1965–74 beneath the present cathedral (cf. p 73). The Bishop's seat, formerly at San Lorenzo (cf. Rte 10) is thought to have been transferred here in the late 7C. By the 13C a new and larger cathedral was deemed necessary. In 1294 *Arnolfo di Cambio* was appointed as architect, and it is not known precisely how far building had progressed by the time of his death in the first decade of the 14C. In 1331 the 'Arte della Lana' (Guild of Wool Merchants) took over responsibility for the cathedral works and *Giotto* was appointed 'capomaestro'. He began the campanile in 1334. It was not until 1355 that work was taken up again on the cathedral itself, this time by *Francesco Talenti*. It seems he followed Arnolfo's original design of a vaulted basilica with a domed octagon flanked by three polygonal tribunes. During the 14C *Alberto Arnoldi, Giovanni d'Ambrogio, Giovanni di Lapo Ghini, Neri di Fioravante, Orcagna*, and others, all joined Talenti as architects, and the octagonal drum was substantially finished by 1417. The construction of the cupola had for long been recognised as a major technical problem. A competition was held and *Brunelleschi* and *Ghiberti* were appointed jointly to the task in 1418. Brunelleschi soon took over full responsibility for the work and the dome was finished up to the base of the lantern by 1436 when pope Eugenius IV consecrated the cathedral. Once a year, on 8 September, visitors are admitted to the galleries and roof of the Duomo (for adm. to the cupola, see below).

Detail of the south side of the Duomo

EXTERIOR. The majestic **CUPOLA (1420–36), the greatest of all *Brunelleschi*'s works, is a feat of engineering skill. It was the first dome to be projected without the need for a wooden supporting frame to sustain the vault during construction. This was possible partly because the upper section was built in bricks in consecutive rings in horizontal courses, bonded together in a vertical herring-bone pattern. However, the exact constructional technique used by Brunelleschi has still not been satisfactorily explained. The dome was the largest and highest of its time. Its pointed shape was probably conditioned by the octagonal drum which already existed over the crossing and from which the eight marble ribs ascend to the lantern. The cupola has two concentric shells, the octagonal vaults of which are evident both on the exterior and interior of the building. This facilitated construction and lessened the weight; the outer shell is thinner than the inner shell. Some of the apparatus invented by Brunelleschi which was used during the building of the dome can be seen in a storeroom on the descent from the dome (see below), and in the Museo dell'Opera (p 79). Since 1980 detailed long-term studies have been carried out by a special commission to establish whether the stability of the cupola is in danger. The weight of the dome on the drum had caused cracks in the drum by the mid 17C, and the structure is now under observation through a sophisticated system of monitors.—On the completion of the cupola Brunelleschi was sub-jected to another competition as his ability to crown it with a lantern was brought into question. It was begun a few months before the architect's death in 1446, and carried on by his friend *Michelozzo*. In the late 1460s *Verrocchio* placed the bronze ball and cross on the summit. Brunelleschi also designed the four decorative little exedrae with niches which he placed around the octagonal drum between the three domed tribunes. The balcony at the base of the cupola, covering the brick work, on the SE side, was added by *Baccio d'Agnolo*, on a design by *Giuliano da Sangallo* and *Cronaca* in 1507–15. According to Vasari, it was never completed because of Michelangelo's stringent criticism that it reminded him of a crickets' cage.

The building of the cathedral was begun on the S side where the decorative pattern of marble can be seen to full advantage. The 14C sculptures of the Annunciation above the Porta del Campanile (1), attributed to Jacopo di Pietro Guidi and a follower of Giovanni Balduccio, have been removed and restored and will be exhibited in the Museo dell'Opera del Duomo. The PORTA DEI CANONICI (2) has fine sculptured decoration (1395–99) by *Lorenzo d'Ambrogio* and *Piero di Giovanni Tedesco*. On the N side, the *PORTA DELLA MANDORLA (3) dates from 1391–1405. The sculptural decoration on the lower part is by *Giovanni d'Ambrogio, Piero di Giovanni Tedesco, Jacopo di Piero Guidi*, and *Niccolò Lamberti*. In the gable is an *Assumption of the Virgin in an almond-shaped frame (or 'mandorla') by *Nanni di Banco* (c 1418–20), continued after his death by his workshop. The two heads in profile carved in relief on either side of the gable of a Prophet and Sibyl are considered early works by *Donatello*. The sculptures have been blackened by the polluted air and are difficult to appreciate from this distance; they had an important influence on early Renaissance sculpture. In the lunette is an Annunciation in mosaic (1491) by *Domenico* and *Davide Ghirlandaio*.—The FAÇADE, erected to a third of its projected height by 1420, was demolished in 1587–88 (cf. p 78), and the present front in the Gothic style was designed by *Emilio De Fabris* and built in

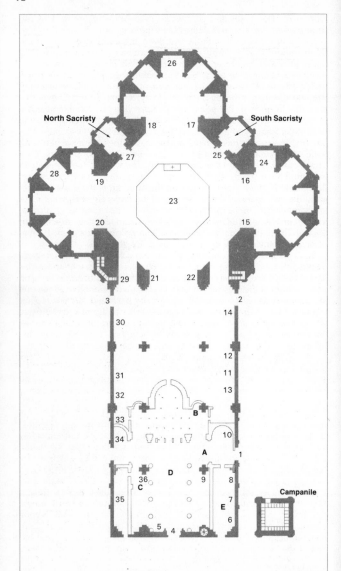

North Sacristy

South Sacristy

Campanile

THE DUOMO

1871–87. Part of it has been under restoration for many years. The bronze doors date from 1899–1903.

The Gothic INTERIOR is somewhat bare and chilly after the warmth of the colour of the exterior, whose splendour it cannot match. The huge grey stone arches of the nave reach the clerestory beneath an elaborate sculptured balcony. The massive pilasters which support the stone vault have unusual composite capitals. The beautiful stained glass windows date mostly from 1434–45. Three dark tribunes with a Gothic coronet of chapels surround the huge dome. The beautiful marble pavement (1526–1660) was designed by *Baccio d'Agnolo*, *Francesco da Sangallo* and others.—WEST WALL. Mosaic (4) of the Coronation of the Virgin, attributed to *Gaddo Gaddi*. *Ghiberti* designed the three round stained-glass windows. The frescoes of the angel musicians are by *Santi di Tito*. The huge clock uses the 'hora italica' method of counting the hours; the last hour of the day (XXIV) ends at sunset or Ave Maria (a system used in Italy until the 18C). *Paolo Uccello* decorated it and painted the four heads of prophets in 1443. The recomposed tomb (5) of Antonio d'Orso, Bishop of Florence (died 1321) by *Tino da Camaino*, includes a fine statue. The painting of St Catherine of Alexandria is by the school of *Bernardo Daddi*.

SOUTH AISLE. In a tondo (6) is the bust of Brunelleschi by *Buggiano*, his adopted son (1446; probably taken from his death mask). In the first 'marble' side altar (7), *Nanni di Banco* (attributed), Statue of a Prophet (1408). Below the bust of Giotto (8; 1490) by *Benedetto da Maiano*, in another tondo, is an inscription by Politian. The elaborate Gothic Stoup (9; c 1380) is attributed to *Urbano da Cortona*. The angel and basin are copies; the originals are in the Opera del Duomo (p 79).

Steps lead down to the entrance (*A*) to the **Excavations of Santa Reparata** (adm. see p 63). At the bottom of the stairs (left) through a grille can be seen the simple tomb-slab (*E*) of Brunelleschi, found here in 1972. The architect of the cupola was the only Florentine granted the privilege of burial in the cathedral. During 1965–74 the ancient cathedral of Santa Reparata (cf. p 69) was uncovered beneath the present cathedral (see the Plan on p 72). The complicated remains, on various levels, include Roman edifices on which the early Christian church was built, a fine mosaic pavement of the palaeochristian church, and remains of the pre-Romanesque and Romanesque reconstructions. Since only a few column bases and parts of the pavement of the earliest church were discovered, its precise plan is not known; the excavated area corresponds to the plan of the Romanesque church with its five apses. Four of the massive nave pilasters of the present cathedral above intrude into this area. The excavations are explained by a detailed model (*C*).

At the entrance, cases of finds from the excavations: gilded bronze sword and spurs of Giovanni de' Medici (cf. below); Roman sculpture, paving tiles, etc; Romanesque architectural fragments; majolica and unglazed pottery from earth fills and tombs dating from the period of the construction of the present cathedral (1296–1375). To the right is the Romanesque crypt of Santa Reparata with 13C tomb slabs in the floor. The fresco fragments include a 14C Christ in Passion (*B*). In the area towards the N aisle is part of the mosaic pavement from the first church with a fragment of Romanesque pavement above it. Plutei of the 8–9C are displayed near the base of the stairs which led up to the raised choir. Beyond the huge square base of one of the nave pillars of the present cathedral are some fragments of Roman buildings below the floor level. A model here (*C*) explains in detail the various levels of excavations. Nearby is part of a pavement thought to be from the pre-Romanesque period and several tomb-slabs. From here a walkway leads across the best preserved part of the palaeochristian mosaic floor, interrupted here and there by fragments of brick, marble, and pietra serena from later buildings. The walkway leads back across a wall of the Roman period to the imposing raised tomb (*D*) of Giovanni de' Medici, buried here in 1351. Nearby are five plans of the excavations.

By the S door (10), St Blaise enthroned by *Rossello di Jacopo Franchi* (1408). On the 2nd altar (11), statue of Isaiah (1427), by *Ciuffagni*, between two painted sepulchral monuments (12 & 13) of Fra' Luigi Marsili and Cardinal Pietro Corsini, by *Bicci di Lorenzo*. The beautiful stained-glass windows, with six saints (1394–95), were designed by *Agnolo Gaddi*. The bust (14) of Marsilio Ficino (1433–99), holding a volume of Plato, the famous philosopher and friend of Cosimo il Vecchio, is by *Andrea Ferrucci* (1521).—Beyond the second S door is an entrance to the steps which ascend the cupola; during restoration work on the dome the steps in the N aisle (5; cf. below) are normally used.

EAST END OF THE CHURCH (open to visitors only when services are not in progress). Above the octagon the great dome soars to a height of 91 metres. The fresco of the Last Judgement by *Vasari* and *Federico Zuccari* (1572–79) has been covered since 1981 by a 'dome' of scaffolding, while restoration work proceeds (expected to take until c 1993). The 15C stained glass in the round windows of the drum is described on p 75. Against the piers of the octagon stand eight 16C statues of Apostles: (15) *Giovanni Bandini*, St Philip, (16) St James the Less; (17) *Benedetto da Rovezzano*, St John; (18) *Baccio Bandinelli*, St Peter; (19) *Andrea Ferrucci*, St Andrew; (20) *Vincenzo de' Rossi*, St Thomas; (21) *Jacopo Sansovino*, St James; (22) *Vincenzo de' Rossi*, St Matthew.—The marble SANCTUARY (23; 1555) by *Bandinelli* with bas-reliefs by himself and *Bandini*, encloses the High Altar, also by Bandinelli, with a wood crucifix by *Benedetto da Maiano*.

Each of the three apses is divided into five chapels with stained glass windows designed by *Lorenzo Ghiberti*. In the right and left apse are frescoes beneath the windows after Paolo Schiavo (c 1440; heavily restored). Right Apse: 5th Chapel (24) 'Madonna del Popolo', fragment of a Giottesque fresco. Above the entrance to the SOUTH SACRISTY (25), large lunette of the Ascension in enamelled terracotta by *Luca della Robbia*. The interesting interior, with a lavabo by *Buggiano* and *Pagno di Lapo*, is not open to the public.—Central Apse: 3rd Chapel (26). On the altar, two graceful kneeling angels by *Luca della Robbia*. Beneath the altar, *Bronze reliquary urn, by *Lorenzo Ghiberti* with exquisite bas-reliefs.—Over the door into the NORTH SACRISTY (27; 'delle Messe') is another fine relief by *Luca della Robbia* of the *Resurrection. This was his earliest important work (1442) in enamelled terracotta. The iconographical composition was copied by later artists. The doors were Luca's only work in bronze (1446–67); he was assisted by *Michelozzo* and *Maso di Bartolomeo*. It was in this sacristy that Lorenzo il Magnifico took refuge on the day of the Pazzi conspiracy in 1478 in order to escape the death which befell his brother, Giuliano. The *Interior has fine intarsia cupboards (restored in 1982) dating from 1436–45. Those on the S wall are by *Agnolo di Lazzaro, Bernardo di Tommaso di Ghigo, Francesco di Giovanni di Guccio*, and *Lo Scheggia*; those on the N wall by *Antonio Manetti*. The end wall was continued by *Giuliano da Maiano* in 1463–65: below are beautiful panels of St Zenobius enthroned between two Saints and above, Annunciation flanked by the prophets Amos and Isiah (possibly on a cartoon by *Antonio del Pollaiolo*). On the entrance wall is a fine marble lavabo by *Buggiano* (1440) probably on a design by Brunelleschi, and a cupboard by *Mino da Fiesole*. The carved frieze of putti supporting a garland is by various hands including, probably, *Benedetto da Maiano*.—Left Apse. In the pavement (usually hidden by pews) is Toscanelli's huge

Gnomon (1475) for solar observations (related to a window in the lantern of the cupola). Toscanelli, a famous scientist, mathematician, and geographer, discussed his calculations concerning perspective with his friend Brunelleschi. In the 2nd chapel (28), dossal painted on both sides by the school of *Giotto*.

In the North Aisle is the entrance (29) to the steps for the *Ascent of the Dome* (adm. see p 60). The climb (463 steps) is not specially arduous, and is highly recommended; it follows a labyrinth of corridors, steps, and spiral staircases (used by the builders of the cupola) as far as the lantern at the top of the dome. During the ascent the structure of the dome (cf. p 71) can be examined, and the views of the inside of the cathedral from the balcony around the drum, and of the city from the small windows and from the lantern, are remarkable.—At the top of the steps which ascend the pier is the interior of one of the small exedrae which Brunelleschi added beneath the drum. From here a spiral staircase continues, at the top of which there is a view of the huge market building of San Lorenzo next to the dome of the Chapel of the Princes. A corridor emerges on the balcony which encircles the octagonal drum. It provides an interesting view of the inside of the cathedral. The frescoes by Vasari and Zuccari (cf. p 74) on the cupola are covered with scaffolding while being restored. The seven stained glass windows in the roundels can be seen to advantage; they were designed in 1443–45 by the following artists: *Paolo Uccello*, Nativity; *Andrea del Castagno*, Deposition; *Paolo Uccello*, Resurrection; *Donatello*, Coronation of the Virgin; *Ghiberti*, Ascension, Prayer in the Garden, and Presentation in the Temple. When Brunelleschi was commissioned to construct the cupola the building of the cathedral had already reached this height; from here can be appreciated the huge space (45.5 metres in diameter) which the architect was required to vault.

A spiral staircase leads to the base of the double dome, the curve of which can clearly be seen. The ascent continues between the two shells, and the little windows frame views of the monuments of the city. The distinctive herring-bone pattern of the bricks (which vary in size; cf. p 71) used in the construction of the dome can be examined here. On the right a steep flight of steps scales the uppermost part of the inner dome. Iron steps continue out on to the lantern, beautifully carved in marble. Access to the bronze ball has been closed for many years; it is large enough to hold about ten people at a time. The view from here (91 metres) embraces the city; the most conspicuous buildings include (right to left): the campanile, Palazzo Strozzi, and the church of the Carmine in the distance; Santo Spirito with its dome and campanile and the huge Palazzo Pitti, and (nearer) the tall Orsanmichele. At the foot of the cathedral is a group of small medieval houses and towers. The Forte di Belvedere can be seen in the distance on its hill behind Palazzo Vecchio, the Uffizi, and the Loggia della Signoria. Farther left is the Badia with its tall tower and the Bargello; the marble façade of Santa Croce with its campanile, and, on the hill behind, San Miniato. Beyond the arcaded façade of the hospital of Santa Maria Nuova rises the green dome of the Synagogue. The straight Via dei Servi leads to Santissima Annunziata, to the right of which are the extensive buildings of the Innocenti with a garden, and nearer at hand the octagonal rotunda of Santa Maria degli Angeli, also by Brunelleschi. In the distance rises the hill of Fiesole. The long façade of Palazzo Medici-Riccardi on Via Cavour can be seen near the tall iron roof of the 19C market building beside the domed church of San Lorenzo. Near the station is Santa Maria Novella with its cloisters and campanile.—On the descent many implements used in the construction and maintenance of the dome can be seen (labelled also in English) in one of the exedrae.

NORTH AISLE. (30) *Domenico di Michelino*, Dante with the 'Divina Commedia' which illuminates Florence (1465; showing the drum of the cupola before it was faced with marble); *Bicci di Lorenzo*, Saints Cosmas and Damian. The two stained glass windows were designed by *Agnolo Gaddi*. On the side altar (31), *Bernardo Ciuffagni*, King David (1434; designed for the old façade of the Cathedral). Beyond are the two splendid *Equestrian memorials (32 and 33) to the famous 'condottieri', the Englishman Sir John Hawkwood ('Giovanni Acuto'), who commanded the Florentine army from 1377 until his death in 1394, and Niccolò da Tolentino (died 1434). They are both frescoes giving the illusion of sculpture: the former by *Paolo Uccello*

(1436) and the latter by *Andrea del Castagno* (1456). The bust (34) of the organist Antonio Squarcialupi is by *Benedetto da Maiano* (1490; the epigraph is thought to be by Politian). On the last altar (35), *Donatello* (attributed), the prophet Joshua (traditionally thought to be a portrait of the humanist friend of Cosimo il Vecchio, Poggio Bracciolini), originally on the façade of the Duomo. On the nave pillar (36) is a painting of St Zenobius by *Giovanni del Biondo* (late 14C).

The *Campanile (Pl.16;4; nearly 85 metres high; being restored) was begun by *Giotto* in 1334 when, as the most distinguished Florentine artist, he was appointed city architect. It was continued by *Andrea Pisano* (1343), and completed by *Francesco Talenti* in 1348–59. It is built of the same coloured marbles as the Duomo, in similar patterns, in a remarkably well-proportioned design. Between the various storeys are horizontal bands of green, white, and pink inlay. The lowest storey bears two rows of bas-reliefs which have been replaced by copies. The originals, now in the Museo dell'Opera, are described on p 80. The lowest row are contemporary with the building, and some of them are thought to have been designed by *Giotto*. They were executed by *Andrea Pisano* and illustrate the Creation of Man, and the Arts and Industries. Five reliefs on the N face were added by *Luca della Robbia*. The upper register has reliefs by pupils of *Andrea Pisano*. The row of niches in the second storey contain casts of the statues of Prophets and Sibyls (1415–36) by *Donatello* and others, also removed to the Museo dell'Opera (see p 80). Above are two storeys, each with a pair of beautiful double-arched windows in each side, then the highest storey, with large and triple-arched openings, and the cornice. The parapet, low roof, and wood mast were all replaced during restoration work in 1981–83.

The **Ascent of the bell-tower** by 414 steps (adm. see p 60) is interesting for its succession of views of the Duomo, the Baptistery, and the rest of the city. Although lower than the cupola, the climb is steeper.—The third and fourth storeys, with their Gothic windows, overlook the Duomo and the Baptistery. The terracotta pots along the roof of the aisle of the Duomo serve to protect the building from the direct fall of rainwater from the gutters. On the highest storey, with its beautiful slender windows, the modern bells can be seen hanging above the original ones (the 'Apostolica' bell, displayed on a platform, dates from the beginning of the 15C). Steep steps continue to emerge beside the simple tiled roof above the cornice.—The splendid panorama of the city includes (right to left): Piazza della Repubblica (with its conspicuous advertisements), with Palazzo Strozzi behind, and the Carmine in the distance. Farther left is Santo Spirito; then Palazzo Pitti with the Boboli gardens stretching as far as the Forte di Belvedere on its hill. Nearer at hand rises the tall Orsanmichele. Farther left is the Loggia della Signoria beside Palazzo Vecchio and the Uffizi, and, at the foot of the campanile, is a group of medieval houses with red-tiled roofs and towers. The Badia is marked by its tall bell-tower next to the Bargello. Beyond Santa Croce, the Synagogue can be seen just to the right of the cupola. On the other side of the dome the long straight Via Ricasoli leads out of the city towards the hills of Fiesole in the distance. On the parallel Via Cavour stands Palazzo Medici-Riccardi. The huge 19C market building is near San Lorenzo with its dome; the large church of Santa Maria Novella can be seen beside the railway station.

2   Piazza San Giovanni and Piazza del Duomo

The Baptistery and the Duomo fill Piazza San Giovanni and Piazza del Duomo (Pl.16;4). Between the Baptistery and the Campanile is the little Gothic *LOGGIA DEL BIGALLO built for the Misericordia (cf. below) in 1351–58 probably by *Alberto Arnoldi*, who carved the reliefs and the lunette of the Madonna and Child (1361) above the door into the Oratory (facing the Baptistery). The Compagnia del Bigallo, founded in 1245, and involved in similar charitable works as the Misercordia, moved to this seat in 1425 when the two confraternities were merged. Beneath the Loggia lost and abandoned children were exhibited for three days before being consigned to foster-mothers. The three 14C statues in tabernacles high up on the façade were moved here from the Bigallo's former headquarters near Orsanmichele. The **Museo del Bigallo** (Pl.16;4; No. 1 Piazza San Giovanni; no longer open regularly) is the smallest museum in the city, but one of the most charming. It preserves most of the works of art commissioned over the centuries by the Misericordia and the Bigallo from Florentine artists.

The SALA DEI CAPITANI is approached through fine inlaid doors (c 1450) which bear the arms of the Misericordia and the Bigallo. The *Madonna of the Misericordia, by an artist in the circle of *Bernardo Daddi*, dates from 1342. The fresco includes the earliest known view of Florence, with the marble Baptistery prominent in the centre near the incomplete campanile and façade of the Duomo. The relief in pietra serena with the Altoviti coat-of-arms is by *Desiderio da Settignano*. Above two wall cupboards containing the archives of the company, is the Madonna in glory with two orphans in adoration, and Charity, both by *Carlo Portelli* (c 1570). Between the windows: *School of Orcagna* (c 1360), St Peter Martyr giving the standard to 12 captains of the Bigallo (with an inscription on the reverse), recording the foundation of the company. Above, *School of Botticelli*, Madonna and Child (removed). The twelve charming frescoed scenes (damaged) from the life of Tobias, patron saint of the Misericordia (c 1360) were detached from the Udienza Vecchia. The fresco fragment of the Captains of the Misericordia consigning lost and abandoned children to foster-mothers outside the Loggia del Bigallo (1386) is by *Niccolò di Pietro Gerini* and *Ambrogio di Baldese*. It was detached from the outside of the building in 1777 (the complete fresco is shown in its original position in the small 18C watercolour).—In the CORRIDOR, Tondo of the Nativity in terracotta (Tuscan, end of 15C).

SACRISTY. '*Maestro di San Miniato*', Madonna and Child; *Bernardo Daddi*, *Portable triptych, dated 1333, one of his most important early works; *Domenico di Michelino*, *Madonna of Humility with two angels; Pupil of Benozzo*, Madonna enthroned with Saints.—ORATORY. The Madonna and Child and two angels by *Alberto Arnoldi* (1359–64), were placed in a gilded wood tabernacle by *Noferi di Antonio Noferi* in 1515. Beneath the statues, predella by *Ridolfo del Ghirlandaio*, including a scene of Tobias burying a corpse in front of the Loggia del Bigallo with hooded members of the Misericordia in their black habits (cf. below) in the background. *Jacopo del Sellaio*, Tondo of the Madonna and Saints in a beautiful contemporary frame; *Alberto Arnoldi* (attributed), Statuette of the Madonna and Child. High up in the lunette above the door, detached sinopia of Christ between angels by *Nardo di Cione*, whose workshop painted the fresco fragment opposite. The 13C painted Crucifix is attributed to the '*Maestro del Bigallo*'. The original base for the statues by Arnoldi is the work of *Ambrogio di Renzo* (1363).

Across Via de' Calzaioli (which leads to Piazza Signoria) is the MISERICORDIA, a charitable institution which gives free help to those in need, and runs an ambulance service. The Order, founded by St Peter Martyr in 1244, moved to this site in 1576 from the Bigallo across the road. In the Middle Ages the brotherhood was specially active during the plague years when they gave medical care to the poor and attended to their burial. The lay confraternity continues its remarkable work through some 2000 volunteers who are a characteristic sight of Florence in their black capes and hoods.

The pretty little ORATORY (left of the main door), decorated in the 17C, contains an enamelled terracotta altarpiece by *Andrea della Robbia* (commissioned by Francesco Sassetti for his chapel in the Badia Fiesolana). The marble statue of St Sebastian by *Benedetto da Maiano* was left unfinished in the sculptor's studio on his death in 1497, and left by him to the Bigallo.—In the SACRISTY is a bronze Crucifix by the circle of *Massimiliano Soldani Benzi*, and a wood Crucifix attributed to *Benedetto da Maiano*. In the VESTIBULE is a delightful relief of the Madonna and Child in painted and gilded stucco by the circle of *Lorenzo Ghiberti*, a relief of the Madonna and Child with angels, by *Giovanni Antonio Amadeo*, and a statue of St Sebastian attributed to *Giovacchino Fortini* (early 18C).—In the busy SALA DI COMPAGNIA (adm. sometimes courteously granted) is a seated statue of the Madonna and Child by *Benedetto da Maiano* (also left by him to the Bigallo; finished by *Battista Lorenzi* in 1575). The two kneeling statues of angels are by *Giovanni della Robbia*, and the busts of the Christ Child and Young St John by the bottega of the Della Robbia. The interesting relief of the Madonna and Child with angels dates from c 1480.—On the upper floor is a room arranged as a MUSEUM (usually kept closed, but sometimes shown on request). Here is kept the good fresco by the late-15C Florentine school of the Madonna and Child with two Saints, detached from the tabernacle outside in Via del Campanile, and recently restored. Among other numerous works of art owned by the Institute are paintings by *Francesco di Giorgio Martini* (or *Neroccio*), *Santi di Tito*, *Giovanni Antonio di Francesco Sogliani*, *Puligo*, *Bachiacca*, and *Dirck van Baburen*.—Outside the building is a painting of one of the brotherhood carrying a sick person by *Pietro Annigoni* (1970).

In the piazza is *Palazzo dei Canonici* with its heavy columns and colossal 19C statues of Arnolfo and Brunelleschi. From this corner of the piazza (by Via del Proconsolo), there is a good view of the Cathedral and dome. On the corner of Via dell' Oriuolo (which leads to the Museo di Firenze com'era, see Rte 14) is the large 17C *Palazzo Strozzi* (formerly Guadagni-Riccardi; being restored as the seat of the Regional Government).

At No. 9 Piazza del Duomo is the *Museo dell'Opera del Duomo (Pl.16;4; adm. see p 61), in a building which has been the seat of the Opera del Duomo (responsible for the maintenance of the cathedral) since the beginning of the 15C. Over the entrance is a bust of Cosimo I by Giovanni Bandini (dell'Opera). One of the pleasantest museums in the city, first opened in 1891, it contains material from the Duomo, the Baptistery, and the Campanile, including important sculpture. The labelling is erratic. There are long-term plans to expand the museum.

COURTYARD. Statues of St John the Baptist in Glory and two angels by *Girolamo Ticciati*, installed over the high altar of the Baptistery in 1732, and two large Roman sarcophagi (2C–3C), removed from outside the Baptistery.—GROUND FLOOR. In the entrance hall, marble bust of Brunelleschi, attributed to *Buggiano* or *Giovanni Bandini*. This is thought to have been commissioned by the Opera del Duomo for its present position. The enamelled terracotta relief of the Madonna and Child, is by *Andrea della Robbia*; the flat lunette of God the Father between two angels is also attributed to *Andrea*. The marble panels from the choir of the Duomo (1547) are fine works by *Baccio Bandinelli* and *Giovanni Bandini*.—The room beyond contains sculptures and architectural fragments from the Duomo and a lunette of St Zenobius by the bottega of *Andrea della Robbia* (1496).

ROOM I. To the right of the door is a facsimile of the drawing (owned by the Opera del Duomo) of the old façade (never completed) _old Façade di Camera_

of the Duomo designed by Arnolfo di Cambio. It was made shortly before its demolition in 1587 by _Bernardino Poccetti_ (and is the most detailed illustration of it which has survived). On the wall opposite are numerous sculptures from the old façade by _Arnolfo di Cambio_ and his bottega, including a *Madonna and Child (a somewhat enigmatic work with striking glass eyes), *St Reparata, St Zenobius, the *Madonna and the Nativity, and (at the end of the room) Boniface VIII (restored). The statuettes from the main door (late 14C) are the work of _Piero di Giovanni Tedesco_. On the other long wall are the four seated Evangelists which were added to the lower part of the façade in the early 15C: _Nanni di Banco_, St Luke 1410–14); _Donatello_, *St John the Evangelist; _Bernardo Ciuffagni_, St Matthew; _Niccolò di Piero Lamberti_, St Mark.—In the centre of the room is the tomb of Piero Farnese (died 1363) which includes a relief from a Roman sarcophagus of the late 2C AD, and the angel and basin of the 14C stoup (attributed to _Urbano da Cortona_) from the Duomo (cf. p 73). In the recess are sculptural fragments including an Etruscan cippus (5C BC), showing musicians and dancers, and a Roman sarcophagus with the story of Orestes. The two small rooms beyond are devoted to _Brunelleschi_. His death mask is displayed beside models in wood of the cupola (probably made by a contemporary of Brunelleschi), and the lantern (thought to date from 1436 and to be by the architect himself). The apparatus which may have been used in the construction of the cupola (or in its maintenance), including pulleys, ropes, technical instruments, etc. is displayed here. It was found in a storeroom at the foot of the cupola, together with Brunelleschi's original brick moulds.—Steps lead up to ROOM II which displays four of the 58 beautiful illuminated antiphonals which belong to the cathedral. All but three of them were seriously damaged in the flood of 1966 and they are being carefully restored. They include works by _Attavante degli Attavanti_, _Monte di Giovanni_, and _Frate Eustachio_. The four large wood models entered in the competition of 1588 for the new façade of the Duomo are thought to be by _Buontalenti, Giambologna, Don Giovanni de' Medici_ and _Giovanni Antonio Dosio_ (or _Cigoli_). The roundel of the Agnus Dei, the 'stemma' of the 'Arte della Lana' who supervised work in the Duomo, has probably always been here since it was commissioned from the workshop of _Andrea della Robbia_. On the opposite wall is another model for the façade of the Duomo made in 1635 by members of the Accademia delle Arti del Disegno.—In the modern chapel is a fine collection of reliquaries (14–18C), including one of 1501 by _Paolo di Giovanni Sogliani_. The Madonna between Saints Catherine and Zenobius, above the altar, is attributed to _Bernardo Daddi_ (1334).

On the Stair landing is displayed the *Pietà of _Michelangelo_, removed in 1981 from a chapel at the E end of the Duomo. A late work, it was intended for Michelangelo's own tomb. According to Vasari, the head of Nicodemus is a self-portrait. Dissatisfied with his work, the sculptor destroyed the arm and left leg of Christ, and his pupil, Tiberio Calcagni, restored the arm and finished the figure of Mary Magdalen.—At the top of the stairs are two frescoed heads (Saints Peter and Paul) by _Bicci di Lorenzo_.

FIRST FLOOR. ROOM I is dominated by the two famous *Cantorie made in the 1430s by _Luca della Robbia_ and _Donatello_, probably as organ-lofts (rather than singing galleries) above the two sacristy doors in the Duomo. The one on the left, by _Luca della Robbia_, was his first important commission. The original panels are displayed

*A carved panel from the Cantoria by Luca della Robbia
(Museo dell' Opera del Duomo)*

beneath the reconstructed Cantoria. As the inscription indicates, the
charming sculptured panels illustrate Psalm 150. The children (some
of them drawn from Classical models), dancing, singing, or playing
musical instruments, are exquisitely carved within a beautiful architectural framework. *Donatello*'s Cantoria, opposite, provides a striking contrast, with a frieze of running putti against a background of
coloured inlay. Beneath it is displayed his expressive statue in wood
of *St Mary Magdalen (formerly in the Baptistery), thought to be a
late work. It was beautifully restored after damage in the flood of
1966.—Around the walls are the 16 statues (most of them in poor
condition) formerly in the niches on the Campanile (cf. p 76):
Donatello, Bearded Prophet, Abraham and Isaac (part of the modell-
ing is attributed to *Nanni di Bartolo*); *Nanni di Bartolo* (attributed),
Prophet; *Donatello*, Beardless Prophet; *Andrea Pisano* (attributed),
four Prophets; *Nanni di Bartolo*, Abdia; *Donatello*, 'Geremiah', *Hab-
bakuk ('lo zuccone'), St John the Baptist (attributed); *Andrea Pisano*,
two Sibyls, Solomon, and David.—The adjoining room exhibits the
original *Bas-reliefs (also badly worn) which decorated the two lower
registers of the Campanile. The lower row, which date from the early
14C, are charming works by *Andrea Pisano* (some perhaps designed
by *Giotto*) they illustrate the Creation of Man, and the Arts and
Industries. Starting on the wall opposite the entrance and going left:
Creation of Adam, Creation of Eve, Labours of Adam and Eve, Jabal
(the Pastoral life), Jubal (Music), Tubalcain (the Smith), Noah,

Gionitus (Astronomy), The Art of Building, Medicine, Hunting, Weaving, Phoroneus the Lawgiver, Daedalus, Navigation, Hercules and Cacus, Agriculture, Theatrica, Architecture, Phidias (Sculpture), Apelles (Painting). The last five reliefs (on the right wall) were made in 1437–39 by *Luca della Robbia* to fill the frames on the N face of the Campanile: Grammar, Philosophy, Orpheus (representing Poetry or Rhetoric), Arithmetic, and Astrology (with the figure of Pythagoras).—The upper row of smaller reliefs by pupils of *Pisano*, illustrate the seven Planets, the Virtues, and the Liberal Arts. The seven Sacraments (right wall) traditionally thought to be by *Alberto Arnoldi*, are now attributed to *Maso di Banco*. The lunette of the Madonna and Child formerly over a door of the Campanile is by *Andrea Pisano*.

ROOM II. The four gilded bronze ·Panels by *Lorenzo Ghiberti* removed from the East Door of the Baptistery have been displayed here since their restoration (cf. p 68); the others will also be housed here when restored. To the right, two Byzantine mosaic tablets of exquisite workmanship, thought to date from the early 14C; '*Maestro del Bigallo*', St Zenobius enthroned and stories from his life; paintings of the 14–15C Florentine school; *Andrea Pisano*, statuettes of the Redeemer and St Reparata; (in cases) 27 needlework ·Panels which formerly adorned vestments made for the Baptistery, with scenes from the life of St John the Baptist worked by the craftsmen of the 'Arte di Calimala' in 1466–87 on a design by *Antonio del Pollaiolo*. At the foot of the steps, Madonna and Annunciatory Angel, by the '*Maestro dell'Annunciazione*' (formerly attributed to *Jacopo della Quercia*), removed from the lunette of the Porta della Mandorla of the Duomo.—*Tino da Camaino* (attributed), Female bust; *Giovanni di Balduccio* (attributed), Crucifix in wood (from the Baptistery); Triptych of the Martyrdom of St Sebastian by *Giovanni del Biondo* (attributed). Above the door, *Benedetto Buglioni*, Mary Magdalen in the Desert.—At the end of the room is the magnificent ·ALTAR of silver-gilt, from the Baptistery, a Gothic work by Florentine goldsmiths (including *Betto di Geri* and *Leonardo di Ser Giovanni*), begun in 1366 and finished in the 15C, illustrating the history of St John the Baptist. The statuette of the Baptist was added by *Michelozzo*. On the left flank, reliefs of the Annunciation to St Zacharias and the Visitation by *Bernardo Cennini*, and the Birth of the Baptist by *Antonio del Pollaiolo*; on the right flank, reliefs of the Banquet of Herod by *Antonio di Salvi* and *Francesco di Giovanni*, and the Beheading of the Baptist by *Verrocchio*. The altar is surmounted by a silver ·Cross by *Betto di Francesco* (1457–59), *Antonio del Pollaiolo*, and probably other artists (*Bernardo Cennini?*).—On the walls, *Monte di Giovanni*, mosaic of St Zenobius (1505); *Pagno di Lapo Portigiani* (attributed), bas-relief of the Madonna and Child; *Jacopo del Casentino* (attributed), Processional painting of St Agatha (removed for restoration).

The piazza follows the curve of the Duomo. At No. 28 (red) the 16C Palazzo Strozzi-Niccolini stands on the site of a house where Donatello had his studio (19C plaque and bust). At the end of Via dei Servi can be seen Piazza Santissima Annunziata with the equestrian statue of the grand-duke Ferdinando I. In Piazza del Duomo are several medieval houses with coats-of-arms (some of them put up in 1390), and one (No. 5) with a pretty loggia. Opposite a side door of the Duomo, the long straight Via Ricasoli leads towards San Marco. Piazza San Giovanni is regained across the busy Via de' Martelli (view of Palazzo Medici-Riccardi). Beside the Baptistery is the *Pillar of St Zenobius*, erected in the 14C to commemorate an elm which came into leaf here when the body of the bishop saint (died c 430) was translated from San Lorenzo to Santa Reparata in the 9C. In the piazza, at No. 7 is the ancient little *Casa dell'Opera di San Giovanni*, with a copy in the lunette of a statuette of St John by Michelozzo (the original is now in the Bargello). The medieval courtyard is used by a florist. The W end of the square is occupied by the huge *Palazzo Arcivescovile*. It incorporates the church of *San Salvatore al Vescovo* (adm. sometimes on request). The interior was entirely frescoed in 1737–38. The quadratura is by Pietro Anderlini. In the vault, Ascension by Vincenzo Meucci, who also frescoed the Resurrection on the right wall. On the left wall, Deposition by Mauro Soderini. The frescoes in the apse and dome, and the monochrome figures of the Apostles are all by Gian Domenico Ferretti. The little Romanesque façade (restored in 1989) of the earlier church can be seen behind, in Piazza dell'Olio.

3   Piazza del Duomo to Piazza della Signoria

Between the Baptistery and the Campanile the straight VIA DE' CALZAIOLI (Pl.16;4,6; a pedestrian precinct) leads due S towards Piazza Signoria. On the line of a Roman road, this was the main thoroughfare of the medieval city, linking the Duomo to Palazzo Vecchio, and passing the guildhall of Orsanmichele. Although many of the shops on the ground floors of the buildings still have arches, the street was transformed when it was widened in the 1840s. Via degli Speziali diverges right for **Piazza della Repubblica** (Pl.16;3), on the site of the Roman forum, and still in the centre of the city. It was laid out at the end of the 19C after the demolition of many medieval buildings, the Mercato Vecchio, and part of the Ghetto (which was created in 1571 and extended from the N side of the present square to Via dei Pecori). Much criticised at the time, the Piazza remains a disappointing intrusion into the historical centre of the city, with its sombre colonnades and undistinguished buildings disfigured by advertisements. The *Colonna dell'Abbondanza*, a granite Roman column, was first set up here in 1428. The statue is a copy of a work by Giovanni Battista Foggini. Several large cafés have tables outside, including the 'Giubbe Rosse', famous meeting place in the first decades of this century of writers and artists. Beneath the arcades is the central Post Office and (on Thursdays) a flower and plant market. The Cinema Edison, beneath the portico, was opened here in 1901. The huge triumphal arch on the W side of the piazza leads into Via Strozzi (cf. p 158).

On the other side of Via de' Calzaioli is the narrow Via del Corso (cf. p 216). Farther on, opposite Via dei Tavolini (with a view of a medieval tower) rises the tall rectangular church of *Orsanmichele (Pl.16;6), on the site of *San Michele ad hortum* founded in the 9C, and destroyed in 1239. It is thought that a grain market was erected here c 1290 by *Arnolfo di Cambio* which was burnt down in 1304. The present building was built as a market by *Francesco Talenti*,

*A detail of the 'Pianta della Catena' of c 1472, showing the
Baptistery, Duomo, Orsanmichele, and the Palazzo and
Loggia della Signoria*

Neri di Fioravante, and *Benci di Cione* in 1337. The arcades were enclosed by huge three-light windows by *Simone Talenti* in 1380. These, in turn, were bricked up shortly after they were finished (but their superb Gothic tracery can still be appreciated). The upper storey, completed in 1404, was intended to be used as a granary. The decoration of the exterior was undertaken by the Guilds (or 'Arti') who commissioned statues of their patron saints for the canopied niches. They competed with each other to command work from the best artists of the age, and the statues are an impressive testimony to the skill of Florentine sculptors over a period of some 200 years. Restoration of the statues and niches has been underway since 1984. So far three statues have been restored and it has been decided, for conservation reasons, that they cannot be returned to the exterior. A cast of one of them (Donatello's St Mark) has been made and will soon be exhibited in situ, and probabaly all the originals will eventually be replaced by casts. The originals may be exhibited after their restoration in rooms above (see below). The empty niches have been beautifully restored.

The 'Arti Maggiori' or Greater Guilds took over control of the government of the city at the end of the 13C and the regime of the 'secondo popolo' lasted for nearly a century. Merchants in the most important trades, bankers, and professional men were members of these guilds: the 'Calimala' (the first guild, named from the street where the wholesale cloth-importers had their warehouses), the 'Giudici e notai' (judges and notaries), the 'Cambio' (bankers), the 'Lana' (woollen-cloth merchants and manufacturers), the 'Por Santa Maria' (named from the street which led to the workshops of the silk-cloth industry), the 'Medici e speziali' (physicians and apothecaries, the guild to which painters belonged), and the 'Vaiai e pellicciai' (furriers). The other corporations, the 'Arti Minori', created in the 13C, represented shopkeepers and skilled artisans.

The tabernacles, and the Guilds to whom they belonged, are described below, beginning at Via de' Calzaioli (corner of Via de' Lamberti) and going round to the right: 1. 'CALIMALA' (wholesale cloth-importers). Tabernacle and St John the Baptist (1414–16) by *Lorenzo Ghiberti*. This was the first life-size statue of the Renaissance to be cast in bronze.—Beyond the door, 2. 'TRIBUNALE DI MERCANZIA' (the merchants' court, where guild matters were adjudicated). Bronze group of the *Incredulity of St Thomas (1466–83; removed for restoration) by *Verrocchio*. The tabernacle was commissioned earlier by the 'Parte Guelfa'; it is the work of *Donatello*, and formerly contained his St Louis of Toulouse now in the Museo dell'Opera di Santa Croce, cf. p 179. Above is the round 'stemma' of the 'Mercanzia' in enamelled terracotta by *Luca della Robbia* (1463).—3. 'GIUDICI E NOTAI' (judges and notaries). Tabernacle by *Niccolò Lamberti* (1403–06), with a bronze statue of St Luke (1601) by *Giambologna*.—4. 'BECCAI' (butchers). St Peter (1408–13) attributed to *Donatello*.—5. 'CONCIAPELLI' (tanners). Tabernacle and St Philip (c 1415) by *Nanni di Banco*.—6. 'MAESTRI DI PIETRA E DI LEGNAME' (stonemasons and carpenters, the guild to which architects and sculptors belonged). Tabernacle and statues of *Four soldier saints (the 'Quattro Santi Coronati'), modelled on Roman statues, by *Nanni di Banco* (c 1415). The *Relief, by the same artist, illustrates the work of the Guild. Above is their 'stemma' in inlaid terracotta by *Luca della Robbia*.—7. 'ARMAIUOLI' (armourers). St George by *Donatello* (copies of the original bas-relief and statue of 1417 removed in 1888 to the Bargello, cf. p 164).—8. 'CAMBIO' (bankers). Tabernacle and bronze statue of *St Matthew (1419–22), by *Ghiberti*.—Beyond the door, 9. 'LANAIUOLI' (wool manufacturers and clothiers). Bronze *St Stephen by *Ghiberti* (1428).—10. 'MANISCALCHI' (farriers). St Eligius (1408–c 1414; removed and restored) and bas-relief of the Saint in a smithy by *Nanni di Banco*.—11. 'LINAIOLI E RIGATTIERI' (linen merchants and used-clothes' dealers). St Mark (1411–13) by *Donatello* (removed and restored in 1986).—12. 'PELLICCIAI' (furriers). St James the Greater (removed and restored in 1988), with a bas-relief of his beheading, attributed to *Niccolò Lamberti*.—13. 'MEDICI E SPEZIALI' (physicians and apothecaries). Gothic tabernacle attributed to *Simone Talenti* (1399), with a *Madonna and Child (the 'Madonna delle Rose') thought to be the work of *Giovanni Tedesco* (also attributed to *Niccolò di Pietro Lamberti* or *Simone Ferrucci*). Above, **'Stemma'* by *Luca della Robbia*.—14. 'SETAIUOLI E ORAFI' (silkweavers and goldsmiths). St John the Evangelist by *Baccio da Montelupo* (1515).

The INTERIOR of the dark rectangular hall (best light in the morning) now serves as a church. It is divided into two aisles by two massive pillars, and on a raised platform at one end are the two altars. The vaults and central and side pilasters are decorated with interesting frescoes of patron saints (many of them damaged, restored, or difficult to see) painted in the late 14C or early 15C by *Jacopo del Casentino, Giovanni del Ponte, Niccolò di Pietro Gerini, Ambrogio di Baldese*, and *Smeraldo di Giovanni*. In the 15–16C more frescoes were added (and some panel paintings) by *Giovanni Antonio Sogliani, Il Poppi, Lorenzo di Credi*, and *Mariotto Albertinelli*. The fine Gothic stained glass windows include one (St Jacob among the shepherds) designed by *Lorenzo Monaco*.—The Gothic *TABERNA-CLE (light on the right) by *Andrea Orcagna* (1349–59), is a master-piece of all the decorative arts, ornamented with marble and coloured glass, as well as with reliefs and statuettes. This is the only important sculptural work by this artist who was also a painter and architect. Around the base are reliefs of the life of the Virgin (including, in front, the Marriage of the Virgin, and the Annuncia-tion). Behind the altar (facing the entrance) is an elaborate sculp-tured relief of the Transition and Assumption of the Virgin. A beautiful frame of carved angels encloses a painting on the altar of the *Madonna by *Bernardo Daddi*.—On the other altar is a statue of the Madonna and Child with St Anne, by *Francesco da Sangallo* (1522).

The two large Gothic halls on the upper floors of Orsanmichele may be used to exhibit the original statues from the niches below. They are approached from an overhead passageway (1569) from *Palazzo dell'Arte della Lana*, described in Rte 21. In Via Orsan-michele is *Palazzo dell'Arte dei Beccai*, see p 209. One of the best-known coffee merchants in the city has its shop and café in Via de' Lamberti.—On the other side of Via de' Calzaioli is the church of *San Carlo dei Lombardi* (1349–1404) with a severe (much ruined) façade. In the unattractive interior is a Deposition by Niccolò di Pietro Gerini. The road ends in Piazza della Signoria, see Rte 4.

4   Piazza della Signoria

Piazza della Signoria (Pl.16;6), dominated by Palazzo Vecchio, the town hall, has been the political centre of the city since the Middle Ages. Here, from the 13C onwards, the 'popolo sovrano' met in 'parlamento' to resolve crises of government, and here in 1530 the return of the Medici was acclaimed by the people. It was the scene of public ceremonies, but also a gathering place in times of trouble. At the instigation of Savonarola, 'immoral luxuries' including works of art were burnt in the piazza, before the Inquisition denounced the Prior of San Marco as a heretic and he, and his two companions, were burnt at the stake here on 23 May 1498. In the life of the city today, the piazza is still the focus of political manifestations. It is now a

Savonarola burnt at the stake in Piazza della Signoria, a detail of a picture by an unknown Florentine painter, c 1500, probably an eye-witness of the event. (Museo di San Marco)

pedestrian precinct (heavy traffic was banned from the piazza as early as 1385), and usually crowded with tourists as well as Florentines. Several cafés and restaurants have tables outside. The piazza has been partly inaccessible for several years during controversial 'restoration' work on the 18C paving. This operation has been complicated by archaeological excavations of Roman remains (now covered over).

The history of the square has followed that of Palazzo Vecchio. The area at the foot of the palace was laid out as 'Piazza del Popolo' in 1307. During the 14C houses were demolished nearby in order to expand the size of the piazza. By 1385, when it was paved, it had nearly reached its present dimensions.

Beside the splendid Palazzo Vecchio (described in Rte 5) is the huge *Loggia della Signoria (Pl.16;6; also known as Loggia dei Lanzi and Loggia dell'Orcagna), with its three beautiful lofty arches (covered with scaffolding since 1987). Their semicircular form, breaking free from Gothic shapes, anticipates the Renaissance. The loggia was built in 1376–82 by Benci di Cione and Simone Talenti (probably on a design by Orcagna) to be used by government officials during public ceremonies, and as an ornament to the square. In the spandrels are statues of Virtues (1384–89) against a blue-enamelled ground, designed by Agnolo Gaddi. The columns are decorated with (worn) statuettes and lions' heads and have composite capitals; there are two elaborate corbels on the back wall. It received its alternative name 'Loggia dei Lanzi' from the bodyguard (the 'Lanzichenecchi') of Cosimo I who were stationed here.

It is only since the end of the 18C that the loggia has been used as an open-air museum of sculpture. In front, on the left, is Cellini's magnificent bronze *Perseus trampling Medusa and exhibiting her severed head. This was commissioned by Cosimo I in 1545 and placed under the loggia near Donatello's Judith (see below); it is considered Cellini's masterpiece. He provides a graphic description in his 'Autobiography' of the great difficulties he encountered while casting it (during which time his studio caught fire and he retired to bed with a fever). He saved the situation at the last moment by seizing all his pewter plates and bowls and throwing them into the melting-pot. The elaborate pedestal, using classical motifs, incorporates bronze statuettes and a bas-relief of Perseus rescuing Andromeda which have been replaced by copies (the originals are in the Bargello, see p 163). On either side of the central arch is a lion, that on the right a Greek work, and the other a 16C copy. Beneath the right arch is Giambologna's last work, the *Rape of the Sabine (1583), a three-figure group. One of the most successful Mannerist sculptures, the elaborate serpentine composition is designed to be seen from every side. The pedestal bears a bronze bas-relief. Under the loggia are Hercules and the Centaur, by Giambologna; Ajax with the body of Patroclus, a Roman copy of a Greek original, and the Rape of Polyxena, by Pio Fedi (1866). Against the back wall are Roman statues. For conservation reasons, the Perseus and Rape of the Sabine may be substituted here by casts and exhibited in the Bargello.

Beyond the corner of the piazza with the Uffizi buildings (see Rte 6) is the main entrance to Palazzo Vecchio. In front stands a copy of Michelangelo's famous DAVID. The huge statue was commissioned by the city of Florence in 1501 and set up here in 1504 as a political symbol representing the victory of Republicanism over tyranny. When it was unveiled it was heralded as a masterpiece and at once established Michelangelo as the greatest Florentine artist of his age. It was removed to the Accademia in 1873 (cf. p 126). The colossal statue of HERCULES AND CACUS was sculpted in 1534 by Bandinelli; it is an unhappy imitation of the David, all the defects of which were pointed out by Cellini to Cosimo I in the presence of the sculptor.

Farther to the left, in front of the palace, is the copy of the statue of Judith and Holofernes by Donatello; the original has been exhibited inside Palazzo Vecchio since its restoration (see p 96). Beyond a copy of Donatello's 'Marzocco', the heraldic lion of Florence (the original is in the Bargello, see p 163) is the NEPTUNE FOUNTAIN (1560–75). The colossal flaccid figure of Neptune, known to Florentines as 'il Biancone', has been restored. It was carved from a block of marble which, despite the efforts of Cellini, was first offered to Bandinelli and on his death to *Ammannati*. In the more successful elegant bronze groups on the basin, Ammannati was assisted by *Giambologna*, *Andrea Calamech*, and others. The porphyry disk with an inscription in the pavement in front of the fountain marks the spot where Savonarola was burnt at the stake (see above). On a line with the statues across the front of Palazzo Vecchio is the fine bronze equestrian monument to Cosimo I by *Giambologna* (1595).

At the end of the piazza (which opens out towards Piazza San Firenze, see Rte 14), and opposite the long flank of Palazzo Vecchio (described on p 91) is the *Tribunale di Mercanzia* (or Merchants' Court), founded in 1308 and established in this building in 1359. Guild matters were discussed here. *Palazzo Uguccioni* (No. 7) has an unusual but handsome façade attributed to Mariotto di Zanobi Folfi (1550; it has been awaiting restoration for years), and a bust of Francesco I by Giovanni Bandini. Above a bank at No. 5, is displayed the COLLEZIONE DELLA RAGIONE (Pl.16;6; adm. see p 60), a representative collection of 20C Italian art left to the city in 1970 by Alberto Della Ragione.

It includes mostly representational works (exhibited on two floors) by *Arturo Tosi, Carlo Carrà, Giorgio Morandi, Ottone Rosai, Gino Severini, Mario Sironi, Felice Casorati, Giorgio De Chirico, Arturo Martini, Virgilio Guidi, Massimo Campigli, Filippo De Pisis, Lucio Fontana, Marino Marini, Carlo Levi, Mario Mafai, Scipione, Giacomo Manzù, Corrado Cagli, Renato Guttuso*, and many others.

5   Palazzo Vecchio

*Palazzo Vecchio (Pl.16;6; adm. see p 62; also known as *Palazzo della Signoria*), the medieval Palazzo del Popolo, is still the town hall of Florence. On a design traditionally attributed to *Arnolfo di Cambio* (1299–1302), it is an imposing fortress-palace built in pietra forte on a trapezoidal plan. The façade has remained virtually unchanged: it has graceful divided windows and a battlemented gallery. It became the prototype of many other Palazzi Comunali in Tuscany. It was the tallest edifice in the city until the 15C; the tower (1310; restored in 1979–81), asymmetrically placed, is 95 metres high. Many of the rooms on the upper floors are open to the public.

The palace stands on part of the site of the Roman theatre of Florence built in the 1C AD. Here the 'priori' lived during their two months' tenure of office in the government of the medieval city. The bell in the tower summoned citizens in times of trouble to 'Parlamento' in the square below. Cosimo il Vecchio was imprisoned in the 'Alberghetto' in the tower in 1433 before being exiled. The building became known as Palazzo della Signoria during the Republican governments of the 15C, and alterations were carried out inside by *Michelozzo, Giuliano* and *Benedetto da Maiano* and *Domenico Ghirlandaio*. After the expulsion of the Medici in 1494 a huge hall (later known as the Sala dei

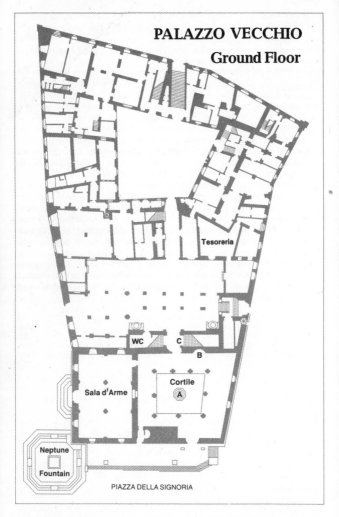

Cinquecento) was built by *Cronaca* to house the new legislative body, the
Consiglio Maggiore, which represented the aristocratic character of the new
regime. Savonarola, at first a supporter of this government, was imprisoned in
the Alberghetto in 1498 before being burnt at the stake in the piazza outside.
One of the most significant moments in the history of the palace occured in 1540
when Cosimo I moved here from the private Medici palace in Via Larga (now
Via Cavour). *Battista del Tasso*, *Vasari*, and later *Buontalenti* were called in to
redecorate the building, now called Palazzo Ducale, and extend it at the back
for the early Medici dukes without, however, altering the exterior aspect on
Piazza della Signoria. It became known as Palazzo Vecchio only after 1549
when the Medici grand-dukes took up residence in Palazzo Pitti. The Provisio-
nal Governments of 1848 and 1859 met here, and from 1865 to 1871 it housed
the Chamber of Deputies and the Foreign Ministry when Florence was capital
of the Kingdom of Italy. Since 1872 it has been the seat of the municipal

government.—The flank of the building on Piazza Signoria includes the battlemented 14C nucleus of the palace, the unfinished exterior of the Salone dei Cinquecento, with a hipped roof and marble window, and the handsome façade added by *Buontalenti* in Via de' Gondi. The 16C additions on the other flank, and at the back of the building on Via dei Leoni, incorporate medieval houses.

The room numbers given below refer to the plans in the text. It is likely that the itinerary of the visit to the upper floors will be changed when more of the building is opened to the public. The palace has been used in recent years for large exhibitions: during the hanging and dismantling of these the rooms normally open to the public may be closed for several months.

The ENTRANCE is guarded by two bizarre terms by *Bandinelli* and *Vincenzo de' Rossi* (the other sculptures outside the palace are described on p 88). Above is a frieze (1528) dedicated to 'Cristo Re' with the monogram of Christ flanked by two symbolic lions. The CORTILE was reconstructed by *Michelozzo* (1453). The elaborate decorations were added in 1565 by *Giorgio Vasari* on the occasion of the marriage between Francesco, son of Cosimo I, and Joanna of Austria. The columns were covered with stucco and the vaults and walls painted with grotesques and views (restored) of Austrian cities. The fountain (A) designed by Vasari bears a copy of *Verrocchio's* popular putto holding a dolphin (c 1470), a bronze made for a fountain at the Medici villa at Careggi. The original is preserved inside the palace (see p 94). The statue of Samson killing the Philistine (B) is by *Pierino da Vinci*. In the large rectangular SALA D'ARME, the only room on this floor which survives from the 14C structure, exhibitions are held. The rest of the ground floor is taken up with busy local government offices. In the entrance to the Tesoreria Comunale is displayed the 15C weather-vane with the Marzocco lion removed from the top of the tower, and replaced there by a copy in 1981. The monumental GRAND STAIRCASE (C) by *Vasari* ascends (right) in a scenographic double flight (past the ticket office) to the first floor.

The immense •**Salone dei Cinquecento** (53.5 × 22 metres, and 18m high) was built by *Cronaca* in 1495 for the meetings of the Consiglio Maggiore of the Republic (addressed here in 1496 by Savonarola). *Leonardo da Vinci* was commissioned in 1503 by the government to decorate one of the two long walls with a huge mural representing the Florentine victory at Anghiari over Milan in 1440. He experimented, without success, with a new technique of mural painting and completed only a fragment of the work before leaving Florence for Milan in 1506. It is not known whether this had disappeared or was destroyed (probably by order of Cosimo I) before the present frescoes were carried out under the direction of Vasari. *Michelangelo* was asked to do a similar composition on the opposite wall, representing the battle of Cascina between Florence and Pisa in 1364, but he only completed the cartoon before being called to Rome by Julius II. The cartoons of both works and the fragment painted by Leonardo were frequently copied and studied by contemporary painters before they were lost (cf. p 94). The room was transformed by Vasari in 1563–65 when the present decoration (designed with the help of Vincenzo Borghini) was carried out in celebration of Cosimo I. In the centre of the magnificent ceiling is the Apotheosis of the Duke surrounded by the 'stemme' of the Guilds. The other panels, by *Vasari*, *Giovanni Stradano*, *Jacopo Zucchi*, and *Giovanni Battista Naldini*, represent allegories of the cities of Tuscany under Florentine dominion, the foundations and early growth of Florence, and the victories over Siena (1554–55) and Pisa (1496–1509). On the walls are

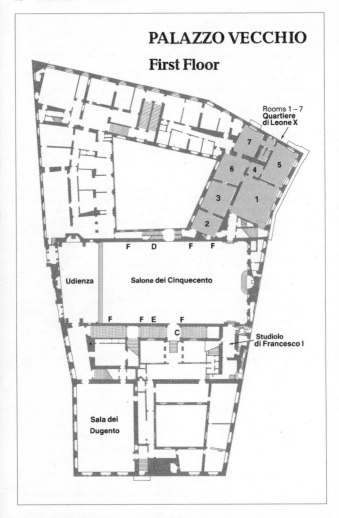

PALAZZO VECCHIO
First Floor

Rooms 1 – 7
Quartiere di Leone X

Udienza

Salone dei Cinquecento

Studiolo di Francesco I

Sala dei Dugento

huge frescoes by the same artists illustrating three more episodes in the wars with Pisa (entrance wall) and Siena. The decoration was completed by *Jacopo Ligozzi, Domenico Passignano*, and *Cigoli*. The raised tribuna ('UDIENZA') contains statues by *Bandinelli* and *Vincenzo de' Rossi* (finished in the following century by *Giovanni Caccini*) of distinguished members of the Medici family. *Michelangelo*'s *Victory (D), a strongly-knit two-figure group, was intended for a niche in the tomb of Julius II in Rome. It was presented to Cosimo I by Michelangelo's nephew in 1565 and set up here by Vasari as a celebration of the victory of Cosimo I over Siena. The serpentine form of the principal figure was frequently copied by later Mannerist sculptors. On the entrance wall (E) is *Giambologna*'s original plaster model for Virtue overcoming Vice (or 'Florence victorious over Pisa') commissioned as a 'pendant' to Michelangelo's Victory. The other statues, representing the Labours of Hercules (F), are *Vincenzo de' Rossi*'s best works. On the end wall, opposite the tribune, are antique Roman statues.

A door in the entrance wall, to the right (inconspicuous as it is sometimes kept closed) gives access to the charming *Studiolo of Francesco I*. This tiny study (with no windows) was created by *Vasari* and his school in 1570–75 on an iconographical scheme devised by Vincenzo Borghini. It is a masterpiece of Florentine Mannerist decoration.

The present entrance is modern; the Studiolo was formerly accessible only by the door on the end wall from the private rooms of the dukes. It is entirely decorated with paintings and bronze statuettes celebrating Francesco's interest in the natural sciences and alchemy. The lower row of paintings conceal cupboards in which he kept his treasures. On the barrel vault, by *Il Poppi*, are allegories of the four Elements and portraits by *Bronzino* of Francesco's parents, Cosimo I and Eleonora di Toledo. The four walls, symbolising the four Elements, include: left wall ('Water'): *Vincenzo Danti*, Venus (bronze); *Vasari*, Perseus liberating Andromeda; *Santi di Tito*, Crossing of the Red Sea; *Giovanni Battista Naldini*, Finding of amber; *Giovanni Stradano*, Circe and the companions of Ulysses; *Alessandro Allori*, Pearl fishing.—On the end wall ('Air'): *Giovanni Bandini*, Juno (bronze); *Maso di San Friano*, Diamond mine, Fall of Icarus.—Right wall ('Fire'): *Giambologna*, Apollo, *Vincenzo de' Rossi*, Vulcan (both bronzes); *Giovanni Maria Butteri*, Glass-blowing factory; *Alessandro Fei*, Goldsmiths' workshop; *Giovanni Stradano*, Alchemist's laboratory.—Entrance wall ('Earth'): *Bartolomeo Ammannati*, Opi (bronze); *Jacopo Zucchi*, Goldmine.—A small staircase leads up to the TESORETTO (adm. only with special permission), the richly decorated private study of Cosimo I. The stuccoes are by *Tommaso Boscoli* and *Leonardo Ricciarelli* and the vault frescoes by *Il Poppi* (1559–62).

Also off the Sala dei Cinquecento (to the left of the dais) is a VESTIBULE (the coved ceiling of which has painted grotesque decorations) which leads into the **Sala dei Dugento** (usually closed), where the town Council meets. This was reconstructed in 1472–77 by *Benedetto* and *Giuliano da Maiano* who also executed the magnificent wood ceiling (with the help of *Domenico, Marco*, and *Giuliano del Tasso*). The name is derived from the council of 200 citizens who met here. The *Tapestries made in Florence in 1546–53 with the story of Joseph, designed by *Bronzino, Pontormo, Salviati*, and *Allori* have been removed since 1983. They are being restored in a special laboratory set up in the Salone delle Bandiere at the top of the palace.

The door opposite the Studiolo leads into the **Quartiere di Leone X** (1–7) decorated by *Vasari* and assistants (including *Marco da Faenza* and *Giovanni Stradano*) in 1555–62 for Cosimo I. The mural paintings illustrate the political history of the Medici family. The SALA DI LEONE X (1) illustrates the life of cardinal Giovanni de' Medici, later Leo X. It has a good terracotta pavement and a fireplace by *Ammannati*. The other rooms are at present closed.

The SALA DI COSIMO IL VECCHIO (2) has a ceiling painting showing Cosimo's return from exile, by *Vasari*.—The SALA DI LORENZO IL MAGNIFICO (3) shows Lorenzo receiving the homage of the ambassadors.—In the CHAPEL (4) the wedding between Isabella, daughter of Cosimo I, and Alfonso d'Este was celebrated, and the secret marriage between Francesco I and Bianca Cappello took place. The altarpiece is an old copy of the Madonna dell'Impannata by Raphael now in the Pitti (p 115). It is flanked by Duke Cosimo as St Damian and Cosimo il Vecchio as St Cosma, the Medici patron saints, both good works by *Vasari*.—The SALA DI CLEMENTE VII (5) contains a mural painting of the siege of Florence by Charles V (1529–30) traditionally attributed to *Vasari* (but now thought to be by *Giovanni Stradano*), with a splendid panorama of the city.—

The SALA DI COSIMO I (6) has the most elaborate historical paintings, with, in the centre, the prisoners from the battle of Montemurlo brought before Cosimo I.

Stairs lead up to the SECOND FLOOR past an interesting fresco (c 1558) by *Giovanni Stradano* of the fireworks in Piazza Signoria celebrating the feast-day of St John the Baptist. At the top of the stairs (left) is the **Quartiere degli Elementi**, five rooms (8–13) decorated with complicated allegories of the Elements by *Vasari* and assistants (including *Cristofano Gherardi*). The SALA DEGLI ELE-MENTI (8) has good panel paintings set into the deeply recessed ceiling.—The TERRAZZA DI SATURNO (9; closed for restoration) was sadly reduced in size in the last century. The ceiling was painted by *Stradano* on a design by *Vasari*. The fine view of Florence to the SE includes the back of the Uffizi with the little round roof and lantern of the tribuna. Across the Arno, on the skyline, stands Forte di Belvedere whose walls can be seen on the green hillside. San Miniato is prominent with its tower, and, lower down at the foot of the hill, Porta San Niccolò. Farther to the left is Santa Croce with its campanile.—The little bronze demon by *Giambologna* was removed from the exterior of Palazzo Vecchietti.—The SALA DI OPI (10) has another fine ceiling and beautiful terracotta floor (1556). In the SALA DI GIOVE (11) with more ceiling paintings, are two fine cabinets in pietre dure, decorated with mythological scenes and birds, fruit, and flowers, both dating from the late-17C. The little TERRAZZO DI GIUNONE (12) was formerly open on three sides and surrounded by a hanging garden, but it was enclosed in the 19C. Here is displayed the *Putto with a dolphin, by *Verrocchio*, the original removed from the courtyard below (p 91). Beyond, a little room with grotteschi decorations has a window with a view of Santa Croce and the hill of San Miniato.—The SALA DI ERCOLE (13) has another good ceiling and a cabinet in pietre dure which belonged to Don Lorenzo de' Medici. It incorporates a view of the Villa della Petraia, on a design by *Giovanni Bilivert*.

A balcony leads across the end of the Sala dei Cinquecento. The following rooms (14–19) form part of the **Quartiere di Eleonora di Toledo**, the apartments of the wife of Cosimo I. The vault in the CAMERA VERDE (14) was painted with grotesques by *Ridolfo del Ghirlandaio* (c 1540). The *CAPPELLA DI ELEONORA (15), entirely decorated by *Bronzino* in 1540–45, is one of his most famous works. The little study has a ceiling painted by *Salviati*.—The next four rooms were decorated in 1561–62 with ceilings by *Battista Botticelli* and paintings (illustrating allegories of the female Virtues) by *Vasari* and *Giovanni Stradano*. The SALA DI ESTER (17) has a pretty frieze of putti intertwined in the letters of the name of Eleonora, and a 15C lavabo from Palazzo di Parte Guelfa. Here is a painting of 1557 which shows the lost fragment of the Battle of Anghiari by Leonardo (cf. above), probably the best copy that has survived. In the SALA DI GUALDRADA (19) there is a series of charming views of the celebrations held in the streets and piazze of Florence.

A passage (20) where remains of the old 14C polychrome ceiling, and parts of the ancient tower are visible, leads into the older rooms of the palace. The CAPPELLA DELLA SIGNORIA (or DEI PRIORI; 1511–14) was decorated by *Ridolfo del Ghirlandaio*, including an Annunciation with a view of the church of Santissima Annunziata in the background (before the addition of the portico). The altarpiece is by his pupil, *Fra Mariano da Pescia*.—The **Sala d'Udienza** has a superb *Ceiling by *Giuliano da Maiano* and assistants. Above the door from

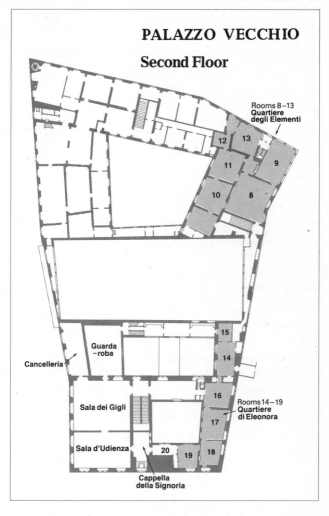

PALAZZO VECCHIO
Second Floor

Rooms 8–13
**Quartiere
degli Elementi**

12 13

11 9

10 8

15

14

Guarda
–roba

Cancelleria

16

Rooms 14–19
**Quartiere
di Eleonora**

17

Sala dei Gigli

Sala d'Udienza 20 19 18

Cappella
della Signoria

the chapel, designed by *Baccio d'Agnolo*, is a dedication to Christ
(1529). The other *Doorway crowned by a statue of Justice is by
Benedetto and *Giuliano da Maiano*. The intarsia doors, with figures
of Dante and Petrarch, are by *Giuliano da Maiano* and *Francione*.
The huge mural paintings illustrating stories from the life of the
Roman hero Marco Camillus, were added c 1545–48 by *Salviati*; they
are one of the major works by this typically Mannerist painter.

The **Sala dei Gigli** takes its name from the lilies, symbol of the city,
which decorate the walls and ceiling. It contains another magnificent
*Ceiling, and the other face of the doorway with a statue of the
young St John the Baptist and putti by *Benedetto* and *Giuliano da
Maiano*. The fresco by *Domenico Ghirlandaio* shows St Zenobius

enthroned between Saints Stephen and Lawrence and two lions, and lunettes with six heroes of ancient Rome. Here is displayed *Donatello*'s bronze statue of *JUDITH AND HOLOFERNES removed since its restoration from Piazza della Signoria. One of his last and most sophisticated works (c 1455), it was commissioned by the Medici and used as a fountain in the garden of their palace. On their expulsion from the city in 1495 it was expropriated by the government and placed under the Loggia della Signoria with an inscription warning against tyrants. A small exhibition illustrates how the statue was cast.—A window of the old palace serves as a doorway into the CANCELLERIA, built in 1511 and used as an office by Niccolò Machiavelli during his term as government secretary. He is here recorded in a fine bust (16C) and a painting by *Santi di Tito*. The stone bas-relief of St George (attributed to *Arnolfo di Cambio*) used to decorate the Porta San Giorgio (cf. p 203).—The GUARDAROBA or SALA DELLE CARTE GEOGRAFICHE (closed for restoration) was decorated with a fine ceiling and wooden cupboards in 1563–65 by *Dionigi di Matteo Nigetti*. On the presses are 57 maps illustrating the entire known world with a remarkable degree of accuracy. Of great scientific and historical interest, they were painted by *Fra Egnazio Danti* for Cosimo I (1563) and completed by *Stefano Bonsignori* by 1581 for Francesco I. The map on the left of the entrance shows the British Isles. The huge globe in the centre is also designed by *Danti*.—From here a door (closed indefinitely) gives access to the Gallery, a covered walk encircling the 13C part of the palace.

Stairs lead down from outside the Sala dei Gigli to the vestibule outside the Sala dei Dugento (see above) and the courtyard of the palace.

The **Quartiere del Mezzanino** is usually kept closed. Beyond some rooms which temporarily house the fine Cherubini collection of old musical instruments (see p 127) is the **Collezione Loeser**, left to the city in 1928 by the distinguished American art critic and connoisseur, Charles Loeser. The finest pieces include: *Gianfrancesco Rustici*, two Battle-scenes in terracotta; *Jacopo Sansovino*, two statuettes of angels; *Piero di Cosimo*, Passion of Christ; *Alonso Berruguete*, *Tondo of the Madonna and Child with the young St John; *Pietro Lorenzetti*, Madonna and Child; *Tino da Camaino*, Angel in adoration (from the Bishop Orso monument in the Duomo); *16C Florentine school*, bust of Machiavelli; *Bronzino*, *Laura Battiferri, wife of Bartolomeo Ammannati, one of his most sophisticated portraits; *Pontormo* (attributed), Portrait of Ludovico Martelli.—The *Alberghetto*, used as a political prison, and the TOWER (*View) have been closed indefinitely to visitors.

6   Galleria degli Uffizi

The massive *Palazzo degli Uffizi** (Pl.16;6) extends from Piazza della Signoria to the Arno. Houses were demolished to create this long narrow site next to Palazzo Vecchio, and *Vasari* was commissioned by Cosimo I to erect a building here to serve as government offices ('uffici', hence 'uffizi'). The unusual U-shaped building with a short 'façade' on the river front was begun in 1560 and completed, according to Vasari's design, after his death in 1574 by *Alfonso Parigi the Elder* and *Bernardo Buontalenti* (who also made provision for an art gallery here for Francesco I). Resting on unstable sandy ground, it is a feat of engineering skill. The use of iron to reinforce the building permitted extraordinary technical solutions during its construction,

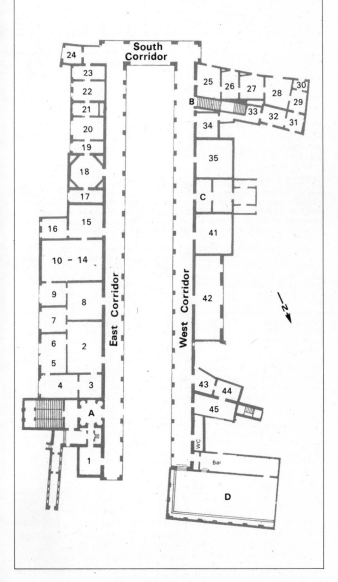

UFFIZI GALLERY

0 — 30 yards
0 — 30 metres

South Corridor

24
23
22
21
20
19
18
17
16
15
10 – 14
9
8
7
6
5
4
3
2
1

A

East Corridor

B
25 26 27 28 30
29
33 32 31
34
35
C
41
42

West Corridor

N

43 44
45
WC
Bar
D

and allowed for the remarkably large number of apertures. A long arcade supports three upper storeys pierced by numerous windows and a loggia in pietra serena. In the niches of the pilasters are 19C statues of illustrious Tuscans. The building now houses the famous Art Gallery.

The ground floor of *Palazzo della Zecca* is incorporated into the fabric of the building (right; with well protected windows). The famous gold 'florins', first issued in 1252, were minted here. The *Sala delle Reali Poste* here, built by Mariano Falcini as a post office in 1866, was restored in 1988 and is used for exhibitions. The fine hall has a huge skylight supported on a cast-iron framework.—At the end of Via Lambertesca is the Porta delle Suppliche added after 1574 by Buontalenti and surmounted by a bust of Francesco I by Bandini.

In Via della Ninna, incorporated into the building, are some of the nave columns of the church of *San Pier Scheraggio* (cf. below). Here also can be seen the beginning of the Corridoio Vasariano, forming a bridge between Palazzo Vecchio and the Uffizi (cf. p 106).

The **Galleria degli Uffizi** is the most important collection of paintings in Italy and one of the great art collections of the world. It is entered by the first door on the left under the colonnade. Admission, see p 61.

The origins of the collection go back to Cosimo I. The galleries were enlarged and the collection augmented by Francesco I. The Medici dynasty continued to add numerous works of art in the following centuries: Ferdinando I transferred sculptures here from the Villa Medici in Rome; Ferdinando II inherited paintings by Raphael, Titian, and Piero della Francesca from Francesco Maria della Rovere of Urbino; and Cardinal Leopoldo began the collection of drawings and self-portraits. The last of the Medici, Anna Maria Lodovica, widow of the Elector Palatine, through a family Pact (1737) settled her inheritance on the people of Florence. The huge collection was partly broken up during the last century when much of the sculpture went to the Bargello and other material was transferred to the Archaeological Museum. This century many paintings removed from Florentine churches have been housed in the gallery.

Since the Archivio di Stato was moved from the building in 1988 plans have been underway to expand the gallery in stages. The rooms on the third floor will probably be used to exhibit paintings up to the 16C, and the piano nobile below for the later works. On the ground floor will be the ticket office, a restaurant, and the tapestries (formerly in the corridors on the third floor), and also some sculptures. In an adjoining building on Piazza de' Castellani there are plans to open a restoration laboratory. The Corridoio Vasariano will be used exclusively for the collection of self-portraits, and in another part of the gallery, the Collezione Contini-Bonacossi (now in the Pitti) will soon be arranged. The modifications at the back of the building in Piazza de' Castellani, already begun some years ago, will eventually be used for an exit from the gallery.

The following description includes only some of the most important paintings and sculptures (and asterisks have been used sparingly). All the works are well labelled, and the collection is arranged chronologically by schools. Round red labels indicate the date a work was restored. Visitors are strongly recommended not to attempt to see the entire collection, for the first time, in one day; the first rooms (up to Room 15) include the major works of the Florentine Renaissance; the later rooms can be combined in a second visit. Usually the gallery is less crowded with tour groups in the late afternoon.

Ground Floor. Beyond the ticket office is a room (not always open) which incorporates remains of the church of San Pier Scheraggio, founded c 1068, and one of the largest churches of its time in Florence. It was altered when the Uffizi was built. Remains have also been found of an 8C Lombard church on this site. Here are displayed detached *Frescoes (c 1450) by *Andrea del Castagno* of illustrious Florentines including Boccaccio, Petrarch, and Dante. These splendid monumental figures decorated a loggia of the Villa Pandolfini at

Legnaia (and were later housed in the monastery of Sant'Apollonia). In 1983 a large painting (the Battle of San Martino, inspired by Paolo Uccello's famous triptych) by Corrado Cagli was also placed here. The room beyond (where the apse of the church has traces of damaged frescoes, c 1294–99) is used to exhibit recently restored paintings from the gallery. It contains the Madonna 'della Ninna' by the *'Maestro di San Martino alla Palma'* (c 1340), and a predella with scenes from the life of St Peter by *Giovanni del Ponte*, both painted for the church.—In an adjacent corridor, *Fresco of the Annunciation by *Botticelli* (from the church of San Martino della Scala), and a column of the church with a 14C fresco of St Francis.—There is a LIFT for the picture galleries on the third floor (although it is now officially reserved for the disabled and for the use of the gallery staff). At the foot of the staircase is a colossal statue (very damaged), attributed to the 16C Tuscan school, from the destroyed Medici theatre. The STAIRCASE, lined with antique busts and statues (including Venus Genetrix, and a Roman Vestal), leads up past part of the huge theatre built in the building by Buontalenti for Francesco I in 1586–89 (over the central door is a bust of Francesco by Giambologna or his workshop). On the left the old entrance now serves as the entrance to the **Prints and Drawings Rooms** (open to scholars with special permission, 9.00–13.00). The collection is one of the finest in the world and is particularly rich in Renaissance and Mannerist works. *Exhibitions are held periodically.

On the **Third Floor**, the VESTIBULE (A) contains antique sculpture including a statue of *Augustus, and two dogs, well preserved Greek works, perhaps of the Pergamenian School. Beyond is the long U-shaped gallery painted with grotesques in 1581; it provides a fine setting for the superb collection of antique sculptures (mostly Hellenistic works). Opposite the windows overlooking the narrow piazza are doors leading into the numerous galleries of paintings (the collection begins in Room 2, to the left).

EAST CORRIDOR. ROOM 1, to the right, is often closed. It contains fine antique *Sculptures which clearly influenced Florentine Renaissance sculptors: neo-Attic relief of dancing Horai; bust of Cicero (1C AD); exquisite Roman decorative relief (1C AD); three copies of the Doryphoros of Polykleitos; Roman reliefs showing a sacrificial scene (2C AD), the dance of the maenads, and the Temple of Vesta in the Roman Forum; and a relief fragment of two horses, an original Greek work of the 5C BC.—Outside in the corridor is (77.), Hercules and the Centaur, a late Hellenistic work restored by Giovanni Battista Caccini in 1589; Roman sarcophagi, and statues of an Athlete (100.), and a Guardian Deity (252.), both from classical Greek originals. The tapestries which used to stretch the whole length of the corridor have been removed for conservation reasons. They included four with grotesques on a yellow ground of the Seasons, by Giovanni Rost on a design by *Bachiacca* (1549–53), and a 16C Flemish series incorporating scenes from the lives of Catherine de' Medici and Henri III.

RÓOM 2. TUSCAN SCHOOL OF THE 13C. Three huge *Paintings of the Madonna enthroned (the 'Maestà') dominate the room and provide a fitting introduction to the painting galleries. On the right (8343.), the Madonna by *Cimabue* (c 1285), painted for the church of Santa Trìnita, marks a final development of the Byzantine style of painting, where a decorative sense still predominates. On the left is another exquisite version of this subject, the so-called 'Rucellai Madonna' by *Duccio di Boninsegna*.

It was commissioned by the Laudesi confraternity in 1285 for their chapel in Santa Maria Novella. Between the 17C and 18C it was put in the Rucellai chapel in the same church and has been housed in the Uffizi since 1948. It was painted on five planks of poplar wood 4.5 metres high and c 60–65 cm wide; since the wood was unseasoned, huge cracks were formed. These were painted over and the picture cleaned and beautifully restored in 1990. The splendid blue mantle of the Virgin was discoved beneath a layer of over-painting carried out in the 17C. The frame, with painted roundels, is original. The painting was traditionally attributed to Cimabue, but is now recognised as the work of the younger Sienese artist, Duccio, who is known to have worked in Cimabue's studio.

The Madonna (8344; removed for restoration), painted some 25 years later for the church of Ognissanti by *Giotto*, heralds a new era in Western painting. Here there is a new idea of the monumentality of the figures in a more clearly defined space.—The *Polyptych of the Badia (Madonna and four Saints) is also by *Giotto*. Also displayed here are two painted Crucifixes, one of the 12C Tuscan school, and one of the 13C Lucchese school; 3493. St Luke by the *'Maestro della Maddalena'*; and (9920.) Madonna and Child by the *'Maestro di San Torpè'*.

ROOM 3 (left). SIENESE SCHOOL OF THE 14C. 8346. *Ambrogio Lorenzetti*, *Presentation in the Temple (1342); 8348., 8349. four scenes from the life of St Nicholas; two small panels by *Niccolò Bonaccorsi*, (3157. Presentation in the Temple), and *Simone de' Crocifissi*, (3475. Nativity); 8347. *Pietro Lorenzetti* (brother of Ambrogio), panels of a dossal with the Story of the Blessed Umiltà; *451.–453. Simone Martini*, Annunciation (1333). The Gothic elegance of the two figures make this one of the masterpieces of the Sienese school. The Saints are by his brother-in-law, *Lippo Memmi*. 8349. *Niccolò di Ser Sozzo*, Madonna and Child; 8731, 8732, 9411. *Ambrogio Lorenzetti*, Madonna and Child, St Nicholas of Bari and St Proculus (a triptych painted for the church of San Procolo recomposed when the central panel was left to the Gallery by Bernard Berenson in 1959). 445. *Pietro Lorenzetti*, Madonna in glory, signed and dated 1340.

ROOM 4. FLORENTINE SCHOOL OF THE 14C. 3073. *Bernardo Daddi*, Madonna between Saints Matthew and Nicholas (1328); 3515. *Nardo di Cione*, Crucifixion; 454. *Giottino* (attributed), Deposition (from the church of San Remigio); 8564. *Bernardo Daddi*, Madonna and Child with Saints; 3163. *Orcagna*, St Matthew with scenes from his life (1367–68, completed by his brother, *Jacopo di Cione*); 459. *Giovanni da Milano*, ten panels of Saints, Martyrs, and Virgins.

ROOMS 5 AND 6. LATER GOTHIC SCHOOLS. 9920. *Masolino* (attributed), Madonna of Humility; 447. *Gherardo Starnina* (also attributed to Fra' Angelico), The Thebaid, a charming panel telling the story of the life of these hermits. 885. *Lorenzo Monaco*, Coronation of the Madonna (1413; to be restored); *Gentile da Fabriano*, 887. Mary Magdalen, St Nicholas of Bari, St John and St George (1425; from the Quaratesi polyptych), *8364. Adoration of the Magi (1423), with a fairy-tale quality, and a striking use of gold. The predella is exquisitely painted. 3344. *Jacopo Bellini*, Madonna and Child; 464. *Agnolo Gaddi*, Crucifixion; *466. *Lorenzo Monaco*, Adoration of the Magi.—From the window there is a view of Santa Croce and the hill of San Miniato.—ROOM 7. FLORENTINE SCHOOL OF THE EARLY 15C. *Fra' Angelico*, 1612. Coronation of the Virgin, 143. Madonna and Child; *884. *Domenico Veneziano*, Madonna enthroned with Saints Francis, John the Baptist, Zenobius, and Lucy, one of the few works known by this artist, painted in beautiful soft colours. 8386. *Masaccio* and *Masolino*, Madonna and Child with St Anne. Masaccio is thought to have added the Madonna and Child to his master's painting, which has, however, otherwise been completely repainted. The tiny painting of the Madonna and Child (9929.), temporarily exhibited here, is an undocumented work attributed to *Masaccio*. *1615. *Piero della Francesca*, a panel with the portraits of Federico di Montefeltro and his duchess, Battista Sforza, with their allegorical triumph on the reverse. Profoundly humanist in spirit, they are exquisite works with detailed landscapes in a transparent light. They were painted in Urbino c 1465 in celebration of this famous Renaissance prince. *479. *Paolo Uccello*, Battle of San Romano, an amusing exercise in perspective. Together with its companions, now in the Louvre and National Gallery, London, it decorated Lorenzo il Magnifico's bedroom in Palazzo Medici-Riccardi in 1492.

ROOM 8. FLORENTINE SCHOOL OF THE EARLY 15C (FILIPPO LIPPI). *8351. *Filippo Lippi*, Predella of the Barbadori altarpiece (now in the Louvre), with a remarkable sense of space; *483. *Alesso Baldovinetti*, Annunciation; 8354. *Filippo Lippi*, Madonna enthroned with Saints; 8355. *Francesco Pesellino*, Predella of No. 8354.; 487. *Alesso Baldovinetti*, Madonna and Child with Saints; *8352. *Filippo Lippi*, Coronation of the Virgin; 474. *Vecchietta*, Triptych of the Madonna and Saints; *Filippino Lippi*, 1566. Adoration of the Magi, 1568. Madonna painted for the Sala degli Otto in Palazzo Vecchio, 3246. Adoration of the Child; *Filippo Lippi*, 8350. Adoration of the Child, *1598. Madonna and Child with two angels (c 1465), justly one of his most famous works, and 8353. Adoration of the Child.

ROOM 9. POLLAIOLO. 495.–499., 1610. *Piero del Pollaiolo*, Six Virtues (including Charity, with a preparatory study on the back by his elder brother *Antonio*); 1606. *Botticelli*, Fortitude, an early work. In the case, four exquisite small *Panels: 1478. 8268. *Antonio del Pollaiolo*, Labours of Hercules, and 1487. 1484. *Botticelli*, Story of Judith and Holofernes (Judith returning from the camp of Holofernes, and the discovery of the decapitated Holofernes in his tent; c 1470). 1491. *Antonio del Pollaiolo*, Portrait of a lady in profile; 1490. *Filippino Lippi*, Young man in a red hat (of doubtful attribution); *1617. *Antonio del Pollaiolo*, Saints Vincent, James, and Eustace, one of the best works by this artist (formerly in the Chapel of the Cardinal of Portugal in San Miniato, where it has been replaced by a copy); 1492. *Antonio* and *Piero del Pollaiolo*, Portrait of Galeazzo Maria Sforza.

ROOMS 10–14 have been converted into one huge room and the rafters of the stage of the old Medici theatre (cf. p 99) exposed. The mistaken illumination has been justly criticised. Here the masterpieces of BOTTICELLI are being rehung. *Botticelli*, 1488. Man with a red hat holding a medallion of Cosimo il Vecchio (being restored), 1601. Madonna of the Rose garden; *1608. Annunciation, showing an extraordinary spiritual bond between the two figures; 881. *Domenico Ghirlandaio*, Madonna enthroned with saints; 1497. *Botticelli*, St Augustine in his study (a small work); 8361. Pala di San Barnaba, with its predella (8390.–8393.). 1619. *Domenico Ghirlandaio*, Tondo with the Adoration of the Magi; *Lorenzo di Credi*, *3094. Venus, one of his best works, and 8399. Adoration of the Shepherds. *Botticelli*'s *Adoration of the Magi (882) includes portraits of the Medici courtiers with Lorenzo il Magnifico and a self-portrait on the extreme right. The *Primavera (8360) is one of *Botticelli*'s most important and most famous paintings.

It was painted probably c 1478 for Lorenzo di Pierfrancesco de' Medici, Lorenzo il Magnifico's younger cousin. An allegory of spring, it is thought to have been inspired by a work of Politian, although its precise significance is still discussed. There is a rhythmical contact between the figures who are placed in a meadow of flowers within a dark orange grove, the Garden of Hesperides of classical myth. To the right Zephyr chases Flora and transforms her into Spring, who is shown bedecked with flowers. In the centre stands Venus with Cupid above her, and beyond the beautiful group of the Three Graces united in dance, is the figure of Mercury (perhaps an idealised portrait of Lorenzo il Magnifico). The work is richly painted on poplar wood. The varnishes which had been added in various restorations were removed in 1982 and the painting cleaned so that the original tones were restored to the surface. The botanical details which have been revealed include a great variety of spring flowers, most of them still to be found in Lorenzo di Pierfrancesco's Villa of Castello (cf. p 245).

Botticelli, *1496. Calumny (painted after 1487). The subject of this very elaborate small painting is taken from Lucian's account of a picture by Apelles described in Alberti's treatise on painting. 1607. Tondo of the Madonna of the Pomegranate (painted in 1487); *29. Pallas and the Centaur, probably intended as an allegory, the significance of which has been much discussed. The *Birth of Venus (878.) is perhaps the most famous of all the works of Botticelli.

This was also probably painted for Lorenzo di Pierfrancesco and hung in the Medici villa of Castello. The pagan subject is taken from a poem by Politian and illustrates Zephyr and Chloris blowing Venus ashore while Hora, her fluttering dress decorated with cornflowers and daisies, hurries to cover her nakedness. The elegant figures are painted with a remarkable lightness of touch in a decorative linear design. The classical nude figure of Venus balances on the edge of a beautiful scallop shell as it floats ashore. A strong wind blows through this harmonious Graeco-Roman world.

*1609. *Botticelli*, Madonna of the Magnificat; *Filippino Lippi*, 1711. Self-portrait (a fresco painted on a terracotta roof tile), 1485. Portrait of an old man; 8389. *Botticelli*, Predella of the Pala of San Marco (removed). The Coronation of the Virgin (1488–90), another beautiful work by *Botticelli* is also to be exhibited here since its restoration. An extremely damaged painting, which had not been exhibited since 1940, it had been the subject of numerous unsuccessful restorations in the past.—In the centre of the room is the huge *Triptych (3191–3.), of the Adoration of the Shepherds, commissioned by the Medici agent in Bruges, Tommaso Portinari from *Hugo van der Goes*, and shipped back to Florence in 1475. On the wings are Saints and members of the Portinari family. The painting had an important influence on contemporary Florentine artists. Behind (1114.), *Rogier van der Weyden*, Deposition.

ROOM 15 displays the early Florentine works of LEONARDO DA VINCI, together with paintings by his master VERROCCHIO. 8368. *Luca Signorelli*, Crucifixion; *1618. *Leonardo da Vinci*, Annunciation, painted in Verrocchio's studio. The extent of his master's intervention is unclear: it is thought he was probably responsible for the design, and for the figure of the Madonna and the classical sarcophagus. 506. *Piero di Cosimo*, Immaculate Conception; *8358. *Verrocchio*, Baptism of Christ, begun c 1470, (according to Vasari and Albertini, the angel on the left was painted by the young Leonardo). *1594. *Leonardo*, Adoration of the Magi (1481). This huge crowded composition is remarkable for its figure studies and unusual iconography. The painting was left unfinished when Leonardo left Florence for Milan; it remains in its preparatory stage of chiaroscuro drawn in a red earth pigment (or 'sinopia', from Sinope in Asia Minor). *8359. *Verrocchio*, Tobias and three Archangels (recently cleaned; also attributed to *Botticini*); 1597. *Lorenzo di Credi*, Annunciation; 1536. *Piero di Cosimo*, Perseus liberating Andromeda (1589); 8369. *Luca Signorelli*, Trinity, with the Madonna and Saints; 8365. *Perugino*, Pietà; 8371. *Signorelli*, Predella of the Trinity.—The walls of the SALA DELLE CARTE GEOGRAFICHE (16; seen from the doorway) are painted with maps of Tuscany by *Stefano Bonsignori* (1589). The rich ceiling is ascribed to *Jacopo Zucchi*. Here is temporarily displayed the best known copy (9953.) of a lost painting by Leonardo of Leda, attributed to *Francesco Melzi*.

ROOM 18. The beautiful octagonal *TRIBUNA was designed by *Buontalenti* (1584) to display the most valuable objects in the Medici collection. It has a mother-of-pearl dome, a fine pavement in pietre dure, and an octagonal *Table, a masterpiece of pietre dure craftsmanship, made in the Florence Opificio between 1633 and 1649 (on a design by *Bernardino Poccetti* and *Jacopo Ligozzi*). Since the 17C it has contained the most important sculptures owned by the Medici. The *Medici Venus, the most famous statue in the Uffizi, is a marble copy (probably of the 1C BC) of the Praxitelean Aphrodite of Cnidos, formerly in the Villa Medici in Rome. The other *Sculptures are: 230. 'Arrotino' (the knife-grinder), now thought to represent a Scythian as part of a group of Apollo and Marsias. It is the only surviving replica of an original by the school of Pergamon (3C or 2C BC), and it was purchased by Cosimo I in 1558 on Vasari's advice. 216. Wrestlers, a restored copy of a bronze original of the school of Pergamon; 220. Dancing Faun, a beautifully restored work; and 229. 'Apollino' (Young Apollo) derived from an Apollo of Praxiteles.—The magnificent cabinet in ebony and pietre dure belonged to Ferdinando II and dates from c 1650. Around the walls are a remarkable series of distinguished court portraits, many of them of the family of Cosimo I commissioned from Bronzino. 1500. *Alessandro Allori*, Bianca Cappello, a mural; 1578. *Vasari*, Lorenzo il Magnifico, and 3574. *Pontormo*, Cosimo il Vecchio, both posthumous and idealised portraits. 1429. *Daniele da Volterra*, Massacre of the Innocents; 4347. *Pontormo*, Madonna and Child with St John;770. *Bronzino*, Young girl with a book; 2155. *Ridolfo del Ghirlandaio*, Young Man; *Bronzino*, *741. and *736. Bartolomeo and Lucrezia Panciatichi; 1672. Maria dei Medici; 1571. Francesco I de' Medici, son of Cosimo I; 1445. *Franciabigio*, Madonna 'del Pozzo' (showing the influence of Raphael); 1446. *Raphael* (and bottega), Young St John in the desert; 2147. *Giulio Romano*, Madonna and Child; 1475. *Bronzino*, Don Giovanni de' Medici as a boy; 1508, *Rosso Fiorentino*, Angel musician; *Bronzino*, 1472. Isabella de' Medici, daughter of Cosimo I, *1575. Portrait of a man, an intellectual typical of his time, *748. Eleonora di Toledo, Cosimo I's wife, with their son Giovanni de' Medici, a fine portrait which speaks eloquently of its period; *783. *Andrea del Sarto*, Girl with a book of Petrarch; *Bronzino*, 28. Cosimo I.—Room 17, the SALA DELL'ERMAFRODITO contains a Sleeping Hermaphrodite, copy of a Greek original of the 2C BC, and small bronzes.

Rooms 19–23 have ceilings decorated with grotteschi and views of Florence etc. carried out in 1588 by *Ludovico Buti* and in 1665 by *Agnolo Gori*. ROOM 19. PERUGINO AND SIGNORELLI. *1435. *Perugino*, Madonna enthroned with Saints John the Baptist and Sebastian; 3282. *Lorenzo Costa*, St Sebastian; 3341. and 3343. *Melozzo da Forlì*, Annunciatory angel, and Madonna annunciate; 1535. *Girolamo Genga*, Martyrdom of St Sebastian; 1474. *Perugino*, Portrait of a young man, possibly Raphael (the work is also attributed to *Lorenzo*

Costa; 1418. *Marco Palmezzano*, Crucifixion; 1444. *Francesco Francia*, Portrait of Evangelista Scappi; *Perugino*, *1700. Portrait of Francesco delle Opere (1494), a Florentine artisan, 8375. and 8376. Don Biagio Milanesi and Baldassare Vallombrosano, two monks. *Luca Signorelli*, *502. Tondo of the Madonna and Child, one of his best works. In the background are allegorical figures, and prophets in the small roundels above; *1605. also by *Signorelli*, Tondo of the Holy Family, in a beautiful frame.—ROOM 20. DÜRER AND THE GERMAN SCHOOL. *1459. and *1458. *Cranach*, Adam and Eve (1528); 8406. *Dürer*, Calvary (a drawing in chiaroscuro, 1505); 1083. *Jan Breughel the Elder*, Calvary; *Dürer*, 1089. and 1099. St James and St Philip, the Apostles, *1434. Adoration of the Magi (1504), 1086. Portrait of the artist's father (painted at the age of 19, his first known work). 1645. *Joos van Cleve*, Portrait of a young man; *Cranach*, 512. Portrait of Luther (1543), 1056. St George (a tiny work), 1631. Portrait of Cranach the Elder (1550; or a self-portrait), 1160. and 1139. Luther and his wife.—ROOM 21. VENETIAN SCHOOL (BELLINI AND GIORGIONE). 901. *Vittore Carpaccio*, Halberdiers (a fragment); 8384. *Lorenzo Costa*, Giovanni il Bentivoglio; 3346. *Bartolomeo Vivarini*, St Louis of Toulouse; 902. *Cima da Conegliano*, Madonna and Child; 1863. *Giovanni Bellini*, Portrait of a gentleman; 3273. *Cosmè Tura*, St Dominic, a strange, late work; *Giovanni Bellini*, *631. Sacred Allegory. An exquisite painting of uncertain meaning, it is infused with an exalted humanist quality. 943. Lamentation over the Dead Christ (an unfinished painting left at the chiaroscuro stage). *Giorgione*, 947. Judgement of Solomon (showing the influence of Bellini), 911. Warrior, the 'Gattamelata', doubtfully attributed to Giorgione (recently restored), 945. Infant Moses brought to Pharoah.— ROOM 22 contains GERMAN AND FLEMISH WORKS. 1460. *16C Northern painter* (formerly attributed to *Lucas van Leyden*), Christ crowned with thorns; *Hans Memling* 1100. Portrait of Benedetto di Tommaso Portinari, 1090. St Benedict, 9970. Portrait of a young man, 1101, 1102, Male portraits, 1024. Madonna enthroned with two angels; 1120. *School of Holbein*, supposed portrait of Thomas More; Dep. N.4 and 5. *Albrecht Altdorfer*, Scenes from the life of St Florian; *Holbein*, 1630. Self-portrait, *1087. Sir Richard Southwell (1536); *1643. 1644. *Joos van Cleve the Elder*, Portrait of a man and his wife; 1140. 1161. *Bernaert van Orley*, Portrait of a man and his wife; 1084. *Joos van Cleve the Elder*, Mater dolorosa; *1029. *Gerard David*, Adoration of the Magi; 1019. '*Master of Hoogstraeten*', Madonna enthroned with St Catherine of Alexandria and St Barbara.—ROOM 23. 3348. *Giovanni Francesco Mainieri*, Christ bearing the Cross; 1454. *Bernardino Luini*, Head of St John the Baptist presented to Herod; *Mantegna* 994. Portrait of Cardinal Carlo de' Medici, *910. Adoration of the Magi, Circumcision, and Ascension, an exquisite small painted triptych, 1348. Madonna; 738. *Sodoma*, Derision of Christ; 2184. *Giovanni Antonio Boltraffio*, Narcissus; *Raphael* (attributed), 1441. Elizabeth Gonzaga, 8538. Guidobaldo da Montefeltro (very ruined); *Correggio*, 1329. Madonna in glory; 1455. Rest on the Flight, 1453. Madonna in adoration of the Child.—The table in pietre dure decorated with flowers was designed by *Jacopo Ligozzi* (1621).—The COLLECTION OF MINIATURES (15–18C) is exhibited in a little oval room (24; only visible through the doorway) designed in 1781 by *Zanobi del Rosso* and painted by *Filippo Lucci*.

The short SOUTH CORRIDOR commands a splendid view of Florence: on the extreme left are San Miniato and Forte di Belvedere; in the centre, beyond the Uffizi building is Palazzo Vecchio and the cupola of the Duomo; at the far end the tiled roof of the Corridoio Vasariano can be seen on its way from the Uffizi to Ponte Vecchio. The Arno flows downstream beneath Ponte Santa Trinita and the bridges beyond. On the S bank the dome and campanile of Santo Spirito are prominent, and, beyond, the dome of San Frediano.— Some of the best pieces of sculpture are displayed here: *Roman matron, seated; Ceres, the so-called 'Night' draped with black marble; Boy with a thorn in his foot, replica of the 'Spinario' in the Capitoline Museum in Rome; *Pedestal for a candelabrum; Sarcophagus with the Fall of Phaeton and chariot-races; *Crouching Venus, and Seated Girl preparing to dance, both from Hellenistic originals of the 3C BC; Mars, Roman copy of a Greek original; and a series of fine busts showing Marcus Aurelius from a very young boy to a middle-aged man. The sculpture is continued in the WEST CORRIDOR: two *Statues of Marsyas, from Hellenistic originals of the 3C BC; Nereid on a sea-horse, Hellenistic; bust of Cicero and of Julia Severus; athletes, warriors, and gods; and, at the far end of the corridor, Laocoön, a copy by *Bandinelli* of the Vatican group.

ROOM 25 (MICHELANGELO). Opposite the entrance is the famous *'Tondo Doni' (1456.) of the Holy Family, the only finished oil painting by *Michelangelo*. It was painted for the marriage of Agnolo Doni with Maddalena Strozzi (1504–05), when the artist was 30 years old. Although owing much to Signorelli (cf. Room 19) it signals a new moment in High Renaissance painting, and points the way forward to the Sistine chapel frescoes. The splendid contemporary frame is by *Domenico del Tasso*. Also in this room: 1587. *Mariotto Albertinelli*, Visitation, probably his best work; 8455. *Fra' Bartolomeo*, Apparition of the Virgin to St Bernard (much repainted, but particularly interesting for the landscape; removed for restoration); 1482. *Raphael* (attributed), Portrait of Perugino; 8380. *Giuliano Bugiardini*, Portrait of a lady; 2152. *Rosso Fiorentino*, Moses defending the children of Jethro (possibly a fragment). The geometrical forms of the nudes in the foreground display a very original and modern tendency. 2152. *Francesco Granacci*, Joseph and his brothers.

ROOM 26 (RAPHAEL). 1489. *Domenico Puligo*, Portrait of Pietro Carnesecchi; 1525. *Pontormo*, Martyrdom of St Maurice and the eleven thousand Martyrs; 8394–6. *Andrea del Sarto*, Dossal with four Saints; 1480. *Pontormo*, Portrait of a lady; 1483. *Pier Francesco di Jacopo Foschi*, Portrait of a man; *Raphael*, 1450. Julius II, a replica of inferior quality to the painting in the National Gallery of London; *40 P. Leo X with cardinals Giulio de' Medici (afterwards Clement VII) and Luigi de' Rossi (1518–19), one of his most powerful portrait groups which was to influence Titian, painted shortly before his death. It provides a vivid picture of the Medici Pope's world. *1447. Madonna del Cardellino (of the Goldfinch, 1506). Painted for the marriage of the artist's friend, Lorenzo Nasi, it was shattered by an earthquake in 1547, but carefully preserved and repaired by the owner, although it remains in a very ruined state. 8760. Francesco Maria della Rovere; 1706. Self-portrait. 8379. *Pontormo*, St Anthony Abbot; *Andrea del Sarto*, *1577. Madonna of the Harpies (1517), 1583. St James and two children.

ROOM 27 (PONTORMO). 8381. *Franciabigio*, Portrait of a young man with gloves (1514); 8377. *Bronzino*, Holy family, commissioned by Bartolomeo Panciatichi (cf. Room 18); 8740. *Pontormo*, Supper at Emmaus (1525), painted for the Certosa di Galluzzo, and an uncharacteristic work by this artist. Above the head of Christ is a surrealist symbol of God the father. 8545. *Bronzino*, Dead Christ with the Madonna and Mary Magdalen; 106. *Rosso Fiorentino* (attributed), Portrait of a man; *Pontormo*, 3565. Portrait of Maria Salviati, widow of Giovanni delle Bande Nere, 743. Portrait of the musician Francesco Dell'Ajolle; 3245. *Rosso Fiorentino*, Portrait of a girl.—ROOM 28 is devoted to TITIAN. *1462. Flora; *1437. Venus of Urbino, commissioned by Guidobaldo della Rovere, later duke of Urbino, in 1538. One of the most beautiful nudes ever painted, it has had a profound influence on European painting. *942. Knight of Malta, a portrait charged with religious fervour. *2183. Portrait of a sick man (formerly attributed to Sebastiano del Piombo). 919. Eleonora Gonzaga della Rovere, duchess of Urbino, and her husband, 926. Francesco Maria della Rovere (restored in 1990), 1431. Venus and Cupid (c 1560, a late work); and works by *Palma Vecchio*.

ROOMS 29 and 30 are devoted to the 16C EMILIAN SCHOOL, notably *Parmigianino*: *230 P. Madonna 'dal collo lungo' ('with the long neck'). This work (1534–36), of extreme elegance and originality, is a fundamental painting of the Mannerist school. 1328. Madonna and Saints (including St Zacharias). Also small works by: *Il Garofalo, Girolamo da Carpi, Lo Scarsellino, Mazzolino*, and *Luca Cambiaso*.— ROOM 31 (VENETO SCHOOL) has a view of Palazzo Vecchio, the Duomo, and the top of Orsanmichele. Works by *Dosso Dossi* and *Girolamo Romanino*.—ROOM 32 (VENETO SCHOOL). *Sebastiano del Piombo*, 916. *Death of Adonis, in an autumnal Venetian landscape, 1443. 'La Fornarina', formerly attributed to Raphael and thought to be a portrait of his mistress; works by *Lorenzo Lotto*, including 1481. Head of a young boy; portraits by *Paris Bordone*.

ROOM 33. 37, *Jean Perréal* (attributed), Portrait of a lady; *987. *François Clouet*, Equestrian portrait of Francis I; 3112. *Luis de Morales*, Christ carrying the Cross; 1108. *Frans Pourbus the Elder*, Portrait of Virgilio van Aytta; 1637. *Antonio Moro*, Self-portrait; 4338. *16C French School*, Christine of Lorraine; 763. *Alessandro Allori*, Torquato Tasso.—In the corridor the small 16C paintings include several works by *Alessandro Allori*, and a Head of Medusa (1479.), by the *16C Flemish school*.

ROOM 34. VERONESE AND THE VENETIAN SCHOOL. 1343. *Paolo Veronese*, Crowning of St Agatha, a tiny work; *Giulio Campi*, 1796. Portrait of a man, 958. Guitar player; 1387. *Jacopo Tintoretto*, Portrait of a man; *Giovanni Battista Moroni*, 933. Portrait of a man with a book, *906. Count Pietro Secco Suardi (1563); 1628. *Giulio Campi*, Padre Galeazzo Campi; *Paolo Veronese*, *899. Annunciation, designed around a perspective device in the centre of the picture. The work is delicately painted in simple colours, in contrast to the rich golden hues of the figure of St Barbara in the *Holy Family with St Barbara (1433.), a work of the artist's maturity.

From the W Corridor a door (B) gives access to the **Corridoio Vasariano**. This can normally be visited by previous appointment at the administrative offices on the third floor near the entrance to the gallery: small groups are accompanied when staff are available. It was built by Vasari in 1565 in five months, on the occasion of the marriage of Francesco de' Medici and Joanna of Austria. Its purpose was to connect Palazzo Vecchio via the Uffizi and Ponte Vecchio with the new residence of the Medici dukes at Palazzo Pitti (cf. p 90), in the form of a covered passage-way. It affords unique views of the city, and is hung with notable paintings including a celebrated collection of self-portraits (begun by Cardinal Leopoldo). A series of rooms (with works by *Gherardo delle Notti* and the school of Caravaggio, including *Artemisia Gentileschi, Borgognone*, and *Annibale Carracci*) precede the entrance to the corridor proper. Here, displayed by regional schools, are 17C works: *Guido Reni* (Susannah and the Elders), *Guercino* (Sleeping Endymion), *Domenico Feti, Domenichino, Maratta, Pietro da Cortona, Mattia Preti, Salvator Rosa, Carlo Dolci, Sassoferrata, Giuseppe Maria Crespi*, and *Sustermans*. There follow 18C paintings by *Vanvitelli, Ricci, Tiepolo*, and others.—The ***Collection of Self-portraits** begins, appropriately, with one by *Vasari*. Arranged chronologically, they include works by *Agnolo, Taddeo*, and *Gaddo Gaddi, Andrea del Sarto, Bandinelli, Beccafumi, Bronzino, Perino del Vaga, Santi di Tito, Cigoli*, etc. Beyond the centre of Ponte Vecchio: *Salimbeni, Federico* and *Taddeo Zuccari, Bernini, Pietro da Cortona, Batoni, Luca Giordano, Salvator Rosa*, and *Giuseppe Maria Crespi*. On the Oltrarno the Corridor continues with 16–18C foreign self-portraits including *Pourbus, Rubens, Gerard Dou, Sustermans, Rembrandt, Van Dyck, Zoffany, Velasquez, Callot, Charles le Brun, Lely, Kneller, Hogarth, Romney*, and *Reynolds*. The Corridor descends past a group of sketches to the collection of 19C self-portraits: *David, Delacroix, Corot, Ingres, Fattori, Millais, Benjamin Constant, Latour*, etc. In the last part of the corridor is a group of 17–18C portraits (mostly of royalty); the 20C self-portraits exhibited in the Gallery in 1982 may also be hung here. Visitors are usually asked to leave the corridor by the Boboli Gardens (cf. p 121).

ROOM 35 (TINTORETTO; sometimes closed). 969. *Jacopo Bassano*, Portrait of an artist, perhaps a self-portrait; *Federico Barocci*, 765. Portrait of a girl, 798. Noli me tangere, *Jacopo Tintoretto*, 924. Portrait of a man with red hair, 921. Portrait of an admiral; 1438. *Federico Barocci* Francesco Maria II della Rovere; 914. *Jacopo Tintoretto*, St Augustine; *El Greco*, Saints John the Evangelist and Francis; 915. *Leandro Bassano*, Family Concert; 751. *Federico Barocci*, Madonna del Popolo; *Jacopo Tintoretto*, 957. Portrait of Jacopo Sansovino, 935. Portrait of an old man in a fur, *3085. Portrait of a man; 965. *Jacopo Bassano*, Two hunting dogs.—In the centre of the room is a table in pietre dure with a view of the port of Livorno (1604, by *Cristofano Gaffurri* on a design by *Jacopo Ligozzi*).—Beyond the stairs down to the exit (C; cf. below), ROOM 41 (not always open) contains some fine works by RUBENS and VAN DYCK. 5404. *Rubens*, Triumphal entry of Ferdinand of Austria into Anversa; 3141. *Jacob Jordaens*, Portrait of an old lady; *Rubens*, *729. Henri IV entering Paris, *722. Henri IV at Ivry, two huge paintings comprising the first part of a cycle depicting the King's history, 779. *Isabella Brandt, 792. Equestrian portrait of Philip IV of Spain. *Van Dyck*, 777. Margaret of Lorraine, 1439. Equestrian portrait of the Emperor Charles V, 726. Susterman's mother, 1436. John of Montfort. 745. *Sustermans*, Galileo Galilei.

The NIOBE ROOM (42; usually closed) was designed by *Gaspare Maria Paoletti* and frescoed in the 1770s by *Tommaso Gherardini*. It contains statues forming a group of Niobe and her Children, found in a vineyard near the Lateran in 1583, and transferred to Florence in 1775 from the Villa Medici in Rome. These are Roman copies of Greek originals of the school of Skopas (early 4C BC); many of the figures are wrongly restored and others do not belong to the group. The Medici Vase in the centre is a neo-Attic work acquired by Lorenzo de' Medici. Recently restored paintings from the collection are sometimes exhibited here.

ROOM 43. Works by *Caravaggio* (*4659. Sacrifice of Isaac, 5312. Young Bacchus, 1351. Medusa head, painted on a shield); 1096. *Claude Lorrain*, Port scene; *Annibale Carracci*, 799. Man with a monkey, 1452. Bacchic scene.—ROOM 44. *Rembrandt*, *3890. Self-portrait, *8435. Portrait of an old man, and *1871. Self-portrait as an old man; 1301. *Jan Steen*, Lunch-party; a fine landscape by *Jacob Ruysdael*, and other Dutch and Flemish works.—ROOM 45 displays 18C paintings: 8419. *Piazzetta*, Susannah and the Elders; 3139.

Giovanni Battista Tiepolo, Erection of an imperial statue (for a ceiling); Venetian views by *Francesco Guardi* and *Canaletto*; Two portraits of children by *Simeon Chardin*. *Francisco Goya*, Two beautiful *Portraits of Maria Theresa; 3573. *Alessandro Longhi*, Portrait of a lady; *Jean Marc Nattier*, Maria Enrichetta of France as Flora, and Maria Adelaide of France as Diana; *Etienne Liotard*, Maria Adelaide of France in Turkish costume; *Françoise Xavier Fabre*, Portrait of Vittorio Alfieri and the Countess of Albany.

A door at the end of the Corridor (beyond a small Bar) gives on to the roof of the Loggia della Signoria (D) with a splendid view over Piazza della Signoria beyond the buildings of the city to the hills of Fiesole.—A long flight of stairs (cf. above), or a lift, descend from the West Corridor to the exit. On the landing is a Hellenistic marble torso of a satyr, and the famous sculptured Boar, a copy of a Hellenistic original, and the model for the 'Porcellino' in the Mercato Nuovo.

7   Galleria degli Uffizi to Palazzo Pitti

This route follows the course of the CORRIDOIO VASARIANO which is described on p 106.

From the river 'façade' of Palazzo degli Uffizi (Pl.16;8; see p 96) there is a striking view of Palazzo Vecchio with its tower. The CORRIDOIO VASARIANO, the covered way built by Vasari in 1565 to link Palazzo Vecchio and the Uffizi with the new residence of the Medici, Palazzo Pitti, can be seen here as it leaves the Uffizi building, crosses above the busy road, and continues on a raised arcade towards Ponte Vecchio. On the bridge, its line of rectangular windows passes above the little picturesque shops which overhang the river. On this very narrow part of the Lungarno is the fine old *Palazzo Girolami* (No. 6) with a pretty loggia and coat-of-arms.

The fame of **Ponte Vecchio** (Pl.16;5,7; open to pedestrians only), lined with quaint medieval-looking houses, saved it from damage in 1944 (although numerous ancient buildings at either end were blown up instead in order to render it impassable). Near the site of the Roman crossing (which was a little farther upstream), it was the only bridge over the Arno until 1218. The present bridge of three arches was reconstructed after a flood in 1345 probably by *Taddeo Gaddi* (also attributed to *Neri di Fioravante*). The bridge on this site has been lined by shops since the 13C; the present jewellers' shops have pretty fronts with wood shutters and awnings; and they overhang the river supported on brackets. They were well restored after severe damage in the flood of 1966. The excellent jewellers here continue the traditional skill of Florentine goldsmiths whose work first became famous in the 15C. Many of the greatest Renaissance artists were trained as goldsmiths (including Ghiberti, Brunelleschi, and Donatello). The most famous Florentine goldsmith, Benvenuto Cellini, is aptly recorded with a bust (1900) in the middle of the bridge. Above the shops on the left side can be seen the round windows of the Corridoio Vasariano. From the opening in the centre there is a view of Ponte Santa Trìnita (p 185). On the corner of a house here is a sundial and worn inscription of 1345. The Corridoio Vasariano leaves the bridge supported on elegant brackets in order not to disturb the medieval angle tower which defended the bridge (Torre dei Mannelli; restored after the War).

Across Borgo San Jacopo (see p 192) is a fountain reconstructed here in 1958 with a 16C bronze statue of Bacchus and a Roman sarcophagus. Via Guicciardini continues towards Piazza Pitti; on the left opens Piazza Santa Felìcita with a granite column of 1381 marking the site of the first Christian cemetery in Florence. Here, behind the Corridoio Vasariano, is **Santa Felìcita** (Pl.16;7), probably the oldest church in Florence after San Lorenzo. Syrian Greek merchants came to settle in the suburbs here, near the river and on a busy Roman consular road, in the 2C, and are thought to have introduced Christianity to the city. The paleochristian church, built at the end of the 4C or the beginning of the 5C, was dedicated to the Roman martyr, St Felicity (a tombstone dated 405 has been found in excavations here). A new church was built in the 11C and the present church was erected in 1736–39 by *Ferdinando Ruggieri*.

In the PORTICO is the funerary monument (right) of Cardinal Luigi De' Rossi (died 1518) by *Giovanni Battista del Tasso*, and (left) beneath the tomb-slab of Barduccio di Cherichino (died 1416), the monument of Arcangiola Paladini by *Agostino Bugiardini* and *Antonio Novelli*.—The fine INTERIOR by *Ferdinando Ruggieri* takes its inspiration from late-16C Florentine architecture. It is chiefly visited for the superb *Works (1525–27) by *Pontormo* in the CAPPELLA CAPPONI (1st on right), which include a remarkable altarpiece of the Deposition, in a magnificent contemporary frame, and a fresco (detached and restored) of the Annunciation. These are considered among the masterpieces of 16C Florentine painting. The tondi in the cupola of the Evangelists are also by Pontormo, except perhaps St Matthew (with the angel), which is usually attributed to *Bronzino* (it is here replaced by a copy). The chapel was originally designed by *Brunelleschi* (c 1420–25), but was altered in the 18C.—Over the 4th altar on the right is a striking painting (the Martyrdom of the Maccabei brothers) by *Antonio Ciseri* (1863). In the S transept, Meeting of St Joachim and St Anne by *Michele di Ridolfo Ghirlandaio.*The CHOIR CHAPEL was designed by *Ludovico Cigoli* in 1610–22. The high altarpiece of the Adoration of the Shepherds, traditionally attributed to Santi di Tito, is now thought to be the work of *Francesco Brina*. NORTH SIDE. The last chapel (beneath the organ) contains a wood Crucifix by *Andrea Ferrucci (da Fiesole)* and the funerary monument of Giacomo Conti by *Girolamo Ticciati*. 4th chapel, *Simone Pignone*, St Louis providing a banquet for the poor (1682); 2nd chapel, *Ignazio Hugford*, Tobias visiting his father. The chapel opposite the Capponi chapel has a fresco of the Miracle of Santa Maria della Neve, by *Bernardino Poccetti*, a vault fresco by *Tommaso Gherardini*, and an altarpiece of the Assumption of the Virgin by *Andrea del Minga*.—The pretty SACRISTY (unlocked on request), in the style of Brunelleschi (off the right transept), has a polyptych of the Madonna and Child with Saints, by *Taddeo Gaddi*, in its original frame; St Felicity and her seven children by *Neri di Bicci* (removed indefinitely for restoration), a Crucifix attributed to *Pacino di Buonaguida*, two detached 14C frescoes of the Nativity and Annunciation, attributed to *Niccolò di Pietro Gerini*, and an early-15C Adoration of the Magi. The beautiful polychrome terracotta half-figure of the Madonna and Child has been attributed to *Luca della Robbia* or his bottega since its restoration in 1980.—The CHAPTER HOUSE has a fresco of the Crucifixion signed and dated 1387–88 by *Niccolò di Pietro Gerini*.

At the end of the road (left) at No. 15 is *Palazzo Guicciardini*, reconstructed on the site of the residence of Luigi di Piero Guicciardini, Gonfalonier of Justice, which was burnt down during the uprising in 1378 of the Ciompi (cloth-workers). Part of the façade has remains of graffiti decoration. The courtyard and garden, created c 1620, can be seen through the grille. Here is a large stucco relief of Hercules and Cacus attributed to Antonio del Pollaiolo. Francesco Guicciardini was born here in 1483. On his retirement from political life in 1530 he wrote his famous 'History of Italy'. Casa Campiglio, nearby, where Machiavelli lived and died in 1527, has been destroyed. The two great statesmen and writers, who had served different causes, became close friends at the end of their careers.

Beyond is Piazza Pitti (p 201) dominated by Palazzo Pitti (Rte 8).

8   Palazzo Pitti and the Boboli Gardens

Palazzo Pitti (Pl.9;4) was built by the merchant Luca Pitti, an effective demonstration of his wealth and power to his rivals the Medici. The majestic golden-coloured palace is built in huge rough-hewn blocks of stone of different sizes. Its design is attributed to *Brunelleschi* although it was begun c 1457 after his death. *Luca Fancelli* is known to have been engaged on the building, but it is generally considered that another architect, whose name is unknown, was also involved. The palace remained incomplete on the death of Luca Pitti in 1472; by then it consisted of the central seven bays with three doorways. Houses were demolished to create the piazza in front of the palace, and its site was chosen here, on the slope of a hillside, to make it more imposing. *Bartolomeo Ammannati* took up work on the building c 1560 and converted the two side doors of the façade into elaborate ground-floor windows. These were then copied after 1616 by *Giulio* and *Alfonso Parigi the Younger* when they enlarged the façade to its present colossal dimensions (possibly following an original design). The two 'rondòs' or wings were added at the end of the 18C (on the right), and in the 19C (on the left).

In 1549 the palace was bought by Eleonora di Toledo, wife of Cosimo I. It became the official seat of the Medici dynasty of grand-dukes after Cosimo I moved here from Palazzo Vecchio (to which he connected the Pitti by means of the Corridoio Vasariano, cf. p 106). The various ruling families of Florence continued to occupy the palace, or part of it, until 1919 when Victor Emmanuel III presented it to the State.

The central door leads into the ATRIUM by *Pasquale Poccianti* (c 1850). The splendid *COURT (1560–70) by *Ammannati* serves as a garden façade to the palace. It is a masterpiece of Florentine Mannerist architecture, with bold rustication in three orders. Nocturnal spectacles were held here from the 16C to the 18C. The lower fourth side is formed by a terrace with the 'Fontana del Carciofo' (cf. p 121), beyond which extend the Boboli gardens (see below). The grotto beneath the terrace has another fountain with a porphyry statue of Moses (Roman, restored in the 16C). Under the portico to the right is the entrance to the celebrated **Galleria di Palazzo Pitti** or **Galleria Palatina**, a splendid collection of paintings acquired by the Medici and Lorraine grand-dukes, including numerous famous works by Raphael, Titian, and Rubens. The gallery maintains the character of a private princely collection of the 17–18C. The aesthetic arrangement of the pictures which decorate the walls produces a remarkable effect of magnificence. The elaborately carved and gilded frames, many of them original, and especially representative of the Mannerist, Baroque, and neo-classical styles, are particularly fine. Only some of the paintings (all of which are well labelled) have been mentioned in the description below, and asterisks have been used sparingly.

History. The collection owes its origins to the 17C Medici grand-dukes, and in particular to Cardinal Leopoldo, brother of Ferdinand II, and to Cosimo III and his eldest son the Crown Prince Ferdinand (died 1713), who added Flemish

PALAZZO PITTI
First Floor
Galleria Palatina

paintings, works of the Bolognese and Veneto schools, and altarpieces from
Tuscan churches. Under the Lorraine grand-dukes, in 1771, the paintings were
installed for the first time in the present rooms which had been decorated by
Pietro da Cortona and Ciro Ferri for Ferdinand II. The gallery was first opened
regularly to the public in 1833, and in 1911 it was acquired by the State.
Unfortunately, many of the paintings which formed the original nucleus of the
collection were removed to the Uffizi in this century. The present arrangement
of the pictures follows, as far as possible, the arrangement of 1833.

Tickets for the Galleria Palatina (which include admission to the Appartamenti
Monumentali, when open) are purchased off the courtyard, left of the stairs up
to the gallery. A separate ticket must be purchased here for the Museo degli
Argenti (which includes admission to the Museo del Costume). Tickets for the
Galleria d'Arte Moderna are sold on the second floor. Off the courtyard there is
also a cloakroom and W.C. There is no lift to the picture galleries.

All the rooms are named as indicated in the description below; room numbers
on the first floor have been given only to correspond with the plan on p 111.

Admission, see p 62. *Galleria Palatina*. The six main rooms of paintings are
numbered 1–6 on the Plan. The other groups of rooms (numbered 7–15 and 18–
27) of the picture gallery are sometimes closed for certain periods of the year.
The *Appartamenti Monumentali* (ex *Reali*) are numbered II–XIV on the plan;
they have been closed for restoration for several years. The remaining rooms on
the first floor (XV–XXII on the plan) are closed except for exhibitions, etc.—On
the SECOND FLOOR, is the *Galleria d'Arte Moderna* (adm. as for the Galleria
Palatina); tickets are purchased at the entrance on the second floor. On the
GROUND FLOOR, off the left side of the courtyard, is the entrance to the *Museo
degli Argenti* (adm. as for the Galleria Palatina; but separate ticket necessary).
The *Galleria del Costume* (adm. as for the Museo degli Argenti), is in the
Palazzina della Meridiana (entered from the Boboli gardens). The *Collezione
Contini-Bonacossi* (for adm. enquire at the Uffizi) is also temporarily housed
here but is to be moved to the Uffizi. The *Museo delle Carrozze* (coach museum)
in a 'rondò' (entered from the piazza) has been closed for many years.

The GRAND STAIRCASE by *Ammannati* ascends past (3rd landing) the
'Genio medoceo', a bronze statue attributed to the circle of Tribolo, to
the entrance of the Galleria Palatina. The ANTICAMERA or SALA
DEGLI STAFFIERI (A) contains statues by *Baccio Bandinelli* (Bacchus),
and *Pietro Francavilla* (Mercury). The GALLERIA DELLE STATUE (B) is
decorated with sculptures and Florentine tapestries by *Pietro Fevère*.
From the windows there is a view of the courtyard and Boboli
gardens (with the Forte di Belvedere on the skyline). Here are
displayed two seascapes by *Van der Velde the Elder*. To the left the
neo-classical SALA DELLE NICCHIE (I) by *Giuseppe Maria Terreni* and
Giuseppe Castagnoli (late 18C) is closed during restoration work on
the Appartamenti Reali. The SALA DEL CASTAGNOLI (C) is named
after the artist who decorated it. It contains a magnificent mosaic
table in pietre dure made in Florence in 1837–50 with Apollo and the
Muses (the bronze base of the four seasons is by *Giovanni Duprè*).
Here is displayed a painting of St Sebastian by *Sodoma*. To the left is
the entrance to the first of the five reception rooms on the piano
nobile overlooking Piazza Pitti. The ceilings were beautifully decorated in the 17C by *Pietro da Cortona* for Ferdinand II. The Baroque
decoration, including fine stuccoes, illustrates the life of the Medici
prince by means of extravagant allegories. These, together with the
19C Sala dell'Iliade, contain the masterpieces of the collection.

The SALA DI VENERE (1) has the earliest ceiling (1641–42) by *Pietro
da Cortona*. The paintings here include: 409. *Sebastiano del Piombo*,
Baccio Valori; *Titian*, *185. Concert (c 1510–12). The attribution of
this famous work has been much discussed and it appears that more
than one hand was involved. It has also been attributed to *Giorgione*
who may have been responsible for the figure on the left. The portrait
of pope Julius II is a copy by *Titian* of an original by Raphael

now in the National Gallery of London (a replica of which is in the Uffizi, see p 105). On the two end walls are two large seascapes (*4. and 15.), painted for cardinal Gian Carlo de' Medici by *Salvator Rosa.*—9. *Rubens,* Ulysses in the Phaecian Isle, a companion to *14. Return from the hayfields, with a superb joyful landscape. Above, 8. *Guercino,* Apollo and Marsyas, and other 17C works by the Tuscan artists, *Matteo Rosselli* and *Rutilio Manetti.*—*54. *Titian,* Pietro Aretino, one of his most forceful portraits, exquisitely painted. After a quarrel with the artist, Aretino presented the painting to Cosimo I in 1545. 84. *Bonifazio Veronese,* Sacred Conversation; *18. *Titian,* Portrait of a lady ('la bella'), commissioned by the Duke of Urbino in 1536.—In the centre, the *'Venus Italica' sculpted by *Canova,* and presented by Napoleon in 1812 in exchange for the Medici Venus which he had carried off to Paris.

SALA DI APOLLO (2). 150. *Anthony Van Dyck,* Charles I and Henrietta Maria; (above) 4263. *Rubens,* Isabella Clara Eugenia, dressed in the habit of a nun; 220. *Guido Reni,* Cleopatra; 41. *Cristofano Allori,* St Julian; *Cigoli,* Portrait of a man; *81. *Andrea del Sarto,* Holy Family.—116. *Sustermans,* Portrait of Vittoria della Rovere dressed as a Roman vestal; 50. *Guercino,* St Peter healing Tabitha; *237. *Rosso Fiorentino,* Madonna enthroned with Saints, a typical Florentine Mannerist work painted in 1522 for the church of Santo Spirito. When it was acquired by the Crown Prince Ferdinand in 1691, he had it enlarged. 55. *Barocci,* Federigo, prince of Urbino in his cradle; 380. *Dosso Dossi,* St John the Baptist.—131. *Tintoretto,* Vincenzo Zeno (recently restored); *58. *Andrea del Sarto,* Deposition (1523); *Titian,* *92. Portrait of a Gentleman (c 1540), once thought to be the Duke of Norfolk. It is justly one of his most famous portraits, revealing the intense character of the unknown sitter. *67. Mary Magdalen, another beautifully painted work by *Titian,* which was frequently copied (removed for restoration).

SALA DI MARTE (3). *83. *Tintoretto,* Luigi Cornaro (recently restored); *82. *Anthony Van Dyck,* Cardinal Guido Bentivoglio, a fine official portrait; 80. *Titian,* Andrea Vesalio.—*201. *Titian,* Cardinal Ippolito de' Medici, in Hungarian costume; *86. *Rubens,* Consequences of War, a huge allegory painted in 1638 and sent to his friend and fellow countryman at the Medici court, Sustermans. One of Rubens' most important works, it shows Venus trying to prevent Mars going to war, while both figures are surrounded by its destructive and tragic consequences. 216. *Paolo Veronese,* Portrait of a man, once thought to be Daniele Barbaro; 256. *Fra' Bartolomeo,* Holy Family.—56., 63. Two paintings of the Madonna and Child, typical works by the Spanish painter *Murillo.* 235. *Rubens* (attributed), Holy Family; *85. *Rubens,* 'The Four Philosophers' (Rubens, his brother Filippo, Justus Lipsius, and Jan van Wouwer), a charming portrait group. Rubens' brother and van Wouwer were both pupils of the great Flemish humanist Lipsius, famous for his studies of Seneca, whose bust is present.

The SALA DI GIOVE (4) was the throne-room of the Medici and has the most refined decoration by *Pietro da Cortona* in this suite of rooms. *110. *Venetian School,* 'Three Ages of Man' (in fact probably representing a concert). This fine work has had various attributions; since its restoration in 1989 the most convincing seems to be *Giorgione.* *245. *Raphael,* Portrait of a lady ('la Velata' or 'la Fornarina'), one of the most beautiful of all Raphael's paintings. The grace and dignity of the sitter pervade the work, which is painted with a skill which anticipates the hand of Titian. It was purchased by

Cosimo II de'Medici. 112. *Borgognone*, Battle Scene; 139. *Rubens*, Holy Family (an early work).—370. *Verrocchio* (attributed), *Head of St Jerome (a small work in an elaborate 19C frame; restored in 1990); 16C *Flemish School*, Jacobina Vogekort; *Andrea del Sarto*, Madonna in glory, Annunciation (an early work); 125. *Fra' Bartolomeo*, St Mark.—149. *Bronzino*, Guidobaldo delle Rovere; 113. *Francesco Salviati*, The Fates; *64. *Fra' Bartolomeo*, Deposition, his last and one of his best works. During its restoration in 1983–88 the two figures of Saints Peter and Paul were revealed in the background: this proves that it is a fragment. (Above) 141. *Rubens*, Nymphs and satyrs in a fine landscape; *272. *Andrea del Sarto*, the Young St John the Baptist (1523; recently restored). One of the best-known representations of the Baptist, this picture was owned by Cosimo I and formerly hung in the Tribuna of the Uffizi. 219. *Perugino*, Madonna in adoration ('del sacco'); 156. *Guercino*, Madonna 'of the house-martin'.—In the centre, marble statue of Victory, by *Vincenzo Consani*.

SALA DI SATURNO (5). The ceiling was completed by Pietro da Cortona's pupil *Ciro Ferri* in 1665. *151. *Raphael*, Madonna 'della Seggiola', a beautifully composed tondo, among the artist's most mature works (c 1514–15). It was purchased by the Medici shortly after Raphael's death, and became one of the most popular paintings of the Madonna. 152. *Andrea Schiavone*, Samson and the Philistine; 158. *Raphael*, Cardinal Bernardo Dovizi da Bibbiena.—207. *Ridolfo del Ghirlandaio*, Portrait of a man (thought to be a goldsmith), showing the influence of Raphael (removed for restoration); 42. *Perugino*, Mary Magdalen (similar to his self-portraits; also removed for restoration); 159. *Fra' Bartolomeo*, The Risen Christ appearing to his Disciples; *164. *Perugino*, Deposition (1495; recently restored); *Raphael*, *59. Maddalena Doni, in the pose of Leonardo's Gioconda, and (61.) Agnolo Doni, her husband (both recently beautifully restored; the splendid landscapes can now be appreciated). *174. Vision of Ezekiel (a tiny work); 165. Madonna 'del Baldacchino', a large altarpiece (1507–08), completed at the top by Niccolò Cassana (restored in 1990); the Risen Christ, an early work by *Rubens*.—171. *Raphael*, Cardinal Tommaso Inghirami (beautifully restored); 166. *Annibale Carracci*, Head of a man; 172. *Andrea del Sarto*, Disputation on the Trinity; *178. *Raphael*, Madonna 'del Granduca', probably an early work (c 1504–05), showing the influence of Leonardo. It received its name after its purchasè in 1800 by Ferdinand III of Lorraine (then in exile); (above the door), 179. *Sebastiano del Piombo*, Martyrdom of St Agatha.

SALA DELL'ILIADE (6), with a ceiling by *Sabatelli* of 1819 illustrating the Iliad. 243. *Velazquez* (attributed), Equestrian portrait of Philip IV of Spain; 186. *Paolo Veronese*, Baptism of Christ; 190. *Sustermans*, Count Valdemar Christian of Denmark; 187. *Frans Pourbus the Younger*, Eleonora de' Medici; *Andrea del Sarto*, *191. and (opposite) 225. two large paintings of the Assumption, the former among the most important late works by this artist; *Artemesia Gentileschi*, 398. Judith, and 142. Mary Magdalen (by one of the few women artists represented in the gallery).—*Titian*, *200. Philip II of Spain, *215. Diego de Mendoza.—224. *Ridolfo del Ghirlandaio*, Portrait of a young woman; *229. *Raphael*, Portrait of a woman expecting a child ('la Gravida', c 1506); 391. *Frans Pourbus the Younger*, Eleonora of Mantua as a child (daughter of Eleonora de' Medici, see No. 187.); 223. *Joos van Cleve* (attributed), Portrait of a man.—4273. 16C *English School*, Elizabeth I.—In the centre of the room, Charity, a fine marble group by *Lorenzo Bartolini*.

The exit from the Gallery in summer (kept locked in winter) is through the VESTIBULE (D) which contains a fountain attributed to *Francesco di Simone Ferrucci* (from the Villa di Castello). The GRAND STAIRCASE, a monumental work by *Luigi del Moro* (c 1895–97) descends to the garden.

The other rooms of the Galleria Palatina were decorated in the neo-classical style in the Napoleonic period when Elisa Baciocchi was in residence. They contain the smaller works in the collection and may be entered from the Sala del Castagnoli (see above; Plan C), or from the Sala dell'Iliade (6), as described below.

The SALA DELL'EDUCAZIONE DI GIOVE (8). *96. *Cristofano Allori*, Judith with the head of Holofernes (with portraits of the artist, his mistress, and her mother), one of the most famous Florentine works of the 17C; typical pious works by *Carlo Dolci; Carletto Caliari*, Christ taking leave of his mother; *183. *Caravaggio*, Sleeping Cupid, painted in Malta in 1608 (in its beautiful original frame); *Carletto Caliari*, The Marys at the sepulchre; two tiny Medici portraits by *Bronzino*; Claude of Lorraine, by *Jean Clouet; Anthony Van Dyck*, Portrait of a man; (above) *Tintoretto* (or his School), Deposition.—The *SALA DELLA STUFA (left; 7) was beautifully frescoed by *Pietro da Cortona* (1637–41; the four Ages of the World) and *Matteo Rosselli* (1622; Fames and Virtues, on the ceiling) for the Grand-Duke Ferdinand II. The restored majolica pavement (Triumph of Bacchus, 1640) is by *Benedetto Bocchi*.—Beyond the splendid 'Empire' bath-room (9) by *Cacialli* is the SALA DI ULISSE (10). 16C *Florentine School*, Portrait of a man; 70. *Tintoretto*, Andrea Frizier, Grand Chancellor of Venice; *Moroni*, 128. and 121. two fine portraits; *338. *Filippino Lippi*, Death of Lucrezia, a beautiful small painting (once part of a 'cassone'), showing the influence of Botticelli. *94. *Raphael*, Madonna 'dell'Impannata' (so named from the window in the back-ground), a mature composition, perhaps with the collaboration of his workshop.—The SALA DI PROMETEO (11). *Giuseppe Ribera* (*Lo Spagnoletto*), St Francis; 379. *Pontormo*, Adoration of the Magi; 167. *Baldassarre Peruzzi*, Dance of Apollo with the Muses (this famous and unusual small work was formerly attributed to Giulio Romano); 364. *Jacopo del Sellaio*, Tondo of the Madonna in adoration; 357. *Botticelli* (attributed), Madonna and Child with the young St John; 347. *Francesco Botticini*, Tondo of the Madonna in adoration with angels; 15C *Umbrian school*, Epiphany; *343. *Filippo Lippi*, Large tondo of the Madonna and Child, a charming composition with scenes from the life of the Virgin in the background. This is one of Lippi's best works, and had a strong influence on his contemporaries. *Guido Reni*, Young Bacchus, a well-known painting (the fine frame dates from the end of the 17C); 355. *Luca Signorelli*, Tondo of the Holy Family, in a lovely frame; 348. *School of Botticelli*, Tondo of the Madonna and Child with angels; 372. *Botticelli*, Portrait of a man (a damaged painting), 353. Portrait of a lady in profile (called the 'Bella Simonetta'; the identification of the sitter, and the author of this interesting work are still much discussed. Since its restoration in 1989 it is generally attributed to the Bottega of Botticelli). 354. *Cosimo Rosselli*, Nativity; 604. *Marco Palmezzano*, Caterina Sforza; 359. *Beccafumi*, Tondo of the Holy Family; 182. *Pontormo*, The eleven thousand martyrs; *Il Bachiacca*, Mary Magdalen; 365. *Mariotto Albertinelli*, Holy Family; *Francesco Salviati*, Portrait of a man.

A door (sometimes closed) leads into the CORRIDOIO DELLE COLONNE (12) hung with small Flemish paintings by *Cornelis van Poelenburgh, Paul Brill, Frans*

Franken, Jan Breughel (Orpheus), *David Rychaert* (Temptations of St Anthony), and others.—SALA DELLA GIUSTIZIA (13). 494. *Titian* (attributed), Portrait of a Gentleman; 228, *Titian*, The Redeemer, an early work, *495. Portrait of a man, once thought to be Vincenzo Mosti; *Tintoretto*, 410. and 65. Two portraits; and works by *Bonifazio Veronese*.—SALA DI FLORA (14). 21 dep., *Pontormo*, Portrait of a lady; *Paolo Veronese*, St Catherine; 88. and 87. *Andrea del Sarto*, Story of Joseph, two beautiful small works; and works by *Domenico Puligo*.—SALA DEI PUTTI (15). *1165. *Rubens*, The Three Graces, a small painting in monochrome, and Dutch works by *Rachele Ruysch, Willem Van Aelst, Ludolf Backhuysen, Jacob Jordaens,* and *Godfried Schalken* (Girl with a candle).

From the Sala di Prometeo (see above) is the entrance to the the GALLERIA DEL POCCETTI (16) which received its name from the traditional attribution of the frescoes in the vault to *Poccetti*; it is now thought these are by *Matteo Rosselli* and his pupils (c 1625). The beautiful table inlaid in pietre dure is attributed to *Giovanni Battista Foggini* (1716). The paintings include: *Rubens*, 761. and 324. Duke and Duchess of Buckingham; 249. *Pontormo*, Francesco da Castiglione; *Gaspare Dughet* (brother-in-law of Poussin), four Landscapes; *Domenico Feti*, two small biblical scenes; *Francesco Furini*, Hylas and the Nymphs; 408. *Peter Lely*, Cromwell; 188. *Niccolò Cassana*, Portrait of an artist (formerly thought to be Salvator Rosa's self-portrait).—Beyond is the neo-classical SALA DELLA MUSICA (17) by Cacialli (1811–21) with drum-shaped commodes. From the Sala del Castagnoli (see above; Plan C) a door (sometimes closed) leads into another series of rooms.

The SALA DELLE ALLEGORIE (18) has a statue of the young Michelangelo by *Emilio Zocchi* (1861). The vault is frescoed by Volterrano. The paintings include: *Volterrano*, 582. The Parson's jest (Pievano Arlotto), 107. Love sleeping, 105. Mercenary Love; *Giovanni da San Giovanni*, 33 dep. Portrait of the pievano Arlotto, 2120. The Wedding Night, 1529. Angels waiting on Christ; *Sustermans*, Portraits of the Puliciani; 2129. *Artemesia Gentileschi*, Madonna and Child; 1344. *Cristofano Allori*, Mary Magdalen in the desert.—On the left of the SALA DELLE BELLE ARTI (19), with paintings by *Cigoli* and *Carlo Dolci*, is the SALA DELL'ARCA (20) with delightful frescoes of 1816 by *Luigi Ademollo*. Recently restored works are sometimes exhibited here. The early-17C chapel was built for Maria Maddalena d'Austria, wife of Cosimo II, and contains paintings by *Matteo Rosselli, Filippo Tarchiani, Fabrizio Boschi,* and *Giovanni Bilivert.* Beyond is a corridor (21) with tiny Dutch paintings acquired by Cosimo III on a trip to Holland in 1667.—The SALONE D'ERCOLE (22) is frescoed with scenes from the life of Hercules by *Pietro Benvenuti* (1828). The huge Sèvres vase dates from 1784.—SALA DELL'AURORA (23). Paintings by *Empoli, Lorenzo Lippi, Cristofano Allori, Jacopo Ligozzi,* and *Jacopo Vignali*.—The SALA DI BERENICE (24) contains works by *Francesco Furini, Carlo Dolci, Orazio Riminaldi, Giovanni Biliverti,* and *Francesco Curradi* (Narcissus).—Rooms 25–27 are temporarily closed. SALA DI PSICHE (25). Fine works by *Salvator Rosa*: 470. The Wood of the Philosophers, and land- and sea-scapes, a battle scene, and sketches on wood.—SALA DELLA FAMA (26). Flemish works (*Willem van Aelst*, etc.).—The Vestibule and Bathroom (27) of Empress Maria Luisa (wife of Napoleon) were designed in neo-classical style by *Giuseppe Cacialli* (c 1805).

The other half of the piano nobile along the façade of the palace is occupied by the **Appartamenti Monumentali (ex Reali)** which have been closed for restoration for several years. They are usually entered from the Sala delle Nicchie (I; cf. above). This series of state apartments, most of them lavishly decorated in the 19C by the Dukes of Lorraine, are notable particularly for their numerous portraits of the Medici by Sustermans, the Flemish painter who was appointed to the Medici court in 1619 and remained in their service until his death in 1681, and a fine group of 18C Gobelins tapestries.

The SALA VERDE (II) has a painting (formerly in the ceiling) of the Allegory of Peace between Florence and Fiesole, by *Luca Giordano*, and a painting showing the studio of an artist (for long thought to be that of Rubens), by *Cornelis de Baelheur*. The ebony Cabinet decorated with pietre dure was made for Vittoria della Rovere in 1680.—The SALA DEL TRONO (III) and SALA CELESTE (IV), contain portraits by *Sustermans* and his master *Frans Pourbus the Younger*.—The CAPPELLA (V) has a Madonna by *Carlo Dolci* (in a rich frame of 1697), and a portrait of Cardinal Carlo de' Medici by *Sustermans*.— SALA DEI PAPPAGALLI (VI). *School of Botticelli*, Tondo of the Madonna and Child with angels; 764. *Titian*, Giulia Verana, Duchess of Urbino (?); *Frans Pourbus the Younger*, Elizabeth of France; *Sustermans*, Vittoria della Rovere, Maria Maddalena d'Austria. The Cabinet in ebony and ivory is by *Giovanni Battista Foggini*.—The SALA GIALLA (VII) and the CAMERA DA LETTO DELLA REGINA MARGHERITA (VIII) contain a magnificent series of hunting tapestries showing Louis XV, on cartoons by *Jean Baptiste Oudry*.—The oval TOILETTE DELLA REGINA (IX), decorated in the Chinese style on a design by *Ignazio Pellegrini*, is next to the circular SALA DI MUSICA DELLA REGINA (X; usually kept closed). From the Sala dei Pappagalli (VI; see above) is the entrance (not always open) to the APPARTAMENTI DI UMBERTO I, four rooms (XI–XIV) elaborately decorated, with more portraits by *Sustermans*—The remaining series of rooms (XV–XXII) are normally kept closed and used only for exhibitions. The 18C SALA BIANCA (XV) or DEL BALLO by *Gaspare Maria Paoletti* has recently been well restored. The SALA DI BONA (XXII) is frescoed by *Bernardino Poccetti* (1608).

On the floor above the Galleria Palatina is the **Galleria d'Arte Moderna** (for adm. see p 62), moved here after 1918. The collection is particularly representative of Tuscan art of the 19C, notably the 'Macchiaioli' school (Giovanni Fattori, Silvestro Lega, Telemaco Signorini, etc.). Many of the rooms were decorated in the 19C by the last grand-dukes, Ferdinand III and Leopold II. In every room there is a detailed catalogue of the works displayed which cover the period from the mid 18C up to the end of the Second World War. They are arranged chronologically and by schools. The gallery is to be expanded.

ROOM 1. Neo-classicism. *Pompeo Batoni*, Hercules at the crossroads (1742), and works by *Stefano Tofanelli* and *Gaspare Landi*.—RR. 2–6 (left; not always open) contain works of the Romantic period, including paintings by *Francesco Hayez* and *Francesco Sabatelli*.—R. 7. Portraits by *Pietro Benvenuti* and *Vincenzo Camuccini*; head of Napoleon I by *Canova* (or a contemporary copy); landscape by *Nicolas Didier Boguet*; (left wall) *Françoise Xavier Fabre*, Antonio Santarelli (1812).—R. 8. Portraits of the last grand-dukes of Tuscany, and a huge Sèvres vase with a bronze mount by Pierre-Philippe Thomire.—R. 9 is devoted to the Demidoff family in Florence, and includes a model by *Lorenzo Bartolini* for his monument on Lungarno Serristori (cf. p 190).—R. 10. On the end wall, a huge painting by *Giuseppe Bezzuoli* showing Charles VIII's entry into Florence. Also here: *Amos Cassioli*, Battle of Legnano; *Aristodemo Costoli*, Dying gladiator; *Giovanni Duprè*, Cain and Abel, two bronze statues; *Pio Fedi*, St Sebastian.—R. 11 (right) contains paintings by *Stefano Ussi*.—R. 12. *Antonio Ciseri*.—The SALA DA BALLO (1825) has two statues of the young Bacchus, by *Giovanni Duprè*.—R. 13. Good portraits by *Giovanni Boldini*, *Giovanni Fattori*, and *Antonio Puccinelli*.—R. 14. Landscapes by *Antonio Fontanesi*.—R. 15. (Cristiano Banti collection). Works by *Cristiano Banti*, *Francesco Altamura*, and *Giovanni Boldini*.—R. 16 (Diego Martelli collection). Works by the 'Macchiaioli', a school of painters founded in Tuscany in the mid 19C whose works were characterised by 'macchie' or spots of colour. Taking their inspiration direct from nature, they could be termed Tuscan Impressionists, and the results they obtained were often of the highest quality. The painters represented here include *Guiseppe Abbati*, *Giovanni Fattori*, *Silvestro Lega*, *Raffaello Sernesi*, *Telemaco Signorini*, and *Federico Zandomeneghi*. The collection also includes two landscapes by *Camille Pissarro*—In R. 17 are genre scenes by *Giuseppe Abbati*, *Giuseppe De Nittis*, *Domenico Induno*, and *Silvestro Lega*, and sculptures by *Adriano Cecioni*.—R. 18. The Risorgimento.

Bust of Mazzini by *Cecioni*, and battle-scenes by *Giovanni Fattori* and *Silvestro Lega*.—R. 19. *Antonio Ciseri*.—R. 20. *Stefano Ussi*.—RR. 23 and 24 (the Ambron collection) display more fine works by the Macchiaioli school including *Giovanni Fattori, Telemaco Signorini, Vito d'Ancona,* and *Vincenzo Cabianca*—R. 25. Peasant scenes by *Egisto Ferroni, Fattori, Signorini,* and *Enrico Banti*.—R. 26. Works by *Eugenio Cecconi*.—R. 27. *Filippo Palizzi, Giuseppe de Nittis, Domenico Morelli, Pio Joris, Gaetano Esposito,* etc.—R. 28. German artists working in Florence in the late 19C, including *Arnold Böcklin* and *Adolf Hildebrand*.—R. 29. *Adolfo De Carolis, Lorenzo Viani, John Singer Sargent,* and sculptures by *Medardo Rosso*.—R. 30 contains works by *Elisabeth Chaplin* and *Armando Spadini,* among others.

To the right of R. 1 the Salone del Ballo (decorated in 1815–30 by *Pasquale Poccianti*) in the Quartiere d'Inverno, and the Sala della Musica (frescoed in 1795 by *Giuseppe Terreni*) were reopened in 1986 to display part of the collection of 20C works (1915–45) by *Virgilio Guidi, Arturo Tosi, Mario Sironi, Guido Peyron, Giovanni Colacicchi, Felice Carena, Primo Conti, Felice Casorati, Ardengo Soffici, De Pisis, Carlo Carrà, Gino Severini, De Chirico, Emanuele Cavalli,* and others.

Palazzo Pitti and Forte di Belvedere, from a tempera lunette by Giusto Utens, 1599. (Museo di Firenze com'era)

The ***Museo degli Argenti** (for adm. see see p 62), arranged in the summer apartments of the grand-dukes, is entered from the left side of the courtyard.

The entrance hall has tapestries and a portrait of Leopoldo de' Medici (later Cardinal) by *Sustermans*.—SALA DI GIOVANNI DI SAN GIOVANNI. The exuberant and colourful frescoes by *Giovanni di San Giovanni* were begun after the marriage of Ferdinando II and Vittoria della Rovere in 1634. They represent the apotheosis of the Medici family. The decoration of the end walls was completed by his pupils *Cecco Bravo, Francesco Furini*, and *Ottavio Vannini*. The pretty little organ by Lorenzo Testa dates from 1703 (concerts are held here in the autumn).— In the room to the left, the SALA BUIA, is displayed (central case) the magnificent *Collection of sixteen vases in pietre dure which belonged to Lorenzo il Magnifico (whose portrait by Girolamo Macchietti is displayed here), and which bear his monogram 'LA V.R.MED'. Most of them date from the Late Imperial Roman era; others are Byzantine or medieval Venetian works. They were mounted in silver-gilt in the 15C (some by *Giusto da Firenze*) or later in the grand-ducal workshops. In the four smaller cases are Antique cups and dishes in pietre dure, and some Byzantine works. Also here are 15C church vestments, and reliquaries (13–15C).—Beyond is the GROTTICINA (restored after damage in a gas explosion in 1984), with a little fountain and a pretty frescoed ceiling with birds by Florentine artists (1623–34). Here are portraits of four grand-duchesses, including Christine of Lorraine, by *Pulzone*. The exquisitely carved limewood relief by *Grinling Gibbons* was presented to Cosimo III in 1682 by Charles II (restored after damage in 1984).—To the right of the Sala di Giovanni di San Giovanni, beyond the CHAPEL decorated by local craftsmen in 1623–34, are three RECEPTION ROOMS with delightful trompe l'oeil frescoes by the Bolognese painters, *Angelo Michele Colonna* and *Agostino Mitelli* (1635–41). The cabinet, brought to Florence in 1628, was made in Augsburg. Also here are several fine tables in pietre dure (16–17C), a 17C prie-dieu (kneeling-desk) in ebony and pietre dure, and a chessboard made in 1619 on a design by *Jacopo Ligozzi*.

The rooms towards the Boboli gardens were the living quarters of the grand-dukes. Here, and on the mezzanine floor, are displayed their eclectic collection of personal keepsakes, gifts presented by other ruling families, objets d'art made specially for them, etc. In the room to the right are vessels in rock crystal and pietre dure including (802.) a lapis lazuli vase (1583, designed by *Buontalenti* with a gold mount by *Jacques Bylivelt*), a rock-crystal vase (721.) in the form of a bird (with a gold enamelled mount, c 1589), and a lapis lazuli shell (413.), with the handle in enamelled gold in the form of a snake. The so-called 'Coppa di Diana di Poitiers' (540.), in rock crystal with an enamelled gold lid, is thought to have been made for Henry II of France. A fiasca (620.) in rock crystal has an incised scene of Parnassus and a gold ornamental chain.—The ivories in the two rooms to the left include statuettes made for Cardinal Leopoldo by the German *Balthazar Stockamer* in the mid 17C, an elaborate composition of Curtius riding his horse into the abyss, and a series of turned vases, also of German manufacture, particularly remarkable from a technical point of view.— Stairs lead up to the MEZZANINE where the grand-ducal collection of jewellery has always been kept. In the two rooms to the right: rings with cameos and intaglio; cameo portraits; the *Jewellery collection of the last of the Medici, the electress Anna Maria; ex-voto in precious stones of Cosimo II in prayer made in the grand-ducal workshops in 1617–24; relief of Cosimo I and his family in pietre dure by *Giovanni Antonio de'Rossi* (1557–62); oval in pietre dure of Piazza Signoria by *Bernardo Gaffurri* (1598); Roman head of Hercules.—The first two rooms to the left of the stairs contain gold and silversmiths' work from the Treasury of Ferdinando III brought to Florence in 1814 (mainly from Salzburg), including elaborate nautilus shells, a double chalice made from an ostrich-egg mounted in silver gilt (c 1370–80), two ornamental cups made from buffalo horns with silver gilt mounts (14C), etc. The series of silver gilt dishes from Salzburg were made by *Paul Hübner*, c 1590.—Beyond a painted 'loggia' (early 17C) with four 17C Mexican vases, is another frescoed room (overlooking the courtyard) which contains exotic and rare objects from all over the world. These include an Islamic powder horn, nautilus shells, 17C shell figurines, a mitre with scenes of the Passion depicted in gold thread and birds' feathers (Mexican, c 1545), etc.—Other rooms (sometimes closed) contain plaster casts of the silver plates belonging to the last Medici grand-dukes which were melted down in 1799; Chinese and Japanese porcelain, church silver, etc.

The ***Galleria del Costume** (adm. see p 62) was opened in 1983 on the ground floor of the PALAZZINA DELLA MERIDIANA, which was begun in 1776 by Gaspare

Maria Paoletti. It is reached from the main Courtyard where stairs lead up to the Boboli gardens. The entrance to the Meridiana is behind the palace to the right. The delightful collection, which is being augmented all the time (most recently by the Umberto Tirelli Collection of theatrical costume), illustrates the history of costume from the 18C to the early 20C. The beautifully displayed clothes are changed round about every two years and frequent exhibitions are held.—On the upper floor the *Collezione Contini-Bonacossi** was temporarily arranged in 1974 (for adm. see p 62). There are plans to move it to the Uffizi building. It includes a fine collection of Italian (and some Spanish) paintings and furniture of the 15–17C, majolica, etc. Some of the most important works include: R. I. *Agnolo Gaddi*, Madonna and Child with Saints.—R. II. *Paolo Veneziano*, Two scenes from the life of St Nicholas.—ROOM III. *Bernardo Zenale*, St Michael archangel, St Bernard; *Sassetta*, Madonna della Neve; *Defendente Ferrari*, Madonna and Child.—R. IV. *Giovanni Bellini*, St Jerome in the desert; *Paolo Veronese*, Count Giuseppe da Porto and his son Adriano; *Vincenzo Catena*, Supper at Emmaus; *Gian Lorenzo Bernini*, Martyrdom of St Lawrence (sculpture).—R. V. *Bramantino*, Madonna and Child with Saints; *Giovanni Antonio Boltraffio*, Portrait of the poet Casio; *Cima da Conegliano*, St Jerome in the desert.—R. VI. *Francisco de Goya*, Bullfighter; *El Greco*, 'The tears of St Peter'; *Diego Velazquez*, The water-carrier.—RR. VII–IX. Della Robbian tondi, statuettes by *Bambaia*, etc.—R. X. *Andrea del Castagno*, Madonna and Child with angels and Saints and two children of the Pazzi family (fresco from the castle of Trebbio).—R. XI. *Jacopo Tintoretto*, Portrait of a man, Minerva, and Venus.

Palazzo Pitti from the Boboli Gardens

On the hillside behind Palazzo Pitti lie the magnificent *Boboli Gardens**, laid out for Cosimo I by *Tribolo*, and continued after his death in 1555 by *Marco del Tasso* and *Ammannati*. After 1569 Francesco I employed *Buontalenti* to direct the works. The gardens were extended in the early 17C by *Giulio* and *Alfonso Parigi*, and were opened to the public for the first time in 1766. The normal entrance is from the piazza through an archway in the left wing of the palace (they can also be reached from the courtyard of Ammannati, cf. p 110). For admission see p 60. The charming garden in front of the Museo delle Porcellane (adm. see p 62) is only open with the museum. There are three additional exits from the gardens: at Porta Romana, at the Annalena gate on Via Romana, and at the Forte di Belvedere gate (cf. the Plan on p 122). The biggest public park in the centre of Florence, the gardens are beautifully maintained. They are always cool even on the hottest days in summer, and are a delightful place to picnic. Many of the statues which decorate the walks are restored Roman works, but some of them still remain unidentified. Two worn statues in the gardens were recognised as works by Cellini only just before the last War (they are now in the Bargello, see p 162). Some of the statues have been restored in situ; others have been removed for restoration and will not be put back in the gardens for conservation reasons. Casts of two of the marble statues have substituted the originals in situ, but it has not yet been decided whether casts in synthetic materials or copies in marble or stone will be made in future of the restored works. There are long-term plans to open a Museum of Statuary from the gardens near Porta Romana in Le Pagliere (a stable block built in 1867), where all the restored statues will be kept.

On the left of the entrance arch is the so-called 'Fontana del Bacco' (1), really an amusing statue of Pietro Barbino, the pot-bellied dwarf of Cosimo I, seated on a turtle, by Valerio Cioli (1560; removed for restoration and replaced here by a cast). Here can be seen the last stretch of the Corridoio Vasariano from the Uffizi (cf. p 106) with remains of graffiti decoration. A path lined with magnolia trees descends to the scenographic *GROTTA GRANDE (2; covered for restoration and usually kept locked), traditionally thought to be the work of Buontalenti, but now considered by some scholars to have been built by Ammannati. The two statues of Apollo and Ceres in the niches on the façade (begun by Vasari) are by Baccio Bandinelli, and the decoration above was added by Giovanni del Tadda. The walls of the first chamber are covered with fantastic figures carved in the limestone by Piero di Tommaso Mati (on a design by Buontalenti). In the four corners are casts of Michelangelo's unfinished 'slaves' (the originals, placed here in 1585, were removed to the Accademia in 1908). The charmingly painted vault is by Bernardino Poccetti. Beyond an erotic group of Paris abducting Helen, by Vincenzo de' Rossi, the innermost grotto contains a beautiful statue of Venus emerging from her bath (c 1565) by Giambologna, and pretty murals by Poccetti.

The carriage-way, flanked by two porphyry and marble Roman statues of Dacian prisoners (brought here from the Villa Medici in Rome, with bas-reliefs of the late 3C on their pedestals), winds up through the gardens. One of the statues has been removed for restoration, and the other has been returned here since its restoration. The ancient square bell-tower of Santa Felìcita can be seen near a rose-garden with a colossal seated figure of Jupiter which may be by Baccio Bandinelli. Beyond two pine trees a narrow path, lined with box hedges, leads to the Grotticina di Madama (usually locked), commissioned by Eleonora di Toledo, and the first grotto to be built in the gardens (1553–55, by Bandinelli and Giovanni Fancelli). It contains stalacites and bizarre goats. The main path emerges on the terrace behind Palazzo Pitti, overlooking the courtyard and Fontana del Carciofo (3), by Francesco Susini (1641), named from the bronze artichoke on top, which has been lost. It replaced a fine fountain by Ammannati (now recomposed in the Bargello). From the terrace there is a magnificent view of the Duomo and Campanile behind Orsanmichele.

The AMPHITHEATRE (4) was laid out as a garden by Ammannati in 1599, in imitation of a Roman circus. The open-air theatre was constructed in 1630–35 by Giulio and Alfonso Parigi for the spectacles held here by the Medici which culminated in the festivities for

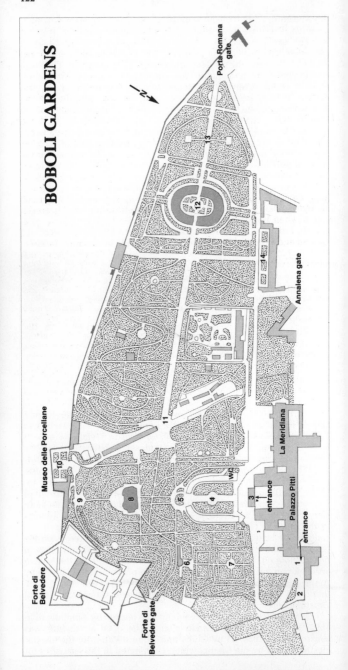

BOBOLI GARDENS

Porta Romana gate

Annalena gate

La Meridiana

Palazzo Pitti

entrance

entrance

Museo delle Porcellane

Forte di Belvedere

Forte di Belvedere gate

WC

the marriage of Cosimo, son of Ferdinand II with Margaret Louise of Orléans in 1661. The huge granite basin comes from the Baths of Caracalla and the obelisk of Rameses II was taken from Heliopolis by the Romans in 30 BC, and found its way to the Villa Medici in Rome in the 17C. It was brought here in 1790 from Rome where its companion now adorns the Dogali Monument. All the restored antique statues from the niches have been removed.—On the first terrace behind the Amphitheatre are three Roman statues (5), standing on funerary altars, including a fine Ceres.—On the upper level is a large fishpond surrounded by terraces planted with trees (above which can be seen the Forte di Belvedere). Here is the *Neptune Fountain* (8) by Stoldo Lorenzi (1565–68). A short detour to the left leads through romantic winding alleys overshadowed by ilexes and a cypress grove, to the rococo *'Kaffeehaus'* (6), built in 1776 by Zanobi del Rosso (a café here is open in summer), with charming frescoes. In the garden in front (with a good view of Florence and Fiesole) is the *Ganymede Fountain* (7; removed for restoration; replaced by a cast), thought to date from the 17C. Behind the Kaffeehaus there is access (open when the gardens are open) to the Forte di Belvedere (see p 203). From the Neptune Fountain steps continue to the top of the garden and a colossal Statue of *'Abundance'* (9), in a niche of bay and ilex. Begun by Giambologna, it was finished by Pietro Tacca, and placed here in 1636 (recently restored). From here the view embraces the whole city, beyond the Pitti and the tower of Santo Spirito.

A short double flight of steps (right) continues to the *Giardino del Cavaliere* (10), a delightful secluded walled garden on a bastion constructed by Michelangelo in 1529. The fountain (removed for restoration) has three bronze monkeys attributed to Pietro Tacca, and a putto attributed to Pierino da Vinci. The view from the terrace is one of the most charming in Florence, embracing the rural outskirts of the city. On the extreme left is the bastion of Forte di Belvedere, then, behind a group of cypresses, San Miniato with its tower. The fields and olive groves are dotted with beautiful old villas. To the right is the residential area of Bobolino beside a splendid stretch of the city walls. Here, in the Casino del Cavaliere, enlarged in the 18C, the MUSEO DELLE PORCELLANE was opened in 1973 (temporarily closed for structural repairs, but for adm. when it reopens, see p 62). It contains a well displayed collection of Italian, German, and French porcelain from the Medici and Lorraine grand-ducal collections. Room 1 displays 18C French porcelain (Tournai, Chantilly, Vincennes, Sèvres, including the delicate 'alzata da ostriche'). In the centre, beneath a Venetian chandelier, the dinner service of Elisa Baciocchi, and a plaque with a portrait of her brother Napoleon in Sèvres porcelain, after Françoise Gérard (1809–10). Also here, 18–19C Doccia and Neapolitan ware.—In the other two rooms, 18–19C works made in the Meissen and Vienna porcelain factories.

At the foot of the double stairs, another flight of steps leads down between seated Muses to the *Prato dell'Uccellare*, with a grove of cedars of Lebanon (view), at the end of a range of garden houses.— To the left the magnificent long VIOTTOLONE (11) descends steeply through the gardens. A majestic cypress avenue planted in 1637 by Alfonso Parigi the Younger, it is lined with statues, many of them restored Roman works (and some of them carved in the 16C and 17C); some of these have been removed for restoration. The 17C arboured walks and little gardens to the right and left, with delightful vistas, provide some of the most beautiful scenery in the park. The paths are laid out between box hedges and laurel avenues. The four statues (one of them has been removed) at the first crossing are by Giovanni Battista Caccini (c 1608), and three of the statues at the next crossing are restored Roman works. A path (left) ends at a colossal bust of Jupiter by the school of Giambologna (here a path lined with late-16C fountains follows a stretch of the city walls). Beyond the end of the avenue are two groups of statues depicting folk games (17–18C). The statues of animals in this part of the garden are by Francesco del Tadda. The ISOLOTTO (12) was laid out by Alfonso Parigi in 1618. It is a circular moat with fine sculptural decorations surrounding an island with a garden and a copy by Romanelli of Giambologna's Fountain of Oceanus (original in the Bargello, p 163), on a huge granite base quarried by Tribolo in Elba. The fanciful groups of statues on the balustrade are 18C copies of works by the school of Giambologna, and works by Alfonso Parigi (1637–39; some of which have been removed and restored). The island recalls the so-called Naval Theatre, Hadrian's retreat at his villa near Tivoli. In the niches in the surrounding hedge are restored 17C statues (many of them propped up by scaffolding) of peasants, etc. (one of them of a Moorish hunter by Domenico Pieratti has been removed and restored). The dogs are by Romolo Ferrucci del Tadda.

Beyond is the _Hemicycle_ (13), surrounded by plane-trees, with two Roman granite columns surmounted by neo-classical vases, purchased from Lord Cowper by Pietro Leopoldo. Some of the colossal busts are Antique. The four statuary groups of folk games, and three grotesque figures once thought to be by Romolo del Tadda have recently been attributed to Tribolo or Caccini. The green provides a cool playground for local children in summer. At the end of the garden are more statuary groups of folk games. On top of a Roman sarcophagus is a fountain of a peasant with a barrel by Giovanni Fancelli. At the exit from the garden through the walls, beside Porta Romana, is a statue of Perseus by Vincenzo Danti.

Just outside the gate (left; entered through another gateway and approached by a park), in the former Royal Stables is the _Istituto d'Arte_, a State art school. It owns a famous *_Gipsoteca_ (or _Museum of Plaster-casts_; admission by appointment at the art school) with casts of numerous famous Antique and Renaissance sculptures, including many by Donatello and Michelangelo. They were mostly made at the end of the 19C and beginning of this century by Giuseppe Lelli; his son left them to the Institute in 1922. The collection, in a splendid hall, is being rearranged.—Nearby is the building known as _Le Pagliere_ which is to house a museum of sculpture from the gardens.

Buses from Porta Romana return to the centre of the city; otherwise a path leads back through the Boboli gardens following the left wall along Via Romana. Beyond the _Fountain of the Vintage_ (1599–1608), by Valerio Cioli, is the handsome _Orangery_ (14) by Zanobi Del Rosso (1785), near the Annalena gate, another exit from the garden. Nearby is a small grotto with statues of Adam and Eve by Michele Naccherino. A path continues past more greenhouses to emerge by the charming 18C Meridiana wing (with the Costume Museum, cf. p 119) of Palazzo Pitti. The hillside here was used probably since Roman times as a quarry for pietra forte (covered over in the 18C). The nearest exit from the gardens is beneath the Fontana del Carciofo into Ammannati's courtyard.

9 Galleria dell' Accademia and Santissima Annunziata

From Piazza San Marco (see Rte 10) the straight Via Ricasoli (Pl.6;6) leads towards the Duomo (view of the Campanile). Beyond the Accademia di Belle Arti (p 135) is the entrance at No. 60 to the *Galleria dell'Accademia (Pl.6;6; adm. see p 60), visited above all for its famous works by Michelangelo, but also containing an important collection of Florentine paintings.

The collection was formed in 1784 with a group of paintings given, for study purposes, to the Academy by Pietro Leopoldo I. Since 1873 some important sculptures by Michelangelo have been housed here, including the David. The works are all well labelled.

The entrance leads into the first room of the PINACOTECA with 15C and early 16C paintings. *Fra' Bartolomeo*, Isaiah and Job; *Francesco Granacci*, Madonna and Child with Saints; *Mariotto Albertinelli*, Annunciation (1510), Madonna enthroned with Saints; two tondi of the Holy Family by *Girolamo del Pacchia* and *Franciabigio*; *Filippino Lippi*, St John the Baptist and St Mary Magdalen; *Francesco Botticini*, Saints Augustine and Monica; *Perugino*, and *Filippino Lippi*, *Descent from the Cross; *Perugino*, Assumption and Saints (being restored); *Ridolfo Ghirlandaio*, Madonna and Child with Saints Francis and Mary Magdalen; *Albertinelli*, The Trinity; *Bartolomeo di Giovanni*, St Jerome; *Fra' Bartolomeo*, *Madonna enthroned with Saints and angels (a painting which may be returned to the Pitti); *Francesco Granacci*, Virgin of the Sacred Girdle.—In the centre, the original plaster model for the Rape of the Sabine (cf. p 88), by *Giambologna*.

The GALLERIA contains **Sculptures by *Michelangelo*. The four SLAVES or PRISONERS (c 1521–23) were begun for the ill-fated tomb of Julius II. They were presented to the Medici in 1564 by Michelangelo's nephew, Leonardo. In 1585 they were placed in the Grotta del Buontalenti in the Boboli gardens (cf. p 121). In the centre of the right side is the ST MATTHEW (1504–08), one of the twelve apostles commissioned from the sculptor by the Opera del Duomo, and the only one he ever began. These are all magnificent examples of Michelangelo's unfinished works, some of them barely blocked out, the famous 'non-finito', much discussed by scholars. They evoke Michelangelo's unique concept expressed in his poetry, that the sculpture already exists within the block of stone, and it is the sculptor's job merely to take away what is superfluous. The way in which Michelangelo confronted his task, as Cellini noted, was to begin from a frontal viewpoint, as if carving a high relief, and thus the statue gradually emerged from the marble.—The Pietà from Santa Rosalia in Palestrina is an undocumented work, and is not now usually considered to be by Michelangelo's own hand.

To the right are three more rooms of the PINACOTECA with 15C paintings. ROOM 2. 8508. *Mariotto di Cristofano*, Scenes from the life of Christ and the Madonna; 3160. *Andrea di Giusto*, Madonna and Child with angels; 8457. Panel, known as the 'Cassone Adimari', by *Lo Scheggia* (1440–45), showing a wedding scene with elegant guests in period dress in front of the Baptistery; 171 dep. 'Master of the Castello Nativity', Nativity (from the Villa di Castello, cf. p 245); 1562. *Cosimo Rosselli*, Madonna and Child with Saints; 4632. *Filippino Lippi*, Annunciation (an early work; a copy from a painting by his father, *Fra' Filippo Lippi*); *Mariotto di Cristofano*, 3162. Resurrection, 3164. Marriage of St Catherine; 8624. *Domenico di Michelino*, St Tobias and three archangels.—Room 3. *3166. *Botticelli*, Madonna and Child with the young St John and angels (an early work); 5381. Pupil of Paolo Uccello (attributed), The Thebaids; *8637. *Alessandro Baldovinetti*, Trinity and Saints (much ruined); 8623. *Sebastiano Mainardi* (attributed), Pietà.—R. 4. *8661. *Lorenzo di Credi*, Adoration of the Child; *8456. *Botticelli* (attributed), Madonna 'of the Sea'; 8663. *Raffaellino* *del Garbo*, Resurrection; 8631–33. *Cosimo Rosselli*, God the Father, Moses and Adam, David and Noah; 8627–29. *Bartolomeo di Giovanni*, Deposition, St Francis, and St Jerome; 1621. *Sebastiano Mainardi*, Saints Stephen, James, and Peter.

The TRIBUNE was specially built in 1882 by De Fabris to exhibit the *DAVID by *Michelangelo* (1501–4) when it was removed from Piazza della Signoria (cf. p 88). It is perhaps the most famous single work of art of Western civilisation, and has become all too familiar through endless reproductions, although it is not the work by which Michelangelo is best judged. It was commissioned by the city of Florence to stand outside Palazzo Vecchio where its huge scale fits its setting. Here it seems out of place in its cold heroic niche. The colossal block of marble, 4.10 metres high, quarried in 1464 for the Opera del Duomo, had been left abandoned in the cathedral work-shop. The marble was offered to several other artists, including Andrea Sansovino and Leonardo da Vinci before it was finally assigned to Michelangelo. The figure of David, uncharacteristic of Michelangelo's works, stands in a classical pose suited to the shallow block of marble. The hero, a young colossus, is shown in the moment before his victory over Goliath. A celebration of the nude, the statue established Michelangelo as the foremost sculptor of his time, at the age of 29.

The walls of the Tribune have recently been hung with Florentine paintings by Michelangelo's contemporaries. On the right, *Bronzino*, Deposition; *Pontormo*, Venus and cupid; *Ridolfo Ghirlandaio*, two oval portraits; works by *Alessandro Allori* and *Francesco Granacci*. In the hall to the left are works by *Giovanni Battista Naldini*, *Carlo Portelli*, *Stefano Pieri*, *Alessandro Allori*, *Santi di Tito*, and *Francesco Salviati*.

To the left are three more rooms of the PINACOTECA displaying early Tuscan works (13–14C). ROOM 5. *3345. Crucifix by the Sienese school. 8459. *Pacino di Buonaguida*, Tree of the Cross (restored); Byzantine works including (8466.) Mary Magdalen with stories from her life by the '*Maestro della Maddalena*'.— R. 6. 3469. *Andrea Orcagna*, Madonna and Child with angels and saints; 8464. *Nardo di Cione*, Triptych with the Trinity and two Saints; works by the *Gaddi*, and by *Bernardo Daddi* and his school; 456. *Jacopo di Cione*, Coronation of the Virgin.—R. 7. *8467. *Giovanni da Milano*, Pietà; 8581–8603. Scenes from the life of Christ and from the life of St Francis by *Taddeo Gaddi* (from the Sacristy of Santa Croce); 442. *Bernardo Daddi*, Crucifix.

The huge light hall at the end of this wing (not yet regularly open) has recently been filled with a splendid display of 19C sculptures and paintings by members of the Accademia di Belle Arti (cf. p 135), including plaster *Models for his marble statues by *Lorenzo Bartolini* (1777–1850).

From the entrance stairs lead up to the **First Floor** where four rooms were opened in 1985 and well arranged with a fine collection of Florentine paintings of the end of the 14C and early 15C. ROOM 1 has two painted Crucifixes by *Lorenzo Monaco*.—The long gallery (2; with a view of the Accademia di Belle Arti) has a rich display of triptychs. *Giovanni del Biondo*, Presentation in the Temple; *Andrea Orcagna*, Pentecost (formerly on the high altar of Santi Apostoli); *Niccolò di Pietro Gerini*, Crucifixion and Saints, Coronation of the Virgin and Saints; *Spinello Aretino*, Madonna and Saints; *Bicci di Lorenzo*, Madonna and Saints; *Lorenzo Monaco*, Prayer in the Garden; *Lorenzo di Bicci*, St Martin; *Giovanni del Biondo*, huge triptych of the Annunciation, St John the Evangelist; *Lorenzo Monaco*, Madonna and Saints, Christ in pietà and symbols of the Passion; *Rossello di Jacopo Franchi*, Madonna and Saints, Coronation of the Virgin; *Giovanni del Ponte*, Coronation of the Virgin; '*Master of the Madonna Straus*', Annunciation; *Niccolò di Pietro Gerini*, Christ in Pietà.— ROOM 3 has 16C Russian works, and cases of 16–18C Russian icons (from the Lorraine grand-ducal collections), as well as more works by *Neri di Bicci*, *Giovanni del Ponte*, and *Bicci di Lorenzo*.—The last room has works by *Lorenzo Monaco* (triptych of the Annunciation and Saints); *Mariotto di Nardo* (Annunciation); and *Agnolo Gaddi*.

At the crossing of Via Ricasoli with Via degli Alfani is a small piazza with the entrance to the *Conservatorio Luigi Cherubini* (Pl.6;6; the building has been in restoration for many years), the conservatory of music named after the greatest Florentine musician Luigi Cherubini (1760–1842) who spent most of his career in Paris. The remarkable *MUSEUM OF OLD MUSICAL INSTRUMENTS, a collection begun by the last of the Medici and the grand-dukes of the House of Lorraine, is one of the most interesting in Italy. It still awaits a definitive arrangement here and is temporarily housed in Palazzo Vecchio. It includes the 'Viola Medicea' built by Antonio Stradivari in 1690; violins and 'cellos by Stradivari, Guarneri, Amati, and Ruggeri; a harpsichord by Bartolomeo Cristofori, etc. The library contains autograph compositions. Via degli Alfani continues left (at the end can be seen the green dome of the synagogue) past the entrance (No. 78) to the OPIFICIO DELLE PIETRE DURE (Pl.6;6), founded here in 1588 by the grand-duke Ferdinando I.

The craft of working hard or semi-precious stones ('pietre dure') was perfected in Florence. Beautiful mosaics were made to decorate cabinets, table-tops, etc. (many of the best examples are preserved in Palazzo Pitti). The workshop is now dedicated to the restoration of stone, marble, bronze, and pietre dure (another branch of the restoration laboratory, largely concerned with paintings and frescoes, operates in the Fortezza da Basso). There is a small MUSEUM (adm. see p 62) here. Room I displays Antique and modern examples of work in porphyry. In R. 2 are 17–19C panels executed for the altar in the Cappella dei Principi in San Lorenzo. In the other rooms on the ground floor are 19C tables, including one with flowers and birds by Niccolò Betti (1855), and inlaid pictures in pietre dure. The two rooms at the top of the stairs contain 19C objects, and the work benches and instruments once used by the craftsmen. In wall cases are numerous samples of semi-precious stones. There are long-term plans to rearrange the museum on the ground floor.

Via degli Alfani continues across Via dei Servi (see below). On the right is an octagonal building, the ROTONDA DI SANTA MARIA DEGLI ANGELI (Pl.6;6; called 'Il Castellaccio' from its fortress-like air; no adm.). It was begun by Brunelleschi in 1434 as a memorial to the soldier Filippo degli Scolari (died 1424), and left unfinished in 1437. Modelled on the Temple of Minerva Medica in Rome, it was one of the first centralised buildings of the Renaissance. After a period of use as a church, then completed as a lecture-hall in 1959, it has recently been inappropriately converted into a language laboratory of the University. In the square behind are the buildings of the Faculty of Letters and Philosophy of the University.

At No. 48 Via Alfani, *Palazzo Giugni* is a characteristic work by Ammannati (1571) with a fine courtyard, and little garden (with a grotto by Lorenzo Migliorini). The interesting garden façade, with a loggia, bears a copy of the stemma of the family (the original can be seen in the courtyard). On the first floor is the Galleria decorated by Alessandro Gherardini (used by the Lyceum club, who organise concerts here). At No. 39 (now the seat of the Amici dei Musei di Firenze) is the entrance of the ex church of *Santa Maria degli Angeli* (remodelled in 1676) and now used for lectures. The unusual interior with a barrel vault has frescoes by Alessandro Gherardini and stuccoes by Vittorio Barbieri and Alessandro Lombardi. In the former Refectory is a fresco of the Last Supper (1543) by Ridolfo del Ghirlandaio. The pretty cloister on the right of the church (to be restored) has graffiti decoration and lunettes by Bernardino Poccetti and Donato Mascagni (detached and restored and to be returned here), and busts attributed to Caccini and Francavilla. Off the cloister is a little chapel (1599) with a fresco in the dome by Poccetti who probably also painted the altarpiece, a detached fresco fragment of the Pietà (14C), and sculptured medallions attributed to Caccini and Francavilla.

Via dei Servi (Pl.6;6), on the line of an ancient thoroughfare leading N from the city, is documented as early as the 12C as far as the Porta di Balla (cf. below). It was extended beyond the city gate in the 13C, and used by Brunelleschi in his Renaissance design of Piazza Santissima Annunziata to provide a magnificent view of the cupola of the Duomo. It is now lined by a number of handsome 16C palaces. Going towards the Duomo, on the right, Nos 15 and 17 were restored in 1959 as government offices. The pretty fountain at No. 17 can be seen from the road. No. 15, *Palazzo Niccolini*, was designed by Baccio d'Agnolo in 1548–50. Its beautiful façade is typical of Florentine palaces of this period. The small courtyard has graffiti decoration, and in the garden beyond is an elaborate double loggia, probably by Giovanni Antonio Dosio. Opposite, *Palazzo Sforza Alimeni* (No. 12), c 1510–20, has two good ground-floor windows; the coat-of-arms on the corner has been replaced by a modern copy. The house across Via del Castellaccio is on the site of the studio of Benedetto da Maiano in 1480–98.

The next crossing, the Canto di Balla, is on the site of the old Porta di Balla, a postern gate in the 12C walls. Here is a worn coat-of-arms by Baccio da Montelupo on the corner of *Palazzo dei Pucci*, among the largest palaces in Florence, which bears the name of one of the oldest families in the city, who still live here. The central part of the long façade (which stretches as far as Via Ricasoli) dates from the 16C, and is in part attributed to Ammannati; the wings on either side are 17C extensions. In the little piazza is the church of **San Michele Visdomini** (Pl.16;2; or *San Michelino*), of ancient foundation, known to have been enlarged by the Visdomini family in the 11C. It was demolished in 1363 in order to make way for the E end of the Duomo, and reconstructed on this site a few years later.

INTERIOR. Right side: *Empoli*, Nativity; *Pontormo*, *Holy Family (1518); left side: *Poppi*, Madonna and Saints; *Passignano*, St John the Baptist; *Poppi*, Immaculate Conception. In the left transept, *Poppi*, Resurrection. The 18C vault fresco in the crossing of the Fall of Satan is by *Niccolò Lapi*. In the chapel to the right of the high altar, interesting frescoes and sinopie, found in 1966 and attributed to *Spinello Aretino*. In the chapel to the left of the high altar is the 14C wood crucifix 'de Bianchi' and more fresco and sinopia fragments.

Opposite the church, *Palazzo Incontri* (reconstructed in 1676) was owned by Piero il Gottoso in 1469. Via de' Pucci leads to Via Ricasoli, and on the corner is the *Tabernacolo delle Cinque Lampade*, with a fresco (right) by Cosimo Rosselli. Via Ricasoli is named after Baron Ricasoli (1809–80), mayor of Florence. He lived at No. 9 which has a courtyard of the late 16C.

Via dei Servi leads N to ***Piazza Santissima Annunziata** (Pl.6;6), designed by Brunelleschi, and surrounded on three sides by porticoes. It is the most beautiful square in Florence.

On the right is the Spedale degli Innocenti; in front is the church of the Annunziata and the convent of the Servite order, with remains of five Gothic windows; to the left, the colonnade (modelled on the earlier one opposite), by *Antonio da Sangallo* and *Baccio d'Agnolo* (1516–25); at the corner of Via dei Servi, Palazzo Riccardi-Mannelli, formerly Grifoni, is now the seat of the President of the Regional Government of Tuscany. It is thought to have been begun in 1557 by *Ammannati* probably on a design by *Giuliano di Baccio d'Agnolo*, and then finished by *Buontalenti* and *Giambologna*. It has two ornate brick façades with decorative friezes. In the middle of the square is an equestrian statue of the Grand-Duke Ferdinando I, by *Giambologna* (his last work, cast by *Tacca* in 1608, who also designed the base). The two little symmetrical bronze fountains with bizarre monsters and marine decorations are delightful Mannerist works also by *Tacca* (with the help of his pupils Bartolomeo Salvini and Francesco Maria Bandini). They were restored in 1987.— On the festival of the Annunziata (25 March) a fair is held in the piazza and adjoining streets; homemade sweet 'biscuits' ('brigidini') are sold from the stalls.

The ***Spedale degli Innocenti** (Pl.6;6; properly, *Ospedale degli Innocenti*), opened in 1445 as a foundling hospital, the first institution of its kind in Europe, is still operating as an orphanage and as an Institute dedicated to the education and care of children. It is also used by UNICEF. Vincenzo Borghini, prior here from 1552–80, was an outstanding figure of 16C Florence, friend of Vasari, and counsellor to Duke Cosimo on artistic and literary matters. The 'Arte della Seta' commissioned *Brunelleschi* (who had, as a goldsmith, become a member of the Guild) to begin work on the building in 1419. The

Piazza Santissima Annunziata

*COLONNADE (1419–26) of nine arches is one of the first master-pieces of Renaissance architecture. It takes inspiration from classical antiquity as well as from local Romanesque buildings. The last bays on the right and left were added in the 19C. In the spandrels are delightful *Medallions, perhaps the best-known work of *Andrea della Robbia* (1487), each with a baby in swaddling-clothes against a bright blue ground (the end ones on each side are 19C). Beneath the portico at the left end is the 'rota' constructed in 1660 to receive abandoned babies (walled up in 1875). The fresco under the central vault of the colonnade is by *Bernardino Poccetti* (1610), that in the lunette above the door of the church is by *Giovanni di Francesco* (1459; very damaged). The CHURCH (open in the early morning only) was remodelled in neo-classical style in 1786 by *Bernardo Fallani*. It contains an altarpiece of the Annunciation by *Mariotto Albertinelli* and *Giovanni Antonio Sogliani*.

The CONVENT may be visited to see the **Museo dello Spedale degli Innocenti** (adm. see p 62). The oldest parts of the convent buildings, around two cloisters, were modified in the 18–19C, but were beautifully restored in 1972 to their original design by *Brunelleschi*. The main 'CHIOSTRO DEGLI UOMINI' (1422–45) was decorated in 1596 with a clock tower, and graffiti (drawn with lime) showing the emblems of the 'Arte della Seta' and the other two hospital foundations (San Gallo and Santa Maria alla Scala), which were united here in the 15C. Over the side door into the church is a beautiful lunette of the Annunciation by *Andrea della Robbia*. A door on the right leads out of the far side of the courtyard to the oblong *'CHIOSTRO DELLE DONNE' (1438), another beautiful work by *Brunelleschi*, with 24 slender Ionic columns beneath a low loggia. The charming perspective of the colonnades is reminiscent of the background in some Renaissance paintings. This part of the convent was reserved for the women who worked in the Institute. There is now a collection of games and toys in rooms off the cloister which is open to children (who can borrow them, as in a lending library). Exhibitions are also held in this part of the convent. The ARCHIVES are preserved intact including the first register of 1445; they are now housed in an 18C room with charming 19C bookcases.

From the main cloister stairs lead up to the GALLERY overlooking the first cloister. Here are displayed detached frescoes, many of them from Ognissanti: 16C *Florentine School*, Crucifixion; 18C *Florentine School*, Adoration of the Shepherds; *Circle of Fra' Bartolomeo*, Crucifixion with Mary Magdalen; *Bicci di Lorenzo*, Madonna enthroned between Saints George and Leonard (sinopia of 1430 from Porta San Giorgio); *Giovanni Battista Naldini*, Deposition; series of large frescoes from Ognissanti by *Alessandro Allori* (1575); *Domenico Ghirlandaio* (and his workshop), Madonna and Child.—In the small rooms off the cloister: terracotta crib by *Matteo Civitali*, beneath a fresco of St Catherine and the Philosophers by *Bernardino Poccetti* (1612). In the room to the left: *Bicci di Lorenzo*, St Anthony Abbot, Madonna and Child between Saints (both sinopie); *Lorenzo Monaco*, Crucifixion, Christ in Pietà. The other room has models and plans of the hospital.—The stairs continue to the Long Gallery (formerly the day nursery) which has been arranged as a **Pinacoteca**: *'Master of the Madonna Straus'*, Coronation of the Virgin; *Giovanni del Biondo*, Annunciation between Saints; *Cenni di Francesco*, Madonna and Child (detached fresco); *Neri di Bicci*, Coronation of the Virgin; *Botticelli*, Madonna and Child with an angel (an early work copied from Filippo Lippi. Beyond an archway is a little room dominated by the splendid *Adoration of the Magi by *Domenico Ghirlandaio*. The brightly coloured work includes a scene of the Massacre of the Innocents and two child Saints in the foreground. The predella is by *Bartolomeo di Giovanni*. The altarpiece was commissioned for the high altar of the church by the prior, Francesco Tesori (died 1497), whose tomb-slab has been placed in the floor here. The *Madonna and Child by *Luca della Robbia* (c 1445–50) is one of his most beautiful works. The Madonna enthroned is by *Piero di Cosimo*. In the long gallery, Bust of Cione Pollini (15C); *Jacopino del Conte* (attributed), Madonna of the Innocenti; *Giovanni di Francesco Toscani*, Triptych of the Madonna and Child with Saints.

The church of the *Santissima Annunziata (Pl.6;6; closed 12.30–16.00) was founded by the seven original Florentine members of the Servite Order in 1250, and rebuilt, along with the cloister, by *Michelozzo* and others in 1444–81.

Of the portico the central arch is ascribed to *Antonio da Sangallo*, the rest is by *Giovanni Battista Caccini* (1600). The middle door, over which is a lunette with an Annunciation in mosaic (very damaged) by *Davide Ghirlandaio*, admits to the **Atrium** or **Chiostrino dei Voti**, by *Manetti* (1447) from a design by *Michelozzo*. The series of frescoes on the walls are particularly interesting since most of them were painted in the second decade of the 16C by the leading painters of the time. They have suffered from humidity and have been detached and returned here after restoration. From right to left: *Rosso Fiorentino*, Assumption (1), a very early work; *Pontormo*, *Visitation (2; showing the influence of Andrea del Sarto); *Franciabigio*, Marriage of the Virgin (3; the head of the Virgin was damaged by the painter himself in a fit of anger). Beyond a marble bas-relief of the Madonna and Child by an unknown sculptor (sometimes attributed to *Michelozzo*), *Andrea del Sarto*, *Birth of the Virgin (4). The Coming of the Magi (5) contains *Andrea del Sarto*'s self-portrait in the right-hand corner. Here intervenes the great door, in front of which are two bronze stoups by *Antonio Susini* (1615). The colours in the fresco of the *Nativity (6) by *Alesso Baldovinetti* (1460–62) have faded because they were badly prepared by the artist. The landscape is particularly beautiful. Beyond the Vocation and Investiture of San Filippo Benizzi (7) by *Cosimo Rosselli* (1476) are more Scenes from the life of San Filippo Benizzi (8–12), interesting (but damaged) works by *Andrea del Sarto* (1509–10).

The heavily decorated and dark INTERIOR, has a rich ceiling by *Pietro Giambelli* (1664–69) on a design by *Volterrano*. The nave has stucco and painted decoration by *Cosimo Ulivelli, Francesco Silvani, Pier Dandini* and *Tommaso Redi* (c 1703). At the W end the shrine of the Madonna (13), highly venerated by Florentines, is bedecked with ex-votos, hanging lamps, and candles. The huge *Tabernacle (almost

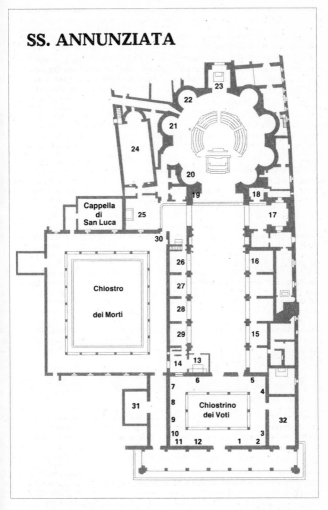

SS. ANNUNZIATA

hidden by the devotional images), commissioned by Piero il Gottoso (dei Medici), was designed by *Michelozzo* and executed by *Pagno di Lapo Portigiani* (1448–61). It has a bronze grille by *Maso di Bartolomeo*, and an incongruous 17C canopy. It protects a painting (also difficult to see) of the Annunciation, traditionally ascribed to a friar who was miraculously assisted by an angel. The adjoining chapel (14) was built as an oratory for the Medici (1453–63). It has five beautiful panels inlaid by the Opificio delle Pietre Dure (cf. p 127) in 1671 with the symbols of the Virgin (the rose, lily, moon, sun, and star). Here, amidst ex-votos, is a small painting by *Andrea del Sarto* of the Head of the Redeemer (1515).

SOUTH SIDE. 1st chapel, Altarpiece of the Madonna by *Empoli*, and vault frescoes by *Matteo Rosselli*; 2nd chapel (15), Crucifix in wood by *Antonio da Sangallo* (1483; removed for restoration); 3rd chapel, the Colloredo chapel, was designed by Matteo Nigetti in 1651. The frescoes in the cupola are by *Volterrano*; 5th chapel (16), Monument to Orlando de' Medici, a delicate work by *Bernardo Rossellino* (1456). In the transept chapel (17), erected on a design by *Ferdinando Fuga* in 1768, a small painted crucifix has recently been restored and attributed to *Andrea del Castagno*. In the next chapel (18), Dead Christ supported by Nicodemus, whose head is a self-portrait of the sculptor *Bandinelli* who is buried here. Behind the monument are the portraits of Bandinelli and his wife in relief. At the end of the aisle is a splendid organ (1521; being restored) by *Domenico di Lorenzo di Lucca*.

The large circular TRIBUNE at the E end of the church was begun by *Michelozzo* and completed in 1477 by *Leon Battista Alberti*, at the expense of Ludovico Gonzaga. It has a very unusual design, a rotonda preceded by a triumphal arch, derived from antique buildings. The huge fresco of the Coronation of the Virgin in the cupola (difficult to see) is by *Volterrano*. The high altar, with a frontal by *Giovanni Battista Foggini* (1682) bears a silver ciborium by *Antonio Merlini* 1656) on a design by *Alfonso Parigi*. Behind (difficult to see) are the choir stalls and two lecterns of English workmanship (15C). On the left of the great arch, in the pavement beneath a statue of St Peter by *Pier Francesco Silvani*, is the burial place of Andrea del Sarto. The *Tomb (19) of Bishop Angelo Marzi Medici, with an expressive effigy of the Bishop, charged with the fervour of the Counter Reformation, is signed by *Francesco da Sangallo* (1546).

The entrance to the nine semicircular chapels which radiate from the Sanctuary is on the left. In the chapel to the right (20), *Alessandro Allori*, Birth of Mary, and Miracles of the Blessed Manetti (one of the founders) by his son, *Cristofano Allori*. In the chapels to the left: Madonna and Saints after *Perugino* (21; removed for restoration); Resurrection by *Bronzino* and a wooden statue of St Roch by *Veit Stoss* (22). The E chapel (23) was reconstructed by *Giambologna* as his own tomb, and contains fine bronze reliefs and a bronze Crucifix by him, and statues by his pupils including *Francavilla*. The Madonna is attributed to *Bernardo Daddi*. Behind the altar, above the sarcophagus of Giambologna and Pietro Tacca, is a Pietà by *Ligozzi*.

The SACRISTY (24), with a fine vault, was built by *Pagno di Lapo* from Michelozzo's design. The chapel in the N transept (25) is also the work of *Michelozzo* (1445–47), covered in 1746 by trompe l'oeil frescoes. It contains a terracotta statue of the Baptist by *Michelozzo* and a Deposition painted by *Ferdinando Folchi* (1855). A door here admits to the cloisters (see below).—The 4th chapel on the N side of the nave (26) contains an Assumption by *Perugino*; 3rd chapel (27), Crucifixion by *Giovanni Stradano*. The Last Judgement by *Alessandro Allori* is a copy of various figures in Michelangelo's fresco in the Sistine Chapel. 2nd chapel (28) *Holy Trinity with St Jerome, a fresco by *Andrea del Castagno*; the Cappella Feroni (29), with elaborate Baroque decoration by *Giovanni Battista Foggini* (1692), contains another fresco by *Castagno*, *St Julian and the Saviour.

The **Chiostro dei Morti**, with its memorial stones, is entered from the door in the N transept of the church (unlocked on request in the Sacristy). Over the door (30) is the so-called *Madonna del Sacco (from the sack on which St Joseph is leaning), an original portrayal of the Rest on the Flight into Egypt. It is one of *Andrea del Sarto's* best works. The other colourful frescoed lunettes (recently restored; others will be returned here after restoration) in the cloister are by *Donato Mascagni, Bernardino Poccetti, Matteo Rosselli*, and *Ventura Salimbeni*. They illustrate the origins of the Servite order and are interesting documents of 17C Florence.—The CAPPELLA DI SAN LUCA (opened on request in the sacristy) has belonged to the Accademia delle Arti del Disegno since 1565 (cf. p 209); a special Mass for artists is held on St Luke's Day. In the vault below are buried Cellini, Pontormo, Franciabigio, Montorsoli, Bartolini, and many other artists. In the vestibule is a Crucifix attributed to *Antonio da Sangallo* and a 15C sinopia of the Madonna enthroned. The chapel altarpiece of St Luke painting the Madonna is an interesting self-portrait by *Vasari*, a founder member of the Academy. On the left wall is a detached (and damaged) fresco by *Pontormo* of the Madonna with Saints (including St Lucy). On the right wall is a fresco of the Trinity by *Alessandro Allori*. On the W wall, *Santi di Tito*, Allegory of Architecture. The ceiling fresco of the Vision of St Bernard is by *Luca Giordano*. The clay statues which lean dramatically out of their niches are the work of various Academicians, including *Montorsoli* (who was also a member of the Servite Order). The little organ (1702) was made by Tommaso Fabbri da Faenza.—In the REFECTORY (no adm.) are sketches made in 1358 by *Francesco Talenti* and *Giovanni di Lapo Ghini* for the columns and capitals in the Duomo and a fresco by Santi di Tito.—In the 17C SAGRESTIA DELLA MADONNA (31), also off the cloister, is an Assumption by *Jacopo Vignali*.—The ORATORIO DI SAN SEBASTIANO (32; usually closed), entered from the portico (right of the Atrium) has a vault fresco by *Poccetti*.—The convent also owns a rich treasury (works of art from the 13–19C).

Via della Colonna leads out of Piazza Santissima Annunziata beneath an archway and skirts *Palazzo della Crocetta*, with its garden. This was built for the grand-duchess Maria Maddalena of Austria in 1620, probably by Giulio Parigi. It has been the home since 1879 of the ***Museo Archeologico** (Pl.7;5; entrance at No. 38; adm. see p 61). which includes one of the most important collections of Etruscan antiquities in existence. The Etruscan Topographical Museum on the ground floor has been closed since 1966 when it was severely damaged in the flood (although some of the more important objects which have been restored are temporarily displayed). The other collections have been in the course of rearrangement for many years, and parts of the museum are often closed.

Many of the most precious objects in the Etruscan Museum, founded in 1870, came from the Medici collections. The Etruscan topographical museum was inaugurated in 1897 by Luigi Adriano Milani. The Egyptian Museum was founded by Leopold II after the Egyptian expedition in 1828–29 organised by François Champollion and Ippolito Rosellini. In 1845 Leopold II also acquired the François vase.

GROUND FLOOR. The small rooms at the foot of the staircase display recently-restored objects from the collections. In the first room is the famous *François Vase, a huge Attic krater made by Ergotimos and painted by Kleitias in Athens (signed; c 570 BC). It was discovered by Alessandro François in an Etruscan tomb at Fonte Rotella, Chiusi in 1845. It had to be restored after it was broken in 1900, and in 1973 it was again reconstructed. It was used at banquets for mixing water with wine. It is decorated with six rows of exquisite black-figure paintings of mythological scenes, identified by inscriptions.—The next room displays important Etruscan works of the 5C BC, recently restored: the stone cover of a cinerary urn from Chianciano (showing Classical influence), an alabaster cinerary urn from near Chiusi, and the famous 'Mater Matuta', a tomb statue of an Etruscan woman on a throne holding a baby.—The adjoining room displays two fine kourai acquired by Milani in 1902. The date of the larger one, known as Apollo, is given by some scholars as 570 BC and by others as 510 BC. The 'Apollino' dates instead from the late 6C BC. Also here is an interesting classical relief showing the niobids.—The rooms beyond are used for exhibitions.

FIRST FLOOR. At the top of the stair is a painting by Giuseppe Angelelli of 1830 showing members of the Franco-Tuscan expedition to Egypt (see above). The **Egyptian Museum** is slowly being rearranged and relabelled; only some rooms have so far been completed. The contents of the other rooms may be moved round when they are modernised. The decoration of the rooms, in Egyptian style, was carried out in 1881–94. ROOM IIA. Prehistoric objects; two fine polychrome statuettes (restored): maidservant preparing yeast for beer, and maidservant kneading dough (2625–2475 BC); material of the XIIth Dynasty (19C BC), including part of a granite statue of a Pharaoh.—R. IIB. Bas-reliefs including one with the plan of a tomb preceded by a courtyard (14C BC); one showing craftsmen at work (7–6C BC); polychrome relief for the tomb of Seti I, representing the goddess Ma'at and Hathor, and the Pharaoh (c 1292 BC); scribes recording objects (fragment; c 1400 BC).—ROOMS III–VIII. Very rare Hittite *Chariot in wood and bone from a Theban tomb of the 14C BC (probably used by the defunct in his lifetime); sarcophagi, mummies, canopic vases, papyri, stelae, and Coptic fabrics; statuettes in limestone and wood; portrait of a young woman, from the Flavian period; statuettes of divinities; amulets, scarabs; plant ornaments; vases and necklaces.

The **Etrusco-Greco-Roman Museum** (partly closed for many years) occupies ROOMS IX–XXII of the First Floor and the whole of the Second Floor. FIRST FLOOR: Etruscan sculpture. ROOM IX. Urns with mythological subjects and from the heroic cycles of the Greek world; in the centre, alabaster sarcophagus from Tarquinia (4C BC) with tempera paintings of a battle between the Greeks and Amazons.—R. X. Sculptured urns, sarcophagi, and statues; urn in the form of an Etruscan house; urn with banqueting and dancing scene; lid of a sarcophagus with an obese Etruscan.

Etruscan, Greek, and Roman bronzes (left). ROOM XI. Etruscan inscribed mirrors and decorative bronzes.—R. XII. Small Greek and Roman bronzes; Roman and Christian lamps; urn with the symbolic ship of the Church.—R. XIII. The *Idolino, a remarkable bronze statue of a young athlete offering a libation, probably a Roman copy of a Greek original by Polykleitos of c 420 BC found at Pesaro in 1530; the base is of 16C workmanship. It is justly the most famous work in the collection. Torso of an athlete, a Greek original of the 6–5C BC. The *Horse's Head probably came from a Greek quadriga group of the late Hellenistic period. It is thought that both Verrocchio and Donatello saw it in the garden of the Palazzo Medici-Riccardi before executing their equestrian statues.—R. XIV, the Long Gallery, contains important Etruscan monumental bronzes. The Minerva from Arezzo is a copy (considerably restored) of a 5C Greek work. The *Chimera, also from Arezzo (found in 1553 and acquired by Cosimo I) probably dates from 380–360 BC. It is a fantastical animal, with the body and head of a lion, the head of a ram (on its back), and a serpent's tail (restored). The *Arringatore, or Orator in a toga, dedicated to Aulus Metullus, was found near Perugia in 1566 and also acquired by Cosimo I. It is the only known Etruscan monumental bronze of the late Hellenistic period. R. XV. Bronze fittings, arms, and various instruments; incribed bronzes and seals, among them the well-known Seal of Magliano, which has a double inscription showing names of divinities and ritual prescriptions.

SECOND FLOOR (often closed). Here the exhibits are poorly labelled and crowded into old-fashioned showcases. PREHISTORIC COLLECTION. In two rooms to the right; objects of the Rinaldone culture, and finds from Campiglia d'Orcia, Populonia, and Montemercano.—ITALIC AND MEDITERRANEAN COMPARISONS. R. III. Examples of the civilisation of Central Italy, including the bronze cap-shaped helmet, chased by Oppeano of Este.—R. IV. Cypriot ceramics and sculpture; antiquities from Asia Minor.—R. V. Cretan ware bronzes.—Vases and Terracottas. R. VI. Vases from Greece and Rhodes, including a huge amphora.—R. VII (with an unusual view of the cupola of the Duomo). Decorated ceramics of the various Greek factories under Oriental influence.—R. VIII. Primitive Italic and Etruscan vases of impasto and black bucchero ware of the 9–8C BC.—R. IX. Etruscan vases of impasto and bucchero ware (7–6C BC).—R. X. Etruscan bucchero ware of the 6–5C BC.

ROOMS XI–XII. GREEK VASES in painted terracotta, with Etruscan imitations, a series largely dating from the finest period of the art, and important for the perfection of the paintings (some of which may be assigned to the school of Polygnotos) and for the light they throw on Greek mythology.—ROOM XII contains two well-known vases from Populonia and various vessels.—R. XIII. Etruscan vases in imitation of the Attic, and Faliscan vases from Southern Italy.—R. XIV. Late Italic vases (3C–1C BC).—R. XV. Etruscan and Roman terracottas.

From Room VI is the entrance to RR. XVII and XVIII which contain reproductions of tomb frescoes of Etruria, and the Tomb of Larthia Scianti, in polychrome terracotta, with a reclining effigy of the deceased. A room containing a complete gilt bronze armour is normally kept closed.—In the garden (not usually open) are reconstructed Etruscan tombs.

The COIN ROOMS (ancient Greek and Roman coins, Medieval and modern Italian coins, especially from Tuscany) and the COLLECTION OF PRECIOUS STONES are visible only with special permission. The latter includes gems, cameos (head of Alexander the Great and Olympia), vitreous paste (*Unguent box of Torrita), silver (bowl with Bacchus, Pan, Ariadne, and Silenus; shield of Flavius Ardaburius Aspar), a silver situla from Chiusi, the *Mirror of Bomarzo, and the seal-ring of Augustus, in gold and jasper, found in his mausoleum. A precious collection of Greek, Etruscan, and Roman sculpture is also on view to students with special permission.

In the same building is the INSTITUTE OF ETRUSCAN AND ITALIC STUDIES, with an extensive library.

10 San Marco, Palazzo Medici-Riccardi, and San Lorenzo

Piazza San Marco (Pl.6;6), one of the liveliest squares in the city with several cafés, is a meeting-place for students of the University and Academy of Art, both of which have their headquarters here. In the garden is a statue of general Manfredo Fanti by Pio Fedi (1873). On one corner is the *Loggia dell'Ospedale di San Matteo, one of the oldest porticoes in Florence (1384). The seven arches may have inspired Brunelleschi's Loggia degli Innocenti (p 129). This is now the seat of the ACCADEMIA DI BELLE ARTI, an art school opened in 1784 by the Grand-Duke Pietro Leopoldo, but formerly part of the Accademia delle Arti del Disegno, founded more than two centuries earlier (cf. p 209).

Over the three doors are fine Della Robbian lunettes. The Mannerist courtyard has unusual columns. A tabernacle with the Rest on the Flight into Egypt, one of the best works of Giovanni di San Giovanni, is preserved in a classroom (sometimes shown on request). The famous Gallery of the Accademia is in the adjoining building (entrance at No. 60 Via Ricasoli; see Rte 9).

Across Via Cesare Battisti (in which, at No. 10–12, is the remarkable cartographic library of the Istituto Geografico Militare) are the administrative

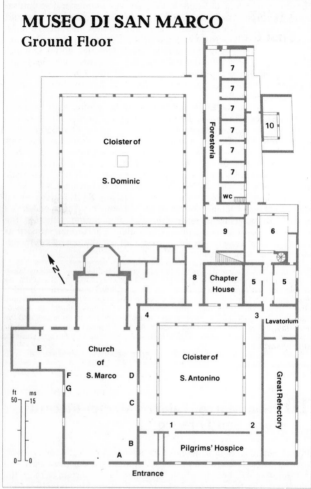

offices of the University of Florence, next to which (entrance on Via Micheli or at No. 4 Via La Pira) is the **Giardino dei Semplici** (Pl.6;4; adm. see p 60), on the site of a botanical garden laid out here in 1545–46 by Tribolo for Cosimo I. It contains medicinal plants, Tuscan flora, azaleas, irises, water plants, coniferous trees, yews, and cork trees. In the greenhouses are tropical plants, palms, ferns, orchids, and citrus fruits.—At No. 4 is the entrance to the Natural History study collections (adm. see p 61) of the University (moved here from Via Romana at the end of the 19C; see p 201). The *Botanical Museum* is the most important in Italy, with some 4 million specimens, the Central Italian Herbarium, the Andrea Cesalpino Herbarium (1563), one of the oldest in the world, and the Philip Barker Webb Herbarium (1854), which contains plants collected by Charles Darwin on his first voyage in 'The Beagle'. The *Museum of Minerals* includes samples of minerals and rocks from Elba, the Medici collection of worked stones, and a huge Brazilian topaz weighing 151kg. The *Geological and Palaeontological Museum*, the largest and most important in Italy, includes interesting material from the grand-ducal collections: vertebrates, skeletons of

MUSEO DI SAN MARCO
First Floor

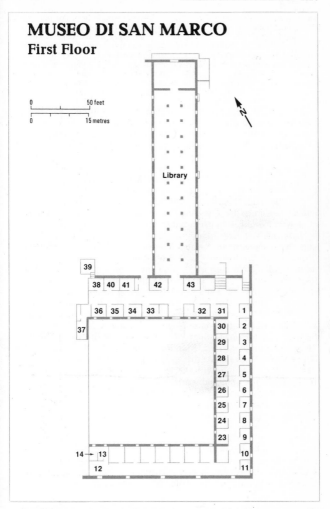

0 ——— 50 feet
0 ——— 15 metres

Library

mammals from the Lower Pleistocene period in Tuscany, a gallery of invertebrates and plants, and a research section.

On the other side of Via La Pira (No. 26 Via Micheli) is the *Waldensian church*
on the site of a church set up by the Anglican community of Florence in 1846. In
1903 the present neo-Gothic church of the Holy Trinity, with stained glass
windows, was erected by G.A. Bodley and C. Hare, owned since 1967 by the
Waldensian community.

The N side of the square is occupied by the Dominican church and
convent of San Marco, which contains the ***Museo di San Marco**
(Pl.6;6; adm. see p 62), famous for its works by the 'Blessed' Fra'
Angelico. The ground floor is still in the course of arrangement, so
that when completed more rooms and the small cloisters of the
monastery will be accessible to the public.

The convent was favoured by Cosimo il Vecchio who ordered *Michelozzo* to enlarge the buildings (1437–52), and who here founded a public library, the first of its kind in Europe. The founding prior, Antonino Pierozzi (1389–1459), was made archbishop of Florence in 1446, and was later canonised. Another famous defender of Republican values, Girolamo Savonarola (1452–98), a native of Ferrara, became prior in 1491. His dramatic preachings ended when he was burnt at the stake in Piazza della Signoria seven years later (cf. p 85). The painters Fra' Angelico and Fra' Bartolomeo were both friars here.

The beautiful **Cloister of St Antonino**, with broad arches and delicate Ionic capitals, was built by *Michelozzo*. In the centre is a venerable cedar of Lebanon. In the lunettes are scenes from the life of St Antonino, by *Bernardino Poccetti* and other painters of the 17C (being restored). In the corners are frescoes by *Fra' Angelico*: St Thomas Aquinas (1; very worn); Christ as a Pilgrim welcomed by two Dominicans (2); Pietà (3; restored); *St Dominic at the foot of the Cross, and a lunette of St Peter Martyr enjoining silence (4).

The **Pilgrims' Hospice**, by *Michelozzo*, contains a superb collection of paintings by *Fra' Angelico*, many of them from Florentine churches: *Deposition (from Santa Trìnita, c 1435–40; the cusps are by *Lorenzo Monaco*); Madonna and Child with St John the Baptist and three Dominican Saints; a predella with the Marriage and Dormition of the Virgin; *Last Judgement (1431; from Santa Maria degli Angioli); Naming of St John the Baptist (c 1430–32); Panels from the Life of Christ (including the *Flight into Egypt). These served as cupboard doors in the Santissima Annunziata. The Marriage at Cana, Baptism of Christ, and the Transfiguration are attributed to *Alesso Baldovinetti*. *Madonna 'della Stella' (a little tabernacle from Santa Maria Novella); Madonna and Child (possibly from the Certosa of Galluzzo); *Deposition (of the Compagnia del Tempio). *Zanobi Strozzi*, Madonna and Child with Angels (from Santa Maria Nuova).—At the end of the room is the famous *Tabernacle of the Linaiuoli, with the Madonna enthroned with Saints, by *Fra' Angelico*, commissioned by the flax-workers guild in 1433 for their headquarters. The beautiful marble frame was designed by *Ghiberti*.—*Fra' Angelico*, Pala 'del Bosco ai Frati' (c 1450); two tiny roundels with the Crucifixion and Coronation of the Virgin; Coronation of the Virgin (a tabernacle from Santa Maria Novella); Madonna enthroned with Saints painted for the high altar of the church of San Marco (c 1438–40), with two scenes (removed for restoration) from the predella of Saints Cosmas and Damian (one showing a leg transplant); Annunciation and Adoration of the Magi (a tabernacle from Santa Maria Novella); Pala 'di Annalena'.

The **Great Refectory** has been restored (but is not always open). In the LAVATORIUM is a Crucifixion with Saints Nicholas of Bari and Francis, by *Fra' Angelico*, a Della Robbian tabernacle, a damaged frescoed lunette of the Madonna and Child attributed to *Paolo Uccello*, and four Saints beneath an Annunciation by *Fra Angelico* (from the Certosa di Galluzzo; to be restored). The Great Refectory contains 16C and 17C works by *Giovanni Antonio Sogliani*, *Fra' Paolino*, *Jacopo Vignali*, *Lorenzo Lippi*, *Jacopo Ligozzi*, and others. On the end wall is a fresco of St Dominic and his brethren fed by Angels by *Sogliani* (1536). From the Lavatorium, a door leads into two more rooms (5; sometimes closed) with more works by *Fra' Bartolomeo*, including a large Madonna with St Anne and other Saints in monochrome, a large detached fresco (very ruined, but restored) of the Last Judgement, and heads of Saints and a tondo of the Madonna and Child. In the room on the left are 15C paintings and frescoes including a processional standard by *Baldovinetti*, a Madonna and Child with two angels by *Cosimo Rosselli*, a predella by *Benozzo Gozzoli*, and works by *Antoniazzo Romano* and *Bartolomeo Caporali*.

From the small cloister ('delle Spese'; 6) beyond there is access (open only in summer) to the MUSEO DI FIRENZE ANTICA (otherwise approached from the Small Refectory, see below). This is still being arranged in the cells of the FORESTERIA (7; guest-quarters of the convent, some of them with a lunette over the door by *Fra' Bartolomeo*). So far only the corridor is open. Here was collected the material salvaged from the demolition at the end of the 19C of the Mercato Vecchio and part of the Ghetto (the central part of this area of the city is now occupied by Piazza della Repubblica; cf. p 82). This includes numerous architectural fragments dating from the medieval and early Renaissance periods. The arrangement of 1904 has been preserved but the rooms have been restored. Material from the Sepolcreto di San Pancrazio is to be arranged in the Chiostrino dei Silvestrini (10).

Chapter House. *Crucifixion and Saints, a large fresco by *Fra' Angelico* and assistants (1441–42). The convent bell is in the style of Donatello.—To the left a door gives access to a corridor (8) with a wood crucifix from the church of San Marco attributed to *Baccio da Montelupo*. At the end may be seen the CLOISTER OF ST DOMINIC (no adm.), also by *Michelozzo*, with early 18C frescoes by *Alessandro Gherardini*, *Cosimo Ulivelli*, and others. To the left, at the foot of the stairs up to the Dormitory, is the **Small Refectory** (9) with a charming Last Supper frescoed by *Domenico Ghirlandaio* and his workshop, and Della Robbian terracottas. From here there is access to the *Foresteria* (see above).

FIRST FLOOR. The *Dormitory consists of 44 small monastic cells beneath a huge wood roof, each with their own vault and adorned with an intimate fresco by *Fra' Angelico* and his assistants. It is still uncertain how many of the frescoes are by the hand of the master alone, and how many are by artists (whose names are unknown) employed in his studio. Others are attributed to *Zanobi Strozzi* and *Benozzo Gozzoli*. All the frescoes have recently been beautifully restored, and the colour of the original plasterwork has been returned to the walls of the cells and corridors. At the head of the staircase is the *Annunciation, justly one of the most famous works by Angelico. In the cells (beginning to the left): 1. *'Noli me tangere'; 3. *Annunciation; 5. Nativity (perhaps with the help of an assistant); 6. *Transfiguration; 7. Mocking of Christ in the presence of the Madonnna and St Dominic (perhaps with the help of an assistant); 8. Marys at the Sepulchre; 9. *Coronation of the Virgin; 10. Presentation in the Temple; 11. Madonna and Child with Saints (probably by an assistant).—At the end of the next corridor (closed for restoration) are the rooms (12–14) occupied by Savonarola as prior, with some mementoes and his *Portrait (with the attributes of St Peter Martyr; c 1497), by his supporter and fellow friar, *Fra' Bartolomeo*. The other cells in this corridor have frescoes of Christ on the Cross by followers of Fra' Angelico.—Cells 23–29 are frescoed by assistants, while on the wall outside in the corridor is a *Madonna enthroned with Saints attributed to the master himself.—In the third corridor is the Cell (31; if closed, sometimes opened on request) of St Antonino, with Christ in Limbo by an assistant of Angelico, who also probably painted the scenes in the next four cells (32–35) showing the Sermon on the Mount, Arrest of Christ, Agony in the Garden, and the Institution of the Eucharist. Cell 36 has an unusual scene of Christ being nailed to the Cross. Cells 38 and 39 were occupied by Cosimo il Vecchio in retreat; the Adoration of the Magi, designed by Angelico, was restored in the 19C. Cells 40–43 have worn frescoes of the Crucifixion by Angelico's workshop.—The *LIBRARY, a light and delicate hall by *Michelozzo* (1441), is one of the most pleasing architectural works of the Florentine Renaissance. It contains illuminated choirbooks

and psalters (mostly 15–16C), and a missal illuminated by Fra'
Angelico as a young man (not always on display).

The church of **San Marco** (Pl.6;6), founded in 1299, and rebuilt with
the rest of the convent in 1442, received its present form in 1588 on a
design by *Giambologna*. The façade dates from 1780.

INTERIOR (see Plan). On the W wall, 14C fresco of the Annunciation (A), a
version of the famous fresco in the Annunziata (see p 131), and, above the door,
a painted Crucifix in the style of Giotto. Right side: Ecce Homo (B), a devotional
figure in wood of the 16C; 2nd altar (C), *Fra' Bartolomeo*, *Madonna and six
Saints (1509; showing the influence of Raphael); 3rd altar (D), *Madonna in
prayer, a remarkable 8C mosaic which had to be cut into two pieces for its
journey from Constantinople.—The tribune was added in 1678 by *Pier Francesco Silvani*; the decoration by *Alessandro Gherardini* dates from 1717. A
small painted Crucifix by *Fra' Angelico* was placed here in 1984.—The CHAPEL
OF ST ANTONINO (E; which contains his body) was designed by *Giambologna*
and was decorated by his contemporaries: in the vestibule are frescoes by
Passignano; the bronze reliefs are by *Giambologna* and *Francavilla*; the
altarpiece of the Descent into Limbo is by *Alessandro Allori*; to the right is the
Calling of St Matthew, by *Battista Naldini*; and to the left, Healing of the Leper,
by *Francesco Morandini*.—On the 3rd altar on the left side (F) is an altarpiece by
Cigoli. On the wall are the tomb-slabs (G) of the great humanist scholar Pico
della Mirandola (1463–94), and of his friend, the poet Politian (Angelo
Ambrogini, 1454–94). On the W wall is an interesting painting of the Transfiguration.

From the N side of Piazza San Marco runs VIA CAVOUR (Pl.6;6) in which, on the
left, is the *Casino Mediceo*, built by Buontalenti (1568–74), and now occupied
by the law courts. A worn plaque on the garden wall records the site of the
Medici Garden here where Cosimo il Vecchio and Lorenzo il Magnifico
collected antique sculpture, and where Bertoldo held a school of art. At No. 69,
beyond, is the *Chiostro dello Scalzo (Pl.6;4; adm. see p 60; ring), a charming
little cloister of the early 16C, with very fine *Frescoes in monochrome, by
Andrea del Sarto (c 1507–26) of the life of St John the Baptist, beneath
decorative friezes also by him. The scenes were not painted in the chronological
order of the story, and two of them were painted by Franciabigio when del Sarto
left for France; but he returned to complete the cycle. To the right of the door:
Faith, c 1523; Angel announcing the birth of the Baptist to St Zacharias
(1523).—Visitation (1524); Naming of the Baptist (1526); Blessing of the young
St John before leaving for the desert (by Franciabigio, 1518–19); Meeting of
Christ with the young St John (Franciabigio, 1518–19).—The scenes on the end
wall are almost totally ruined (Baptism of Christ, c 1507–8, and the Preaching of
the Baptist, 1515).—Baptism of the multitude (1517); Capture of the Baptist
(1517); Dance of Salome (1521); Beheading of the Baptist (1523).—On the
entrance wall, Banquet of Herod (1523).—The terracotta bust of St Antonino
dates from the early 16C.

From Piazza San Marco Via Cavour leads in the other direction S towards the
Duomo. On the right is the *Biblioteca Marucelliana* (Pl.6;6), founded by
Francesco di Alessandro Marucelli (1625–1703) and opened to the public in
1752. On the other side of the road are two palaces (Nos 22 and 4) by Gherardo
Silvani. Opposite Palazzo Medici-Riccardi (see below), on the bend of the road,
is Palazzo del Cardinale Panciatichi, by Antonio Ferri (1696). Set back from the
road, at the beginning of Via de' Martelli is the little church of **San Giovannino
degli Scolopi** (Pl.6;2), begun by Ammannati in 1579. The 4th chapel on the
right was built in 1692–1712 for the grand-duke Cosimo III. The altarpiece of
the Preaching of St Francis Xavier is the best work of Francesco Curradi. The
vault fresco is by Pier Dandini and the stucco angels by Girolamo Ticciati. The
1st chapel on the left has Angels, Jacob's Dream, and the Fall of Lucifer, by
Jacopo Ligozzi. The 2nd chapel on the left was designed by Ammannati as his
burial place (1592); the altarpiece is by Alessandro Allori. The confessionals
date from the late 17C.

From Piazza San Marco Via degli Arazzieri (the site of the Florentine
tapestry factory) leads into Via XXVII Aprile. Here on the left is the
former convent of **Sant'Apollonia** (Pl.6;4; adm. see p 60), founded in
1339 and enlarged in 1445. The vestibule contains works by *Paolo
Schiavo*, and *Neri di Bicci*. In the Refectory is a *Last Supper, the

masterpiece *of Andrea del Castagno* c 1450; recently restor
an unusual painted marble 'loggia'. Above are equally fine ...coves
(much ruined) also by him, of the Crucifixion, Deposition, and
Resurrection. The sinopia is displayed on the opposite wall. Among
other frescoes by him displayed here are lunettes with the Crucifixion between the Madonna and Saints, and a Pietà with two angels.
The sinopia is from his fresco of St Jerome in Santissima Annunziata.
The large wooden Crucifix is by *Raffaello da Montelupo*.

VIA SAN GALLO (Pl.6;4) leads towards Piazza della Libertà (Rte 22). To the right
is the church of *Gesù Pellegrino* (or Oratorio dei Pretoni; usually closed), rebuilt
in 1588 by Giovanni Antonio Dosio with a fresco cycle of 1590 and three
altarpieces by Giovanni Balducci (Il Cosci). In the nave is the tomb slab of the
Pievano Arlotto (1400–84), rector of the church, with an amusing inscription. To
the right is the *Loggia dei Tessitori*, part of the weavers' guild-house (c 1500; the
columns have been poorly restored). Farther on (No. 66) is the church of **San
Giovannino dei Cavalieri** (Pl.6;4; usually closed), preceded by an unusual
vestibule, with original cupboards. In the tribune, surrounded by worn frescoes
of 1703 by Alessandro Gherardini, is a large Crucifixion by Lorenzo Monaco. At
the end of the right aisle is an Annunciation, a good painting by the 'Master of
the Castello Nativity'. On the right wall is a worn fresco of St Michael Archangel
by Francesco Granacci. In the left aisle is a Nativity by Bicci di Lorenzo, and a
Coronation of the Virgin by his son, Neri di Bicci. On the W wall, Birth of the
Baptist, by Santi di Tito, and Beheading of the Baptist by Pier Dandini. The two
altars in the nave are attributed to Giovanni Tedesco.—Beyond is *Palazzo
Pandolfini* (No. 74), built as a villa on the outskirts of the town for Bishop
Giannozzo Pandolfini with a terrace on the first floor, and a big garden and
orchard. It was designed by Raphael (the most important architectural work by
him to survive), and executed by Giovanni Francesco and Aristotile da Sangallo
(1516–20). When the 'Portone' is open the pretty garden façade can be seen.—
Farther on, at No. 110, is the church of *Sant'Agata* (used by the Military hospital
and rarely open), with a façade designed by Allori in 1592, who also painted the
high altarpiece of the Marriage at Cana (in a handsome frame). The church also
contains frescoes by Giovanni Bizzelli, and paintings attributed to Lorenzo di
Credi, Lorenzo Lippi, and Neri di Bicci.

Via San Gallo leads S from Via XXVII Aprile. On the left (No. 10) is
Palazzo Marucelli, built by Gherardo Silvani c 1630. The coat-of-
arms over the elaborate doorway (with sculptured caryatids by
Raffaello Curradi) was set up by its later owner Emanuele Fenzi
(1784–1875), a banker who financed the Florence–Livorno railway.
Across Via Guelfa VIA DE' GINORI (Pl.6;5,6) continues, lined with a
number of fine palaces on the right. No. 15, *Palazzo Taddei* was built
by Baccio d'Agnolo for the merchant Taddei who commissioned from
Michelangelo the tondo which now bears his name and is owned by
the Royal Academy, London. Raphael, while staying here as a friend
of the family in 1505 saw and copied the tondo (the plaque is on the
wrong house). The tabernacle in Via Taddei has a Crucifixion by
Giovanni Antonio Sogliani. *Palazzo Ginori* (No. 11; Pl.6;5) is also
attributed to Baccio d'Agnolo (c 1516–20). *Palazzo Montauto* (No. 9)
has remains of 15C graffiti and two ground-floor windows attributed
to Ammannati. Diotisalvi Neroni lived at *Palazzo Neroni* (No. 7; with
pronounced rustication) before his exile as an enemy of the Medici in
1466. On the left (No. 14) is the entrance to the BIBLIOTECA RICCAR-
DIANA founded by Riccardo Riccardi and opened to the public in
1718 (open weekdays 8–14; closed Easter week and the last half of
August). It is a fine example of a private library, with a delightful
reading room frescoed by Luca Giordano. The original bookshelves
contain illuminated MSS. and incunabula. It forms part of the 17C
extension of Palazzo Medici-Riccardi which stands on the corner

of Piazza San Lorenzo (see below). Via Gori leads left, skirting its imposing flank.

•Palazzo Medici-Riccardi (Pl.16; 2; entrance on Via Cavour) is now the seat of the Prefect. This town mansion on Via Larga (renamed Via Cavour) was built for Cosimo il Vecchio by *Michelozzo* after 1444, and was the residence of the Medici until 1540 when Cosimo I moved into Palazzo Vecchio. Its rusticated façade served as a model for other famous Florentine palaces, including those built by the Strozzi and Pitti. Charles VIII of France stayed here in 1494 and the Emperor Charles V in 1536. It was bought by the Riccardi in 1659 and before the end of the century was extended towards Via de' Ginori, and the façade on Via Cavour was lengthened by seven bays.

The dignified COURTYARD, with composite colonnades, is decorated with medallions ascribed to *Bertoldo*, inspired by antique gems. Some ancient sculptures, mainly Roman, are preserved here and in the pretty second court. The first door on the right gives access to the staircase which leads up to the dark little **•Chapel** (closed for restoration, but for admission times when it reopens, see p 62), the only unaltered part of *Michelozzo*'s work, with a beautiful ceiling and marble inlaid floor. The walls are entirely covered with decorative •Frescoes, the masterpiece of *Benozzo Gozzoli* (1459–60), of the Procession of the Magi to Bethlehem. It is one of the most pleasing, even if not one of the most important fresco cycles of the Renaissance. It was commissioned by Piero di Cosimo. It is thought the vividly coloured frescoes must have been painted before the altar wall was bricked up in order to make use of the daylight (details of the frescoes are illuminated on request by the custodian). The decorative cavalcade is shown in a charming landscape with hunting scenes. The personalities of the Medici family are shown with their emblem of the three ostrich feathers.

The procession is seen approaching along the distant hills on the right wall. The figures in the foreground are led by the third King, perhaps an idealised portrait of Lorenzo il Magnifico, on a splendid grey charger. In the crowd behind on the extreme left, can be seen Benozzo Gozzoli's self-portrait, with his signature in gold lettering on his red beret.—On the wall opposite the altar is the second King in splendid Oriental dress.—On the last wall, the painting of the first King (seated on a mule) was cut in two when the wall was moved to accommodate the staircase in the 17C.—On either side of the altar are beautiful landscapes with angels, recalling those of the painter's master, Fra' Angelico. The altarpiece is a copy by Pseudo Pier Francesco Fiorentino of a Madonna by Filippo Lippi.

The next door on the right in the courtyard admits to the stairs up to the first-floor •GALLERY (lift), an elaborate Baroque loggia (1670–88) covered by a fresco of the Apotheosis of the second Medici dynasty, by *Luca Giordano* (1683). The stucco decoration was designed by *Giovanni Battista Foggini*. The four painted mirrors are by *Antonio Domenico Gabbiani, Bartolomeo Bimbi,* and *Pandolfo Reschi.* A beautiful painting of the Madonna and Child by *Filippo Lippi* is exhibited here.—In the former private apartments of the Medici, on the ground floor, important exhibitions are now held. The *Medici Museum,* with a collection of portraits and memorials to the Medici family, has been closed indefinitely.

The back of Palazzo Medici-Riccardi stands on the corner of PIAZZA SAN LORENZO (Pl.16;2), filled with a busy street market (open all day except Monday in winter and Saturday in summer); the stalls have leather-goods, clothing, straw, jewellery, etc. for sale (and they continue the length of Via dell'Ariento, see below). The seated statue

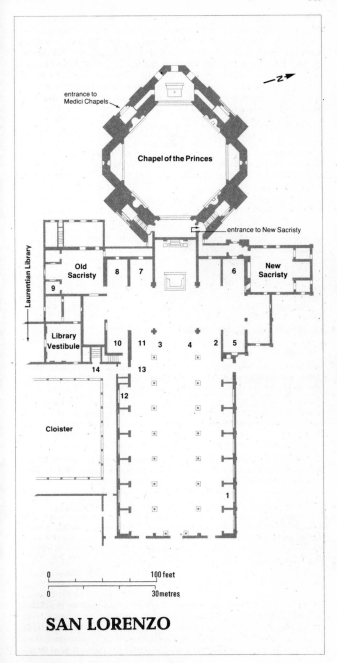

SAN LORENZO

of Giovanni delle Bande Nere is by Baccio Bandinelli (1540). The long façade (14–15C) of Palazzo della Stufa (No. 4) overlooks the piazza. Above the market awnings rises the pretty flank of the church with the large dome of the Chapel of the Princes, and the smaller cupola of the New Sacristy, and the campanile (1740). *San Lorenzo (Pl.16;1; closed 12.00–15.30) was intimately connected with the Medici after they commissioned *Brunelleschi* to rebuild it in 1425–46. It is the burial place of all the principal members of the family from Cosimo il Vecchio to Cosimo III.

A basilica on this site, outside the walls, was consecrated by St Ambrose of Milan in 393, thought to be the earliest church in Florence. The church of St Zenobius, the most famous Bishop of Florence, it served as cathedral of the city before the bishop's seat was transferred, probably in the late 7C, to Santa Reparata (on the site of the present cathedral). Michelangelo spent much time in designing a grandiose façade by order of Leo X (his model survives in the Casa Buonarroti, cf. p 181), but only the interior façade was ever built; the exterior remains in rough-hewn brick. On 14 July 1564 a solemn memorial service was held here in honour of the 'divine' Michelangelo, organised by the Accademia del Disegno.

The grey cruciform INTERIOR, built with pietra serena, with pulvins above the Corinthian columns in pietra forte, is one of the earliest and most harmonious architectural works of the Renaissance. It was completed on Brunelleschi's design by *Antonio Manetti* (1447–60) and *Pagno di Lapo Portigiani* (1463). In the right aisle (2nd chapel; 1), *Rosso Fiorentino*, *Marriage of the Virgin (1523); gothic tomb-slab of the organist Francesco Landini (1398). At the end of this aisle is a *Tabernacle (2) by *Desiderio da Settignano*, of extremely fine workmanship. In the nave are two bronze *Pulpits (3 and 4; raised on columns in the 17C) by *Donatello* (c 1460). These were his last works and they were finished by his pupils *Bertoldo* and *Bartolomeo Bellano*.

The beautifully carved panels have a border of classical motifs around the top. Many of the scenes are crowded and grim and present a unique iconography. The pulpit on the N side (3) shows the Agony in the Garden, St John the Evangelist and the Flagellation (these last two both 17C imitations in wood); Christ before Pilate and Christ before Caiaphas; the Crucifixion and Lamentation over the Dead Christ; and the Entombment. The pulpit on the S side (4) shows the Marys at the Sepulchre; Christ in Limbo, the Resurrection, and Christ appearing to the Apostles; Pentecost; the Martyrdom of St Lawrence, St Luke and the Mocking of Christ (the last two both 17C imitations in wood).

Beneath the dome three grilles in the pavement and a simple inscription with the Medici arms mark the grave of Cosimo Il Vecchio 'Pater Patriae' (died 1464). The high altar in pietre dure of 1787 incorporates a panel of the Fall of Manna designed by *Bernardino Poccetti*. Above is a Crucifix by *Baccio da Montelupo*.—RIGHT TRANSEPT. Nativity and Saints attributed to *Cosimo Rosselli* or *Davide Ghirlandaio*. 1st chapel (5), a Roman sarcophagus, and a fresco fragment of a female saint (attributed to *Nardo di Cione*), and a wooden Crucifix by *Antonio del Pollaiolo*. In the chapel opposite (6) is a monument of 1871 (left) to the goldsmith Bernardo Cennini, who printed the first book in Florence in 1471.—LEFT TRANSEPT. 1st chapel (7), Madonna and Child, a charming statue in polychrome wood attributed to *Alberto Arnoldi*, and two paintings attributed to *Raffaellino del Garbo*. 2nd chapel (8), a good painting by the *School of Ghirlandaio* of Saints Anthony Abbot, Leonard, and Julian.

Inlaid doors give access to the *Sagrestia Vecchia, or Old Sacristy (1420–29), the first part of the church to be rebuilt. One of the earliest and purest monuments of the Renaissance by *Brunelleschi*, it was built at the expense of Giovanni Bicci de' Medici. The vault is particularly noteworthy. The decorative details are mainly by *Donatello*: above the frieze of cherubs' heads, the *Tondi in the pendentives and lunettes depict the four Evangelists and scenes from the life of St John the Evangelist. Modelled in terracotta and plaster they are remarkable for their composition. Over the two little doors are large reliefs of Saints Cosmas and Damian and Saints Lawrence and Stephen. Excellent restoration work was carried out on the sculptural details in 1989. The remarkable dark blue frescoes in the little dome over the altar, depicting the sky as it was in 1442 with the signs of the zodiac, have also been restored. The bronze *Doors have figures of the Apostles and Martyrs in animated discussion. The terracotta *Bust of St Lawrence (or St Leonard) has been attributed to Donatello or Desiderio da Settignano. The raised seats and presses are decorated with inlay. In the centre is the sarcophagus of Giovanni Bicci de' Medici (died 1429) and Piccarda Bueri, the parents of Cosimo il Vecchio, by *Buggiano* (1434). Set into the wall is the magnificent porphyry and bronze sarcophagus of Giovanni and Piero de' Medici the sons of Cosimo il Vecchio. This was commissioned from Verrocchio in 1472 by Lorenzo il Magnifico and his brother Giuliano. In the little chapel (9; being restored) is a lavabo with fantastic creatures, by the workshop of Donatello.

In the last chapel in the left transept (10) is a monument (1896) to Donatello (died 1466; buried in the vault below) and an *Annunciation by *Filippo Lippi*. The marble sarcophagus of Niccolò Martelli is by the school of Donatello. In the LEFT AISLE (11) is a huge fresco of the Martyrdom of St Lawrence, by *Bronzino* (restored in 1989). The Cantoria above the door into the Cloister (see below) is after Donatello. In the last chapel in this aisle (12) is a painting of Christ in the carpenter's workshop by *Pietro Annigoni*.

The CLOISTER, by Manetti (1457–62), entered from the left aisle (13) or from the left of the façade, has graceful arcades in the style of Brunelleschi. In the centre is an orange tree. From here there is an entrance (kept closed; but sometimes open for exhibitions) to the crypt of San Lorenzo and the vaults with the tombs of Cosimo il Vecchio and Donatello. A staircase (14), near a statue of the historian Paolo Giovio, by Francesco da Sangallo (1560) ascends to the *Biblioteca Laurenziana** (or *Laurentian Library*; Pl.16;1; adm. see p 60). It was begun by *Michelangelo* c 1524 at the order of Clement VII (Giulio de' Medici) to house the collection of MSS. made by Cosimo il Vecchio and Lorenzo il Magnifico. It is a remarkable monument of Mannerist architecture.

The solemn **Vestibule**, filled with an elaborate staircase, was constructed by *Vasari* and *Ammannati* on *Michelangelo*'s design in 1559–71. A somewhat disturbing work, it has been interpreted by scholars in numerous different ways. It testifies to Michelangelo's sculptural conception of architecture, with a pronounced use of pietra serena in the tall room.—The peaceful **Reading Room**, a long hall, provides an unexpected contrast. Here the angle at which the architectural decoration can be seen has been carefully calculated, and the inlaid desks, also by Michelangelo, form an intricate part of the design. It is interesting to note that the heavily decorated vestibule is invisible from the aisle (only a blank wall is framed in the doorway). The fine wood ceiling and terracotta floor were added by *Tribolo*.

The collection is famous above all for its Greek and Latin MSS.; it has been augmented over the centuries and now includes 11,000 MSS. and 4000 incunabula. *Exhibitions are held every year, here and in the adjoining rooms (the circular 'tribune' was added in 1841). The oldest codex is a famous 5C Virgil. Other works owned by the library include: Syrian gospels of the 6C; the oldest MS. of Justinian's Pandects (6–7C); the Codex Amiatinus (From Monte

Amiata) written in the monastery of Jarrow in England in the 8C; a Choir Book illuminated by Lorenzo Monaco and Attavante; a Book of Hours which belonged to Lorenzo il Magnifico; the Città di Vita of Matteo Palmieri, with illuminations in the style of Pollaiolo and Botticelli; a Treatise on Architecture with MS. notes by Leonardo da Vinci; the MS. of Cellini's autobiography; and a parchment of the Union of Greek and Roman churches recording the abortive effort of the Council of Florence in 1439.

The entrance to the **Cappelle Medicee** (Pl.6;5; adm. see p 60), or Medici Chapels, is from outside San Lorenzo, in Piazza Madonna degli Aldobrandini. In the Crypt of the Chapel of the Princes, built on a design by *Buontalenti*, are the tomb slabs of numerous members of the Medici family. A staircase leads up to the ***Cappella dei Principi**, the opulent, if gloomy, mausoleum of the Medici grand-dukes, begun by *Matteo Nigetti* (1604) on a plan by Don Giovanni de' Medici, illegitimate son of Cosimo I. It is a high octagon, 28 metres in diameter, entirely lined with dark-coloured marbles and semi-precious stones, a tour de force of craftsmanship in pietre dure. The mosaic arms of the 16 towns of Tuscany are especially notable (1589–1609). Between them are 32 vases in red and green jasper carried out in the early 17C. In the sarcophagi round the walls, from right to left, are buried Ferdinando II, Cosimo II, Ferdinando I, Cosimo I, Francesco I, and Cosimo III. The second and third sarcophagi are surmounted by colossal statues in gilded bronze, by *Pietro* and *Ferdinando Tacca* (1626–42). Work continued until 1836 when the decoration on the drum of the cupola was completed. The vault frescoes carried out at this time are by *Pietro Benvenuti*. The pavement was executed in 1882–1962. The altar is a model in wood hastily set up in 1938 which bears pietre dure panels of various dates, including the Supper at Emmaus (1853–61) and four fine panels with liturgical emblems (1821–53). Behind the altar two treasuries of the Medici popes contain the mitre of Leo X and reliquaries presented by Clement VII.

A passage to the left leads past two trophies attributed to *Silvio Cosini*, intended to decorate a tomb in the New Sacristy. The so-called ***Sagrestia Nuova**, or New Sacristy, built by *Michelangelo* in 1520–24 and 1530–33, was left unfinished when he finally left Florence in 1534 in anger at the political climate in the city. It balances Brunelleschi's Old Sacristy (see above) and drew inspiration from it, but was used from its inception as a funerary chapel for the Medici family. It is built in dark pietra serena and white marble in a severe and idiosyncratic style. It produces a strange, cold atmosphere, in part due to the diffusion of light exclusively from above, and the odd perspective devices on the upper parts of the walls. *Michelangelo* executed only two of the famous ****Medici Tombs**, out of the three or more originally projected. The sculptures were carefully cleaned in 1990. To the left of the entrance is that of LORENZO, DUKE OF URBINO (1492–1519), grandson of Lorenzo il Magnifico. The statue of the Duke shows him seated, absorbed in meditation, and on the sarcophagus below are the reclining figures of Dawn and Dusk. Opposite is the tomb of GIULIANO, DUKE OF NEMOURS (1479–1516), the third son of Lorenzo il Magnifico. Both these comparatively insignificant members of the Medici family are shown through idealised portraits; only their tombs ensured their fame. Beneath are the figures of Day and Night, the last, with the symbols of darkness (the moon, the owl, and a mask), is considered to be among the finest of all Michelangelo's sculptures.—The entrance wall was intended to have contained the architectural monument to

Lorenzo il Magnifico and his brother Giuliano; the only part carried out by Michelangelo is the *Madonna and Child. It is his last statue of a Madonna and one of his most beautiful. The figures on either side of St Cosmas and St Damian, the medical saints who were the patrons of the Medici, are by Montorsoli and Raffaello da Montelupo. Lorenzo il Magnifico's coffin was transferred here from the Old Sacristy in 1559.

On the walls behind the altar architectural graffiti have recently been uncovered. Some of these are attributed to *Michelangelo*, and others to his pupils, including *Tribolo*. The door to the left of the altar gives access to a little room where charcoal *Drawings of great interest were discovered on the walls in 1975. Small groups are usually conducted c every 30 minutes (by appointment at the ticket office, 9.30–12.00). The drawings have aroused much discussion among art historians, most of whom recognise them as works by *Michelangelo*. It is thought that he hid here for a time under the protection of his friend, the prior of San Lorenzo, after the return of the Medici in 1530. They clearly refer to works by Michelangelo, such as his statue of Giuliano in the adjoining chapel. The large figure study for a Resurrection of Christ on the entrance wall is particularly remarkable.

At No. 4 in Piazza Madonna, *Palazzo Mannelli-Riccardi* has a painted façade of the mid 16C (very ruined) and a bust of Ferdinando I by Giovanni dell'Opera. Off Via de' Conti, which leads out of the piazza, is Via Zanetti (Pl.16;1). Here at No. 8 is *Palazzo Martelli*, onced owned by the family who were famous as patrons of Donatello. It contains one of the most important private collections in Florence, in rooms decorated in the 18C. On the stair landing is the family coat-of-arms attributed to Donatello. It was left by the last member of the Martelli family to the Curia Vescovile in 1986 on condition that it was preserved as a gallery, and it is hoped that it will be purchased by the State and opened to the public. The tabernacle on the exterior contains a Madonna and Child with St John attributed to Mino da Fiesole.

The animated VIA DELL'ARIENTO leads away from San Lorenzo. It is lined with numerous market stalls (cf. p 142), and passes the huge *Mercato Centrale* (Pl.6;5), the principal food market in the town (open Monday–Saturday, 7.00–13.00; also 16.30–19.30 on Saturday except in July and August), well worth a visit. The magnificent cast-iron building by Giuseppe Mengoni (1874) was restored in 1980 when a mezzanine floor was constructed for the sale of fruit and vegetables, and a car park opened in the basement. The market produce is generally of good value. Via Sant' Antonino is another crowded street with popular food shops, and in Via Panicale are more market stalls selling clothes (locally known as 'Shanghai'). Via Chiara was Cellini's birthplace. Via dell'Ariento ends in VIA NAZIONALE, a busy street typical of the anonymous areas around railway stations. Here is a huge tabernacle attributed to Giovanni della Robbia (1522), above a fountain. In Via Faenza, just to the left, by a tabernacle by Giovanni di San Giovanni (1615), is the entrance (No. 42; closed since 1987) to the so-called **Cenacolo di Foligno** (Pl.6;5), a fresco of the *Last Supper by *Perugino* (c 1493–96) painted in the refectory of the ex-convent of Sant'Onofrio (or Foligno). In the background is a lovely landscape with the Agony in the Garden. There are long-term plans to open a small museum here.—On the next corner (left) the poet Lamartine, then a diplomatic secretary, lived in 1826–29.

In VIA GUELFA (Pl.6;5), which also traverses Via Nazionale, is the church of **San Barnaba**. It preserves a 14C portal with a Della Robbian lunette. The pretty

interior was remodelled in 1700 and there is a Baroque organ above the nuns'
choir. On the left wall is a painting of the Madonna and Saints by Pier Francesco
Toschi, and a fragment of a fresco of Saints enthroned attributed to Spinello
Aretino.—Nearby is a big edifice (which has been awaiting restoration for
years) built by Bartolomeo Silvestri on the site of the Convent of Sant'Orsola as
a tobacco manufactory in 1810. At the NW end of Via Guelfa, then on the
outskirts of the city, Luca della Robbia and his nephew Andrea probably had
their house and kiln (after 1446). Opposite the end of Via Montanelli is the
Istituto Sant'Agnese (No. 79), an old people's home run by the Bigallo, with a
pretty little Baroque chapel (early 18C; frescoes by the school of Sagrestani).

11 Santa Maria Novella and Ognissanti

*Santa Maria Novella (Pl.5;6; closed 11.30–15.30) is the most import-
ant Gothic church in Tuscany. The first church (the foundations of
which have recently been found during excavations), called Santa
Maria delle Vigne, was built in 1094 on the site of a chapel (probably
9C). The Dominicans were given the property in 1221, and building
was begun in 1246 at the E end of the present church. The Dominican
friars *Sisto* and *Ristoro* are thought to have been the architects of the
impressive nave, begun in 1279. The church was completed under
the direction of *Fra' Jacopo Talenti* in the mid 14C, when the great
Dominican preacher Jacopo Passavanti was Prior.

The lower part of the beautiful marble *FAÇADE, in a typical
Tuscan Romanesque style, is attributed to *Fra' Jacopo Talenti*. In
1456–70 *Leon Battista Alberti* was commissioned by Giovanni di
Paolo Rucellai to complete the upper part of the façade. Its classical
lines are in perfect harmony with the earlier work. He also added the
main portal (executed by *Giovanni di Bertino*). Exquisite inlaid
friezes bear the emblems of the Rucellai (a billowing ship's sail) and
of the Medici (a ring with ostrich feathers); in 1461 Giovanni
Rucellai's son Bernardo married Nannina, daughter of Piero de'
Medici. Below the tympanum an inscription in handsome classical
lettering records the name of the benefactor and the date 1470. The
use of scrolls to connect the nave roof with the lower aisle roofs was
an innovation which was frequently copied in church façades of later
centuries. The two astronomical instruments (a quadrant and an
armilla) by Egnazio Danti were placed here in 1572. To the right of
the façade is a long line of Gothic arcaded recesses, the 'avelli' or
family-vaults of Florentine nobles. These extend around the old
cemetery, with its cypresses, on the right side of the church. The
painter Domenico Ghirlandaio (died 1494) was buried here (4th
'avello').—The CAMPANILE also attributed to *Fra' Jacopo Talenti*, was
grafted onto an ancient watch tower.

INTERIOR. The spacious nave has remarkably bold stone vaulting,
its arches given prominence by bands of dark grey pietra serena. 14C
frescoes of Saints on the intrados of the arches have been exposed.
The composite pillars between nave and aisles have classical capitals. The bays decrease in width as they approach the three fine
stained glass lancet windows at the E end. The interior was altered
by *Vasari* in 1565 when the rood-screen (which formerly divided the
church at the steps in the fourth bay) and the friars' choir were
demolished, and side altars were set up in the nave (replaced by the
present neo-Gothic ones in the 19C).—On the W wall (1) is a fresco
by the Florentine school (late 14C). The stained glass in the rose
window is thought to have been designed by *Andrea di Bonaiuto*

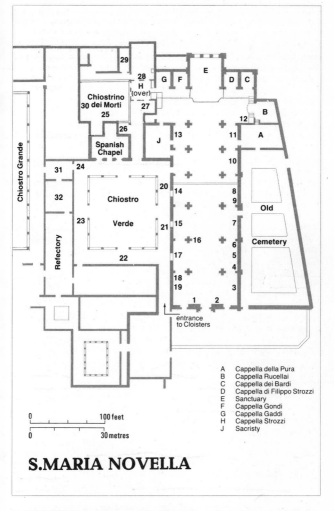

S.MARIA NOVELLA

A Cappella della Pura
B Cappella Rucellai
C Cappella dei Bardi
D Cappella di Filippo Strozzi
E Sanctuary
F Cappella Gondi
G Cappella Gaddi
H Cappella Strozzi
J Sacristy

0   100 feet

0   30 metres

(c 1365). The fresco lunette of the Nativity attributed as an early work to *Botticelli*, over the W door, has recently been restored. On the left of the door (2), Annunciation, by *Santi di Tito*.

SOUTH AISLE. 1st altar (3), *Girolamo Macchietti*, Martyrdom of St Lawrence; Monument (4) to the Blessed Villana delle Botti (died 1361) by *Bernardo Rossellino* (1451), with two pretty angels. 2nd altar (5) *Giovanni Battista Naldini*, Nativity; 16C Monument (6) to Giovanni da Salerno, founder of the convent, by *Vincenzo Danti*, in imitation of Rossellino's monument. The next two altarpieces (7 and 8) are also by *Naldini*. On the right of the Deposition is a monument (9) to Ruggero Minerbetti (died 1210), by *Silvio Cosini* (c 1528) with bizarre Mannerist trophies. Beyond a highly venerated modern statue of the Madonna of the Rosary with St Dominic, the 5th altar (10) has a painting of St Vincent Ferrer by *Jacopo del Meglio*.—In the 15C CAPPELLA DELLA PURA (or 'Purità'; A; sometimes closed) the 14C fresco of the Madonna and Child with St Catherine, and a donor, was detached from an 'avello' outside the church. The wood Crucifix over the other altar is by *Baccio da Montelupo*.—On the 6th altar (11), Miracle of St Raymond, by *Jacopo Ligozzi*.

SOUTH TRANSEPT. Three Gothic tombs (12): Tomb of Bishop Aliotti (died 1336), once attributed to *Tino da Camaino*; (left) Tomb of Fra' Aldovrando Cavalcanti (died 1279); and, below, tomb of Joseph, Patriarch of Constantinople (who attended the Council of Florence in 1439 and died in the convent in the following year), with a contemporary fresco of him.—The simple classical sarcophagus tomb of Paolo Rucellai precedes the CAPPELLA RUCELLAI (B), which housed Duccio's famous Madonna in the 18C (removed to the Uffizi in 1948, see p 99). It now contains a marble *Statue of the Madonna and Child signed by *Nino Pisano*, and the bronze tomb-slab of the Dominican general Francesco Lionardo Dati, by *Ghiberti* (1425; removed from the nave in front of the high altar). The walls have traces of 14C frescoes: those flanking the closed Gothic window are attributed to the circle of the 'St Cecilia Master' (c 1305–10). The large painting of the Martyrdom of St Catherine is an interesting work by *Giuliano Bugiardini*. On the wall outside the chapel is the tomb-slab of Corrado della Penna, Bishop of Fiesole (died 1313).—The CAPPELLA DEI BARDI (C) was formerly used by the Laudesi brotherhood (founded c 1245 by St Peter Martyr) who commissioned the 'Rucellai' Madonna from Duccio for this chapel (later moved to the Cappella Rucellai, cf. above) in 1285. The bas relief of Riccardo di Ricco Bardi kneeling before St Gregory dates from the year after his death in 1334 when his heirs took possession of the chapel. Frescoes of the late 14C (restored in 1989) partially cover earlier fresco fragments. The lunettes above (with the Madonna enthroned) of c 1285 have recently been attributed to *Cimabue*. The altarpiece of the Madonna of the Rosary is by *Vasari*.—The CAPPELLA DI FILIPPO STROZZI (D); light on left) was acquired by the great Florentine banker in 1486. He commissioned *Filippino Lippi* to decorate it. The exuberant *Frescoes were not finished until after 1502 on the artist's return from Rome. They are full of allusions to Antiquity and are conspicuously different from other fresco cycles in Florence of this period. On the right wall is the Crucifixion of St Philip the Apostle, and his miracle before the Temple of Mars (the terrible stench of the monster he conjures forth from its steps kills the king's son). On the left wall is the Martyrdom of St John the Evangelist, and the raising of Drusiana. In the vault, Adam, Noah, Abraham, and Jacob. *Filippino* also designed the beautiful stained-glass window and the splendid classical trompe l'oeil frescoes in grisaille on the altar wall, which were restored in 1985. Behind the altar, *Tomb of Filippo Strozzi, exquisitely carved by *Benedetto da Maiano* (who had also been involved in the building of Palazzo Strozzi for his patron). Boccaccio in the *Decameron* takes this chapel as the meeting-place of a group of young people during the Plague year of 1348.

On the MAIN ALTAR is a bronze Crucifix by *Giambologna*. In the SANCTUARY (E; light behind the altar) the stalls are attributed to *Baccio d'Agnolo*. The delightul *Frescoes (those on the left wall have been restored; those on the right wall are now covered for restoration), commissioned by Giovanni Tornabuoni, are the masterpiece of *Domenico Ghirlandaio* (assisted by his brother *Davide*, his

brother-in-law, *Sebastiano Mainardi*, and his pupils, including perhaps the young Michelangelo).

They replaced a fresco cycle by Orcagna (fragments of which, with heads of
Prophets, have been detached from the vault), and may follow a similar
iconographical design. Many of the figures are portraits of the artist's contemporaries, and the whole cycle mirrors Florentine life in the late 15C. On the right
wall are scenes from the life of St John the Baptist, including (lower register) the
Angel appearing to St Zacharias in the temple (with portraits of the Tornabuoni
and famous humanist scholars), the Visitation, and (above) Birth of St John
(showing ladies of the Tornabuoni family).—On the left wall, scenes from the
life of the Virgin, including (lower register) the Expulsion of St Joachim from the
Temple (with members of the Tornabuoni family, and, in the group on the right,
the self-portraits of the artists), and the Birth of the Virgin (with portraits of the
Tornabuoni ladies).—On the end wall, Coronation of the Virgin, Miracle of St
Dominic, Death of St Peter Martyr, Annunciation, St John the Baptist in the
desert, and the two kneeling figures of the donors, Giovanni Tornabuoni and his
wife Francesca Pitti.—In the vault, the four Evangelists. The stained glass
windows (c 1491) were also designed by *Ghirlandaio*.

NORTH TRANSEPT. The CAPPELLA GONDI (F) has handsome marble
decoration by *Giuliano da Sangallo*. Here is the famous *Crucifix by
Brunelleschi*, traditionally thought to have been carved to show
Donatello how the Redeemer should be represented (cf. p 175). It is
his only sculpture to survive in wood (restored in 1977). It was made
to wear a loin-cloth. The damaged vault frescoes of the four Evangelists are thought to date from the end of the 13C.—The CAPPELLA
GADDI (G), by *Giovanni Antonio Dosio* (1575–77) has a cupola
decorated by *Alessandro Allori*, and a painting of Christ raising the
daughter of Jairus by *Bronzino*. The two bas-reliefs on the walls are
by *Giovanni Bandini*.—At the end of the transept the *CAPPELLA
STROZZI (H) is a remarkably well-preserved example of a Tuscan
chapel of the mid 14C. It contains celebrated *Frescoes by *Nardo di
Cione*, his most famous work (c 1357; recently detached and
restored), carefully designed to cover the entire chapel. They represent (in the vault), St Thomas Aquinas and the Virtues; on the end
wall, the Last Judgement; on the left wall, Paradise, a huge crowded
composition; and on the right wall, Inferno, a pictorial commentary
on Dante's 'Inferno'. The splendid frescoed decoration is completed
on the intrados of the entrance arch with a frieze of Saints. The
stained-glass window is designed by *Nardo di Cione* and his brother
Andrea di Cione (Orcagna), who painted the fine *Altarpiece of the
Redeemer giving the Keys to St Peter and the book of wisdom to
St Thomas Aquinas (1357), remarkable also for its unusual
iconography.—On the outside wall of the ancient chapel at the base
of the Campanile (closed, but containing very old frescoes) is a
ruined fresco (recently restored) of the Coronation of the Virgin,
traditionally attributed to *Buffalmacco*.

The SACRISTY (J) has a fine cross-vault by *Fra' Jacopo Talenti*
(c 1350). The stained-glass windows date from 1386, and are thought to
have been designed by *Niccolò Gerini* (restored in 1975). On the
left of the door is a Lavabo in terracotta with a charming landscape
by *Giovanni della Robbia* (1498); the upper part may be by *Andrea
della Robbia*. Above the entrance, *Crucifix, an early work by *Giotto*
(removed for restoration since 1987). The huge cupboard on the
opposite wall was designed by *Buontalenti* (1593). On the walls:
Jacopo Ligozzi, Conversion of St Paul; *Giovanni Stradano*, Baptism
of Christ; *Pietro Dandini*, St Vincent Ferrer; *Vasari*, Crucifixion
(being restored in situ). A 15C bust of St Antonino in terracotta

(formerly in the South Transept) is kept in a cupboard here (shown on request).

NORTH AISLE. 6th altar (13), *Alessandro Allori*, Saints; 4th altar (14), *Vasari*, Resurrection and Saints; (15) Fresco of the Trinity and the Virgin and St John the Evangelist with donors, above a skeleton on a sarcophagus, a remarkable work by *Masaccio* (c 1428). It is famous for its perfect composition and accurate perspective which gives it an almost metaphysical atmosphere. The architecture of the shadowy niche owes much to Brunelleschi.—To the left, St Lucy with a donor by *Davide Ghirlandaio*. The Pulpit (16) from which Caccini denounced Galileo's astronomical theories, was designed by *Brunelleschi* and executed by his adopted son *Buggiano*. On the 2nd altar (17), *Alessandro Allori*, Christ at the well; to the left, Annunciation, in the manner of *Bicci di Lorenzo*. The monument (18) to Antonio Strozzi (1524) is by *Andrea Ferrucci*, with a Madonna by his pupil, *Silvio Cosini*. 1st altar (19), *Santi di Tito*, Resurrection of Lazarus.

To the left of the church is the entrance to the *Cloisters (adm. see p 60), which now belong to the city. They were reopened after restoration in 1983, and excavation and restoration work continues here. Foundations of the church of 1094 have recently been found. There are long-term plans to open a museum of miniatures belonging to the Convent. The Convent of Santa Maria Novella was one of the richest and largest in Florence, and it remains an oasis of calm in this busy part of the city. Eugenius IV transferred the Papal court here in 1434–43 during sessions of the Council of Florence (1439) which attempted to heal the Eastern schism. The Romanesque *CHIOSTRO VERDE (c 1330–50) receives its name from the green tone of its decoration (in the vaults are roundels of Dominican Saints). Four cypresses surround the raised well, and there is a good view of the side of the church, the exterior of the sacristy with its stained-glass windows, and of the campanile. The damaged *Frescoes by *Paolo Uccello* and assistants, painted in terraverde, have all been returned here after restoration.

They illustrate stories from Genesis (the biblical references are given below each scene), and the cycle begins at the far end of the East (entrance) walk beside the door into the church. The numerous frescoes with animals are particularly charming. The *Creation of Adam, and of the Animals, and the Creation and Temptation of Eve (c 1425; 20), and the *Flood, and the Recession of the Flood (with Noah's ark), and the Sacrifice and Drunkenness of Noah (c 1446; 21), are considered to be by *Paolo Uccello* himself. Although much damaged, they are remarkable for their figure studies and perspective devices; the later works are among the most mysterious and disturbing paintings of the Florentine Renaissance. The frescoes in the South Walk (22) are attributed to a Florentine painter of the first half of the 15C. In the West Walk (23) the first fresco is attributed to Dello Delli, and the others to another Florentine painter of the first half of the 15C. Over the door into the Refectory (see below) is a detached fresco of Christ on the Cross with Saints Dominic and Thomas Aquinas, attributed to *Stefano Fiorentino* (mid 14C). At the beginning of the N walk (24) is a fresco attributed to *Bernardino Poccetti* (c 1592), and a lunette of the Madonna and Child, a Sienese work of c 1330 (Lippo Memmi?).

Off the cloister opens the *Cappellone degli Spagnuoli, or *Spanish Chapel*. It received its name in the 16C when it was assigned by Duchess Eleonora di Toledo to the Spanish members of her suite. It was originally the Chapter House, built by *Jacopo Talenti* in the mid 14C with a splendid cross-vault and two fine Gothic windows. The walls and vault are entirely covered with colourful *Frescoes by

Andrea di Bonaiuto (sometimes called *Andrea da Firenze*) and
assistants (c 1365), the most important work by this otherwise little-
known artist who was influenced by the Sienese school of painting.

The pictorial decoration, on a monumental scale, is carefully designed to fit the
wall space. The subjects are: in the vault, the Resurrection, Ascension, the
Navicella, and Descent of the Holy Ghost; altar wall, Via Dolorosa, Crucifixion,
Descent into Limbo.—On the right wall, the Mission, Works, and Triumph of the
Dominican Order illustrated by various scenes. In front of the elaborate church,
the artist's vision of the completed Duomo, is the Church Militant with the Pope
and Emperor and Church dignitaries. In the foreground (right), behind a group
of kneeling pilgrims, are the presumed portraits of Cimabue, Giotto, Boccaccio,
Petrarch, Dante, etc. The scene on the bottom right shows St Dominic sending
forth the hounds of the Lord ('Domini canes'), with St Peter Martyr and St
Thomas Aquinas. Above, four seated figures symbolising the Vices are surrounded by representations of dancing, etc. A Dominican friar taking confession
shows the way to salvation, and those absolved are sent on towards the Gate of
Paradise guarded by St Peter. On the other side of the gate the Blessed look up
towards Christ in Judgement surrounded by angels.—The opposite wall shows
the Triumph of Catholic doctrine personified in St Thomas Aquinas, who is
shown enthroned beneath the winged Virtues. On his right and left are Doctors
of the Church. In the Gothic choir-stalls below are 14 female figures symbolising the Arts and Sciences, with, at their feet, historical personages representing
these virtues.—On the entrance wall is the Life of St Peter Martyr (damaged).—
The polyptych by *Bernardo Daddi* (restored) was painted for the Chapter House
in 1344. The apse chapel (recently restored) was decorated in 1592 by
Alessandro Allori (including the altarpiece of the martyrdom of St Jacob) and
Bernardino Poccetti (vault frescoes).

On the right of the Chapel is the entrance to the CHIOSTRINO DEI
MORTI (25), the oldest part of the convent (c 1270). The chapel on the
left (26) is frescoed with a Nativity and a Crucifixion, which probably
date from the mid 14C (formerly attributed to Giottino). On the right
is the chapel of St Anthony Abott (27) with very ruined frescoes
(c 1349), and the Chapel of St Anne (28; closed for restoration), with
frescoes of the life of St Anne and the Virgin, and figures of Saints
Thomas Aquinas, Luke, John the Evangelist, and Dominic, attributed
to a follower of *Nardo di Cione*. In another chapel (29) are displayed
sinopie from this cloister, and a colossal statue of St John of Salerno
by *Girolamo Ticciati*. The lunette fresco of St Thomas Aquinas is
attributed to *Stefano Fiorentino*. A tabernacle (30) in the cloister
contains a terracotta by the workshop of *Giovanni della Robbia*.—
From the Chiostro Verde a passage (31), with the sinopie of the
frescoes of Paradise by Nardo di Cione in the Cappella Strozzi (see
p 151) leads towards the imposing GREAT CLOISTER (no adm.; in use
as a police barracks), which can be seen through a glass door.

The frescoes (gradually being returned after restoration) in the Great Cloister,
carried out in the early 1580s by *Poccetti*, with the help of *Bernardino Monaldi*
and *Cosimo Gheri*, are the first example in Florence of religious painting
inspired by the Counter Reformation. There are also frescoes by Cigoli and
Bronzino here. Also in the cloister is the charming little doorway of the Farmacia
di Santa Maria Novella (see below) and an interesting 14C carved architrave
with the Adoration of the Magi. Off the cloister is the remarkable vaulted
dormitory (now used as a refectory). Upstairs is the *Cappella dei Papi* (adm. only
by special permission) built in 1515 for Leo X. The frescoes of the Veronica and
of putti on the barrel vault are by Pontormo. The Coronation of the Virgin is by
Ridolfo del Ghirlandaio.

From the passage (31; see above), on the left is the entrance to the
CAPPELLA DEGLI UBRIACHI (32) and the Refectory, built by *Francesco*

Jacopo Talenti (1365–66), where a MUSEO D'ARTE SACRA was opened in 1983 to display the reliquaries, vestments, etc. formerly in the Sacristy of the church. In the chapel is the tomb-slab of the Ubriachi family and traces of wall decoration showing their emblem. Here also are displayed busts of prophets by *Andrea Orcagna* and his school, detached from the vault of the main chapel in the church, and the sinopie of the first frescoes by *Paolo Uccello* from the East walk of the Chiostro Verde. In the show cases are charming reliquary busts (Sienese school, late 14C), and a frontal made for the high altar of the church, beautifully embroidered with scenes from the life of the Virgin (Florentine, c 1460–66; recently restored).

The large **Refectory** has superb cross-vaulting in three bays by Talenti. On the entrance wall, a large fresco of the Manna in the desert, by *Alessandro Allori* surrounds a good fresco attributed to a follower of *Agnolo Gaddi*, contemporary with the building, and probably part of a larger composition which covered the entire wall. It shows the Madonna enthroned between St Thomas Aquinas, St Dominic (at whose feet is the Prior of the convent, Fra' Jacopo Passavanti), St John the Baptist, and St Peter Martyr. On the left wall, *Alessandro Allori*, Last Supper (1583); this formerly covered the Madonna enthroned. The show cases display 16C and 17C reliquaries, church silver, vestments, etc. belonging to the convent.

PIAZZA SANTA MARIA NOVELLA, with its irregular shape, was created by the Dominicans at the end of the 13C. The two obelisks were set up in 1608 (resting on bronze tortoises by Giambologna) as turning posts in the course of the annual chariot race (Palio dei Cocchi) which was first held here in 1563. The *Loggia di San Paolo* was erected on the SW side of the square in 1489–96. It is a free copy of Brunelleschi's Loggia degli Innocenti, with terracottas by Giovanni della Robbia. The beautiful *Lunette beneath the arcade (right) of the Meeting of St Francis and St Dominic is by Andrea della Robbia. The tabernacle on the corner of Via della Scala contains a fresco by Francesco d'Antonio (recently restored). In the house on the corner here Henry James began 'Roderick Hudson' in 1874. In Via della Scala (No. 16) is the FARMACIA DI SANTA MARIA NOVELLA (open 8.30–12.30, 15–19 except Monday morning).

The pharmacy attached to the convent of Santa Maria Novella had become important as a chemist's shop by the mid 16C, and it is still famous as such in Florence, producing its own perfumes, etc. The present shop is in the ex-14C chapel of San Niccolò decorated in a delightful neo-Gothic style in 1848 by Enrico Romoli. It has Art Nouveau lamps and frescoes representing the four continents by Paolino Sarti. The other rooms are shown on request: one overlooking the former physic garden, has late-18C furnishings, pharmacy jars (including Montelupo ware), and a carved Medici coat-of-arms with a painted portrait of St Peter Martyr by Matteo Rosselli. The charming old chemist's shop, overlooking the Great Cloister of Santa Maria Novella (see above) has 17C vases including albarelli, mortars, etc. The sacristy of San Niccolò has frescoes of the Passion formerly attributed to Spinello Aretino and now thought to be by Mariotto di Nardo.

Off the E side of Piazza Santa Maria Novella, the winding Via delle Belle Donne leads shortly to a crossroads in the middle of which stands the *Croce del Trebbio* (from 'trivium'), a granite column reconsecrated in 1338 with a Gothic capital bearing symbols of the Evangelists. Above this is a Cross of the Pisan school protected by a wooden tabernacle. It is traditionally thought to commemorate a massacre of heretics which took place here in 1244, but the date of its erection is unknown.

Via de' Fossi leads towards the Arno. It takes its name from the ditch outside the city walls built here in 1173–75, and contains a number of well-known antique shops. The church of Ognissanti may be reached from here either by Via de' Fossi and then Borgo Ognissanti, or by Via Palazzuolo (right) and then (left) Via del Porcellana.

In Via Palazzuolo is the church of *San Paolino* (Pl.5;7; usually closed) of 10C foundation, with a bare façade, rebuilt in 1669 by Giovanni Battista Balatri. It contains 17–18C paintings by Volterrano, Giovanni Domenico Ferretti, Vincenzo Meucci, Ignazio Hugford, and Ottaviano Dandini. At No. 17 Via Palazzuolo is the *Oratorio di San Francesco dei Vanchetoni* (usually closed) built in 1602 by Giovanni Nigetti, with a vestibule and façade by Matteo Nigetti (1620). The ceiling frescoes are by Pietro Liberi, Volterrano, Cecco Bravo, and others (possibly including Giovanni da San Giovanni and Lorenzo Lippi). The chapel behind the altar contains a 16C Crucifix, and the charming sacristy has inlaid cupboards.

In the wide Borgo Ognissanti is the church of *San Giovanni di Dio* (open for services), built by Carlo Marcellini (1702–13) next to the ex-hospital of *San Giovanni di Dio*, founded in 1380 by the Vespucci family. It was enlarged in 1702–13 by Carlo Marcellini incorporating the Vespucci house on this site, including the birthplace of Amerigo (cf. below). In the fine atrium (1735) are sculptures by Girolamo Ticciati. At No. 8, then the Albergo Aquila Nera, Mozart stayed in 1770 when he came to give a concert at Poggio Imperiale. At No 26 is an Art Nouveau house designed by Giovanni Michelazzi (1921).

The Church of **Ognissanti** (Pl.5;7) was founded in 1256 by the Umiliati, a Benedictine Order particularly skilled in manufacturing wool. This area of the city became one of the main centres of the woollen cloth industry, on which medieval Florence based her economy. Mills on the Arno were used for washing, fulling, and dyeing the cloth. Since 1561 the church has been owned by the Franciscans; it was rebuilt in a Baroque style in the 17C. The façade by *Nigetti* (1637) incorporates a glazed terracotta Coronation of the Virgin ascribed to *Benedetto Buglioni*.

The INTERIOR was restored after severe flood damage in 1966. The trompe l'oeil ceiling fresco by Giuseppe Romei dates from 1770. SOUTH SIDE. 1st altar, Ascension by *Lodovico Buti*; 2nd altar, frescoes of the Pietà and the Madonna della Misericordia, early works by *Domenico* and *Davide Ghirlandaio*. The Madonna protects the Vespucci (Amerigo is supposed to be the young boy whose head appears between the Madonna and the man in the dark cloak). The family tombstone (1471) is in the pavement left of the altar. The Vespucci (see above), merchants involved in the manufacture of silk, held political office in the 15C as supporters of the Medici. Amerigo (1451–1512), a Medici agent in Seville, gave his name to America having made two voyages in 1499 and 1501–02 following the route charted by his Italian contemporary Columbus.—3rd altar, *Santi di Tito*, Madonna and Saints. Between the 3rd and 4th altars, *Botticelli*, *St Augustine's vision of St Jerome (a fresco of c 1481). 4th altar, *Nicodemo Ferrucci*, St Francis. The 17C pulpit has bas-reliefs by a pupil of *Benedetto da Rovezzano*. The 5th altarpiece is by *Vincenzo Dandini*.—The frescoes in the Baroque chapels in the SOUTH TRANSEPT date from c 1717–22. 1st altar (on the right), *Jacopo Ligozzi*, San Diego healing the sick. In the adjacent chapel, with a dome frescoed by *Matteo Bonechi*, the round tombstone in the pavement marks the burial place of Sandro Filipepi (Botticelli). In the chapel at the end of the transept, ceiling frescoes by *Gian Domenico Ferretti*. In the next chapel, with the dome frescoed by *Ranieri del Pace*, are two paintings (including the Martyrdom of St Andrew) by *Matteo Rosselli*. In the 2nd chapel right of the high altar, frescoes by *Giovanni Cinqui*, and in the 1st chapel right of the high altar, altarpiece by *Pier Dandini*.—The CHOIR CHAPEL has frescoes in the dome by *Giovanni da San Giovanni* (1616–17), and the high altar (1593–1605) has a tabernacle above in pietre dure perhaps on a design by *Jacopo Ligozzi*.—NORTH TRANSEPT. In the 1st chapel left of the high altar, paintings by *Pier Dandini*. Next to a chapel with a Crucifix by *Viet Stoss* on the wall, a door leads into the Sacristy where decorative wall paintings of the late 13C have been uncovered. The Crucifixion, with its sinopia, is by *Taddeo Gaddi*, and the Resurrection and fragment of the Ascension is attributed to *Agnolo Gaddi*.

The painted Crucifix is by the school of *Giotto*—North side, 3rd altar, *Maso di San Friano*, Assumption (the angels are by *Santi di Tito*). Between the 3rd and the 4th altars, *Domenico Ghirlandaio*, *St Jerome, painted, like Botticelli's fresco opposite, c 1481.

On the left of the church is the entrance (No. 42) to the CONVENT (ring for adm.; see p 60; offering). The Cloister, in the style of Michelozzo, incorporates octagonal pilasters which support part of the Gothic church. The old campanile can also be seen here. The 17C frescoes (*Giovanni da San Giovanni, Jacopo Ligozzi*, etc.) have been detached and restored and returned here. The pretty vaulted REFECTORY, with its lavaboes and pulpit in pietra serena, contains a *Last Supper, by *Domenico Ghirlandaio* (1480). The delightful background includes plants and birds which are Christian symbols. Its sinopia is displayed on another wall. The fresco of the Annunciation dates from 1369.—A small MUSEUM (usually locked), on the other side of the cloister, has a 15C Madonna and Child in polychrome terracotta (by *Nanni di Bartolo*), and vestments, etc. from the sacristy.

Piazza Ognissanti opens onto the Arno. On the right is *Palazzo Lenzi*, built c 1470. The graffiti were repainted when the palace was restored in 1885. It is now occupied by the French Consul and French Institute, founded in Florence by Julien Luchaire for the University of Grenoble in 1907–08. Across the Arno, the domed church of San Frediano in Cestello and the green hill of Bellosguardo are prominent.

12 Via Tornabuoni: Santa Trìnita and Palazzo Strozzi. Palazzo Rucellai

Ponte Santa Trìnita (see p 185) crosses the Arno at the beginning of **Via Tornabuoni** (Pl.16;5,3), the most elegant street in Florence, famous for its fashionable shops (including Ferragamo and Gucci). At the beginning on the right is the splendid battlemented *PALAZZO SPINI-FERONI (Pl.16;5), one of the best-preserved and largest private medieval palaces in the city. It was built for Geri degli Spini in 1289 possibly by Lapo Tedesco, master of Arnolfo di Cambio (and restored in the 19C). Opposite is the church of *Santa Trìnita (Pl.9;2; closed 12–16). The Latin pronunciation of its name betrays its ancient foundation. A church of the Vallombrosan Order existed on this site at least by 1077. Probably rebuilt in 1250–60, its present Gothic form dates from the end of the 14C and is attributed to *Neri di Fioravante*. The FAÇADE (being restored) was added by *Buontalenti* in 1593–94. The relief of the Trinity is by *Giovanni Caccini*. The bell-tower (1396–97) can just be seen behind to the left.

The fine INTERIOR has the austerity characteristic of Cistercian churches. On the entrance wall the interior façade of the Romanesque building survives. The church is unusually dark (best light in morning); each chapel has a light: the switches are inconspicuously placed to the left. High up on the outside arches of many of the chapels are remains of 14–15C frescoes (some restored); the most interesting are those by *Giovanni del Ponte* outside the choir chapels. SOUTH AISLE. 1st chapel, Wood Crucifix and detached fresco and sinopia of the 14C; 3rd chapel, altarpiece of the Madonna enthroned with four Saints, by *Neri di Bicci*. On the walls, detached fresco and sinopia by *Spinello Aretino* (considerably ruined) found beneath a fresco by Lorenzo Monaco in the adjoining chapel.—The 4th chapel is entirely frescoed (including the entrance arch) by *Lorenzo Monaco* (1422; covered for restoration). The *Altarpiece of the Annunciation is also by him.—5th chapel, Pietà, fresco attributed to *Giovanni Toscani*, and a noble altar by *Benedetto da Rovezzano*, part of a monument to St John Gualberto, founder of the Vallombrosan Order (damaged in the siege of Florence, 1530). The painting of Christ resurrected, and Saints, is by *Maso di San Friano*. In the side entrance porch are six worn 'avelli', or Gothic tombs.—In the SACRISTY is the tomb of Onofrio Strozzi, by *Piero di Niccolò Lamberti* (1421) with painted decoration on the arch by *Gentile da Fabriano*. Here are displayed detached frescoes of the 14C, including a Pietà and 'Noli me tangere'.

CHOIR CHAPELS. *SASSETTI CHAPEL, with frescoes (coin-operated light in chapel) of the life of St Francis by *Domenico Ghirlandaio* commissioned in 1483 by Francesco Sassetti, a merchant and typical figure of Renaissance Florence. The scene in the lunette above the altar (St Francis receiving the Rule of the Order from Pope Honorius) takes place in Piazza della Signoria and those present include: (in the foreground, right) Lorenzo il Magnifico with Sassetti and his son, and, to his right, Antonio Pucci. On the stairs are Agnolo Poliziano with Lorenzo il Magnifico's sons, Piero, Giovanni, and Giuliano. In the Miracle of the boy brought back to life (beneath) is Piazza Santa Trìnita (with the Romanesque façade of the church and the old Ponte Santa Trìnita). The altarpiece, the *Adoration of the Shepherds (1485), also by *Ghirlandaio*, is flanked by the kneeling figures of the donors, Francesco Sassetti and Nera Corsi, his wife. Their tombs, with black porphyry sarcophagi, are attributed to *Giuliano da Sangallo*. The decoration of the chapel includes numerous references to classical antiquity (the Sibyl announcing the coming of Christ to Augustus on the outside arch; the four Sibyls on the vault; the Roman sarcophagus used as a manger in the Adoration of the Shepherds; and the carved details on the tombs).—In the chapel to the right of the main altar, the painted Crucifix is said to have bowed approvingly to St John Gualberto when he pardoned his brother's assassin. The bust of the Saviour in painted terracotta is attributed to *Pietro Torrigiano* (c 1519).—In the Sanctuary, on the wall to the right of the 15C classical main altar is a Triptych of the Trinity, by *Mariotto di Nardo*. The fine figures in the vault of David, Abraham, Noah, and Moses are almost all that remains of the fresco decoration of the sanctuary by *Alesso Baldovinetti*.—The 1st chapel left of the altar was redecorated in 1635. The bronze altar frontal of the Martyrdom of St Lawrence is by *Tiziano Aspetti*; on the left wall, St Peter receiving the keys, by *Empoli*; the two lunette frescoes are by *Giovanni di San Giovanni*.—In the 2nd chapel left of the altar, *Tomb of Benozzo Federighi, Bishop of Fiesole (died 1450), by *Luca della Robbia* (1454–57). This was made for San Pancrazio and was moved here in 1896. The beautiful marble effigy is surrounded by an exquisite frame of enamelled terracotta mosaic on a gold ground. On the walls are detached fresco fragments by *Giovanni del Ponte*.—The little chapel in the N transept decorated by *Passignano* (1574) contains a reliquary of St John Gualberto.

NORTH AISLE. 5th chapel, Mary Magdalen, a fine wooden statue by *Desiderio da Settignano*, finished by Benedetto da Maiano (this has not yet been returned here since its restoration).—4th chapel, detached fresco of St John Gualberto surrounded by Vallombrosian saints, by *Neri di Bicci*, and (on the outside arch) fresco of St John Gualberto pardoning his brother's assassin, by *Bicci di Lorenzo*.—3rd chapel, 14C frescoes, and an Annunciation by *Neri di Bicci*. The tomb of Giuliano Davanzati (1444) was adapted from a Paleochristian sarcophagus with a relief of the Good Shepherd.—2nd chapel, Annunciation and St Jerome, good works by *Ridolfo del Ghirlandaio*.—The vault of the 1st chapel (1603) was painted by *Bernardino Poccetti*. It contains two statues by *Giovanni Caccini*, and an altarpiece of the Annunciation by *Empoli*. The statue from a niche on the façade, also by Caccini, is temporarily displayed here.—The CRYPT (with remains of the Romanesque church) dates from the 11C (approached from the nave, lights on left; shown by the sacristan on request).

In the little Piazza Santa Trìnita stands the *Column of Justice*, a granite monolith from the Baths of Caracalla in Rome, presented by Pius IV to Cosimo I in 1560. The prophyry figure of Justice, by Tadda (1581) has a bronze cloak added subsequently. The three narrow medieval streets leading out of the E side of the piazza are described in Rte 21. Opposite the impressive curving façade of Palazzo Spini-Feroni is *Palazzo Buondelmonti* (No. 2) with a façade of c 1530 attributed to Baccio d'Agnolo. In 1819 the Swiss scholar Gian Pietro Vieusseux here founded a scientific and literary association (cf. below) which became a famous intellectual centre in Italy; it was attended by Manzoni, D'Azeglio, Leopardi, Stendhal, and Dumas, among others. Across Via delle Terme is *Palazzo Bartolini-Salimbeni* (No. 1), perhaps the best work of Baccio d'Agnolo (1520–

23). Various types of stone were used in the fine façade, and the unusual courtyard has good graffiti decoration. The Hôtel du Nord was opened here in 1839, and the American writers Ralph Waldo Emerson, James Russell Lowell, and Herman Melville all stayed here.

Beyond Via Porta Rossa (with a good view of Palazzo Davanzati, see p 210) Via Tornabuoni continues, lined with handsome mansions. On the left *Palazzo Minerbetti* (No. 3) dates from the 14–15C *Palazzo Strozzi del Poeta* (No. 5) was reconstructed by Gherardo Silvani in 1626. The *Palazzo del Circolo dell'Unione* (No. 7) may have been designed by Vasari. The pretty doorway is surmounted by a bust of Francesco I by Giambologna. On the right a shop has recently replaced *Doney's*, a famous café, once frequented by foreigners in Florence, including Edmond and Jules Goncourt in the mid 19C, and, in this century, 'Ouida', D.H. Lawrence, Norman Douglas and the Sitwells. Beyond rises the huge *Palazzo Strozzi (Pl.16;3; the exterior has been propped up by scaffolding for many years, awaiting its restoration), the last and grandest of the magnificent Renaissance palaces in Florence, built for Filippo Strozzi (died 1491).

It is typical of the 15C town-mansion, half fortress, half palace, with all three storeys of equal emphasis constructed with large rough blocks of stone. It was begun by *Benedetto da Maiano* in 1489. *Giuliano da Sangallo* executed a model (cf. below), but he is not now thought to have been involved in the building. The wrought-iron torch-holders and fantastic lanterns were designed by Benedetto da Maiano and executed by *Caparra*. The side most nearly complete faces Piazza Strozzi; *Cronaca* continued the building and was responsible for the great projecting cornice, suggested by Antique examples, which was left half-finished when money ran out after the death of Filippo Strozzi. *Cronaca* also built the courtyard (finished in 1503); an incongruous iron fire escape was 'temporarily' installed here some years ago to enable the palace to be used for huge exhibitions. The palace is now the seat of the *Gabinetto Vieusseux*, an excellent lending library (cf. above), and various learned institutes, and is used for exhibitions and lectures. A small *Museum* (adm. see p 62) illustrates the history of the palace and preserves the model by Giuliano da Sangallo.—In Piazza Strozzi, *Palazzo dello Strozzino*, also built for the Strozzi family, has a façade begun by Michelozzo and completed by Giuliano da Maiano.

The crossroads in Via Tornabuoni with Via Strozzi, Via della Vigna Nuova, and Via della Spada, marks the centre of the Roman colony, and subsequently the W gate of the Roman city (cf. Plan on pp 30–1). The palace fitting the awkward site between Via della Vigna Nuova and Via della Spada was the home from 1614 of Sir Robert Dudley (1573–1649), Duke of Northumberland, who, on leaving England, became a naval engineer and took charge of the Arsenal in Livorno for Cosimo II and Ferdinando II (plaque placed in Via della Vigna Nuova in the 19C by his biographer John Temple Leader). In the corner house (left) George Eliot stayed while gathering material for 'Romola'. Via della Vigna Nuova, on the site of a huge orchard, leads past the narrow old Via dell'Inferno (left) to a little opening in front of *Palazzo Rucellai* (Pl.5;8). This was the town house of Giovanni Rucellai (1403–81), one of the most respected intellectual figures of Renaissance Florence (author of the 'Zibaldone', his memoirs), as well as one of the wealthiest businessmen in Europe. It was almost certainly designed for him by *Leon Battista Alberti* and executed by *Bernardo Rossellino* (c 1446–51).

Its dignified façade with incised decoration is in striking contrast to the heavy rustication of other Florentine palaces of the period. The three storeys, with classical pilasters and capitals of the three orders, are divided by delicately carved friezes bearing the Rucellai and Medici emblems. The five bays of the front were later increased on the right to seven bays. The design of the façade had a lasting influence on Italian architecture.—The small **Museo di Storia della Fotografia Fratelli Alinari** (adm. see p 62) has recently been opened in modernised rooms on the ground floor of the palace. It illustrates the history of the firm of Alinari, founded in 1852 and famous in black-and-white photography. Periodic exhibitions are held and the *Photo Archive* on the first floor is open to the public.—The *Loggia dei Rucellai* has three arches also attributed to Alberti and a graffiti frieze.

Via della Vigna Nuova continues to the Arno; Via dei Palchetti skirts Palazzo Rucellai (right) and Via de' Federighi (view left of the garden of Palazzo Niccolini above a high wall) continues into Piazza San Pancrazio. Here is the ex-church of SAN PANCRAZIO (Pl.5;8), one of the oldest in the city, founded before 1000. Deconsecrated in 1809, it was later used as a tobacco factory, and as a military store. The beautiful classical *Porch is by Alberti. It has been converted into a Museum (adm. see p 61) for works by Marino Marini (1901–80) which were left to the city by the sculptor. Exhibitions are held in the 15C crypt.—In Via della Spada (No. 18) is the entrance (usually open only on Sat at 17.30) to the remarkable *Cappella di San Sepolcro*, built in 1467 by Alberti for Giovanni Rucellai. In the middle of a lovely barrel-vaulted chapel is a perfectly preserved *Model in inlaid marble with exquisite carving of the Sanctuary of the Holy Sepulchre in Jerusalem. Inside is a much blackened Resurrection attributed to Giovanni di Piamonte. Via della Spada, a local shopping street, returns to Via Tornabuoni (view of Palazzo Strozzi).

At No. 19 Via Tornabuoni, *Palazzo Larderel* (Pl.16;3), attributed to Giovanni Antonio Dosio (begun 1580), is a model of High Renaissance architecture. On the right, preceded by a wide flight of steps is **San Gaetano** (properly *Santi Michele e Gaetano*; Pl.16;3; open 17–18.30 or Sunday morning), the most important 17C church in Florence. The fine façade (1648–83) was designed by *Pier Francesco Silvani*.

The dark grey INTERIOR (best light in the morning) in pietra serena was built in 1604–49 by *Matteo Nigetti* (possibly influenced by a design of *Bernardo Buontalenti*) and (after 1630) by *Gherardo Silvani*. The sombre decoration in various precious marbles and dark wood survives almost totally intact and nearly all the frescoes and altarpieces were painted in the 1630s and 1640s (unless otherwise indicated below). The colossal white marble statues (with bas reliefs below) of the Apostles and Evangelists (1640–90) are by *Giovanni Battista Foggini* (Saints Peter and Paul on the triumphal arch), *Antonio Novelli* and others. SOUTH SIDE. 1st chapel, Madonna in glazed terracotta by *Andrea della Robbia*, and two paintings and vault frescoes by *Ottaviano Vannini*. 2nd chapel, two paintings by *Jacopo Vignali* and vault frescoes by *Angelo Michele Colonna*. 3rd chapel, Altarpiece of Saints by *Matteo Rosselli* and vault frescoes by *Sigismondo Coccapanni*.—SOUTH TRANSEPT. Adoration of the Magi, by *Ottaviano Vannini*. Chapel to the right of the high altar, *Matteo Rosselli*, Nativity and Visitation, and vault frescoes, and Annunciation by *Fabrizio Boschi*.—CHOIR CHAPEL. The dome was frescoed by *Filippo Maria Galletti* in the late 17C, and on the E wall is a bronze Crucifix by *Giovanni Francesco Susini*, his most important work (1634–5).—NORTH TRANSEPT. In the chapel to the left of the high altar, Finding of the True Cross by *Matteo Rosselli*, two paintings on the side walls by *Giovanni Bilivert*, and vault frescoes by *Jacopo Vignali*. The Exaltation of the Cross on the end wall of the transept is by *Giovanni Bilivert*.—NORTH SIDE. 3rd chapel, Death of St Andrea Avellina, signed and dated by *Ignazio Hugford* (1738), and (on the right wall) a 15C Madonna surrounded by angels painted by *Francesco Boschi*. On the opposite wall, Presentation in the Temple, by his brother *Alfonso*. The vault frescoes of the Coronation of the Virgin surrounded by putti, and the three lunettes of angels (very difficult to see) are by *Lorenzo Lippi*. 2nd chapel, *Pietro da Cortona*, Martyrdom of St Lawrence (c 1653); on the right wall, Madonna appearing to St Francis by *Jacopo da Empoli*, and on the left wall, St Lawrence giving to the poor, by *Matteo Rosselli*. The vault frescoes are by *Angelo Michele Colonna*.

1st chapel, altarpiece of St Michael Archangel by *Jacopo Vignali*, and vault frescoes by *Filippo Maria Galletti* (late 17C).—The ANTINORI CHAPEL (usually kept locked) on the left side of the church, was erected in 1635–37. It contains a Crucifix and Saints by the school of *Filippo Lippi*, three bas-reliefs from the Romanesque church, and a monument to Alessandro Antinori (died 1557).

In Piazza Antinori is *Palazzo Antinori*, owned by the Antinori since 1506 and one of the most beautiful smaller Renaissance palaces in Florence. Built in 1461–69, with a pretty courtyard, it is attributed to Giuliano da Maiano.

Via degli Agli and Via Vecchietti (left) lead to the church of **Santa Maria Maggiore** (Pl.16;3; entered by the side doors), with a rough exterior in pietra forte. Probably founded in the 8C, it was rebuilt in its present Gothic Cistercian form at the end of the 13C. At the corner of the façade is the Romanesque bell-tower. In the dark interior the 17C altarpieces (3rd chapel right, and 2nd chapel left), by *Pier Dandini* and *Onorio Marinari*, are obscured by candles. On the pilasters and on the W wall are 13–14C frescoes, some by *Mariotto di Nardo*. The internal façade was designed by *Buontalenti*. In the chapel to the left of the choir: *Madonna enthroned, a Byzantine relief in painted wood, attributed to *Coppo di Marcovaldo*; (right) a column which survives from the tomb of Brunello Latini (died 1294), Dante's teacher, and (left) tomb (1272) of Bruno Beccuti with the figure of the deceased attributed to *Tino da Camaino*. The two detached frescoes (very ruined) in the sanctuary are attributed to a contemporary of Spinello Aretino.

13   Museo Nazionale del Bargello

*Palazzo del Bargello** (Pl.16;6; *Palazzo del Podestà*), a massive battlemented medieval fortress-building in pietra forte, stands in Piazza San Firenze. Built in 1255 as the 'Palazzo del Popolo' it is the oldest seat of government which survives in the city.

It was begun, according to Vasari, to a design by a certain 'Lapo', the master of Arnolfo di Cambio. Building continued until 1330–50; the splendid upper hall was vaulted by Neri di Fioravante and Benci di Cione in 1345. The ancient *Tower* (restored in 1987) is 57 metres high. Well restored in 1857–65, and at present undergoing another lengthy restoration, the building still preserves its 14C aspect. It was at first the seat of the 'Capitano del Popolo', who, during his one-year term of office held supreme authority in the government of the city. From the end of the 13C until 1502 the palace was the official residence of the 'Podestà', the governing magistrate of the city, who was traditionally a foreigner. In the 16C the building became known as the 'Bargello', when the police headquarters were moved here and prisons were installed (in use until 1858–59). In 1786, when the grand-duke Pietro Leopoldo abolished the death sentence, instruments of torture were burnt in the courtyard.

The palace now contains the **Museo Nazionale del Bargello**, famous for its superb collection of Florentine Renaissance sculpture, including numerous works by Donatello and the Della Robbia family. 16C Florentine sculpture is well represented by Michelangelo, Cellini, and Giambologna, among others, and an exquisite collection of small Mannerist bronzes. In no other museum of the city can the Florentine Renaissance be better understood. The building also houses a notable collection of decorative arts. The Museum was first

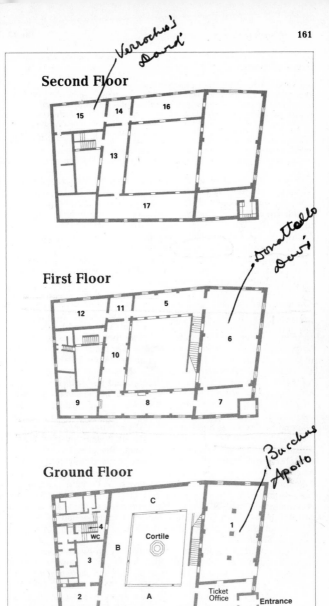

Verrochio's David

Second Floor

15 14 16
13
17

Donatello David

First Floor

12 11 5
10
6
9 8 7

Bacchus Apollo

Ground Floor

C
4
WC
B Cortile
3
1
2 A
Ticket Office
Entrance

MUSEO NAZIONALE DEL BARGELLO

opened to the public in 1865. The entrance is in Via del Proconsolo (adm. see p 61).

The museum came into being in 1859 when the collection of sculpture and applied arts formerly in the Uffizi (cf. p 98) was tranferred here. In 1888 the important Carrand Collection was left to the museum, and later acquisitions included the Ressmann collection of armour and Franchetti collection of fabrics. The whole of the ground floor was submerged to a height of nearly four metres in the flood of 1966. The 16C sculpture and armoury which suffered most damage have since been beautifully restored. The rooms of sculpture are arranged mostly by period and school. Room numbers refer to the numbers on the plans in the text. Rooms 7–9 & 17 are closed for restoration.

Ground Floor. ROOM 1, a fine hall, contains 16C sculpture by Michelangelo and his Florentine contemporaries. By the door is a fresco of the Madonna and Child with Saints attributed to *Taddeo Gaddi.* (In wall case) *Rustici,* terracotta group of horsemen engaged in battle (after Leonardo da Vinci); *Andrea Sansovino,* Madonna and Child (terracotta). In the centre, three superb works by *Michelangelo:* *Bacchus drunk, made on his first visit to Rome c 1497 for the banker, Jacopo Galli. It was kept in his garden for over 50 years and was then purchased by the Medici and brought to Florence. Michelangelo's first important piece of sculpture, it shows the influence of classical works. The *Tondo of the Madonna and Child with the infant St John was made for Bartolommeo Pitti c 1503–05. It is a charming work, and a fine example of the sculptor's 'schiacciato' technique. The *Bust of Brutus is a much later work (c 1539–40), derived from Imperial Roman portrait busts, and is the only bust Michelangelo ever sculpted. It was made after the murder of Duke Alessandro de' Medici and is an exaltation of Republicanism as against the tyranny of the Medici. It was left unfinished, and Michelangelo's pupil Tiberio Calcagni added the drapery.—Behind Michelangelo's tondo there is another tondo of the same subject by *Rustici.* Beyond the door, *Jacopo Sansovino,* *Bacchus, which takes its inspiration from Michelangelo's statue. The small figure called *Apollo (or David) is another beautiful work by *Michelangelo* in a 'contrapposto' position. According to Vasari, it was carved for Baccio Valori, but later formed part of the Medici collection. The statuettes, models, and replicas (in cases against the wall) by followers of Michelangelo include works by *Pietro Francavilla, Tribolo, Giambologna* (a model for his giant 'Appennino' at Pratolino), *Bartolommeo Ammannati,* and *Vincenzo Danti.* The marble figure of Leda by *Ammannati* (c 1540–50) is one of the best copies which has survived of the famous painting by Michelangelo commissioned by Alfonso d'Este and later destroyed. The marble bust of Cosimo I is a good work by *Bandinelli.*

In the second part of the hall: *De' Rossi,* *Dying Adonis; *Bandinelli,* colossal statues of Adam and Eve, which were not considered suitable for the Duomo. The two statues by *Ammannati* were intended for the Nari tomb in Santissima Annunziata (1540), but because of the opposition of Bandinelli they were never set up there. The clay bas-reliefs of the Passion of Christ displayed in wall-cases are by *De' Rossi* (formerly attributed to Donatello). There follow a group of *Works by *Cellini.* The Narcissus, carved from a worn block of marble with two holes, was damaged in Cellini's studio during an Arno flood. Together with the Apollo and Hyacinth, also displayed here, it later found its way to the Boboli gardens, and the two statues were only re-identified and brought under cover just before the last War. The splendid bronzes exhibited here include a scale model of

Cellini's famous statue of Perseus (in the Loggia della Signoria, p 88), and the relief (Perseus releasing Andromeda) and statuettes (Danae and Perseus, Mercury, Minerva, and Jove) from the pedestal of this statue. The marble Ganymede is an Antique statue restored by *Cellini*. *Vincenzo Danti*'s statue representing Honour overcoming Deceit (his first work in marble, which was placed in the Boboli gardens in 1775) is exhibited near *Giambologna*'s colossal Virtue repressing Vice (or Florence victorious over Pisa). The bronze *Mercury is *Giambologna*'s most successful and influential statue: it seems almost on the point of flying away and invites the beholder to walk around it. The bronze cupboard door was made by *Vincenzo Danti* for Cosimo I. The colossal *Bust of Cosimo I was the first work *Cellini* cast in bronze (1545–48). His talent as a goldsmith can be seen in the delicate carved details of the armour. Beyond another bronze relief (Moses and the Serpent) by *Danti*, is a portrait bust of Michelangelo by *Daniele da Volterra*.

The Gothic *CORTILE, the finest part of the palace, is adorned with a large number of coats-of-arms of the former Podestà. Here is displayed more 16C sculpture: under the colonnade (A): *Vincenzo Danti*, idealised statue of Cosimo I dressed as a Roman; *Benedetto da Maiano*, large high relief of the Coronation of Ferdinand of Aragon, with six boy musicians; *Niccolò di Pietro Lamberti*, St Luke the Evangelist (formerly in a niche of Orsanmichele). The cannon, cast by *Cosimo Cenni* in 1620 shows the planet Jupiter with its four satellites discovered by Galileo in 1610. Against the far wall (B) are six fine statues (including Juno) by *Ammannati* (1556–63) from an allegorical fountain intended for the S end of the Sala dei Cinquecento in Palazzo Vecchio, but instead set up first in the Villa di Pratolino, and then in 1588 in the courtyard of Palazzo Pitti (cf. p 121). On the last wall (C): *Giambologna*, Oceanus, a colossal statue from the Boboli gardens (see p 124); *Tribolo*, *Fiesole (in pietra serena) from the garden of the Villa di Castello; *Domenico Poggini*, Clio. The Fisherboy (1877) is by the Neapolitan sculptor, *Vincenzo Gemito*. The *Cannon of St Paul is a wonderful piece of casting by *Cenni* (1638). It was commissioned by Grand-Duke Ferdinando II for Livorno castle.—Off the courtyard is the SALA DEL TRECENTO (2) with 14C sculpture. Here are displayed statues from Orsanmichele, capitals from the Badia, and colossal statues of the Madonna and Child and Saints Peter and Paul from the Porta Romana, by *Paolo di Giovanni*. The three acolytes are by *Arnolfo di Cambio*, and works by *Tino da Camaino* include a fine Madonna and Child. Two more statues of the Madonna and Child are from the bottega of the Sicilian sculptor *Domenico Gagini*, and by a 14C French sculptor.—The room next door (3) is used for exhibitions. Here also is a restored statue of St John the Baptist by *Battista Lorenzi* (removed from the Boboli).

The **First Floor** may be reached by the staircase (4) or from the open stairway in the courtyard. The LOGGIA (5) provides a charming setting for works by the Flemish-born *Giambologna*, perhaps the greatest Mannerist sculptor who worked in Florence, who had a wide influence on his contemporaries. The life-like group of bronze birds was made for a grotto at the Villa di Castello. The female statue in marble represents Architecture.

The SALONE DEL CONSIGLIO GENERALE (6) is a splendid 14C vaulted hall. Here are displayed works by *Donatello*, the greatest sculptor of the Quattrocento, and his contemporaries. In the middle of the room is his Marzocco, the Florentine heraldic lion, in pietra serena. On the end wall is the reconstructed tabernacle from

Orsanmichele (cf. p 84) which contains *St George, made for the guild of armourers c 1416. By endowing the statue with a sense of movement, Donatello here resolves the difficult problem of placing a figure within a niche, but at the same time not letting it appear to be confined. The remarkably well-composed statue, at once recognised as a new departure from Gothic forms, shows the Saint as the young Champion of Christendom. The *Bas-relief of St George and the Dragon was removed from Orsanmichele in 1974 and beautifully restored in 1982. It is a remarkable work in low relief, using the 'schiacciato' technique, showing a new interest in linear perspective and pictorial space. Other works by _Donatello_ include (left) *David with the head of Goliath, in bronze. One of the earliest and most beautiful free-standing male statues of the Renaissance, it was probably made between 1430–40 for the Medici. On their expulsion from Florence it was moved in 1495 to Palazzo della Signoria. The other *David, in marble (between the windows) is an early work by _Donatello_, begun in 1408. It was commissioned by the Opera del Duomo, but placed in Palazzo della Signoria in 1416. Opposite, St John the Baptist is attributed to the _school of Donatello_ (_Michelozzo?_), and the Young St John from the Casa Martelli is attributed to _Donatello_ or _Desiderio da Settignano_. In the centre of the room: _Desiderio da Settignano_, *Busts of a young woman and a boy; _Donatello_ (attributed), *Bust in coloured terracotta, full of character, traditionally thought to be a portrait of Niccolò da Uzzano; _Donatello_, *'Atys-Amorino', a humorous putto, in bronze. It represents a mythological subject of uncertain significance and dates from 1430–40. The statuette of a cupid in bronze is by _Bonacolsi_.

Around the walls (from the entrance door): _Vecchietta_, St Bernard, a statue in wood; a lunette from Via dell' Agnolo with the Madonna and two angels attributed to _Andrea della Robbia_; _Donatello_ (attributed), bronze statuette of a dancing Putto. The two trial *Reliefs of the Sacrifice of Isaac were executed by _Ghiberti_ and _Brunelleschi_ in competition for the second bronze doors of the Baptistery (cf. p 68). In 1403 Ghiberti was given the commission, a decision reached by a narrow majority, but which reflected approval for his new conception of art. The *Reliquary Urn (1428), beneath, is also by _Ghiberti_. The fine works by _Giovanni di Bertoldo_, Donatello's pupil, include: *Battle scene, a relief based on a Roman sarcophagus at Pisa, Statuette of Apollo or Orpheus (unfinished), and (end wall) reliefs of the Pietà, Triumph of Bacchus, and the Crucifixion. The gilded relief of the Crucifixion was made in Donatello's workshop. The *Bust of a youth with a medallion at his neck is instead thought to be by _Donatello_ himself (or possibly _Bertoldo_). One of the fine marriage-chests (early 15C) below shows the procession of San Giovanni (with a view of the Baptistery), _Desiderio da Settignano_, Relief of the Young St John.—On the next wall: _Donatello_ (attributed), Head of a marine divinity in bronze; _Agostino di Duccio_, Madonna and Child (a coloured relief), *Madonna and Child with angels (a tabernacle); _Desiderio da Settignano_, Madonna and Child (from Palazzo Panciatichi); _Michelozzo_, *Reliefs of the Madonna and Child (one in marble and one in terracotta). There follow a number of charming Madonnas by _Luca della Robbia_, who invented a special technique of enamelled terracotta sculpture which was a jealously guarded secret of his workshop for most of the 15C. The *Madonna and Child in a Rose-garden is by _Luca_; the tondo of the Madonna and Child with two angels is now thought to be an early work by his nephew _Andrea_. Below, tomb statue of Mariano Sozzino by

Vecchietta.—On the short wall: *Luca della Robbia,* two marble
*Reliefs made for an altar in the Duomo and left unfinished in 1439.
They show the Deliverance and Crucifixion of St Peter. The
Madonna and Child from Santa Maria Nuova in its original gilt wood
tabernacle is attributed to the *Della Robbia* workshop. *Michelozzo,*
Young St John, from the Casa dell'Opera di San Giovanni, Madonna
and Child. *Luca della Robbia,* *Madonna of the Apple (c 1460),
which formed part of the Medici collection.

Rooms 7–9 are closed for restoration. They are dedicated to the decorative arts,
including a *Collection (well labelled) from all over Europe dating from earliest
times up until the 17C, made by the wealthy Lyons art-collector Louis Carrand
and bequeathed to the museum in 1888. In the SALA DELLA TORRE (7) is a
collection of Islamic art including 15C armour, 16C and 17C brocade,
damascened dishes, works in brass and ivory, and a case of ceramics (Persian
tiles, etc.).—SALONE DEL PODESTÀ (8). *Marinus van Reymerswale,* The Money-
changer and his wife (1540); Limoges enamels; French and Italian cutlery (15–
16C); European clocks; ecclesiastical ornaments, many of them enamelled,
including reliquary caskets, pastoral staves, processional crosses, ewers, etc.;
15–16C metalwork from France; a 15C Venetian astrolabe in gilt bronze;
diptych of the Annunciation and the Presentation in the Temple (with monochrome figures on the reverse), a 15C Flemish work; a chimneypiece of 1478;
and Venetian and Bohemian glass (16–17C). At the end of the room, flat cases
contain a beautiful collection of jewellery and goldsmiths' work from the Roman
period to the 17C. The tiny Flemish and Italian paintings displayed together
here include three fragments by *Agnolo Gaddi,* a Madonna and Child by *Dirk
Bouts,* and a Coronation of the Virgin, and 'Noli me tangere', by the *'Master of
the St George Codex'.*
    The CAPPELLA DEL PODESTÀ or DI SANTA MARIA MADDALENA (9) dates from
the early 14C. The damaged frescoes (restored) were attributed to Giotto when
they were discovered in 1841, but they are now considered to be the work of his
school. On the altar wall, the scene of Paradise includes a portrait of Dante as a
young man (in the group to the right, dressed in maroon). Also on this wall there
is a frescoed roundel of the Madonna and Child by *Bastiano Mainardi* (1490).
The triptych of the Madonna and Saints by *Giovanni di Francesco* (mid 15C) has
been restored recently. The high lectern decorated with intarsia, from San
Miniato, is dated 1498. The stalls are of the same period. In the small adjoining
room cases contain two paxes decorated with niello by *Tommaso Finiguerra*
and *Matteo di Giovanni Dei,* and a bronze dove by *Luca della Robbia* which
comes from his tabernacle in Peretola (see p 247). Also here, goldsmiths' work,
chalices, processional crosses, reliquaries, etc.
    ROOM 10 has a fine collection of *Ivories, from the Etruscan period onwards. In
the first flat case: Persian, Arabic, German, and Sicilian ivories, and Carolingian
reliefs (9C); in the 2nd flat case; valve of a diptych which belonged to the
Roman Consul Basilio (6C); part of a Byzantine diptych with the Empress
Arianna (8C); an early Christian diptych (5C) showing Adam in earthly Paradise
and scenes from the life of St Peter in Malta. In a wall case, fragment of an
Anglo-Saxon coffer (8C) in whale-bone (the rest is in the British Museum). In
another central case: Byzantine coffer; French Pastoral staves (11–14C), and a
12C liturgical Flabellum. The Chessboard with intarsia ornament and bas
reliefs is a 15C Burgundian work.—Also displayed here are wood statues
including a Madonna of the Misericordia (Umbrian, late 14C), and a seated
female statue by *Mariano d'Angelo Romanelli* (c 1390), and a painted and
gilded 14C statue of a Bishop Saint (restored in 1982). The painting of the
Coronation of the Virgin is attributed to *Giottino.* ROOM 11 displays the
collection of furniture recently donated to the museum by the Florentine
antiquarian Giovanni Bruzzichelli. Also here: *Jacopo Sansovino,* Madonna and
Child, a large relief in papier mâché.—The SALA DELLE MAIOLICHE (12) contains
part of the Medici collection of Italian majolica (mostly 15C and 16C) including
works from the Deruta, Montelupo, Faenza, and Urbino potteries, and part of a
service which belonged to Guidobaldo II della Rovere, Duke of Urbino. The
beautiful *Garland with the Bartolini-Salimbeni and Medici emblems is the
work of *Giovanni della Robbia.*

The **Second Floor** is reached from Room 10 (see above). At the top of
the stairs ROOM 13 contains colourful and elaborate enamelled

terracottas, many of them by *Giovanni della Robbia*, son of Andrea. These include (No. 44) a fine *Tondo of the Madonna and Child and young St John. The large relief in white terracotta (Noli me tangere) is by *Rustici* (perhaps with the collaboration of *Giovanni della Robbia*). Works by *Benedetto Buglioni* include a polychrome terracotta statue of the Madonna and Child and a relief of the Noli me tangere. In the cases are displayed bronze medals and palquettes by *Il Riccio*, *Valerio Belli*, *'Moderno'*, and others.—ROOM 14 contains beautiful works in enamelled terracotta by *Andrea della Robbia*: Bust of a boy; *Madonna 'of the cushion', in a pretty tabernacle; *Madonna of the Stonemasons (1475). The portrait of a lady (a circular high relief) has recently been attributed to Andrea's uncle, *Luca della Robbia*.

ROOM 15 displays works by *Verrocchio* and fine Renaissance portrait busts. In the centre is *Verrocchio*'s bronze ⟨David⟩ made for the Medici, and then acquired by the Signoria in 1476. It owes much to Donatello's earlier statue of the same subject (see p 164). To the right of the door are charming marble works by *Mino da Fiesole*: busts of Cosimo il Vecchio's two sons, Giovanni and *Piero il Gottoso (1453; the first dated portrait bust of the Renaissance); two Madonnas; portrait of Rinaldo della Luna; and a tabernacle.—On the window wall: *Benedetto da Maiano*, *Pietro Mellini, signed and dated 1474, a remarkable portrait of this rich Florentine merchant as an old man; 15C *Florentine School*, Bust of Giuliano di Piero de' Medici, murdered in the Pazzi conspiracy; *Gian Francesco Romano* (attributed), Profile relief of Federico da Montefeltro and Francesco Sforza; exquisite tabernacle by *Desiderio da Settignano*.—On the end wall, the works by *Antonio Rossellino* include a bust of Francesco Sassetti; a painted relief of the Madonna in a tabernacle; a marble tondo of the Nativity; busts of a young boy, and of the young St John the Baptist; and the portrait bust of Matteo Palmieri, Renaissance statesman and scholar (1468). This was on the façade of his Florentine palace until the 19C, which accounts for its weathered surface.—On the wall opposite the windows: *Antonio del Pollaiolo*, *Young cavalier, a bust thought to be a portrait of a member of the Medici family (in terracotta); works by *Verrocchio*: Portrait bust of Piero di Lorenzo de' Medici (in terracotta); also attributed to Piero del Pollaiolo); Resurrection, a polychrome relief; bas-relief in terracotta of the Madonna and Child from Santa Maria Nuova; *Bust of a lady holding flowers. Formerly part of the Medici collection, this is one of the loveliest of all Renaissance portrait busts, and was once attributed to Verrocchio's pupil, Leonardo da Vinci. *Antonio del Pollaiolo*, *Portrait of a man, another marble bust; *Verrocchio*, Death of Francesca Tornabuoni-Pitti, a tomb relief; *Matteo Civitali*, Faith, Portrait relief of a lady; *Francesco Laurana* (a Dalmatian artist who worked at the Court of Urbino), *Battista Sforza, duchess of Urbino (a marble bust).

The **Medagliere Mediceo** (beautifully displayed in RR 18 & 19) was reopened in 1990. This huge collection of Italian medals was started by Lorenzo il Magnifico. Room 18. Case A. *L'Antico (Jacopo Alari Bonacolsi)*, Two circular reliefs with the Labours of Hercules; Case I. *Medals by *Pisanello*, the *15C Ferrarese school*, and *Matteo de' Pasti*.—The chronological order of the display continues in the next room (19). Beyond the marble bust of Virginia Pucci Ridolfi, by *Domenico Poggini*, Cases II & III have medals including works by *Francesco di Giorgio Martini*, *Sperandio*, and *Niccolò di Francesco Spinelli*. On the wall, 1C Roman relief (reworked in the 17C) of Ganymede. On the end wall, *Jacopo Sansovino*, *Christ in Glory, a bas-relief in a tabernacle. Case IV contains medals by Florentine artists (*Francesco da Sangallo*, *Domenico Poggini*). Cases

V & VI, medals by *Gasparo Mola* and 16C Roman artists. On the walls, three late-15C reliefs of allegorical triumphs. Case VII, medals by *Leone Leoni*. Wall case B has a selection of medals from the Carrand collection.—In R. 18, *Bernini*, *Bust of his mistress Costanza Bonarelli, and a small model in terracotta for a fountain in Pistoia. Case IX, medals by *Massimiliano Soldani*. The bust of Cardinal Paolo Emilio Zacchia Rondanini is by *Alessandro Algardi*. Cases XI–XII, Baroque and neo-classical medals. On the walls, two high reliefs of St Teresa and St Joseph by *Massimiliano Soldani*. Case XIII has 16–18C foreign medals.

From Room 14 there is access to the SALONE DEL CAMINO (16), with a superb display of small Renaissance *Bronzes*, the most important collection in Italy. The fashion of collecting small bronzes was begun by Lorenzo il Magnifico following a Roman tradition. The statuettes, animals, bizarre figures, candelabra, bells, etc. were often copies of Antique works, or small replicas of Renaissance statues. In the wall cases on the right: splendid bronzes by *Giambologna* including several statuettes of Venus, animals, Architecture, and Hercules and the Hydra; *Benvenuto Cellini*, relief of a dog.—Works by *Danese Catteneo* (including Fortune), *Tribolo*, and a fine group of statuettes by *Baccio Bandinelli*.—The splendid *Chimneypiece is the work of *Benedetto da Rovezzano*, and the firedogs are by *Niccolò Roccatagliata*. The Ganymede is attributed to *Cellini* or *Tribolo*.—The wall cases on the opposite wall contain: an Anatomical figure, a famous work made in wax by *Lodovico Cigoli* (1598–1600) and fused in bronze by *Giovanni Battista Foggini* after 1678. Beyond are charming animals by 15C and 16C artists from the Veneto and Padua; fantastical works by *Il Riccio*; and works by *Giovanni Battista Foggini* and *Pietro da Barga*.—On the entrance wall, works by *Pier Jacopo Alari* and copies from Antique statues. The 'Frightened Man' is attributed to *Donatello*.—The central cases contain copies from works by Giambologna, as well as the dwarf Morgante riding a monster by *Giambologna* and *Vincenzo della Nera*; works by *Giovanni Francesco Susini*; a satyr by *Massimiliano Soldani Benzi*; and 16–18C bronzes from the Veneto. In the centre of the room, *Hercules and Anteneas, by *Antonio del Pollaiolo*, a beautiful small bronze group, also the subject of a painting (now in the Uffizi, see p 101) by the same artist.

From Room 13 a door leads into the SALA DELLE ARMI (17; closed) with a magnificent display of *Arms and armour from the Medici, Carrand, and Ressmann collections (well labelled). It includes saddles decorated with gold, silver, and ivory, a shield by Gaspar Mola (17C), and numerous sporting guns, dress armour, oriental arms, etc. Also, a fine bust in marble by *Francesco da Sangallo*, an idealised portrait of Giovanni delle Bande Nere. The bronze bust of Ferdinando I is by *Pietro Tacca*.—The SALA FRANCHETTI may be reopened to be used as an exhibition hall and to display the study collection of materials.

14 From the Badia Fiorentina to Santa Maria Nuova

In **Piazza San Firenze** (Pl.16;6), where seven streets converge, a miscellany of buildings are assembled. Opposite the corner of Palazzo Vecchio stands *Palazzo Gondi* (No. 2), a beautiful palace built c 1489 by Giuliano da Sangallo with a pretty little courtyard. It was completed (and the façade on Via de' Gondi added) with great taste by Giuseppe Poggi in 1872–84. The square is dominated by SAN FIRENZE, a huge Baroque building, now occupied by the law courts, by Francesco Zanobi del Rosso (1772–75). It is flanked by two church façades designed by Ferdinando Ruggieri (1715). The church of *San Filippo Neri* (left), by Gherardo and Pier Francesco Silvani (1633–48) has an unusually tall interior, decorated in 1712–14 (the ceiling was painted by Giovanni Camillo Sagrestani).—At the end of the piazza the slender tower of the Badia rises opposite the battlemented Bargello (see Rte 13). At the beginning of Via del Proconsolo (left) is a portal by Benedetto da Rovezzano (1495), with a Madonna in enamelled terracotta by Benedetto Buglioni, which leads into the courtyard of the **Badia Fiorentina** (Pl.16;6), the church of a Benedictine abbey founded in 978.

Willa, the widow of Uberto, Margrave of Tuscany, founded the monastery in his memory, richly endowing it with property. Their son Count Ugo, a benefactor of the monastery, is buried in the church. One of the first hospitals in the city was established here in 1031. The tolling of the bell, mentioned by Dante ('Paradiso', XV, 97–98), regulated life in the medieval city. At one time the 'Consiglio del Popolo' met here. The church was rebuilt on a Latin cross plan in 1284–1310 probably by *Arnolfo di Cambio*. This building was radically altered in 1627–31 when *Matteo Segaloni* reconstructed the interior.

The VESTIBULE, with a Corinthian portico, is by *Benedetto da Rovezzano*. From here there is a good view of the graceful CAMPANILE, Romanesque below (1307) and Gothic (after 1330) above.—The 17C INTERIOR preserves fragments of frescoes from the old church on the W wall. The carved wood ceiling by Felice Gamberai (1629) has been restored. On the left, *Madonna appearing to St Bernard, a large panel of great charm by *Filippino Lippi* (c 1485). On the right, tomb of Giannozzo Pandolfini, from the workshop of *Rossellino*, and a sculpted altarpiece of the Madonna and Saints (1464–69) by *Mino da Fiesole*. In the right transept, tomb of Bernardo Giugni, the Florentine statesman (1396–1466), with a good effigy and statue of Justice, also by *Mino*. A Baroque chapel here has vault frescoes by *Vincenzo Meucci*, and an altarpiece by *Onorio Marinari* (1663). Above is a fine organ (1558; well restored) by *Onofrio Zeffirini* with paintings by *Francesco Furini* and *Baccio del Bianco*. In the chapel to the left of the presbytery, Way to Calvary, by *Giovanni Battista Naldini*. In the left transept, *Monument to Ugo (died 1001), Margrave of Tuscany, son of the foundress of the church, an exquisite work by *Mino da Fiesole* (1469–81). Above is a good painting of the Assumption and two Saints by *Vasari*. In the chapel are displayed four damaged frescoes detached from a wall of the church. They illustrate the Passion of Christ (including the suicide of Judas) and are attributed to *Nardo di Cione*. The two 19C statuettes are by *Amalia Duprè*.

Interesting fragments of 14C frescoes with scenes from the life of the Virgin (some attributed to *Giotto*) were detached with their sinopia from the Choir. These have been restored but have not been returned here. On the right of the Choir (with stalls of 1501), a door gives access to a flight of stairs which lead to the upper loggia of the **Chiostro degli Aranci** (open 9–11.45, 16.30–18), by *Bernardo Rossellino* (c 1434–36), a peaceful cloister where orange trees were once cultivated. The interesting and well-preserved *Fresco cycle illustrates scenes from the life of St Benedict (restored in 1973, when the sinopie were also detached). By an unknown master (usually known as the 'Master of the Chiostro degli Aranci') working in the decade after the death of Masaccio, they have been attributed to *Giovanni di Consalvo*, a Portuguese artist and follower of Fra' Angelico. One of the lunettes in the N walk contains an early fresco by *Bronzino*.

In Via del Proconsolo (right) rises the handsome *Palazzo Pazzi-Quaratesi* (No. 10; no adm.) attributed to Giuliano da Maiano (1458–69). The Pazzi coat-of-arms (removed from the exterior) is displayed in the vestibule which leads to a pretty courtyard (with good capitals). The Pazzi, one of the oldest Florentine families, who made their fortune as bankers, organised a notorious conspiracy in 1478 against the Medici (cf. p 33) when Giuliano, brother of Lorenzo il Magnifico, was killed by Francesco de' Pazzi. Francesco, who was wounded, hid here before being seized by the mob and hung from a window of Palazzo Vecchio.—Across Borgo degli Albizi, a street lined with fine palaces described on p 216, is *Palazzo Nonfinito*, begun in 1593 by Buontalenti. The great courtyard is attributed to Cigoli. The building was continued by Vincenzo Scamozzi and others, but was left unfinished. It now houses the **Museo Nazionale di Antropologia ed Etnologia** (Pl.16;4), founded in 1869 by Paolo Mantegazza, the first museum of its kind in Italy (adm. see p 61).

The collection, displayed in some 35 rooms, is probably the most important ethnological and anthropological museum in Italy. It covers: *Africa* (notably

Ethiopia, Eritrea, Somalia, and Libya); *North Pakistan*, (a rare *Collection made in 1955–60 by Paolo Graziosi of material relating to the Kafiri); *South America* (including mummies, etc. from Peru, collected in 1883) and *Mexico*; *Asia* (Melanesia, the Islands of Sumatra, including the Modigliani collection c 1880, Tibet, and Japan, with the Fosco Maraini collection of Ainu material); and material from the Pacific Ocean probably acquired by Captain Cook on his last voyage in 1776–79.

Via del Proconsolo emerges in Piazza del Duomo (see Rte 2); to the right Via dell'Oriuolo leads to the ex-*Convento delle Oblate* (No. 24) which now houses the **Museo di Firenze com'era** (Pl.6;8; adm. see p 61), a topographical historical museum of the city. The maps, paintings and prints displayed in several rooms of the old convent illustrate the life of the city since the 15C.

Of particular interest are the prospect of the city, a 19C copy in tempera of the 'Pianta della Catena', an engraving of 1470 now in Berlin, and the first topographical plan of Florence drawn by *Stefano Bonsignori* in 1584 for the grand-duke Francesco I.—In the second room is a charming series of Lunettes of the Medici villas by the Flemish painter, *Giusto Utens* (1599) from the Villa di Artimino. The cartographical collection is continued with works by *Valerio Spada* (1650), *F.B. Werner* (1705), and *Federigo Fantozzi* (1843 and 1866). The views of Florence include paintings by *Thomas Patch* and *Giuseppe Maria Terreni*, and engravings by *Telemaco Signorini* of the Mercato Vecchio in 1874 before its demolition.—In the last hall are a fine series of engravings (1754) with views of the city and villas in the environs, by *Giuseppe Zocchi*, and lithographs by *A. Durand* (1863). The elevations and sections of the Duomo, Baptistery, and Campanile published by *Sgrilli* in 1755, were drawn by *Giovanni Battista Nelli* (1661–1725) who made the first measured survey of these buildings for the Opera del Duomo. The famous 'Fiera' of Impruneta was engraved by *Jacopo Callôt* in 1620. Plans by *Giuseppe Poggi*, architect when Florence was capital of Italy, complete the collection.

Via Folco Portinari leads N from Via dell'Oriuolo to SANTA MARIA NUOVA (Pl.6;8), a hospital founded in 1286 by Folco Portinari, believed to be the father of Dante's Beatrice. It is still operating as one of the main hospitals of Florence. The unusual portico (1574–1612) is a good work by Bernardo Buontalenti. Beneath it, in the centre, is the church of SANT'EGIDIO (c 1420) with a cast of a terracotta by Dello Delli (1424) in the lunette above (original see below).

In the Interior, immediately on the right, are the remains of the Portinari tomb. The first altarpiece on the right (Madonna and Child with Saints) is by *Felice Ficherelli* (1654–57). The splendid high altar with a ciborium in pietre dure dates from 1666. To the left is a small marble tabernacle by *Bernardo Rossellino* (1450); the bronze door by *Lorenzo Ghiberti* is replaced here by a copy (the original is kept in the offices of the Presidenza, see below).—A door to the right of the church (usually kept closed; admission through the hospital buildings) leads into a cloister, the oldest part of the hospital, with a Pietà by *Giovanni della Robbia*. To the left of the church, in another old courtyard, is the tomb-slab of Monna Tessa, the servant of Portinari who persuaded him to found the hospital, and a small tabernacle with a fresco of Charity by *Giovanni di San Giovanni*. The incongruous neo-classical pavilion is a monument to Count Galli Tassi, benefactor of the hospital.—In the offices of the Presidenza, above (adm. granted to scholars by appointment), are the original lunette by *Delli* (cf. above), a fresco of the Crucifixion, an early work by *Andrea del Castagno*, and a Madonna and Child by *Andrea della Robbia* (formerly in Sant'Egidio). The Salone di Martino V (sometimes shown on request) contains detached frescoes (formerly flanking the church doorway) of Martin V consecrating the church, by *Bicci di Lorenzo* (with its sinopia), and the same pope confirming its privileges, by *Andrea di Giusto* (repainted). Also a detached fresco of the Resurrection (damaged), recently discovered, attributed to *Pietro Gerini*.

At No. 1 Via Bufalini a plaque marks the site of Ghiberti's workshop, where the Baptistery doors were cast.—In Via Sant'Egidio (No. 21) is the entrance to the **Museo Fiorentino di Preistoria** (Pl.6;8; adm. see p 61), a museum of

prehistory founded in 1946. Exhibited in three large rooms, the material is well
labelled and arranged chronologically and geographically. The lower hall is
dedicated to Italy, and includes a human skull of the Paleolithic era found at
Olmo near Arezzo in 1865; in the upper hall material from Europe, Africa, and
Asia is displayed, including an interesting collection from the Graziosi expedition to the Sahara, with photographs of rock carvings.—In Via della Pergola is
the house (No. 59) where Cellini cast his 'Perseus' (cf. Rte 4), and where he died
in 1571. The **Teatro della Pergola** (Pl.7;7), on the site of a wooden theatre
erected in 1656 by Ferdinando Tacca (famous for the comedies performed here),
dates in its present form from the 19C. When Gordon Craig was director in 1906
'Rosmersholm' was produced with Eleonora Duse. Plays and chamber music
concerts are now given here (cf. p 58).

15   Santa Croce and Casa Buonarroti

PIAZZA SANTA CROCE (Pl.10;2; closed to cars), one of the most
attractive and spacious squares in the city, has been used since the
14C for tournaments, festivals, and public spectacles, and the traditional football game was held here for many centuries (cf. p 58). It is
the centre of a distinctive district of the city, with numerous narrow
old streets of small houses above artisans' workshops. In medieval
Florence the area was a centre of the wool industry. One side of the
piazza is lined with houses whose projecting upper storeys rest on
brackets. These are the characteristic 'sporti', a familiar architectural
feature of the medieval city. The wooden brackets were replaced in
the 15C and 16C by stone supports. *Palazzo dell'Antella* (No. 2) was
built by Giulio Parigi and its polychrome façade (now very worn) is
supposed to have been painted in three weeks in 1619 by Giovanni
di San Giovanni, Passignano, Matteo Rosselli, Ottavio Vannini, and
others.—The unusual palace at the end of the square facing the
church is *Palazzo Cocchi* (*Serristori*; restored in 1990), built above a
14C house c 1470–80, and recently attributed to Giuliano da Sangallo. The ungainly monument to Dante, beside the church façade,
was erected by Enrico Pazzi (1865).

   Santa Croce (Pl.11;1; closed 12.30–15), the Franciscan church of
Florence, was rebuilt in 1294 possibly by *Arnolfo di Cambio*. The
nave was still unfinished in 1375 and it was not consecrated until
1442. Remains of an earlier 13C church were found beneath the nave
in 1967. The CAMPANILE was added in 1842 by *Gaetano Baccani*.
The bare stone front was covered with a neo-Gothic FAÇADE in
1857–63 by *Niccolò Matas*; its cost was defrayed by an English
benefactor, Francis Sloane. It is a tour de force of local craftsmanship.
The lunette above the main door of the Triumph of the Cross is by
Giovanni Duprè. Along the left flank of the church a picturesque 14C
arcade survives. The church is much visited by tourist groups.

   The huge wide INTERIOR has an open timber roof. The vista is closed
by the polygonal sanctuary and the 14C stained glass in the E
windows. The Gothic church was rearranged by *Vasari* in 1560 when
the choir and rood-screen were demolished and the side altars added,
with tabernacles by *Francesco da Sangallo*. Fragments of frescoes by
Orcagna which formerly decorated the nave have been uncovered,
and some are exhibited in the Museum (see below). In the pavement
are numerous fine tomb-slabs. For 500 years it has been the custom to
bury or erect monuments to notable citizens of Florence in this church;
it is the burial place of Ghiberti, Michelangelo, Machiavelli, and
Galileo.—WEST WALL. In the round window the stained-glass

Deposition was composed from a cartoon attributed to *Giovanni del Ponte*. Monuments here commemorate the 19C patriots Gino Capponi and Giovanni Battista Niccolini (by Pio Fedi).

SOUTH AISLE. 1st pillar (1) *Madonna 'del Latte', a charming relief by *Antonio Rossellino* (1478), above the tomb of Francesco Nori, killed in the Pazzi conspiracy. The Tomb of Michelangelo (2) was designed by *Vasari* and includes a statue of architecture by *Giovanni dell'Opera*. Michelangelo died in Rome in 1564 but his body was transported to Florence for an elaborate funeral service (cf. p. 144). 2nd altar (3), *Vasari*, Way to Calvary. The cenotaph to Dante (4) is a neo-classical work by *Stefano Ricci* (1829). Dante, exiled in 1302 as an opponent of the Guelf faction in the government, never returned to his native city. He died in 1321 in Ravenna where he was buried. 3rd altar (5), *Jacopo Coppi di Meglio*, Ecce Homo. On the nave pillar (6), *Pulpit by *Benedetto da Maiano* (1472–76), a beautifully composed work decorated with delicately carved scenes from the life of St Francis and five Virtues. The monument (7) to Vittorio Alfieri (1749–1803), the poet, by *Antonio Canova*, was erected at the expense of the Countess of Albany. 4th altar (8), *Alessandro del Barbiere*, Flagellation of Christ, a good work. The monument (9) to Niccolò Machiavelli (died 1527), who is buried here, is by *Innocenzo Spinazzi* (1787). 5th altar (10) *Andrea del Minga*, Agony in the Garden, an unusual painting. By the side door (probably moved from another part of the church) is the Cavalcanti *Tabernacle (11) with a beautiful high relief in gilded limestone of the Annunciation, by *Donatello*. A very unusual work, there is a remarkable bond between the two figures.—On the other side of the door, *Tomb of Leonardo Bruni (12), by *Bernardo Rossellino* (c 1446–47), one of the most harmonious and influential sepulchral monuments of the Renaissance. The architectural setting takes its inspiration from Brunelleschi. Bruni, who died in 1444, was an eminent Florentine humanist, a Greek scholar, a historian of the city, and Chancellor of the Republic. He is shown crowned with a laurel wreath in a beautiful serene effigy. The touching epitaph was composed by Carlo Marsuppini, his successor as Chancellor, who is buried opposite (see below).—The monument (13) to Gioacchino Rossini (1792–1868), the composer, is by *Giuseppe Cassioli*, a sad imitation of the Bruni tomb, and placed too close to it. 6th altar (14), *Cigoli*, Entry into Jerusalem. The sepulchral statue (15) of Ugo Foscolo, the poet, who is buried here, is by *Antonio Berti* (1939). On the nave pillar, monument to Giovanni Antonio Degli Alberti by *Emilio Santarelli* (1836).

SOUTH TRANSEPT. The CASTELLANI CHAPEL (A) contains decorative *Frescoes by *Agnolo Gaddi* and assistants (among them probably *Gherardo Starnina*). They depict (right) the histories of St Nicholas of Bari and St John the Baptist, and (left) St Anthony Abbot and St John the Evangelist. On each wall is a white terracotta statue of a saint by the *Della Robbia*. The altar relief of the Marys at the Sepulchre is by a follower of *Nicola Pisano*. Behind is a tabernacle by *Mino da Fiesole* and a painted Crucifix by *Niccolò di Pietro Gerini*. Among the monuments is one by *Emilio Santarelli* to the Countess of Albany (died 1824; cf. p 185).—The BARONCELLI CHAPEL (B; light) has stained glass and *Frescoes by *Taddeo Gaddi* (father of Agnolo) who worked with Giotto for many years and was his most faithful pupil. These are considered among his best works, executed in 1332–38, and reveal his talent as an innovator within the Giottesque school (they include one of the earliest known night scenes in fresco

Piazza Santa Croce at the start of the traditional football game, an engraving by Alexander Cecchini, 1600. (Kunsthistoriches Institut)

painting). On either side of the entrance arch, Prophets, and tomb (right) of a member of the Baroncelli family (1327) with a Madonna and Child in the lunette also by *Gaddi*. The two statuettes of the Annunciation are attributed to *Giovanni di Balduccio*. The fresco cycle in the chapel illustrates the Life of the Virgin. The altarpiece of the Coronation of the Virgin (restored) is by *Giotto*, perhaps with the intervention of his workshop (including possibly Taddeo Gaddi). On the back wall (right), Madonna of the Girdle, a large 15C fresco by *Bastiano Mainardi* and a 16C statue of the Madonna and Child, a good work by *Vincenzo Danti*.

A portal by *Michelozzo*, with an inlaid door attributed to *Giovanni di Michele* leads into a CORRIDOR (C) also by *Michelozzo*. Here is a large Deposition by *Alessandro Allori* (1560) and a monument to Lorenzo Bartolini, who sculpted a

number of monuments in the church (died 1850), by his pupil, *Pasquale Romanelli*. On the left another carved and inlaid door gives access to the *SACRISTY (D) with frescoes of the Crucifixion by *Taddeo Gaddi*, the Way to Calvary, attributed to *Spinello Aretino*, and the Resurrection by *Niccolò di Pietro Gerini*. The fine inlaid cupboards (restored after serious flood damage in 1966), by *Giovanni di Michele*, contain antiphonals. The bust of the Redeemer is by *Giovanni della Robbia*. The RINUCCINI CHAPEL (E) is closed by a Gothic grille (1371). It is entirely covered with *Frescoes by *Giovanni da Milano* representing scenes from the life of the Virgin and St Mary Magdalen (c 1365). This Lombard artist who worked in Florence was one of the best and most sophisticated followers of Giotto. Over the altar is a polyptych by *Giovanni del Biondo* (1372).—Remains of an old courtyard can be seen from an adjoining room.—The MEDICI CHAPEL (F), also by *Michelozzo* (1434) is entered through a door by *Giovanni di Michele*. It contains a Madonna with Saints by *Paolo Schiavo* and St John the Baptist by *Spinello Aretino*. The terracotta *Altarpiece of the Madonna and Child with angels is by *Andrea della Robbia* (c 1480; the Saints were probably added by an assistant).

The small rectangular vaulted CHAPELS AT THE EAST END OF THE CHURCH are notable for their frescoes by Giotto and his school. The

VELLUTI CHAPEL (G) has damaged frescoes of St Michael Archangel by a follower of *Cimabue* (possibly *Jacopo del Casentino*). The polyptych on the altar is by *Giovanni del Biondo*.—The CALDERINI CHAPEL (H), by *Gherardo Silvani* (c 1620) has a damaged vault painting by *Giovanni di San Giovanni*, and an altarpiece by *Giovanni Biliverti* (The Finding of the True Cross, 1621).—The GIUGNI CHAPEL (J) contains the tomb of Charlotte Bonaparte (died 1839) by *Lorenzo Bartolini*.—The following two chapels were decorated by *Giotto*, born in the Mugello just to the N of Florence, for the Peruzzi and Bardi, two of the richest merchant families of the city. The frescoes were discovered in 1841–52; the lower scenes had been irreparably damaged by funerary monuments. They were restored by Gaetano Bianchi and others and the missing parts repainted, but in another restoration in 1957–61 the repainting was removed. Giotto's works here had a fundamental influence on Florentine painting and the Giottesque school continued to flourish throughout the 14C. The *PERUZZI CHAPEL (K) was painted by *Giotto* in his maturity, probably after his return to Florence from Padua; the frescoes are damaged and in extremely poor condition. The architectural settings contain references to classical Antiquity. In the archivolt, eight heads of Prophets; in the vault, symbols of the Evangelists; on right wall, scenes from the life of St John the Evangelist (Vision at Patmos, Raising of Drusiana, Ascent into Heaven); and on left wall, scenes from the life of St John the Baptist (Zaccharias and the Angel, Birth of St John, Herod's Feast). A drawing by Michelangelo survives of the two male figures on the left in the Ascension of St John the Evangelist.—The *BARDI CHAPEL (L) also contains frescoes by *Giotto*. Certainly designed by the master, it is possible that some of the frescoes were executed by his pupils. They represent the story of St Francis: on the entrance arch, the Saint receiving the stigmata; in the vault, Poverty, Chastity, Obedience, and the Triumph of St Francis. On the end wall, Franciscan Saints, including St Catherine. Left wall: the Saint stripping off his garments; the Saint appearing to St Anthony at Arles; Death of St Francis. Right wall: the Saint giving the Rule of the Order; the Saint being tried by fire before the Sultan (a particularly fine work); and the Saint appearing to Brother Augustine and Bishop Guido of Assisi.—On the altar, St Francis and scenes from his life by a Florentine artist of the 13C.

The polygonal vaulted SANCTUARY (M) is frescoed by *Agnolo Gaddi* (c 1380), and has fine stained glass lancet windows also designed by him. In the vault, Christ, the Evangelists, and St Francis, and (on the walls) the *Legend of the Cross. Over the altar is a large polyptych made up from panels by various hands including the Madonna and Saints by *Niccolò Gerini*, and four Fathers of the Church by *Giovanni del Biondo*. Above hangs a fine Crucifix by the 'Master of Figline'.—The TOSINGHI AND SPINELLI CHAPEL (N) has an Assumption of the Virgin above the entrance arch, also attributed to the 'Master of Figline'.—The CAPPONI CHAPEL (O) contains sculptures including a Pietà by the Florentine sculptor *Libero Andreotti* (1926). The next chapel was decorated in 1828–36 by *Giuseppe* and *Francesco Sabatelli*.—The BARDI DI LIBERTÀ CHAPEL (P) contains an altarpiece by *Giovanni della Robbia*, and frescoes of the Lives of St Lawrence and St Stephen by *Bernardo Daddi*.—The BARDI DI VERNIO CHAPEL (Q) has colourful and well-preserved *Frescoes of the Life of St Sylvester by *Maso di Banco* (after 1367), perhaps the most original follower of Giotto. The first Gothic tomb contains a Last Judgement with the figure of Bettino de' Bardi (c 1367), also attributed to *Maso di*

Banco; in the second niche, Deposition attributed to *Taddeo Gaddi*. The stained glass is also by *Maso*. The altarpiece by *Giovanni del Biondo* has been removed for restoration.

NORTH TRANSEPT. The NICCOLINI CHAPEL (R) was designed by *Giovanni Antonio Dosio* c 1580, using a profusion of rare marbles. The dome has good frescoes by *Volterrano* (1652–64). The statues are by *Francavilla* and the paintings by *Alessandro Allori*.—The second BARDI CHAPEL (S) contains the celebrated wooden *Crucifix by Donatello* (not seen to advantage here). The story is told by Vasari of Brunelleschi's complaint that it was a mere 'peasant on the cross' (cf. p 151).—In the SALVIATI CHAPEL (T) is the *Tomb of Sofia Zamoyska Czartoryska (died 1837), with a Romantic effigy by *Lorenzo Bartolini*. Outside the chapel (16) is a monument by Odoardo Fantacchiotti to the composer Luigi Cherubini (died 1842; born at No. 22 Via Fiesolana not far N of the church).

NORTH AISLE. Monument (17) to Raffaello Morgheni (died 1833), the engraver, by *Fantacchiotti*. On the nave pillar (18), monument to Leon Battista Alberti (died 1472), by *Lorenzo Bartolini*.—On the right of the side door, *Monument to Carlo Marsuppini (19), the humanist scholar and Chancellor of the Republic (died 1453), by *Desiderio da Settignano*. It takes its inspiration from the Bruni monument opposite (see above) and incorporates some exquisite carved figures. The fine classical sarcophagus may possibly be the work of *Verrocchio*. The organ above the door is by *Nofri da Cortona* (1579; restored).—Beyond the door (20) monument to Vittorio Fossombroni (died 1844) by *Bartolini*. 5th altar (21), Ascension by *Giovanni Stradano*. The painting of the Deposition is by *Bronzino*. In the pavement between the 5th and 4th altar (22) is the handsome tomb-slab with niello decoration and the emblem of an eagle which marks the burial place of Lorenzo Ghiberti, and his son Vittorio. 4th altar (23), *Vasari*, Incredulity of St Thomas. On either side are neo-classical funerary monuments by *Innocenzo Spinazzi*. The next two altarpieces (Supper at Emaus and the Resurrection; 24 and 25) are good works by *Santi di Tito*. Between them is a funerary monument by *Stefano Ricci*.—Galileo Galilei (1564–1642), the great scientist who spent the latter part of his life in Florence, was tried by the Inquisition for his contention that the earth was not at the centre of the Universe. He was not allowed Christian burial inside the church until 1737 when a Monument (26) was set up to him on a design by *Giulio Foggini*. *Giovanni Battista Foggini* carved the bust and the statues are by *Girolamo Ticciati* (Geometry, on the right), and *Vincenzo Foggini* (Astronomy). In the pavement in the centre of the nave (27) is the tomb-slab with a relief of his ancestor and namesake Galileo Galilei, a well-known physician in 15C Florence. The remains of frescoes on the wall (28) have been attributed to *Mariotto di Nardo*. 1st altar (29), *Giovanni Battista Naldini*, Deposition. On the wall (30) are remains of frescoes of three Saints (15C).

On the right of the church is the entrance to the conventual buildings and the **Museo dell'Opera di Santa Croce** (Pl.11;1; adm. see p 62). Here in 1966 the water of the Arno reached a height of nearly 6m (marked by the highest plaque to the left of the Pazzi Chapel); the buildings and works of art have since been carefully restored. The FIRST CLOISTER dates from the 14C; opposite the arcade along the bare Gothic flank of the church is a portico and loggia. On the green lawn is a group of cypresses with acanthus plants (and two incongruous statues: the seated figure of God the Father by Baccio

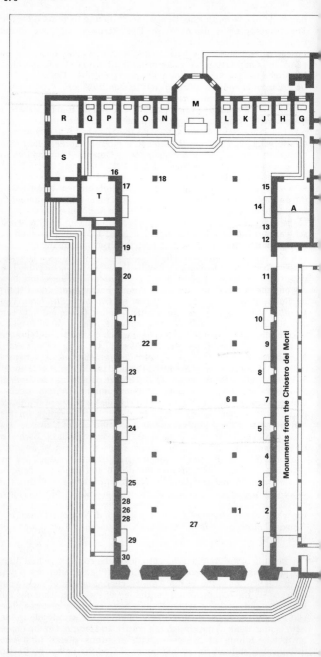

Monuments from the Chiostro dei Morti

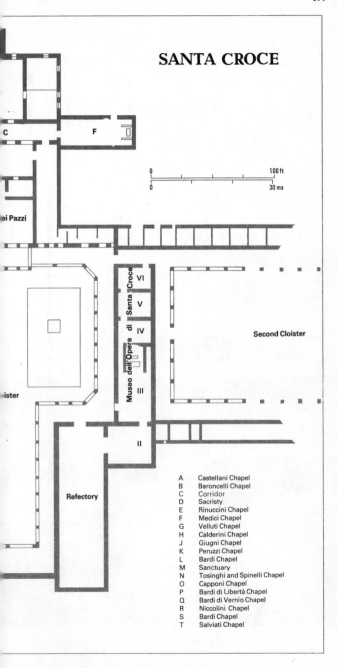

SANTA CROCE

C   F

0   100 ft
0   30 ms

ei Pazzi

VI

V

IV

Second Cloister

Museo dell'Opera di Santa Croce

III

ister

II

Refectory

A	Castellani Chapel
B	Baroncelli Chapel
C	Corridor
D	Sacristy
E	Rinuccini Chapel
F	Medici Chapel
G	Velluti Chapel
H	Calderini Chapel
J	Giugni Chapel
K	Peruzzi Chapel
L	Bardi Chapel
M	Sanctuary
N	Tosinghi and Spinelli Chapel
O	Capponi Chapel
P	Bardi di Libertà Chapel
Q	Bardi di Vernio Chapel
R	Niccolini Chapel
S	Bardi Chapel
T	Salviati Chapel

Bandinelli, which serves as a war memorial, and the statue of a warrior donated to the city by Henry Moore). The neo-Gothic campanile rises behind the charming dome and lantern of the ***Cappella dei Pazzi**, one of the most famous works by *Brunelleschi*. It was commissioned as a Chapter House by Andrea de' Pazzi in 1429 or 1430. Most of the work was carried out by Brunelleschi from 1442 until his death in 1446, but it was not finished until the 1470s.

The PORTICO (being restored) may have been designed by *Giuliano da Maiano*. It bears a terracotta frieze of cherubs' heads attributed to the *Della Robbia* workshop. Beneath the colonnade is a barrel vault and a shallow cupola lined with a delightul polychrome enamelled terracotta decoration by *Luca della Robbia*, with a garland of fruit surrounding the Pazzi arms. Over the door is a medallion with *St Andrew, also by *Luca* (c 1461). The carved wooden door is by the brothers *Da Maiano*.—The beautiful calm INTERIOR is one of the masterpieces of the early Renaissance. Delicately carved pietra serena is used to pronounce the architectural features against a plain white ground. The illumination in the chapel is increased by little oculi in the rib-vaulted dome. The twelve *Roundels in enamelled terracotta of the seated Apostles (c 1442–52) are by *Luca della Robbia*. In the pendentives of the cupola are polychrome roundels of the Evangelists, thought to have been added c 1460. These may have been designed by *Donatello* and glazed by the *Della Robbia* (although some scholars attribute them to Brunelleschi). In the sanctuary are decorations by the school of Donatello and a stained-glass window attributed to *Alesso Baldovinetti*.

On the left of the chapel is an exhibition room, and, beyond, a small courtyard between the Pazzi chapel, the corridor outside the sacristy with windows by Michelozzo, and the exterior of the Baroncelli chapel of the church. The remarkable series of 19C monuments (including works by *Aristodemo Costoli* and *Ulisse Cambi*) from the Romantic *Chiostro dei Morti* (demolished in 1869), were restored in 1986 and set up in a gallery beneath the arcade along the flank of the church.—The *SECOND CLOISTER (being restored) is reached through a doorway by *Michelozzo*. This is another beautiful work by *Brunelleschi*, finished in 1453 after his death. It is one of the most peaceful spots in the city.

Off the First Cloister is the entrance to the **Museo dell'Opera di Santa Croce** (cf. the Plan on p 176–7). The REFECTORY is a fine Gothic hall with large windows.

Detail of a fresco of the Last Supper by Taddeo Gaddi (in the Refectory of Santa Croce)

Here is displayed *Cimabue*'s great *Crucifix* which has been restored after it was almost completely destroyed in the flood. It was the greatest single loss of a work of art in 1966. The end wall is decorated with a huge *Fresco by *Taddeo Gaddi* (detached in one piece and restored) of the Last Supper below the Tree of the Cross* and four scenes showing St Louis of Toulouse, St Francis, St Benedict, and Mary Magdalen annointing the feet of Christ in the house of Simon the Pharisee. On the two long walls (below roundels of Saints) are detached fragments of a large fresco by *Orcagna* of the Triumph of Death and Inferno which used to decorate the nave of the church before Vasari's side altars were set up. The detached 14C fresco (attributed to *Giovanni del Biondo*) includes one of the earliest views of the city (including the Baptistery and Duomo). In a reconstructed tabernacle (a cast) is *Donatello*'s colossal gilded bronze *St Louis of Toulouse, commissioned by the Parte Guelfa for a niche in Orsanmichele. On the entrance wall, Christ carrying the Cross and Crucifixion, two fine detached frescoes by *Andrea di Giusto*. Above the door into the next room, Coronation of the Virgin, by *Maso di Banco*, and to the right, Saints John the Baptist and Francis by *Domenico Veneziano*.

ROOM II. 14–15C stained glass from the church; a fresco of St Francis by *Jacopo Ligozzi*; Madonna and Child (fresco), by the 15C Florentine school, attributed by some scholars to *Paolo Uccello* (and by others to a 14C artist); an unusual detached fresco showing the young Madonna sewing, a charming work attributed to the *'Master of the Bambino Vispo'*.—ROOM III, formerly the Cappella dei Cerchi, has traces of late-13C painted decorations. He e are displayed enamelled terracottas by *Andrea della Robbia* and his workshop, and frescoes by *Niccolò di Pietro Gerini*. In the corridor is a fine detached fresco from the tomb of a Cardinal.—ROOM IV. The three large sketches were detached from the walls of the Cappella dei Pazzi during restoration work in 1966. These interesting studies include a colossal head of St John the Baptist and an architectural study, which have been attributed by some scholars to *Donatello*; and another colossal head (with a halo) attributed to *Desiderio da Settignano*. The detached frescoes include: 15C Tuscan School, Martyrdom of St Thomas; *'Master of the Straus Madonna'*, Madonna enthroned (a sinopia); 14C Florentine School, St John the Baptist.—ROOM V contains sculptural fragments including the reconstructed tomb of Gastone della Torre, by *Tino da Camaino*; a relief of St Martin dividing his cloak with a beggar, in pietra serena, from a demolished rood-screen chapel in the church (15C); and a Madonna annunciate by *Tino da Camaino*.—The last room (VI) displays 17C works including ceiling paintings of two angels by *Matteo Rosselli*, a ciborium, and the sinopia of the fresco by *Ligozzi* in R. II. Other works of art owned by the convent will be returned here after restoration.—Beneath the colonnade, just before the exit from the cloister, is a memorial to Florence Nightingale, named after the city where she was born.

To the right of the monastic buildings of Santa Croce is the modern extension of the **Biblioteca Nazionale** (Pl.11;3), the older buildings of which extend to the entrance on Piazza dei Cavalleggeri. The main building was erected in 1911–35 by Cesare Bazzani. The National Library was formed from the collection bequeathed by Antonio Magliabechi (died 1714) and first opened to the public in 1747. To the original collection were joined the Biblioteca Palatina-Medicea (1711) and the library of Ferdinando III (1861), together with several monastic collections. It includes an important collection of material relating to Dante and Galileo. It became a copyright library for books published in Italy in 1870. In 1966 nearly a third of the library's holdings was damaged in the flood and a restoration centre here will be at work salvaging the books for many years to come.

Corso dei Tintori takes it name from the dyers' workshops documented here as early as 1313.—Nearby is *Borgo Santa Croce*, a handsome street in which Palazzo Spinelli (No. 10), built in 1460–70, has good graffiti decoration on the façade and in the courtyard. No. 8, the *Casa Morra* (no adm.), belonged to Vasari and contains frescoes by him. Palazzo Antinori-Corsini (No. 6) has a beautiful courtyard dating from the end of the 15C.

On the left side of Santa Croce is Via di San Giuseppe, where, in the house next to the church, the Trollope family lived in 1843–45. The little church of *Santa Maria della Croce al Tempio* (closed), contained frescoes attributed to Bicci di Lorenzo.These have been detached for restoration. Beyond is the church of SAN GIUSEPPE (Santa Maria del

Giglio; open 17–19; Wednesday also 9.30–12), built in 1519 on a design by *Baccio d'Agnolo*. The portal dates from 1852 (thought to be based on a design by Michelangelo). The Oratory with graffiti decoration and the elegant campanile both date from 1934.

The handsome INTERIOR has been restored since 1966. The pretty frescoes in the centre of the vault and in the choir are by *Sigismondo Betti* (1754), with architectural perspectives by *Pietro Anderlini*. The fine organ, with its original mechanism, is by the workshop of the Agati of Pistoia (1764). SOUTH SIDE. 1st chapel, 16C lunette (left side), and an unusual funerary monument by *Odoardo Fantacchiotti* (1854). The 2nd chapel was decorated in 1705 with a cupola frescoed by *Atanasio Bimbacci*. The damaged triptych (recently restored) attributed to *Taddeo Gaddi* and the 14C carved wood Crucifix both belonged to the Compagnia di Santa Maria della Croce al Tempio. The third chapel has frescoes by *Luigi Ademollo* (1840), and on the altar is a Nativity, an early work by *Santi di Tito*. Above the high altar inlaid with a floral decoration in pietre dure in 1930, is a painted Crucifix of the early 15C Florentine school. The 17C stalls and 16C paintings in octagonal frames complete the decoration of the choir.—NORTH SIDE. 3rd chapel (left wall) *'Maestro di Serumidio'* (attributed), Annunciation; 2nd chapel, early-16C copy of the fresco of the Madonna del Giglio (formerly in the tabernacle outside the church), and a painted Crucifix attributed to *Lorenzo Monaco*. 1st chapel (left wall) *Santi di Tito*, San Francesco di Paola healing a sick man, and, on the altar, a polychrome wood Crucifix of the 17C and two figures in stucco of the 18C. Two more paintings by *Cigoli* and *Giovanni Antonio Sogliani* have been removed for restoration since 1966.

Opposite the side of Santa Croce, Via delle Pinzochere leads past a fine palace (No. 3) to ***Casa Buonarroti** (Pl.11;1; adm. see p 60), a house in Via Ghibellina (No. 70). Three houses on this site were purchased in 1508 by Michelangelo. He left the property to his only descendant, his nephew Leonardo, who united the houses into one building following a plan already drawn up by Michelangelo. In turn, his son, called Michelangelo, an art collector and man of letters, made part of the house into a gallery in 1612 as a memorial to his great-uncle. The last member of this branch of the Buonarroti family founded the present museum in 1858. In the charming little rooms of the house are displayed some important sculptures by Michelangelo, and some of his drawings owned by the museum, as well as an interesting small eclectic collection of works of art made by Michelangelo's descendants. The rooms are un-numbered, but have been numbered in the text below according to the most obvious itinerary for a visit.

Ground Floor. The room to the left of the entrance hall and several rooms beyond (see below), are open only for exhibitions relating to Michelangelo. The first room has a ceiling fresco of the dream of Jacob by *Jacopo Vignali* (1621) and an unfinished 16C statue of a slave (identified in 1965 by the former director of the museum and attributed by him to Michelangelo).

In the vestibule, to the right of the entrance hall, is a fine bronze head of Michelangelo by *Daniele da Volterra*. In Room I are 16–19C portraits of Michelangelo based on a prototype by *Jacopino del Conte*. The other rooms on this floor contain part of the collection of Antiquities and Renaissance works begun by Michelangelo Buonarroti the Younger (1568–1647), and continued by the archaeologist Filippo Buonarroti (1661–1733). Room II. Portraits including an old man, traditionally attributed to *Guido Reni*; *Gregorio Pagani*, Three nephews of Michelangelo Buonarroti the Younger; 16C head of a woman. The *Love scene of Cornelia and Pompey is thought to be a copy of a lost work by *Titian* (removed for restoration). The statue of Venus and two cupids is attributed to *Vincenzo Danti*.—R III. Works by the Bottega of *Andrea della Robbia*; beautiful terracotta head of a child attributed to the school of Verrocchio or Antonio Rossellino; 16C majolica plates; wooden casket (c 1373). The 19C marble sculpture of Michelangelo at work as a boy is by *Cesare Zocchi*. R. IV. Collection of minerals and semi-precious stones, and coins. The two archaic stelae from Fiesole in pietra serena, one showing a seated satyr playing a lyre (beginning of the 5C BC; found in 1720), and the other with a warrior (late 6C

BC), are among the best preserved Etruscan stelae of this period. The five Etruscan urns include two polychrome terracotta urns from Chiusi (2C BC) with battle scenes, and a fragment of an alabaster urn representing Ulysses and the Sirens.—Other works in the rooms on the other side of the courtyard (used for exhibitions) include: a statue made up from a classical head and a medieval draped toga, two Roman statues of Florentine magistrates; a little relief with two goats (1C AD), and an ancient Ionic capital used as a model by Giuliano da Sangallo in the cloister of Santa Maria Maddalena dei Pazzi (see p 183).

First Floor. At the top of the stairs, sword thought to have belonged to Buonarroto Buonarroti, Captain of the Guelf party in 1392. The room to the left (V) contains two small sculptures by *Michelangelo*: the *Madonna of the Steps, a marble bas-relief, is his earliest known work, carved at the age of 15 or 16. The low 'schiacciato' relief shows the influence of Donatello. The *Battle relief is also one of his earliest works, carved just before the death of Lorenzo il Magnifico in 1492, and left unfinished. Modelled on ancient sarcophagi, it represents a mythological battle between Greeks and centaurs.—R. VI (left) contains the wooden model by *Pietro Urbano* for the façade of San Lorenzo designed by *Michelangelo*. It was commissioned by Leo X in 1516 but never carried out, and a colossal *Torso by *Michelangelo*, a model in clay and wood for a river god, intended for the Medici Chapel. It was presented by Ammannati to the Accademia del Disegno in 1583.—In Room VII, in front of the stairs, are displayed in rotation five or six *Drawings by *Michelangelo* owned by the museum. The four rooms beyond Room VII were decorated for Michelangelo Buonarroti the Younger c 1613–37 as a celebration of his famous great-uncle and his family. The first room, finished in 1620, illustrates Michelangelo's life and apotheosis, with paintings by *Giovanni Biliverti, Empoli, Francesco Furini, Giovanni di San Giovanni, Passignano* and *Matteo Rosselli*. On the wall opposite the statue of Michelangelo by *Antonio Novelli* is a copy of the cartoon of the so-called Epiphany by Michelangelo's pupil, *Ascanio Condivi*.—The next room is dedicated to the Buonarroti family, with a bust of Michelangelo the Younger by *Giuliano Finelli*, Bernini's pupil, and a painting of him by *Cristofano Allori*. The portrait of Michelangelo in a turban is attributed to *Giuliano Bugiardini*. Also here, *Predella with scenes from the life of St Nicholas of Bari by *Giovanni di Francesco*, and a marble cupid by *Andrea Ferrucci*.—The Chapel has a pretty ceiling, and frescoes of Florentine Saints by *Jacopo Vignali*. Here is a 16C bronze copy of the Madonna of the Steps.—The Library is decorated with an engaging frieze of illustrious Florentines by *Cecco Bravo* and *Domenico Pugliani*. Here are displayed Roman and Etruscan small bronzes, and Roman fragments in marble and terracotta. In an alcove are displayed Roman sculptures, including a statuette of Apollo, and the right arm and hand from a good Roman copy of the Discobolos of Myron.

In the room to the right of the stairs (VIII) is a *Crucifix in painted poplar wood, found in Santo Spirito in 1963, a documented work thought to have been lost. Its attribution to *Michelangelo* has been accepted by most scholars. It shows the slight figure of Christ in an unusual 'contrapposto' position, a design subsequently frequently copied.—R. IX. Cases of small bozzetti (models). The study in terracotta by Michelangelo for Hercules and Cacus was intended as a pair to his David outside Palazzo Vecchio (the commission was given instead to Bandinelli). The torso of Hermaphrodite, and the framgment of a female allegorical figure, perhaps for a niche in the funerary monument of Giuliano de' Medici, are attributed to Michelangelo. The tiny model in wood (1562) may have been made for a Crucifix which Michelangelo intended to carve in the last years of his life. The river god in black wax, and a fragment of the Madonna in the Medici chapel are copies from Michelangelo, and the torso in terracotta is attributed to him. The David and Hercules are attributed to *Tribolo*, and the St Jerome, to *Baccio Bandinelli*, or *Francesco da Sangallo*.—Beyond the early-18C Sala dei Paesaggi, is the last room (X) with works derived from Michelangelo. The copy from the Last Judgement is attributed to *Alessandro Allori*. The two paintings of 'Noli me tangere' are attributed to *Bronzino* and *Battista Franco*. The Crucifixion is attributed to *Marcello Venusti* and is a copy of a drawing made by Michelangelo for Vittoria Colonna. The relief in stucco of the Deposition was made in the 16C from a design by Michelangelo. The collection also includes two anatomical drawings by *Eugène Delacroix* and an etching by *Albrecht Dürer*.—On the Second Floor is a LIBRARY with material relating to Michelangelo.

16   Sant'Ambrogio and Santa Maria Maddalena dei Pazzi

This route, which covers the area to the N of Santa Croce, is of secondary importance apart from the churches, and can be combined with Rte 15.

The church of **Sant'Ambrogio** (Pl.11;1) was rebuilt in the late 13C. It has a 19C façade. The interior has pretty Renaissance side altars, and an open timber roof. Badly damaged in the flood of 1966, the works of art have been returned here after restoration.

The tribune, with its side chapels, was designed in 1716 by *Giovanni Battista Foggini.* SOUTH SIDE: Deposition, a fresco by the school of *Niccolò Gerini* (its sinopia is displayed nearby). In the pavement beside the 1st altar is the tomb-slab of Cronaca (died 1508), the architect of a number of fine palaces in the city. 1st altar, Annunciation, a very damaged 14C fresco; 2nd altar, *Madonna enthroned with St John the Baptist and St Bartholomew, a beautiful fresco attributed to the school of Orcagna. Above the 4th altar is an interesting fragment of a mural drawing of St Onuphrius, recently attributed to the 'Master of the Fogg Pietà' (14C). At the end of this wall is a triptych (recently restored) by *Bicci di Lorenzo.*—The Chapel on the left of the high altar (CAPPELLA DEL MIRACOLO) contains an exquisite *Tabernacle by *Mino da Fiesole* (1481), who is buried here (tomb-slab in the pavement at the entrance to the chapel, 1484). The tabernacle contains a miraculous chalice, and the large *Fresco by *Cosimo Rosselli* shows a procession with the chalice in front of the church. It includes portraits of many of the artist's contemporaries, and his self-portrait (to the left). On the wall nearby is displayed the sinopia.—NORTH SIDE: 4th altar, *Raffaellino del Garbo* (attributed), Saints and Annunciation. In the pavement is the tomb-slab of Verrocchio (died 1488). 3rd altar, *Cosimo Rosselli,* Madonna in glory with Saints. Between the 3rd and 2nd altars, a wooden statuette of St Sebastian by *Leonardo del Tasso* stands in a graceful niche with a tiny painted roundel of the Annunciation, attributed to the workshop of Filippino Lippi. 2nd altar, *Andrea Boscoli,* Visitation. On the wall, *Alesso Baldovinetti,* *Angels and Saints surrounding a Nativity by his pupil *Graffione.* On the W wall is a strange fresco of the Martyrdom of St Sebastian, attributed to *Agnolo Gaddi.*

Just to the S of the church (off Via de' Macci) is the *Market of Sant'Ambrogio* (Pl.11;1), a cast-iron building opened in 1873. This is the biggest produce market in the town after the central market at San Lorenzo. Fruit and vegetables, some grown locally, are sold from stalls outside.

From Piazza Sant'Ambrogio Via Pietrapiana leads to PIAZZA DEI CIOMPI (Pl.11;1), named after the famous revolt of Florentine cloth-workers in 1378. The graceful *Loggia del Pesce,* designed in 1568 by Vasari for the sale of fish, was reconstructed here after the demolition of the Mercato Vecchio (cf. p 82). It looks somewhat incongruous in these humble surroundings. In the square is the *Mercatino,* a 'junk' and 'antique' market where bargains can sometimes be found. On a house here a damaged inscription records the home of Lorenzo Ghiberti. Cimabue lived in Borgo Allegri, which was given this name, according to Vasari, after Cimabue's painting of the Madonna left his studio in a joyous procession down the street. In this street is a little public garden opened and kept in order by the old age pensioners who live in the district. At the end of Via Pietrapiana is a tabernacle with a fine relief of the Madonna and Child attributed to Donatello.

From Piazza Sant'Ambrogio Via dei Pilastri leads towards Borgo Pinti passing (right) Via Farini with the huge SYNAGOGUE (Pl.7;7; open daily except Saturday, 11–13; 14–17; 15 June–15 September, 9.30–17.30), an elaborate building in the Spanish-Moresque style with a tall green dome. It was built in 1874–82 by Marco Treves, Mariano Falcini, and Vincenzo Michele.

The Jews are first mentioned as a community in Florence in the 15C when they were called by the Republican government to operate in the city as money-lenders. In 1571 they were confined to a ghetto (in the area of the present Piazza della Repubblica, see Rte 3) by Cosimo I and this was not opened until 1848. At the end of the 19C the ghetto was demolished. A small MUSEUM was opened on the upper floor of the synagogue in 1981 (adm. see p 61); the display is well labelled and includes ceremonial objects, silver and vestments, dating from the 17–18C. In the garden is a Jewish School.

At the end of Via Farini can be seen the large *Piazza d'Azeglio*, planted with plane trees and reminiscent of a London square.—Via dei Pilastri continues to BORGO PINTI (Pl.7;7,5), a long narrow old street leading out of the city. On the corner is the church of *Santa Maria dei Candeli* (usually closed) redesigned by Giovanni Battista Foggini in 1704, with a ceiling fresco by Niccolò Lapi. At the beginning (left) are two 17C palaces, Palazzo Caccini (No. 33) and Palazzo Roffia (No. 13). Palazzo Caccini, now Geddes da Filicaia, was famous for its garden in the 17C. Beneath the portico are neo-classical frescoes. To the right, just before No. 58, is the entrance to the Convent of **Santa Maria Maddalena dei Pazzi** (Pl.7;7; if closed ring at the Convent at No. 58) which has been beautifully restored after severe flood damage. It is named after a Florentine Carmelite nun (1566–1607) who was canonised during the Counter Reformation. It is famous for its fresco by Perugino.

A Cistercian convent, founded here in 1321, was taken over by the Carmelites in 1628. Since 1926 fathers of the Assumption of the Augustinian order have been here (and the church is used by the French community of Florence). On the right of the entrance is the domed CAPPELLA DEL GIGLIO (Neri; for admission ask at the convent), built c 1505, which is beautifully frescoed by *Bernardino Poccetti* and assistants (1598–1600). The altarpiece of the Marytrdom of Saints Nereus and Achilleus is by *Passignano*. In the *CLOISTER by *Giuliano da Sangallo* (1492) beautiful large Ionic capitals support a low architrave. The new bronze panels intended for the door of the church are by *Marcello Tommasi*.

The CHURCH, first built in 1257, has side chapels added in 1488–1526, with pretty carved arches in pietra serena by *Piero di Giovanni Della Bella* and his bottega. The trompe l'oeil ceiling painting is by *Jacopo Chiavistelli* and *Marco Antonio Molinari* (1677), and the paintings in the nave are by *Cosimo Ulivelli* (c 1700). SOUTH SIDE. 1st chapel, *Carlo Portelli*, Martyrdom of St Romulus (a fine work signed and dated 1557); the 2nd chapel was decorated in 1778. 3rd chapel, *Matteo Rosselli*, Coronation of the Virgin, in a fine frame of c 1490. 4th chapel, *Domenico Puligo*, Madonna and Child with saints (1526; with a good frame). 5th chapel, stained glass window of St Francis (c 1500); the 6th chapel has early-19C frescoes by *Luigi Catani* and a small Crucifix attributed as an early work to *Bernardo Buontalenti*.—The well-lit MAIN CHAPEL, with colourful marbles, is one of the most important and complete examples of Florentine Baroque church decoration. It was designed in 1675 by *Ciro Ferri*, who painted the high altarpiece, and by *Pier Francesco Silvani*. On the side walls are two paintings by *Luca Giordano*. The statues are by (left) *Antonio Montauti* (c 1690) and (right) *Innocenzo Spinazzi* (1781). The cupola was frescoed in 1701 by *Piero Dandini*.—NORTH SIDE. 5th chapel, Martyrdom of St James, by *Giovanni Bizzelli* (1601); 4th chapel, *Raffaellino del Garbo*, St Ignatius and St Roch (in a pretty frame). The 3rd chapel has stained glass designed by *Domenico del Ghirlandaio* and an altarpiece of the Agony in the Garden by *Santi di Tito*, signed and dated 1591. The 2nd chapel contains a Coronation of the Virgin by *Cosimo Rosselli*, in another fine frame.

The CHAPTER HOUSE (entered from the crypt; adm. see p 63) contains a beautiful and very well preserved *Fresco of the Crucifixion and Saints by *Perugino* (1493–96), one of his masterpieces. Also here, Christ on the Cross and St Bernard, a detached fresco with its sinopia, by his workshop.

Borgo Pinti continues across Via della Colonna, with the Museo Archeologico (see Rte 9). On the right (No. 68) is *Palazzo Ximenes*, home of the Sangallo brothers (c 1499). The Borgo next crosses Via Giusti.

In Via Giuseppe Giusti (left) is the German Institute (No. 44) with an excellent art history library. No. 43 is a bizarre little house built as a studio by Federico Zuccari, the Roman painter, in 1579. It is connected by a little garden to a larger house built by Andrea del Sarto in 1520 on his return from France and where he died ten years later (plaque on No. 22 Via Gino Capponi). This was also owned by Zuccari, and in 1988 was acquired by the German Institute.—Via Gino Capponi, beyond, honours Gino Capponi (1792–1876), the statesman-historian whose grandiose home, Palazzo Capponi (No. 26) was built in 1698–1713 by Carlo Fontana. The huge palace has a fine garden and part of it is now the Italian headquarters of Sotheby Parke Bernet, the auctioneers. Here the poet Giuseppe Giusti died suddenly in 1850. Palazzo di San Clemente (No. 15), on the corner of Via Micheli, is an interesting building by Gherardo Silvani. It was bought by Charles Stuart, the Young Pretender in 1777, and from here, in 1780, his wife, the Countess of Albany, fled to the nearby Convento delle Bianchette. At the other end of Via Capponi (just out of Piazza Santissima Annunziata) is the **Cloister of the ex-Compagnia della Santissima Annunziata** (or **'di San Pierino'**; No. 4; ring for admission at the Società Dante Alighieri). Above the entrance is a lunette in glazed terracotta of the Annunciation with two members of the confraternity in white hooded robes, the work of Santi Buglioni. The delightful little cloister has frescoes (c 1585–90) by Bernardino Poccetti, Andrea Boscoli, Cosimo Gheri, Bernardino Monaldi, and Giovanni Balducci. The lunettes, representing the martyrdom of the Apostles, are separated by mono-chrome figures of the Christian Virtues, and, above the doors, the Resurrection and Pietà (explained by a diagram in situ). They were detached after the flood of 1966, and restored and returned here in 1989. In the vestibule beyond are two damaged frescoes (also restored) of Christ at the Column and the Crown of Thorns, also by Poccetti, and a small triptych in glazed terracotta by Giovanni della Robbia. The ex-Oratorio has more frescoed lunettes by Poccetti (very damaged).

At the end of Borgo Pinti is the once-famous garden of Palazzo Salviati (No. 76), which is usually closed, and now of little interest. Opposite stands Palazzo della Gherardesca (No. 99), with a fine 19C garden. The palace, built by Giuliano da Sangallo for Bartolomeo Scala in the 15C (with interesting bas-reliefs in the courtyard), was enlarged in the 18C by Antonio Ferri.—The Borgo ends at Piazza Donatello (p 224).

17 The Arno between Ponte alla Carraia and Ponte alle Grazie

This route follows the right and left banks of the Arno between the four bridges in the centre of the city, all of them built for the first time in the 13C (the other bridges, up and down stream, were added after 1836). The roads along the Arno (recorded as early as the 13C) are known as the 'Lungarni' (singular, 'Lungarno'). Lined with handsome palaces and some elegant shops they provide magnificent views of the city on the river.

Ponte alla Carraia (Pl.9;1) was the second bridge to be built over the Arno after Ponte Vecchio. Constructed in wood on stone piles in 1218–20, it was known as 'Ponte Nuovo'. It was reconstructed after floods in 1269 and 1333; the 14C bridge may have been designed by Giotto. It was repaired by Ammannati in 1559, enlarged in 1867, and replaced by a new bridge (a copy of the original) after it was blown up in 1944. From the foot of the bridge is a view to the SE of the campanile of Santo Spirito, with, on the skyline, the Forte di Belvedere and the bell-tower of San Miniato.—At the N end in the busy Piazza Goldoni is a statue of Carlo Goldoni (by Ulisse Cambi,

1873) and *Palazzo Ricasoli* (No. 2, with several coats-of-arms) built c 1475. A road leads to the church of Ognissanti (described on p 155). Lungarno Vespucci, opened in the 19C, leads away from the centre of the city towards the park of the Cascine past two modern bridges which can also be seen downstream, Ponte Vespucci and Ponte della Vittoria. Also downstream on the left bank is the domed church of San Frediano in Cestello.

LUNGARNO CORSINI leads past the huge *Palazzo Corsini* (Pl.9;2) built from 1656 to c 1737 in a grandiose Roman Baroque style. The architects included Alfonso Parigi the Younger and Ferdinando Tacca, and (after 1685) Antonio Ferri (perhaps to a design of Pier Francesco Silvani). The façade, is crowned by statues and has a terrace overlooking the river. The palace contains the GALLERIA CORSINI, the most important private art collection in Florence (adm. by appointment only at 11 Via Parione).

In the left wing is an ingenious spiral staircase by *Pier Francesco Silvani*. The monumental staircase in the other wing by *Antonio Ferri* leads up to the piano nobile and the splendid Salone del Trono designed by Ferri with statues and busts and two huge wood chandeliers made for the room. The fresco of the Apotheosis of the Corsini family is by *Antonio Domenico Gabbiani*. The collection formed in the 17C by Marchese Bartolommeo Corsini and his son Filippo, is arranged in six rooms frescoed in 1692–1700 by *Alessandro Gherardini* and *Antonio Domenico Gabbiani*, with stucco decoration by the *Passardi* and *Rinaldo Botti*. The fine paintings, particularly representative of the 17C Florentine school, in magnificent frames, are arranged aesthetically. They include: *Carlo Maratta*, Portrait of Filippo di Bartolomeo Corsini; *Luca Giordano*, bozzetto for the vault fresco in the Cappella Corsini in the Carmine; *Carlo Dolci*, Poetry; *Luca Signorelli* and his bottega, Tondo of the Madonna; *Giovanni Santi, Timoteo Viti*, and others, Apollo and the muses painted for the Ducal palace at Urbino; *Sustermans*, Portrait of Geri della Rena; *Giovanni Bellini*, Crucifix; *Pier Francesco Toschi*, Portrait of a man; *Pontormo*, Madonna and Child with the young St John; *Botticelli* (or his bottega), Tondo of the Madonna and angels; *Filippino Lippi* (attributed as early works), Five allegorical figures; *Ridolfo del Ghirlandaio*, Portrait of a man; *Sustermans*, Portrait of his friend Pietro Fevre, tapestry maker to the Medici (his first portrait painted in Florence); four scenes of the Passion of Christ by *Domenico Fetti*; cartoon of *Raphael*'s portrait of Julius II, attributed to the master; *Lodovico Cigoli*, Head of Christ; works by *Giacinto Gimignani*; *Hyacinthe Rigaud*, Portrait of Neri Corsini. The marble bust of the Corsini pope Clement XII is by *Bouchardon*. The Deposition in porcelain made in the Doccia factory c 1752 was designed by *Massimiliano Soldani Benzi*.

Farther along the Lungarno is (No. 4) *Palazzo Gianfigliazzi* (1459; reconstructed). Alessandro Manzoni stayed in a hotel here in 1827 (plaque). Next door the British Consulate now occupies *Palazzo Masetti (Castelbarco)* where the Countess of Albany, widow of Prince Charles Edward Stuart, lived from 1793 until her death. Her 'salon' was frequented by Chateaubriand, Shelley, Byron, Foscolo, and Von Platen. Here in 1803 died the dramatist Alfieri, her second husband, and here later she was joined by Xavier Fabre, the painter.

The next bridge is ***Ponte a Santa Trìnita** (Pl.9;2), first built in 1252 and several times rebuilt after flood damage. The present bridge is an exact replica (beautifully executed by Riccardo Gizdulich) of the bridge begun by Ammannati in 1567 and destroyed in 1944. The finest of all the bridges across the Arno, it was commissioned by Cosimo I and it is probable that Ammannati submitted his design to Michelangelo for his approval. The high flat arches which span the river are perfectly proportioned and provide a magnificent view of the city. The four statues were set up on the parapet for the marriage of Cosimo II; Spring (left), the best work of Pietro Francavilla (1593), was recovered from the Arno.

The Lungarno Nuovo (now Vespucci) photographed from Piazza Goldoni c 1890, shortly after it was opened.

At the beginning of Via Tornabuoni (Rte 12; Pl.16;5) stands Palazzo Spini-Feroni. LUNGARNO ACCIAIOLI continues with a good view of Ponte Vecchio. In a group of old houses overhanging the opposite bank of the river is the little tower and river gate of the church of San Jacopo sopr'Arno. The Lungarno becomes narrower and an old lane (signposted) leads to the ancient church of Santi Apostoli (see p 214). The modern buildings on both banks of the river here replace the medieval houses which were blown up in 1944 in order to render Ponte Vecchio impassable. **Ponte Vecchio**, the most famous bridge across the Arno, is described on p 108. At the foot of the bridge is the busy Por Santa Maria, at the bend of which can be seen the lantern of the Duomo above the top of Orsanmichele. Lungarno Archibusieri continues parallel to the raised Corridoio Vasariano, described in Rte 7. The narrow road skirts the façade of the Uffizi; from the little terrace on the river there is a view of the huge Uffizi building with Palazzo Vecchio at the end. In Piazza dei

Giudici (with a view of the tower of Palazzo Vecchio) stands *Palazzo Castellani*, a fine medieval palace owned in the 14C by an important Florentine family whose wealth was based on the cloth trade. It now contains the ***Museo di Storia della Scienza** (Pl.16;8; adm. see p 62), with a beautifully displayed and well-maintained collection of scientific instruments, many of them restored after severe flood damage in 1966. The second floor is still in the process of rearrangement, but is expected to reopen soon.

A large part of the collection was owned by the Medici grand-dukes, and the Museum of Physics and Natural Sciences, directed by Felice Fontana and opened in 1775 by the grand-duke Pietro Leopoldo of Lorraine, was moved to these premises in 1929. Excellent hand lists (also available in English) are lent to visitors. There is a lift.

   Ground Floor. The **Library** of the *Istituto di Storia della Scienza* (open 9–13) has some 80,000 vols including many which belonged to the Medici and Lorraine grand-dukes.

First Floor. Room I. Mathematical instruments in Florence. Arab globe showing the constellations (c 1080). In the central case, 17C compasses, including a pair of the 16C traditionally thought to have been used by Michelangelo; sundials and odometers. In the wall cases: 10–16C astrolabes and quadrants; 16–18C

Night and Day clocks; 17C cases for mathematical instruments.—Room 11. Foreign mathematical instruments, many of them brought back from Germany by Prince Mattias, brother of Ferdinando II in 1635, made by Christoph Schissler and his son, including an astrolabe of 1560 and a quadrant of 1590.—Another case contains surveying instruments including a quadrant of 1608 by Thobias Volckmer, and a compass made in 1572 by Christof Tressler.—Three cases display the nautical instruments invented and used by Sir Robert Dudley, Duke of Northumberland, favourite of Queen Elizabeth I. He left England for Italy and was made director of the Arsenal of Livorno by Ferdinando II. Many of the astrolabes, quadrants and sextants were constructed by Charles Whitwell.—In the last case are more astrolabes and a calculator invented by Sir Samuel Morland in 1666.—Room III. Tuscan instruments, including compasses by Antonio Bianchini (1564), quadrants, and a celestial globe by Mario Cartaro (1577), an armillary sphere attributed to Carlo Plato, and 17C mathematical instruments by the Lusvergs.—The 16C astrolabe, traditionally associated with Galileo, is attributed to Egnazio Danti.—In a wall case, quadrants by Giovanni Battista Giusti, instruments by Egnazio Danti, and a 'perpendiculum' designed by Antonio Santucci.—In the last case are instruments made by the Della Volpaia and Stefano Buonsignori (Night and Day clocks, compasses, armillary spheres, astrolabes, sundials), and a pair of compasses used by Vincenzo Viviani, disciple of Galileo.

Room IV is devoted to Galileo (1564–1642). In the showcase, the lens (in an ivory frame) he used in discovering the four largest moons of Jupiter (cracked by the scientist himself before he presented it to Ferdinando II); the model made in 1877 by Eugenio Porcellotti of the pendulum clock designed by Galileo. The bones of Galileo's right middle finger were removed from his tomb when his remains were transferred to the church of Santa Croce. On the middle shelf: 'Giovilabio' a brass instrument made from sketches by Galileo, and a pair of compasses used by him. On the bottom shelf are loadstones probably used by the scientist. The models made in the 18C by order of the grand-duke Pietro Leopoldo I of inventions by Galileo include a water pump and an instrument for measuring the acceleration of gravity. The loadstone (of natural magnetic rock) was given by Galileo to Ferdinando II.—Room V. Telescopes. In the case to the left, Galileo's two telescopes.—In another case, lenses (1665) by Eustachio Divini and Giuseppe Campani. Among the numerous telescopes here are some by Campani, Divini, and Torricelli.—Room VI. Instruments used in optical experiments. Magnifying glasses, lenses, 18C spectacles, models of the eye, and 17C optical games.

Room VII contains a superb display of *Globes around the huge Ptolemaic armillary sphere built by Antonio Santucci in 1588. Along the left wall, celestial globes by Jansz Willem Blaeu; the 'Wheel of the Heavens' by Santucci; two showcases of armillary Ptolemaic spheres and a Copernican one. Standing in the far corner is an armillary sphere made of painted wood attributed to Vincenzo Viviani. In this part of the room, four large globes by Vincenzo Coronelli. An 18C 'planatarium', and celestial globe by Adrianus Veen and Jodocus Hondius (1613) and two globes with covers by Mathaus Greuter.—The maps include a copy of Fra Mauro's map of the world, and a map by Lopo Homen (1554).—Room VIII. Microscopes, including one designed by Galileo.— Room IX is devoted to the Accademia del Cimento, an experimental academy founded by Cardinal Leopoldo in 1657. Here are displayed a pedometer probably made by Schissler used to measure the shape of the earth; a model of the hygrometer invented by Ferdinando II, and a quadrant by Carlo Rinaldini. The splendid display of glass made in Florence for the Academy includes elaborate thermometers.—Room X. Meteorology. In the first case, barometers by Gian Domenico Tamburini, Daniel Quare, and De Luc; 17C and 18C anemometers (to determine the direction of the wind); a barometer on a marble base by Felice Fontana; thermometers including some by Dollond and Fontana; hygrometers (and, hanging on the wall above, a large hygrometer by Viviani).—Room XI. Astronomy in Florence in the 18C and 19C. On the left is a fine display of 18C telescopes. The large burning lens was made by Benedetto Bregans of Dresden and given by him to Cosimo III (used in the early 19C by Davy and Faraday to experiment with high temperature chemicals). Hanging on the wall is a large telescope made by Giovanni Battista Amici of Modena, and on a stand below another telescope by him. Also here is a telescope made by James Dollond, and a repeating circle by Reichenbach.

Second Floor. This is still closed for rearrangement, but is to be reopened soon. In ten rooms the Lorraine scientifical collections are to be exhibited, as well as the desk used by Pietro Leopoldo, grand-duke in 1765–90, for his chemical experiments. The exhibits include: instruments concerning fluids and gases (fountains, pumps, pneumatic machines); electrostatic machines; clocks, including a pendulum clock made by Filippo Treffler for Ferdinando II; calculators; a curious 'writing machine' constructed in the 18C by Federigo Knaus; 18C and 19C mathematical instruments; anatomical models by Giuseppe Ferrini in wax, for use in obstetrics; surgical instruments of Alessandro Brambilla (1728–1800); weights and measures.—Interesting exhibitions are held on the **Third Floor** where the collection of bicycles, showing their development from 1818–70 (including a primitive wooden bicycle made by Carl Friedrich Drais in 1817 and penny-farthings), may also be shown.

Lungarno Diaz continues past the heavy neo-classical colonnade of the Camera di Commercio and Piazza Mentana (monument to those who fell at Mentana in 1867). Just before the bridge is the garden of Palazzo Malenchini. Via de' Benci leads away from the Arno towards Santa Croce, lined with a number of fine palaces described on p 218. *Palazzo Corsi*, at No. 6, formerly thought to be the work of Giuliano da Sangallo, is now generally attributed to Cronaca. It is an attractive small palace open to the public as the **Museo Horne** (Pl.10;4; adm. see p 61). The interesting collection of 14–16C paintings, sculpture, and decorative arts (notable furniture and majolica) was presented to the nation, along with his house, by the English art historian Herbert Percy Horne (1864–1916). Many of the contents, charmingly displayed, have been restored after damage in the 1966 flood. The important collection of 17–18C drawings (Italian and English schools) is now housed in the Uffizi. The works (unlabelled) are numbered (on the wall) to correspond to a handlist lent to visitors at the entrance.

The courtyard has interesting capitals. **Ground Floor**. A room here contains bronzes, medals, coins, majolica, etc., as well as a stone bas-relief of the Madonna and Child by *Jacopo Sansovino*.—The room beyond is used for exhibitions.
   First Floor. ROOM I. 38. *Dosso Dossi*, Allegory of Music; (wall case) 48. *Masaccio* (attributed), Story of St Julian (a tiny work, unfortunately very ruined).—55. *Filippino Lippi*, Crucifix (a late work, much faded, once used as a processional standard).—On the table in the centre, bozzetti by *Ammannati, Giambologna*, and *Gianfrancesco Rustici*.—Above a 'cassone' (63.) in the style of Ammannati, 61. *Pietro Lorenzetti*, Saints John Gualberto, Catherine of Alexandria, and Margaret (a fragment of a polyptych).—67. *Bernardo Daddi*, Madonna enthroned and Crucifixion (a diptych); 69. *Benozzo Gozzoli*, Deposition, a crowded composition left unfinished at the death of the painter (the colours have darkened with time, and it is at present removed for restoration); 75. *Bartolommeo di Giovanni*, Mythological scene.—R. II. 83, 84, & 100. Paintings by *Francesco Furini*; 85. *Luca Signorelli*, Redeemer; 86. *Domenico Beccafumi*, Mythological scene; 87. *Boccaccio Boccaccino*, Redeemer; 88. *Jacopo del Casentino*, Madonna and Child; 91. *Giotto*, *St Stephen (part of a polyptych), the most precious piece in the collection; 98. *Neri di Bicci*, Madonna and two angels (very ruined); 105. *School of Lorenzo di Credi*, Tondo of the Nativity.—R. III. 111, 116. *Niccolò di Tommaso*, Saints John the Evangelist and Paul; 114. frontal of a 15C 'cassone' with a battle scene; 113. '*Master of the Croce dei Da Filicaia*', Madonna enthroned with Saints. In cupboard, *Lorenzo Monaco or his school*, Portable Crucifix. Over the fireplace, *Desiderio da Settignano*, Relief of the head of the young St John the Baptist (replica of a work in the Bargello).—127. *13C Tuscan School*, Madonna and Child with a donor; 128. *Beccafumi*, *Tondo of the Holy Family, with a beautiful contemporary frame. The statue of St Paul is by *Vecchietta*.
   Second Floor. ROOM IV (left) contains several fine pieces of 15C furniture. 155. *Ercole dei Roberti* (attributed), St Sebastian (removed for restoration); 158. *Bartolommeo della Gatta*, St Roch (restored).—In wall case, 168. *Filippo Lippi*, Pietà (a pax); 170. *Antonio Rossellino*, Madonna and Child, a relief in polychrome terracotta.—177. *Filippino Lippi*, Scene from the Story of Esther (panel of a marriage chest); (above) 182. *School of Sodoma*, Scene from the Battle of Anghiari (of historical interest as a contemporary copy of Leonardo's lost fresco in Palazzo Vecchio); 183. '*Master of the Horne Triptych*' (14C Florentine),

Madonna and Saints (restored in 1987). In a case in the centre of the room 193. *Simone Martini* (attributed), Portable diptych of the Madonna and Child and Pietà.—ROOM V. 216. *Neri di Bicci*, Archangel Raphael, Tobias, and St Jerome; 209. *Beccafumi* (attributed), Drunkenness of Noah (in a tondo surrounded by putti).—The old kitchen also on this floor (with cutlery, utensils, etc.) is opened on request.

Ponte alle Grazie (Pl.10;4) was first built in 1237 and called 'Ponte Rubaconte'. Its present name is taken from an oratory of Santa Maria delle Grazie which formerly stood on the bridge. Destroyed in 1944, it was replaced by a bridge of modern design. From here the view embraces Lungarno delle Grazie with the monumental entrance and two square towers of the Biblioteca Nazionale and the tall spire of Santa Croce; in the distance upstream can be seen the rural banks of the Arno; and across the river the tall Porta San Niccolò is conspicuous beyond the garden of Palazzo Demidoff (and above, on the skyline, stands San Miniato). At the S end of the bridge is PIAZZA DEI MOZZI.

Lungarno Serristori leads away from the Oltrarno district past a little public garden with a pavilion and a good monument (recently restored) to Niccolò Demidoff by Lorenzo Bartolini. *Palazzo Serristori* (1515; with a river front of 1873) was the home of the traitor Baglioni. It is now owned by the State, and is to become the seat of the Soprintendenza Archeologica della Toscana.

At No. 1 Piazza dei Mozzi stands the large *Palazzo Bardini*, built by the famous antiquarian and collector Stefano Bardini in 1883 to house his huge collection of works of art bequeathed to the city in 1922 as the **Museo Bardini** (Pl.10;4; adm. see p 61). His eclectic collection includes architectural fragments, medieval and Renaissance sculpture, paintings, the decorative arts, furniture, ceramics, carpets, arms and armour, musical instruments, etc. Many of the rooms were built specially to contain the fine doorways, staircases, and ceilings from demolished buildings. The rooms are crowded with a miscellany of works, all well labelled.

Ground Floor. From the vestibule is the entrance (right) to ROOM 1 with numerous medieval and Renaissance architectural fragments, including a carved 16C window from Sassari and sculptural reliefs attributed to *Francesco di Simone Ferrucci*. The bust of St John the Baptist dates from the early 16C (formerly attributed to Andrea Sansovino).—Beyond is R. 2 with interesting classical sculpture including a sarcophagus with Medusa's head, used again in the Middle Ages.—RR. 3–5 have been closed for many years.—Beyond R. 6, with a well-head and more architectural fragments, is a large room (7) formerly a courtyard, covered by a coffered ceiling with glass inserted in the panels. Here is displayed a remarkable statue of *Charity ascribed to *Tino da Camaino*. The large Gothic aedicule behind the statue was made up by Bardini using various statuettes and reliefs (including two statuettes of angels in adoration by the Sienese school).The Romanesque architectural fragments here include capitals, pilasters, column-bearing lions, etc. The little console in the form of a female head (on the right wall) has recently been attributed to *Nicola Pisano*.—In the small adjacent room (8) is a well-head of red Veronese marble, and the tomb effigy of Riccardo Gattula (1417), by *Paolo di Gualdo Cattaneo*.—R. 9 (off the vestibule) is approached through a fine doorway. Here are two chimneypieces (one from the bottega di Desiderio da Settignano, and the other, with the Este coat-of-arms, a Lombard work). The amusing putto was made for a fountain in the late 15C.—Stairs lead to R. 10, a large vaulted room built in the form of a crypt to display tomb slabs and wall-tombs. The wall-tomb in relief with the effigy of a bishop attended by an acolyte is ascribed to the circle of *Arnolfo di Cambio*. The relief of St Jerome from San Francesco della Vigna in Venice is by *Giovanni Buora*. The floor tomb-slabs include one of a friar from the circle of *Donatello*, and one (next to it) of Colomba Ghezzi dalla Casa, abbess of San Martino alla Scala, commissioned by her in 1540 from *Francesco da Sangallo*. An Antique sarcophagus bears a relief sculpted with the three faces of the Trinity attributed to *Michelozzo*. The *Altarpiece of the Madonna and Child with angels in Adoration in enamelled terracotta is an early work by *Andrea della Robbia*.

First Floor. A fine staircase leads up from R. 9. At the top of the stairs are displayed 14C wooden statues. Three rooms to the left display an interesting collection of arms and armour. In the first room, 16C decorated swords, crossbows, and weapons used by infantry. In the case, bronze helmets including one (811.) dating from the 6C BC, and a 14C painted crest in the form of a dragon's head.—The main room has 15–17C halberds, pikes, and spears, and 15–16C painted shields, some with plaster reliefs, and a large pavise (shield) painted with the coat-of-arms of the Sienese Bonamici family, attributed to Taddeo Bartoli. In the cases, swords and rapiers, including a French sword of the early 15C, daggers, spurs, tournament weapons, etc. Also here is a rare battle lantern such as those depicted in the frescoes in the Sala dei Cinquecento in Palazzo Vecchio. The cannon include a mortar possibly dating from the end of the 14C. In the last room are displayed 16C Venetian shields and two cases of 16–17C firearms.

Room 14, facing the stair-head, is entered through a marble doorway of 1548. Here are displayed two works sometimes attributed to *Donatello*: a charming high relief of the *Madonna and Child in polychrome terracotta (recently attributed, as an early work, to *Luca della Robbia*), and the Madonna 'dei Cordai', a very unusual polychrome work in stucco, glass, and mosaic. Two other reliefs of the Madonna and Child are by the circle of *Verrocchio* and a copy from a work by Benedetto da Maiano (removed). A painted tondo fragment is attributed to *Spinello Aretino.*—R. 15 (right; beyond R. 16), is notable for its 17C carpets and portraits (including works by *Francesco Salviati*), and its furniture. The central cases contain bronze medals, plaques, and statuettes. Also here, detached frescoes (from Palazzo Pucci) by *Giovanni di San Giovanni*, and two tondi by *Volterrano.*—R. 16, a hall furnished like a sacristy, with a fine chimneypiece and ceiling. The paintings include a large Crucifix attributed to a follower of Bernardo Daddi; *Michele Giambono*, St John the Baptist; *Giuliano Bugiardini* (?), Madonna and Child. The sculpture in stucco and terracotta includes (left of the window) a relief of the Nativity and a damaged Madonna and Child both attributed to the circle of *Donatello*. On the sacristy cupboard are displayed more charming statuettes and high reliefs of the Madonna and Child dating from the early 15C (including one of the Madonna and the sleeping Child by the bottega of *Nanni di Bartolo*), and a Madonna in Adoration dating from the end of the 15C. Above, in a Gothic tabernacle, is a 15C Venetian statue of St Peter enthroned.—Room 17 continues the collection of furniture, paintings, and majolica. The 15C sculptural reliefs include two tondi in stucco of the Madonna and Child, one attributed to *Michelozzo* and one after *Francesco di Simone Ferrucci*, and a Madonna and Child by the bottega of *Jacopo della Quercia.*—Room 18 has 15C wood statues including a Madonna, and St Catherine of Siena by the circle of *Domenico di Niccolò de' Cori*. The Virgin Annunciate in terracotta, in the centre of the room, has for long been considered a Sienese work of the 15C. The damaged bust of a woman is now attributed to *Tullio Lombardo*, and the fine bust of Gerolamo Andreasi is considered to be the work of *Gian Cristoforo Romano*. The painting of *St Michael is by *Antonio Pollaiolo.*—R. 19 displays old musical instruments (including a spinet made in Rome in 1577).—On the upper floor the GALLERIA CORSI (adm. only with special permission) contains the large artistic bequests of Alice and Arnaldo Corsi (1939). Among the 15C and 16C paintings is a Madonna and Child with St Anthony Abbott, attributed to Bartolo di Fredi.— From R. 18 a small staircase descends to R. 20, the Sala del Crocifisso, named from a large realistic Crucifix; here also are fine inlaid stalls (15C); 15–16C furniture, a 17C wood model of Pisa Baptistery, and thr e reliefs of the Nativity by the school of Donatello. The wood ceiling is notable.

At the end of Piazza dei Mozzi, on Via de' Bardi, the three 13C palaces of the Mozzi family, owned by Ugo Bardini, son of Stefano, also an art collector, and left to the state in 1965, are described in Rte 19. LUNGARNO TORRIGIANI (Pl.10;4) follows the S bank of the Arno back towards Ponte Vecchio. Next to the 16C *Palazzo Torrigiani* is a little public garden with the Lutheran church (1899). Across the Arno can be seen the cupola of the Duomo with (right) the towers of the Badia and the Bargello, and (left) the Campanile and tower of Palazzo Vecchio. Beyond the garden of Palazzo Canigiani the lungarno merges with Via de' Bardi (cf. Rte 19) at a road fork. The old

Costa dei Magnoli runs uphill beneath an arch of Palazzo Tempi to Costa San Giorgio (p 203), also reached by steps at the end of Vicolo del Canneto. Via de' Bardi continues to the foot of Ponte Vecchio, passing beneath the Corridoio Vasariano. Via Guicciardini, which leads left to Piazza Pitti, and the bronze fountain on the corner are described on p 109. Here the houses front the Arno; **Borgo San Jacopo** (Pl.9;2), continues parallel to the river. The Borgo, an ancient road leading out of the city, is mentioned as early as 1182. By a modern hotel a terrace opens onto the river opposite the campanile of Santi Apostoli, with a good view left and right of Ponte Santa Trìnita and Ponte Vecchio. Amongst the buildings here rebuilt after the war some restored medieval towers survive. On the corner of the pretty Via Toscanella, *Torre Marsili di Borgo* (No. 17) is a fine towerhouse. Above the door is an Annunciation from the Della Robbia workshop and two angels (restored). On the right of the road is the church of SAN JACOPO SOPR'ARNO (Pl.9;2), with an old portico of three arches transported here in 1529 from the demolished church of San Donato a Scopeto.

The church (which had a river gate) is used by a cultural organisation for concerts and exhibitions. In the Baroque interior (open only for concerts) of 1709, when almost all the painted decoration was carried out, the Romanesque columns were revealed (with questionable taste) during restoration work. The vaults of the two side aisles are decorated with six oval frescoes. Right aisle, 1st and 2nd bay, frescoes by *Niccolò Lapi*; 3rd bay, altarpiece by *Antonio Puglieschi*, and vault fresco by *Ottaviano Dandini*. The cupola over the sanctuary and the spandrels are frescoed by *Matteo Bonechi*. The high altarpiece is by *Pier Dandini* flanked by two Saints in grisaille by *Matteo Bonechi*. Left aisle, 3rd altarpiece by *Jacopo Vignali*; 2nd altarpiece of the Annunciation, by *Ignazio Hugford*; and 1st altarpiece of the Martyrdom of St Lucy, by *Giovanni Casini* (vault by *Matteo Bonechi*).

The Borgo ends in the busy Piazza Frescobaldi with a pretty corner fountain. Via Maggio, described in Rte 19, leads away from the river. The Arno is regained at the end of Ponte Santa Trìnita. The elaborate *Palazzo Frescobaldi* (right) was reconstructed in the 17C. LUNGARNO GUICCIARDINI (Pl.9;1,2) provides a splendid view of the opposite bank of the river (with the imposing Palazzo Corsini) as far as the park of the Cascine. Beyond the red façade of Palazzo Capponi (No. 1; with a salone frescoed by Bernardino Poccetti in 1583) is Via dei Coverelli with a palace with restored graffiti. The famous garden (no adm.) of the yellow *Palazzo Guicciardini* (No. 7) includes a magnolia tree planted in 1787. *Palazzo Lanfredini* (No. 9), by Baccio d'Agnolo, has bright graffiti decoration (restored). On the first floor are the Library and Reading Room, and the Director's office of the *British Institute of Florence*. A non-profit making independent Institution, it was founded in 1917, and received a Royal Charter in 1923. Its scope is to promote British culture in Italy and Italian culture to English-speaking visitors. Beyond the Presbyterian church (No. 19), Ponte alla Carraia is regained.

Lungarno Soderini (Pl.9;1) continues beyond the bridge past a little pavilion-house, with a view of the huge church of San Frediano in Cestello and the Seminary. The diagonal stone dike in the river, the Pescaia di Santa Rosa, was built at the same time as the water mills on the Arno. In Piazza del Cestello is the rough-hewn façade of the church of San Frediano (p 199) and the *Granaio di Cosimo III* (1695) a good building by Giovanni Battista Foggini (now used as a barracks). From the piazza is a view across the river of Ognissanti and its bell-tower, with the campanile of Santa Maria Novella behind. Beyond the modern Ponte Vespucci is the wall of Porta San Frediano (see Rte 19).

18 The Oltrarno: Santo Spirito and Santa Maria del Carmine

In the characteristic district on the S bank of the Arno known as the 'Oltrarno', the two most important churches are Santo Spirito and Santa Maria del Carmine, and around them focuses the life of this part of the city. From the S end of Ponte Santa Trìnita Via di Santo Spirito and Via del Presto (left) lead shortly to the church of *Santo Spirito (Pl.9;1; closed 12–15.30). Its modest 18C façade fronts a pretty square. On the left is the rough stone wall of the convent Refectory, and behind rises Baccio d'Agnolo's slender campanile (1503).

The Augustinian foundation dates from 1250 and the first church was begun in 1292. The convent became a centre of intellectual life in the city at the end of the 14C. In 1428 *Brunelleschi* was commissioned to design a new church, the project for which he had completed by 1434–35. However, building was not begun until 1444 just two years before the great architect's death. Construction continued for most of the 15C, first under the direction of his collaborator *Antonio Manetti*, and then by *Giovanni da Gaiole, Giuliano Sandrini*, and *Giovanni di Mariano*. *Salvi d'Andrea* completed the cupola in 1481.—A crucifix found in the convent in 1963 has been identified by most scholars as the one known to have been made by Michelangelo for the Augustinians. It is displayed in the Casa Buonarroti.

The *INTERIOR was designed by *Brunelleschi* but mostly executed after his death and modified in the late 15C. While it remains a superb creation of the Renaissance, remarkable for its harmonious proportions, its solemn colour, and the perspective of the colonnades and vaulted aisles, it also points the way forward to the more elaborate and less delicate 16C style of architecture. The plan is a Latin cross, with a dome over the crossing. The colonnade, whose 35 columns in pietra forte (including the four piers of the dome) have fine Corinthian capitals with imposts above, is carried round the transepts and E end forming an unbroken arcade. Around the walls is a continuous line of 38 chapels formed by semicircular niches. Some of these have 15C painted wood altar frontals in imitation of precious materials. Although in itself an admirable Baroque work, the elaborate HIGH ALTAR (1599–1607), with a ciborium in pietre dure by *Giovanni Battista Caccini*, beneath a high baldacchino, disturbs the harmony of the architecture. The church was restored in 1976–81.

The handsome interior façade was designed by *Salvi d'Andrea* (1483–87). The stained-glass oculus is from a cartoon by *Perugino*. The side chapels contain interesting works of art which are, however, very poorly lit (difficult to see on a dark day or late in the afternoon). Coin-operated lights have been installed in some chapels. A number of altarpieces are being restored in situ; they will be removed for restoration when possible; others have been restored and will be returned here.—SOUTH AISLE CHAPELS. 1st altar, 1. *Pier Francesco di Jacopo Foschi*, Immaculate Conception; 2. Pietà, a free copy of Michelangelo's famous sculpture in St Peter's, by *Nanni di Baccio Bigio*; 3. The prettily decorated niche contains St Nicholas of Tolentino, a polychrome wood statue by *Nanni Unghero* (on a design by *Jacopo Sansovino*), and two angels painted by *Franciabigio*; 4. *Giovanni Stradano*, Christ expelling the money-changers from the Temple; 5. *Alessandro Gherardini*, Coronation of the Virgin and Saints. Beyond the side door, 6. *Passignano*, Martyrdom of St

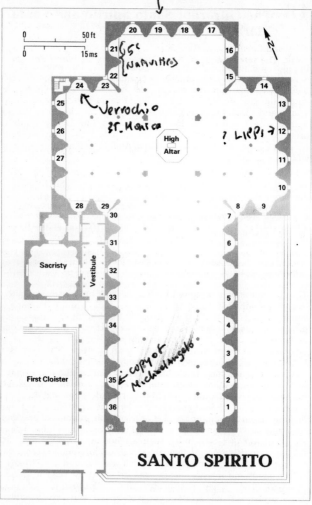

SANTO SPIRITO

Annotations on the plan:
- Allori – P.[?] & Adulteress (at chapels 19/20)
- 5C Nativities (at chapel 21)
- Verrochio St. Monica (at chapel 24)
- ? Lippi → (at chapel 12)
- copy of Michaelangelo (at chapel 35)

Stephen, a good work; 7. Tobias and the Archangel, a large altar-piece in stucco and marble by *Giovanni Baratta*.

SOUTH TRANSEPT CHAPELS. 8. *Francesco Curradi*, Crucifixion; 9. *Pier Francesco di Jacopo Foschi*, Transfiguration; 10. Madonna del Soccorso, a painting of the early 15C, recently attributed to the *'Master of the Johnson Nativity'*. Within the polychrome marble altar (11) by *Buontalenti* is a 14C wood crucifix from the earlier church; 12. *Filippino Lippi*, *Madonna and Child, with the young St John, Saints, and Tanai and Nanna dei Nerli, the donors. In the background is a view of Palazzo dei Nerli near Porta San Frediano. This is one of Filippino's best and most mature works (not yet returned here since its restoration). The Vision of St Bernard by Perugino (now in Munich) has been replaced by a beautiful (and almost indistinguishable) copy (13) by *Felice Ficherelli*, in a prettily decorated niche; 14. *Giovanni Camillo Sagrestani*, Marriage of the Virgin (1713), his best work. The sarcophagus of Neri Capponi is by *Bernardo Rossellino* (1458).

CHAPELS AT THE EAST END. 15. Madonna and Saints, a good painting in the style of *Lorenzo di Credi*; 16. *Maso di Banco*, Madonna and Child with Saints (a polyptych; removed for restoration); 17. *Aurelio Lomi*, Epiphany; 18. *Alessandro Allori*, Martyred Saints (1574), with a predella including an interesting view of Palazzo Pitti before it was enlarged; 19. *Alessandro Allori*, *Christ and the adulteress, a beautiful painting foreshadowing the 17C; 20. *Jacopo Vignali*, Mystical Communion of the Blessed Clara of Montefalco; 21. *15C Florentine School*, Annunciation (showing the influence of the German and Flemish schools); 22. *Florentine Master of the late 15C*, Nativity.

NORTH TRANSEPT CHAPELS. 23. *'Master of Santo Spirito'* (late 15C), Madonna enthroned between Saints John the Evangelist and Bartholomew; 24. *St Monica and Augustinian nuns in black habits, traditionally attributed to *Botticelli*, but now thought by many scholars to be the work of *Verrocchio*. It is a very unusual and beautifully composed painting. 25. *Cosimo Rosselli*, Madonna enthroned between Saints; the Cappella Corbinelli (26) has beautiful marble decoration and an *Altarpiece sculpted by *Andrea Sansovino*. 27. *Trinity with Saints Mary Magdalen and Catherine, a good painting of the late 15C, attributed to the *'Master of Santo Spirito'* (removed for restoration); 28. *Raffaelo dei Carli*, *Madonna enthroned with Saints; 29. Way to Calvary, copy by *Michele Ghirlandaio* of a painting by Ridolfo del Ghirlandaio, and a stained-glass window showing the Incredulity of St Thomas.

NORTH AISLE CHAPELS. 30. *School of Fra' Bartolomeo*, Madonna enthroned and Saints. The marble bust (right) of Tommaso Cavalcanti is by *Montorsoli*. 31. Copy by *Francesco Petrucci* of the 'Pala Dei' by Rosso Fiorentino, which was ordered by Prince Ferdinand in 1691 when he removed the original to Palazzo Pitti (see p 113). The copy shows the original dimensions of the altarpiece (which was enlarged when it was hung in the Pitti).—A door (32) beneath the organ, leads into a grandiose *VESTIBULE with 12 Corinthian columns supporting a barrel vault elaborately coffered, built by *Cronaca* in 1491. The adjoining *SACRISTY is an octagonal chamber inspired by the architectural works of Brunelleschi, with Corinthian pilasters, designed by *Giuliano da Sangallo* (1489), with a lantern and dome executed on a model of *Antonio del Pollaiolo* and *Salvi d'Andrea* (1495). Off the vestibule is the FIRST CLOISTER (no adm.) by *Alfonso* and *Giulio Parigi* (early 17C).—In the remaining chapels in the N aisle: 33. *Ridolfo del Ghirlandaio* (attributed), Madonna with St Anne and other Saints; 34. *Rutilio Manetti*, St Thomas of Villanova; 35. Copy by *Taddeo Landini* (1579) of a statue of the risen Christ by Michelangelo in the church of the Minerva in Rome; 36. *Pier Francesco di Jacopo Foschi*, Resurrection.

The SECOND CLOISTER is a beautiful work by *Ammannati* c 1565. It is now part of a military barracks (no adm.). Off the cloister is the CAPPELLA CORSINI (also closed to the public) with the Gothic tombs of Tommaso Corsini (died 1366) and of Neri Corsini, Bishop of Fiesole (died 1377) with a contemporary fresco of the Resurrection and two Saints. Also here (right wall) is a red porphyry monument with a bust of Bartolomeo Corsini (died 1613) and two children sculpted by

Gherardo Silvani, and a monument to Lorenzo Corsini (Pope Clement XII) with a bust by Girolamo Ticciati (1731).

To the left of the church, at No. 29, is the entrance to the REFECTORY (adm. see p 60), the only part of the 14C convent to survive. Above a fresco of the Last Supper (almost totally ruined) is a huge *Crucifixion (also damaged), both of them painted c 1360–65. They are attributed to *Andrea Orcagna* and his bottega, probably including his brother *Nardo di Cione*. A partial restoration after years of neglect revealed one of the most dramatic scenes of the Crucifixion in 14C Florentine painting. Here is displayed the **Fondazione Salvatore Romano**, left to the city in 1946, with an interesting collection of sculpture (including many works from the Romanesque period). Beneath the fresco, two sea lions (3), Romanesque works from Campania, flank a polychrome high relief (5) of the Madonna of the Misericordia (15C Sienese school).—Against the far wall: Madonna and Child (8), large polychrome relief attributed to *Jacopo della Quercia*, and a fountain (15) attributed to *Ammannati*.—On the end wall the two damaged fragments of bas-reliefs of two Bishop Saints (21) found in Padua are thought to be works by *Donatello* from the church of the Santo. The stone portal is signed by *Natale di Ragusa* (1471).—In the centre of the room: Angel (44) and Virtue (38), both fine statuettes by *Tino da Camaino*; numerous 11C sculptural fragments and primitive stone reliefs; and a marble font (45) from Torcello (6C). The collection also includes detached frescoes of the 14–15C.

PIAZZA SANTO SPIRITO is one of the most attractive small squares in the city, planted with a few trees, and the scene of a little daily market. It is the centre of a distinctive district with numerous medieval houses and artisans' workshops. The most handsome house in the piazza is *Palazzo Guadagni* (No. 10), probably built by Cronaca c 1505. Its pleasing, well-proportioned façade with a top-floor loggia became the model for many 16C Florentine mansions.

Borgo Tegolaio which leads out of one corner of the piazza is a medieval street which takes its name from the brick factories which were once here. In *Via delle Caldaie* the wool-dyers had their workshops.

Palazzo Guadagni in Piazza Santo Spirito, from a lithograph by A. Durand, 1863. (Museo di Firenze com'era)

Via Sant'Agostino, a local shopping street, with public baths, leads from Piazza Santo Spirito across Via de' Serragli (Rte 19) into Via Santa Monica. On the corner is a tabernacle with the Madonna enthroned and Saints by Lorenzo di Bicci (1427). The church of *Santa Monica* (usually closed) contains a circular fresco by Cosimo Ulivelli in the pretty vault. The 16C high altar encloses a Deposition by Giovanni Maria Butteri (1583). The 17C panelling and organ above the nuns' choir are also notable. In Via dell'Ardiglione (left) a plaque on a little house just beyond the arch across the road records the birthplace of Filippo Lippi in 1406. Via Santa Monica ends in Piazza del Carmine, a large square used as a car park. Here is the interesting rough stone façade of the church of **Santa Maria del Carmine** (Pl.9;1; open 9–12, 16–17), famous for its frescoes by Masaccio in the Cappella Brancacci, which, at the time of writing, is open 10–16.30 (fest. 13–16.30, closed Tuesday) and entered at No. 14 in the piazza. A maximum of 30 people at a time are allowed into the chapel.

A Carmelite convent was founded here in 1250 and the first church begun in 1268. This was almost completely ruined by fire in 1771 when the sacristy and two chapels alone escaped destruction. The huge wide interior was rebuilt in an undistinguished late Baroque style (1782). The trompe l'oeil cieling is by Domenico Stagi and Giuseppe Romei. In the APSE of the church is a fine monument (difficult to see) to Piero Soderini (died 1522) by *Benedetto da Rovezzano*. At the end of the left transept is the sumptuous *CHAPEL OF SANT'ANDREA CORSINI* (died 1373) by *Pier Francesco Silvani* (1675–83), one of the best Baroque works in Florence, with a ceiling by *Luca Giordano* (1682) and marble and silver reliefs by *Giovanni Battista Foggini*.—The Gothic SACRISTY (with a 15C statuette of the Madonna over the door) contains a choir chapel frescoed with scenes from the life of St Cecilia by a master influenced by Bicci di Lorenzo, and a polyptych (entrance wall) attributed to Andrea da Firenze, and the Martyrdom of an apostle by Lorenzo Lippi.

The small * *BRANCACCI CHAPEL at the end of the right transept now has to be approached via the early-17C Cloisters (entrance on the right of the façade; cf. above). The frescoes, illustrating the life of St Peter, were commissioned by Felice Brancacci, a rich Florentine merchant and statesman, c 1424, from *Masolino* and *Masaccio*. The frescoes were beautifully restored in 1983–89, and the chapel was reopened to the public in 1990. The design of the whole fresco cycle may be due to *Masolino* who probably worked on the frescoes in 1425 and again in 1427 together with his pupil *Masaccio* who seems to have taken over full responsibility for them after Masolino's departure for Rome in 1428. Later that year Masaccio himself broke off work abruptly on the frescoes for an unknown reason, and left for Rome, where, by the end of the year, he had died at the early age of 27. Brancacci was exiled from Florence in 1436 as an enemy of the Medici and the cycle was only completed some 50 years later by *Filippino Lippi* (c 1480–85) who carefully integrated his style with that of Masaccio, possibly following an earlier design. In 1690 the chapel was saved from demolition through the efforts of the Accademia del Disegno and Vittoria della Rovere, mother of Cosimo III. In the 18C the lunettes and vault of the chapel, probably frescoed by Masolino, were destroyed. The frescoes by *Masaccio* were at once recognised as a masterpiece and profoundly influenced the Florentine Renaissance. All the major artists of the 15C came here to study the frescoes which combine a perfect application of the new rules of perspective with a remarkable use of chiaroscuro. 'Masaccio ... like Giotto a century earlier—himself the Giotto of an artistically more propitious world—was, as an artist, a great master of the significant, and, as a painter, endowed to the highest degree with a sense of tactile values, and with a skill in rendering them. In a career of but a few years he gave to Florentine painting the direction it pursued to the end.' (Bernard Berenson, 'The Italian Painters of the Renaissance'.)

The frescoes are arranged in two registers. UPPER ROW: (right to left). On the entrance arch, *Masolino*, Temptation of Adam and Eve.—*Masolino*, St Peter, accompanied by St John, brings Tabitha to life, and heals a lame man (with a charming view of Florence in the background). The figures on the extreme left and some details in the background may be by the hand of *Masaccio*.—On the right of the altar: *Masaccio*, •St Peter Baptising; (left of the altar): *Masolino*, St Peter preaching.—*Masaccio*, •The Tribute money, perhaps the painter's masterpiece. Three episodes are depicted in the same scene: in the centre, Christ, surrounded by the Apostles, outside the gates of the city is asked by an official (with his back to us) to pay the tribute money owing to the city. Christ indicates to St Peter a lake, and (on the left) Peter is shown extracting the money from the mouth of a fish at the side of a lake. The scene on the right shows Peter handing over the tribute money to the official. The head of Christ has been attributed by some scholars to *Masolino*.—On the entrance arch: *Masaccio*, •Expulsion from Paradise, one of the most moving works of the Renaissance.—LOWER ROW: (right to left). On the entrance arch, *Filippino Lippi*, •Release of St Peter from prison.—*Filippino Lippi*, Saints Peter and Paul before the proconsul, and Crucifixion of St Peter.—On the right of the altar, *Masaccio*, Saints Peter and John distributing alms; (left of the altar) *Masaccio*, •St Peter, followed by St John, healing the sick with his shadow.—*Masaccio*, •St Peter enthroned with portraits of friars, his last work; the next half of this panel was begun by *Masaccio* and finished by *Filippino*. It shows Peter bringing to life the Emperor's nephew (the faces executed by Masaccio are more strongly illuminated; Filippino's figures are, in contrast, flatter and stand as if in shadow).—On the entrance arch, *Filippino Lippi*, St Peter in prison visited by St Paul (on a design by *Masaccio*).—The altarpiece, the •Madonna del Carmine, has been attributed to *Coppo di Marcovaldo* since its restoration in 1986.

During restoration work in 1983–89 it was found that an egg-based substance had been applied to the surface of the frescoes in the late 18C. As a result mould had formed and obscured the colour. This has been eliminated and the superb colouring and details of the landscapes can again be appreciated. During restoration work fragments of frescoes attributed to Masaccio including two heads and part of the scene with St Peter healing the sick with his shadow were found behind the 18C altar. Lengthy and heated debate ensued as to how to redesign the altar in order that these fragments could be permanently visible, and it has at last been decided to replace the huge ungainly altar but install it some centimetres out from the wall.

The rooms off the cloister which display frescoes detached from the cloister buildings have been closed since 1987. In the first room, once part of the Refectory: *Alessandro Allori*, Last Supper and monochrome frescoes. In the 2nd room, detached fresco fragments from the Cappella di San Girolamo, by *Starnina*; *Filippo Lippi*, the •Rule of the Order (partly destroyed); Crucifixion, a beautiful work by an unknown hand; *Giovanni da Milano*, Madonna enthroned with Saints. In the second refectory, known as the 'SALA VANNI' (open for concerts) is the Supper in the House of the Pharisee by *Francesco Vanni*, and detached frescoes from the Cappella della Passione attributed to *Lippo Fiorentino*.

19 The Oltrarno: Porta San Frediano to Porta San Niccolò

Porta San Frediano (Pl.8;2), and the adjoining stretch of wall with crenellations which runs to the Torrino di Santa Rosa on the banks of the Arno, is the best-preserved part of the last circle of walls built by the Comune in 1284–1333 (cf. the Plan on pp 30–1). The Gate, built in 1324 (perhaps by Andrea Pisano), with its high tower, protected the road for Pisa. It preserves interesting ironwork, and its huge wooden doors, decorated with nail heads, with their old locks. High up on the tower is the emblem of the city in stone. By the Torrino di Santa Rosa a large 19C tabernacle protects a fresco of the Pietà (16C; very difficult to see).

BORGO SAN FREDIANO (Pl.8;2) gives its name to a characteristic district with numerous artisans' houses and workshops. Among the local shops are a number of simple antique shops in the side streets. On the corner of Via San Giovanni is a tabernacle with the Madonna and Child with angels (15C). Farther on (left) is the bare stone exterior of the large church of **San Frediano in Cestello** (Pl.9;1), with its main entrance facing the Arno. The church was rebuilt in 1680–89 by Antonio Maria Ferri. Its fine dome is a conspicuous feature of this part of the city.

INTERIOR. All six side chapels have good frescoed decoration in the domes, spandrels, and lunettes carried out at the end of the 17C and the beginning of the 18C by Florentine painters, as well as stuccoes by *Carlo Marcellini*. Right side, 1st chapel, altarpiece of Santa Maria Maddalena dei Pazzi by *Giovanni Camillo Sagrestani*; frescoes by *Matteo Bonechi*. 3rd chapel, Altarpiece and frescoes by *Alessandro Gherardini*. Right transept, Virgin in Glory and Saints by *Francesco Curradi*. The dome was frescoed by *Antonio Domenico Gabbiani*. The elaborate altar also dates from the 18C. Left transept, *Jacopo del Sellaio*, Crucifixion and Martyrdom of St Laurence. Left side, 3rd chapel, frescoes by *Pier Dandini* and polychrome wood statue of the Madonna and Child by the 14C Pisan-Florentine school. 2nd chapel, altarpiece and frescoes by *Antonio Franchi*.—Next to the church is the huge Seminary, and, on the right, opens Piazza del Carmine with the fine bare stone façade of its church (described on p 197). The Borgo ends near the foot of Ponte alla Carraia.

Via de' Serragli (Pl.9;1), a long straight road, first laid out in the 13C, leads away from the Arno past a number of handsome 17–18C palaces. Beyond the crossroads with Via Santa Monica (which leads right to Santa Maria del Carmine, p 197) and Via Sant'Agostino (which leads left to Santo Spirito, p 193), Via de' Serragli continues, now lined with simple low medieval houses, through a local shopping area. Farther on, Via del Campuccio diverges right, skirting the garden wall of *Palazzo Torrigiani*. This is the biggest private garden in Florence (no adm.) created by Pietro Torrigiani (1773–1848). It has fine trees and a 'hypodrome' with sculpture by Pio Fedi (who had his studio at No. 99 Via de' Serragli), and encloses a conspicuous stretch of town walls built by Cosimo I. The fantastic neo-Gothic tower was built by Gaetano Baccani in 1821 as an astronomical observatory. From the nursery at No. 146 Via de' Serragli a corner of the garden can be seen. On the Cinema Goldoni in Via de' Serragli is a plaque recording Gordon Craig's theatre workshop here in 1913.—Via del Campuccio (see above) ends in Piazza Tasso (Pl.8;4) where, on fine days, old furniture, etc. is sometimes sold from lorries by dealers who drive up from the S of Italy. Here, in a ramshackle mews between the Torrigiani garden wall and the defensive walls built by Cosimo I, horses and carriages are stabled when not serving as horse-cabs for tourists.—Off the other side of Piazza Tasso (entrance in Viale Ariosto; Pl.8;2) is the *Convent of San Francesco di Sales* (now a school), built in 1700 by Anton Maria Ferri. The church (usually closed) contains four monuments with busts of the Da Verrazzano family, 18C frescoes by Giovanni Antonio Pucci, and an altarpiece by Ignazio Hugford.

From Piazza Sauro at the S end of Ponte alla Carraia VIA SANTO SPIRITO (Pl.9;1) continues parallel to the Arno. Here on the right (No. 39) is the 17C *Palazzo Rinuccini* by Cigoli (enlarged by Ferdinando Ruggieri); the other Palazzo Rinuccini (No. 41) was built by Pier Francesco Silvani (with a coat-of-arms on the corner of Via de' Serragli by Giovanni Battista Foggini). *Palazzo Manetti* (No. 23) has a 15C façade. This was the home of Sir Horace Mann in 1740–86 while serving as English envoy to the Tuscan court. His famous correspondence with Horace Walpole provides a remarkable picture of 18C Florence. Lord and Lady Holland lived in the neighbouring Palazzo Feroni, with George Frederick Watts as their guest in 1844–47. *Palazzo Frescobaldi* (No. 5–13) has a very long façade with several interior courtyards and a garden (view of Santo Spirito), and one flank supported on 'sporti' in Via dei Coverelli. Opposite is *Palazzo Guicciardini* (No. 14), and, on the corner of Via dei Coverelli, can be seen the restored graffiti decoration on the side of Palazzo Covarelli. Via Santo Spirito ends at a busy intersection of narrow streets near the foot of Ponte Santa Trìnita.

   Via Maggio (Pl.9;2,4) leads away from the Arno. Its name (from 'Maggiore') is a reminder of its origin as the principal and widest street of the Oltrarno. It was opened soon after Ponte Santa Trìnita was built in 1252, and it became a fashionable residential street after the grand-dukes moved to Palazzo Pitti in the 16C. It now has a number of antique shops. On the left, *Palazzo Ricasoli* (No. 7), the largest palace on Via Maggio, was built at the end of the 15C or beginning of the 16C with a fine courtyard. On the right is *Palazzo di Bianca Cappello* (No. 26) with good graffiti decoration attributed to Bernardino Poccetti (c 1579; restored in 1987). The house was built by the grand-duke Francesco I for the beautiful Venetian girl Bianca Cappello who was first his mistress and afterwards his wife. Opposite, *Palazzo Ridolfi* (No. 13), built in the late 16C (attributed to Santi di Tito), stands next to *Palazzo di Cosimo Ridolfi*, a small palace built at the beginning of the 15C. The numerous narrow old streets on the left of the road lead to Piazza Pitti (see below). Farther on is *Palazzo Corsini Suarez* (or *Commenda di Firenze*; No. 42; being restored), named after Baldassare Suarez of Portugal who acquired the palace in 1590. It was built in the late 14C and reconstructed in the 16C partly by Gherardo Silvani. It is now owned by the State and since 1979 has been the seat of the Archivio Contemporaneo, a branch of the Vieusseux Library (see p 158). It is also used as a restoration laboratory for books. In the Saletta dell'Alcova are tempera decorations attributed to Sagrestani. The courtyard is also notable.

   Via Maggio ends in Piazza San Felice. No. 8 is the CASA GUIDI, built in the 15C by the Ridolfi and acquired in 1619 by Count Camillo Guidi, Secretary of State for the Medici. Here Robert and Elizabeth Barrett Browning rented a flat on the first floor and lived after their secret marriage in 1846 until Elizabeth's death in 1861 (inscription; for adm. see p 60; ring). Here both poets wrote many of their most important works and were visited by Walter Savage Landor, Anthony Trollope, Bulwer-Lytton, Nathaniel Hawthorne and 'Father Prout' (Francis Mahony), the Roman correspondent for Dickens' 'Daily News'. The Brownings' son 'Pen' who was born here in 1849 purchased the house after their death. The apartment has been owned by the Browning Institute since 1971. It contains a few mementoes of the Brownings. The collection is to be augmented and the rooms furnished, and a study centre opened.—**San Felice**

(Pl.9;3) is a Gothic church with a Renaissance façade by *Michelozzo* (1457).

INTERIOR. The first half of the nave contains a closed gallery supported by eight columns and a pretty vault. SOUTH SIDE: 1st altar, remains of a fresco of the Pietà, attributed to *Nicolò Gerini* (interesting for its iconography); above the side door, large *Crucifix (removed for restoration many years ago) from the workshop of *Giotto*; 5th altar, Pietà, terracotta group attributed to *Cieco da Gambassi*; 6th altar, Madonna and Saints by *Ridolfo* and *Michele Ghirlandaio*; 7th altar, lunette fresco of the Virgin of the Sacred Girdle (late 14C Florentine).—In the presbytery the altarpiece has a 15C Madonna and Child and two Saints of the 16C.—NORTH SIDE: 7th altar, fresco by *Giovanni da San Giovanni* (the angels are by *Volterrano*); 6th altar, triptych by *Neri di Bicci* beneath a frescoed lunette of the 14C; 1st altar, triptych by a follower of Botticelli (known as the 'Master of Apollo and Daphne').

Via Romana (Pl.9;3), one of the most important thoroughfares of the Oltrarno, continues SW towards Porta Romana. At No. 17 (left) *Palazzo Torrigiani* was built in 1775 by Gaspare Maria Paoletti as a natural history museum. It is known as 'LA SPECOLA' from the astronomical Observatory founded here by the grand-duke Pietro Leopoldo. Here, in 1814 Sir Humphry Davy and Michael Faraday used Galileo's 'great burning glass' (see p 188) to explode the diamond. It is now the seat of the natural sciences schools of the University and (on the third floor) of a ZOOLOGICAL MUSEUM (adm. see p 62) with a comprehensive natural history display, including invertebrates, vertebrates, insects, shells, etc. The remarkable and unique collection of anatomical models in wax made in 1775–1814 by *Clemente Susini*, includes 'lo scorticato', a life-size model of a man (recently restored). There are also numerous anatomical wax models and compositions by *Gaetano Zumbo* (late 17C).

Farther on, nearly opposite the Annalena gate to the Boboli gardens (see p 121) is the *Giardino Corsi*, a delightful little raised garden (no adm.) laid out in 1801–10 by Giuseppe Manetti, with fine trees and a neo-classical loggia overlooking Via Romana. Via Romana ends at *Piazza della Calza*, named after a church and convent (now an old peoples' home; No. 6 Via de' Serragli), with a delightful asymmetrical loggia. In the refectory is a Last Supper by Franciabigio and on the walls pretty pietra serena frames with 18C frescoes. In another room is a polychrome stucco bas-relief, a 15C copy of Donatello's Madonna de' Pazzi and a 15C wood Crucifix. *Porta Romana* (Pl.8;6) is a well-preserved gate built in 1327 on a design by Andrea Orcagna. Outside the gate is a busy intersection where Viale Machiavelli (see p 208) and Viale Poggio Imperiale (see p 237) terminate.

Just out of Piazza San Felice is Piazza Pitti, with Palazzo Pitti, described in Rte 8. The pretty row of houses facing the palace includes No. 16, the home of Paolo dal Pozzo Toscanelli (1397–1482), the famous scientist and greatest geographer of his time. While staying at No. 21 in 1868 Dostoyevsky wrote 'The Idiot'. Via Guicciardini (described in Rte 7) leads past the church of Santa Felìcita (p 109) to Ponte Vecchio. Here begins *Via de' Bardi (Pl.10;1), named from the palaces on the street which were the residence of the Bardi, one of the richest mercantile families in medieval Florence, who, however, were bankrupt by 1340. Among the old houses at the end of the bridge destroyed in 1944 was the Casa Ambrogi, guest house of Horace Mann, where Gray and Walpole stayed in 1740. At the fork with Lungarno Torrigiani can be seen the tall Porta San Niccolò (see below). Via de' Bardi continues on a winding course past a series of noble town houses. On the left is the rough stone façade of *Palazzo Capponi delle Rovinate* (No. 36) with a remarkable courtyard. The palace was built for Niccolò da Uzzano in the early 15C. It is still owned by the Capponi family whose archives and private art collection survive here in period rooms. The family chapel has a Madonna and Child (repainted) by Pontormo and a stained glass window by Guglielmo di Marcillat. The family paintings include

works attributed to Bilivert, Sustermans, Pontormo, Andrea da Bres-
cianino, Cigoli, and Andrea del Sarto. *Palazzo Canigiani* (Larioni dei
Bardi; No. 30), with its garden across the road, has a courtyard (in
need of repair) attributed to Michelozzo. At No. 24 is the little church
of *Santa Lucia dei Magnoli* (open only for evensong).

The glazed terracotta lunette over the door is by *Benedetto Buglioni*. Inside on
the 1st altar on the left, *St Lucy by *Pietro Lorenzetti*; on the wall to the left are
two good panels of the Annunciation, ascribed to *Jacopo del Sellaio*. The other
altarpieces on the left side are by *Jacopo da Empoli* and *Francesco Curradi*. The
high altarpiece of the Madonna and Child with St Anne and four Saints is by the
late-15C Florentine school. The choir, decorated in 1732 with a painting of the
Martyrdom of St Lucy attributed to *Pier Dandini* is partially hidden by the ugly
organ. A photographic reproduction of the famous altarpiece painted for this
church by *Domenico Veneziano* (now in the Uffizi; the predella was divided up
between various musuems) has been placed on the entrance wall.

Opposite the church the pretty old Costa Scarpuccia climbs up the
hill between gardens to Costa San Giorgio. Via de' Bardi ends in
Piazza dei Mozzi. On the bend are the fine old PALAZZI DEI MOZZI
(Pl.10;4) built in the 13–14C and among the most noble private
houses of medieval Florence. The severe façades in pietra forte have
arches on the ground floor. The Mozzi were one of the richest
Florentine families in the 13C, but, like the Bardi, they too lost most
of their wealth in the 14C. Gregory X was their guest here in 1273
when he came to Florence to arrange a peace between the Guelfs
and Ghibellines. The huge garden up to the walls was acquired by
the Mozzi in the 16C. The building, garden, and Villa Bardini were
left indirectly to the State in 1965, together with a vast collection of
decorative arts (including 16C and 17C furniture), and marble
architectural fragments recovered during the demolition of the old
centre of the city, by Ugo Bardini. There are long-term plans to open
a museum here. The piazza opens out onto the Arno with, at No. 1,
the Museo Bardini (described on p 190), left to the Comune by Ugo's
father Stefano.

*VIA DI SAN NICCOLÒ, another narrow street of medieval houses,
continues beyond Piazza de' Mozzi. On the left *Palazzo Alemanni*
(No. 68) was built in the 14C and 15C and reconstructed later. It is
decorated with a row of little demons, copies from Giambologna.
Beyond, at a bend in the road with local shops, is the church of **San
Niccolò sopr' Arno** (or *'Oltrarno'*; Pl.10;4; closed 11–17), founded in
the 11C and rebuilt at the end of the 14C.

In the tall INTERIOR, with an open timber roof, several interesting frescoes were
found beneath the 16C altars during restoration work after 1966. On the W wall,
School of Neri di Bicci, St James the Apostle. SOUTH SIDE: 1st altar, St Anthony
Abbot (15C); 2nd altar, *Michelozzo*, Wood Crucifix; 3rd altar, Pope St Gregory
(15C).—In the SACRISTY (off the S side), *Madonna della Cintola, a beautiful
fresco of the late 15C Florentine school (attributed to Baldovinetti), within a
tabernacle in pietra serena by the bottega of Michelozzo. Also here are two
small paintings of St Michael and St Gabriel Archangel by *Il Poppi*. The
Madonna and Saints by *Bicci di Lorenzo* has been removed for restoration.—In
the chapels to the left and right of the high altar, *Empoli*, St John the Baptist,
and *Il Poppi*, Marriage of the Virgin.—NORTH SIDE: 3rd Altar, *Il Poppi*, Christ
bringing to life the widow's son (recently restored); 2nd altar, Sinopia for the
fresco of *St Ansano, attributed to *Francesco d'Antonio* on the 1st altar. Other
works to be returned here after restoration include a triptych by the *'Master of
San Niccolò'* (late 14C), an Annunciation by *Alessandro Fei*, the Martyrdom of
St Catherine by *Alessandro Allori*, and the Miracle of St Nicholas by *Francesco
Curradi*.

At the end of Via San Miniato (right) can be seen the pretty 14C *Porta San Miniato* in the walls. Via San Niccolò continues past simple houses with workshops on the ground floor, to the massive **Porta San Niccolò** (Pl.11;3), whose high tower remains intact. Built c 1340, it was restored in 1979 (the staircase which leads to the top is sometimes accessible with special permission). From here a ramp leads up the hill towards San Miniato (see Rte 20).

20 Forte di Belvedere and the Basilica of San Miniato

San Miniato can be reached directly from the Station or Piazza del Duomo by BUS No. 13 which traverses Viale dei Colli (Viale Machiavelli, Viale Galileo, and Viale Michelangelo). The church can also be reached on foot by the steps from Porta San Niccolò (Pl.11;3). However, for those with time, the following route on foot is highly recommended (and Bus 13 can be taken from San Miniato to return to the centre of the city).

From the little piazza adjoining Piazza Santa Felìcita (see p 109) the narrow COSTA SAN GIORGIO (Pl.10;3) winds up the hill towards Forte di Belvedere. At the junction with Costa Scarpuccia (a beautiful road which leads downhill to Via de' Bardi, cf. Rte 19) is the church of SAN GIORGIO SULLA COSTA (or *Spirito Santo*; Pl.10;3).

The church has been undergoing restoration for many years and it is at present used by the Romanian Orthodox community of Florence (open only for a service at 10.30 on fest.). The Baroque INTERIOR by *Giovanni Battista Foggini* (1705) is one of the best in Florence. The altarpieces are by *Tommaso Redi, Jacopo Vignali,* and *Passignano,* and on the ceiling is the Glory of St George by *Alessandro Gherardini.* The high altar is also by Foggini. A *Madonna and Child with two angels, an early work by *Giotto* was removed many years ago, and has been stored in the Uffizi since its restoration. The church also contains a precious mechanical organ.

Farther up the street is the house (No. 19; with a portrait on the façade) purchased by Galileo for his son Vincenzio. Here the great scientist was visited in 1620 by Ferdinando II, under whose protection Galileo was able to live in Florence from 1610 until his death. To the left is the *Villa Bardini* (entrance at No. 8) with a huge park (Pl.10;4; no adm.) which extends down the hillside to Palazzo dei Mozzi. A loggia was reconstructed here by Bardini at the top of a long staircase; it has a magnificent view of Florence. The park is owned by the State and may one day be opened to the public (cf. p 202). The pretty Costa San Giorgio continues between the high walls of rural villas to (left) PORTA SAN GIORGIO (Pl.10;5), with a fresco by Bicci di Lorenzo, and, on the outer face, the copy of a stone relief of St George (1284; original in Palazzo Vecchio). Dating from 1260, it is part of the walls built to protect the Oltrarno in 1258 (cf. the Plan on pp. 30–1), and is the oldest gate to have survived in the city. Here is the entrance to *Forte di Belvedere (or *di San Giorgio*; Pl.10;5), a huge fortress designed by Buontalenti (probably using plans drawn up by Don Giovanni de' Medici) in the shape of a six-pointed star.

It was built by order of Ferdinando I in 1590, ostensibly for the defence of the city, but in reality to dominate the supposedly republican citizens. Entered from the Boboli gardens by a secret door, guarded day and night until 1850 by a sentry, it remained inaccessible to the public until 1958. It can now also be visited from the Boboli gardens (cf. p 121). From the ramparts (adm. 9–20) there is a splendid *View in every direction. The Palazzetto at the centre of the fortress has a loggia and two façades, one facing the city and one facing S. The empty interior is only opened from large exhibitions which are held periodically in this magnificent setting.

Here begins *VIA DI SAN LEONARDO (Pl.10;5) one of the most beautiful and best-preserved roads on the outskirts of Florence (but beware of cars). It leads through countryside past villas and their gardens between olive groves behind high walls. A short way along on the left, preceded by a charming little garden with four cypresses, is the church of SAN LEONARDO IN ARCETRI (Pl.10;5; open for services at 17 or 18 on Sat, and 8–11 on fest.; at other times ring at No. 25), founded in the 11C.

The church contains a celebrated *Pulpit of the early 13C removed from the church of San Pier Scheraggio, with beautiful bas-reliefs. Over the high altar, *Lorenzo di Niccolò*, Triptych of the Madonna and Child with Saints, and, on either side, Madonna of the Sacred Girdle with Saints, and an Annunciation with angels and Saints (decorating a tabernacle), both by *Neri di Bicci*. The damaged painting of Tobias and the angel is by the 'Master of San Miniato'.

Via San Leonardo continues past the house (right; No. 64) where a plaque records the stay of Tchaikovsky in 1878, to Viale Galileo (see p 208). The continuation of Via San Leonardo and Arcetri and Pian de' Giullari are described in Rte 25.

From Forte di Belvedere *VIA DI BELVEDERE (Pl.10;6), a picturesque country lane with olive trees, follows the straight line of the city walls built in 1258, reinforced in 1299–1333, and again in the 16C. Even though greatly reduced in height they are the best stretch of fortifications to survive in Florence. The path descends steeply with a fine view of the defensive towers and the tall Porta San Niccolò beyond. At the bottom by *Porta San Miniato*, a simple 14C arch in the wall, Via del Monte alle Croce returns uphill (view back of the walls). This road continues up to the busy Viale Galileo. For pedestrians the prettiest route is by the stepped Via di San Salvatore al Monte, lined with cypresses, which ascends past the wall of a little rose garden (open to the public). Across Viale Galileo a monumental flight of steps or a winding road lead up past a cemetery (1839) to *San Miniato al Monte (Pl.11;7; closed in winter 12–14, in summer 13–15). The finest of all Tuscan Romanesque basilicas, with a famous façade, it is one of the most beautiful churches in Italy. Together with the Baptistery and San Lorenzo it was the most important church in 11C Florence. Its position on a green hill above the city is incomparable. However, the hillside is subject to landslips and has had to be shored up.

The deacon Minias was a member of the early Christian community from the East who settled in Florence. A legend even suggested he was an oriental prince, the son of the King of Armenia. He is thought to have been martyred c 250 during the persecutions of the emperor Decius, and buried on this hillside. The present church, built in 1013 by Bishop Hildebrand, is on the site of a shrine protecting the tomb of St Minias. The Benedictine Cluniac monastery, founded here at the same time by the emperor Henry II, was one of the first important religious houses in Tuscany.

The *FAÇADE, begun c 1090, is built of white and dark-greenish marble in a beautiful geometrical design reminiscent of the Baptistery. Above the exquisite little window in the form of an aedicule is a 13C mosaic (restored) of Christ between the Virgin and St Minias, the warrior-martyr. In the tympanum, supported by two small figures in relief, the marble inlay is repeated in the motifs of the pavement

The façade of San Miniato al Monte

inside. It is crowned by an eagle holding a bale of cloth, emblem of the 'Arte di Calimala' who looked after the fabric of the building.

The very fine *INTERIOR built in 1018–63 is practically in its original state. Its design is unique in Florentine church architecture with a raised choir above a large hall crypt. (The Sacristan will switch on lights on request.) Many of the capitals of the columns come from Roman temples in the city. In the PAVEMENT are tomb-slabs, and, in the centre of the nave, seven superb marble intarsia *Panels (1207) with signs of the Zodiac and animal motifs. The decoration on the inside of the upper part of the nave walls, in imitation of the façade, was carried out at the end of the last century. The open timber roof, with polychrome decoration, was also restored at that time. At the end of the nave is the *CAPPELLA DEL CROCIFISSO (1), an exquisite tabernacle commissioned by Piero il Gottoso from *Michelozzo* in 1448. It is superbly carved and beautifully designed to fit its setting built some 400 years earlier. It was made to house the Crucifix which spoke to St John Gualberto (later removed to Santa Trìnita); the painted panels of the doors of the cupboard which protected the miraculous crucifix are by *Agnolo Gaddi* (1394–96). The enamelled terracotta roof and ceiling are the work of *Luca della Robbia*. The inlaid coloured marble frieze bears the emblem of Piero de' Medici (whose arms also appear on the back of the tabernacle). The copper eagles on the roof, emblems of the 'Arte di Calimala', are by *Maso di Bartolomeo*.—On the outer stone walls of the aisles are a number of frescoes. In the S aisle: (2) *Paolo Schiavo*, Madonna enthroned with six Saints (1436) and a huge figure of St Christopher (3) dating from the 14C or earlier. Most of the other frescoes on this wall are by 15C artists. Also here is a fine painted Crucifix, probably dating from

1260–70. In the N aisle are two detached frescoes (Madonna and Child with Saints, and a Crucifixion with seven Saints) by *Mariotto di Nardo*. By the steps up to the choir is a fresco (4) of the Virgin Annunciate and a fragment of a nativity scene (restored) dating from the late 13C.

Built onto the N wall of the church is the *CHAPEL OF THE CARDINAL OF PORTUGAL, the funerary chapel of Cardinal Iacopo di Lusitania who died in Florence at the age of 25. It was begun by *Antonio Manetti*, Brunelleschi's pupil, in 1460 (and finished, after his death in the same year, probably under the direction of *Antonio Rossellino*). It incorporates some of the best workmanship of the Florentine Renaissance. The exquisitely carved *Tomb of the

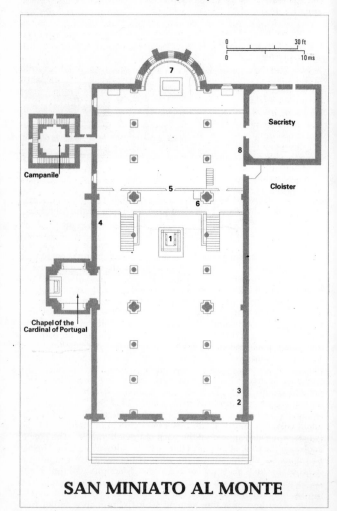

SAN MINIATO AL MONTE

Cardinal is by *Antonio Rossellino* (1461–66). The ceiling has five *Medallions (1461) by *Luca della Robbia* representing the Cardinal Virtues and the Holy Ghost, against a background of tiles decorated with classical cubes in yellow, green, and purple, among the masterpieces of Luca's enamelled terracotta work. The altarpiece of Three Saints, by *Antonio* and *Piero del Pollaiolo* (1466–67) has been replaced by a copy (original in the Uffizi). The frescoed decoration of this wall, including two angels, is by the same artists. Above the marble Bishop's throne on the W wall is a painting of the *Annunciation by *Alesso Baldovinetti* (1466–73), who also frescoed the Evangelists and Fathers of the Church in the lunettes beside the windows, and in the spandrels.

Steps lead up to the raised CHOIR with a beautiful marble *Transenna (5) dating from 1207, and *Pulpit (6), also faced with marble. The lectern is supported by an eagle above a carved figure standing on a lion's head. The low columns in the choir have huge antique capitals. The APSE (7; light) has a beautiful inlaid blind arcade with six small Roman columns between opaque windows. The large apse mosaic representing Christ between the Virgin and St Minias with symbols of the Evangelists (1297) was first restored in 1491 by Alesso Baldovinetti. The Crucifix behind the simple Renaissance altar is attributed to the Della Robbia. The carved and inlaid stalls by *Giovanni di Domenico da Gaiole* and *Francesco di Domenico (Il Monciatto)* date from 1466–70. To the right of the apse is an altarpiece by *Jacopo del Casentino* showing St Minias and scenes from his life. On the S side is the SACRISTY (1387), entirely frescoed by *Spinello Aretino*; in the vault are the Evangelists and in the lunettes the *Life of St Benedict, one of his best works (restored in 1840). Here also are a polychrome bust of St Minias (wearing a crown) attributed to *Nanni di Bartolo*, two Della Robbia statuettes, and stalls like those in the choir. In the lunette above the little door is a Pietà recently attributed to *Giovanni di Piamonte* (1470–72).—Among the frescoes on the walls of the choir are some very early panels of Saints (8; 13C).

The 11C CRYPT beneath the choir has beautiful slender columns, many of them with antique capitals. The original 11C altar contains the relics of St Minias. The little vaults are decorated with frescoes of Saints and Prophets against a blue ground by *Taddeo Gaddi*.

The fine **Cloister** (adm. only by special permission), on the right side of the church, was begun c 1425. On the upper walk fragments of frescoes in terraverde attributed to *Paolo Uccello*, illustrating scenes from monastic legends, were revealed during restoration work, and a sinopia attributed to *Andrea del Castagno*.

The massive stone CAMPANILE (which replaces one that fell in 1499) was begun after 1523 from a design by Baccio d'Agnolo, but never finished. During the siege of Florence (1530) Michelangelo mounted two cannon here, and protected the bell-tower from hostile artillery by a screen of mattresses.—The battlemented *Bishop's Palace*, with well-designed twin windows, dates from 1295 when it was used as a summer residence. It was enlarged in 1320 and again by Bishop Agnolo Ricasoli. In later centuries it was used as a barracks and hospital, and was restored in this century.—The *Fortezza* which now encloses a monumental cemetery laid out in 1854 by *Nicolò Matas* (entrance on the left side of the church) originated in a hastily improvised defence-work planned by Michelangelo during the months preceding the siege. In 1553 Cosimo I converted it into a real fortress with the help of Francesco da Sangallo, Tribolo and others.—

The splendid view from the terrace in front of the church includes the walls climbing the hillside to Forte di Belvedere, and beyond the Lungarno across the river, the Duomo, Campanile, and white roof of the Baptistery, the dome of the Chapel of the Princes beside San Lorenzo, the tower of Palazzo Vecchio (and, in front, the towers of the Badia and Bargello).

Near San Miniato, in a grove of cypresses on the side of the hill, is the church of **San Salvatore al Monte** (Pl.11;5), a building of gracious simplicity by *Cronaca*, called by Michelangelo his 'bella villanella'— his pretty country maid.

The INTERIOR has an open timber roof. On the W wall is a bust of Marcello Adriani (died 1521) by *Andrea Ferrucci*. In the 2nd N chapel, Deposition, a large terracotta group (restored) attributed to *Giovanni della Robbia*. Over the N door is another terracotta Deposition group, an unusual 16C work. In the sanctuary are two early-15C paintings, one of the Pietà attributed to *Neri di Bicci*.

Steps lead down behind the *Palazzina del Caffè* (now a restaurant), built in 1873 by Giuseppe Poggi, to **Piazzale Michelangelo** (Pl.11;5), a celebrated viewpoint, much visited by tourists. From the balustrade on the huge terrace is a remarkable panorama of the city, its surrounding hills, and beyond (on a clear day) the plain as far as Pistoia and the peaks of the Apennines.

From the parapet the view includes (on the extreme left), the olive fields on the hillside below Forte di Belvedere, from which the city walls descend to Porta San Niccolò. The view down the Arno takes in Ponte Vecchio. On the other side of the river can be seen Palazzo Vecchio, the dome of the Chapel of the Princes (San Lorenzo), the campanile and cupola of the Duomo, with the stone towers of the Badia and Bargello in front. Nearer at hand is the huge church of Santa Croce and the green dome of the synagogue.—The monument to Michelangelo (1875) on the terrace is made up of reproductions in bronze of some of the sculptor's famous marble statues in the city.—A delightful *Iris Garden* is open here in May (entrance on the right of the balustrade). On the hillside are some 2500 varieties of iris; a red iris on a white ground is the symbol of Florence. An international competition has been held here annually since 1957.

VIALE DEI COLLI (Pl.11, 10, & 9; Viale Michelangelo, Viale Galileo, and Viale Machiavelli), a fine roadway 6km long, was laid out by Giuseppe Poggi in 1865–70. It is one of the most panoramic drives near Florence, following a winding course from Piazza Ferrucci (Pl.11;4) via Piazzale Michelangelo and San Miniato to Porta Romana. It is traversed by Bus No. 13 which can be taken from Piazzale Michelangelo back to the centre of the city. Beyond San Miniato, off Viale Galileo, Via dei Giramontino leads up to Torre del Gallo, Arcetri, and Pian de' Giullari (described in Rte 25). Viale Machiavelli, from Piazzale Galileo (Pl.9;8) to Porta Romana is particularly attractive, and traverses shady gardens.

Off Viale Michelangelo, near Ponte San Niccolò (Pl.11;6) Via Marsuppini leads into Via Benedetto Fortini where at No. 30 is *Villa Il Tasso* where Roberto Longhi, the art historian, lived from 1939 to 1970. This is now the seat of the Fondazione Longhi, and here is preserved Longhi's interesting collection of paintings (including works by Caravaggio and Guido Reni; not open to the public, but shown to scholars by previous appointment).

21 Medieval Florence

This route follows an itinerary through many of the oldest streets in the city N of the Arno. Important monuments are indicated but described in full in other routes; it has been the intention here to describe as many as possible of the medieval palaces and towers which survive in the city. Towers were first built in the 12C by wealthy Florentines next to their houses, as refuges in times of trouble, as well as status symbols. The towers had to be lowered after 1250 by order of the regime of the 'primo popolo'. Later in the 14C many of them were adapted as houses. The medieval streets often lie on the courses of their Roman predecessors. Destruction of much of the old city took place at the end of the 19C when Piazza della Repubblica and its surrounding thoroughfares were laid out, and during the last War when the old towers and houses in Via Por Santa Maria and at either end of Ponte Vecchio were destroyed. The old streets of the Oltrarno are described in Rte 19.

Orsanmichele (Pl.16;6), one of the most significant medieval monuments in the city, is described on p 82. Next to it is PALAZZO DELL'ARTE DELLA LANA, built in 1308 by the Guild of Wool Merchants, but arbitrarily restored in 1905. The 'Arte della Lana' represented the most important Florentine industry which was responsible for the city's economic growth in the 13C (it has been estimated that a third of the population was employed in the woollen cloth industry in the 13–14C). Among the 'stemme' on the building is that of the Guild, the Agnus Dei. At the base of the tower is the little oratory of *Santa Maria della Tromba* (late 14C), one of the largest of the many tabernacles in the city. It was moved here from the Mercato Vecchio, nearby, the commercial centre of the city until the 19C, which was destroyed to make way for Piazza della Repubblica. Behind the grille is a painting of the Madonna enthroned, by Jacopo del Casentino. On Via Calimala the 13C Torre Compiobbesi is incorporated in the building. In a shop here are remains of frescoes, including a Madonna and Child and two Saints. On the first floor (adm sometimes granted by the Società Dantesca) are 14C frescoes.—In Via Orsanmichele (No. 4) is *Palazzo dell'Arte dei Beccai*, headquarters of the Butchers' Guild until 1534; their 'stemma' (a goat) can be seen high up on the façade.

The palace (c 1415–20) has recently been restored as the seat of the *Accademia delle Arti del Disegno*, the first of all Art Academies, founded in 1563 by members of the Compagnia di San Luca which already existed by 1339. The founders included Vasari, Bronzino, Francesco di Giuliano da Sangallo, Ammannati, Vincenzo de' Rossi, and Montorsoli. Cosimo I and Michelangelo were elected the first Academicians.—Admission to the interior is usually granted on written application. It houses some interesting works of art including a frescoed Crucifix removed from a tabernacle in Via dell'Osservatorio, near the Villa della Petraia (see p 244), and a painting of the Madonna and Saints, both by *Pontormo*; a bronze bust of Michelangelo by *Daniele da Volterra*; and a fresco of the Madonna and Child with Saints by *Mariotto di Nardo*.

Via dell'Arte della Lana crosses Via Lamberti. On the corner here was the site of the first headquarters of the Medici bank, set up in 1397 by Giovanni di Bicci, father of Cosimo il Vecchio. At the next intersection, Via Porta Rossa (so-named since at least the beginning of the 13C) leads (right) past the **Mercato Nuovo** (Pl.16;5), the Florentine straw-market (open daily in summer; closed Monday and Sunday in winter). It has been the site of a market since the beginning of the 11C. The loggia was erected by Cosimo I in 1547–51 on a design by Giovanni Battista del Tasso for the sale of silk and gold. It is now a market-place for cheap lace, straw work, leather goods, and souvenirs. It is known to Florentines as 'Il Porcellino' from a popular statue on the far side of the loggia. The bronze boar was copied by Tacca from the antique statue in the Uffizi; the delightful base is a copy of the original by Tacca. Coins thrown into the fountain are given to charity. The medieval buildings in Via Por Santa Maria which leads to Ponte Vecchio (p 108) were all destroyed in 1944. Via Porta Rossa continues to **Palazzo Davanzati** (Pl.16;5; adm. see p 62), now the MUSEO DELLA CASA FIORENTINA ANTICA, and the best surviving example of a medieval nobleman's house in Florence (despite numerous restorations). It is particularly interesting as an illustration of Florentine life in the Middle Ages.

The palace was built in the mid 14C by the Davizzi family and became the property of Bernardo Davanzati, the successful merchant and scholar, in 1578. It remained in his family until the end of the 19C. In 1904 the palace was bought by the antiquarian Elia Volpi who restored it and turned it into a private museum of antiques, which were later sold to various museums all over the world. The Italian State purchased the house in 1951. Interesting graffiti and drawings referring to contemporary events (1441–1516) have been found on many of the walls.

The typical 14C FAÇADE consists of three storeys above large arches on the ground floor. The proportions have been altered by the loggia at the top which was added in the 16C and probably replaced battlements. The ironwork is interesting and includes brackets which carry diagonal poles across the windows. These were used to hang out the washing, to suspend birdcages, etc., or for the hangings which decorated the façade on special occasions. The huge Davanzati coat-of-arms dates from the 16C; it was brought from another family house. The palace is separated from the smaller medieval house on the right by a narrow alley spanned by stone girders.

The INTERIOR, of great interest for its architecture and contemporary wall paintings (rare survivals of a decorative form typical of 14C houses), has been beautifully arranged with the furnishings of a Florentine house of the 15–17C (including tapestries, lacework, ceramics, sculpture, paintings, decorative arts, domestic objects, etc.). The 16–17C furniture is a special feature of the house. The spacious vaulted ENTRANCE HALL runs the whole width of the building and was used as a loggia, for family ceremonies, and later as shops.—The INTERIOR COURTYARD could be entirely cut off from the street in times of trouble. The storerooms here were replenished directly from the alley-ways at the back and side of the building. The well served all five floors of the house. The corner pilaster bears carved heads traditionally supposed to be portraits of the Davizzi family. A detached fresco of a hunting scene (15C Florentine) has been placed here.—The staircase ascends to the upper floors; the lower steps are in stone, the higher in wood. Beyond a detached fresco of the Madonna enthroned by the Umbrian school (13–14C), on the **First Floor** landing, is a faded fresco of St Christopher (14–15C). To the right is the SALA MADORNALE which runs the width of the building and was used for family gatherings. It has a painted wood ceiling (14–15C). Wall hangings were attached to the hooks at the top of the walls to decorate the room for special occasions. Four holes in the floor were used for defence against intruders in the entrance hall below. The fine table of Florentine workmanship dates from the late 16C, and the painted wood cupboard (16C) stored the family arms. Here are exhibited a series of small coffers (probably used as jewel cases) in decorated wood (15C), the bust of a boy by *Antonio Rossellino*, and a painted tondo showing a Florentine street scene (by *Giovanni di Ser Giovanni*, known as 'Lo Scheggia').—Two small rooms were opened in 1981 with a charming display of •Lace (examples of Flemish, French, and Italian work from the end of the 16C to the present day). A conservation centre for lace has been set up here.—The SALA DEI PAPPAGALLI, or Dining Room has delightful wall paintings. The lower part of the walls imitate wall hangings with a motif of parrots, while above is a painted terrace with trees and flowering shrubs. The fireplace, which bears the arms of the Davizzi and Alberti, was probably installed at the end of the 14C. Here the furniture has been used to display collections of pottery, including 14C household ceramics contemporary with the building of the house.—The SALA PICCOLA, probably a child's bedroom, nearby, contains an elaborate 16C safe, a desk, and 17C Montelupo ceramics. The terracotta Madonna of the Annunciation is attributed to *Andrea Rizzo* or *Nanni di Bartolo*. The paintings include: *Andrea del Sarto* (attributed), Daedalus and Icarus, and *Francesco Granacci*, •Joseph led to prison.—Off this room is one of several W.C.s in the house.—The last room on this floor is the CAMERA NUZIALE, or 'dei pavoni', the bedroom. The fine wall paintings bear the coats-of-arms of families related to the Davizzi between a delightful frieze of birds. The rare linen *Bed cover, a Sicilian work of the end of the 14C, is decorated with storeys of Tristan (sometimes removed for conservation reasons).

Second Floor. To the right is the second SALONE. The interesting portrait of Giovanni di Bicci de' Medici (father of Cosimo Il Vecchio) is attributed to *Zanobi Strozzi*. The ceramics include a tile with two figures made in central Italy at the end of the 14C, a charming series of hand-warmers in the form of shoes (18C), and two fine pharmacy jars. Here is hung the family tree of the Davanzati painted in the 17C. A small room has another display of lace babies' clothes made in the 19C and 20C.—The DINING ROOM is decorated with a pretty series of small Flemish tapestries illustrating biblical scenes (15C; very well preserved; temporarily removed). Here are more ceramics including a series of salt cellars in enamelled terracotta (17–18C), and an inlaid 'cassone' (end of the 16C). the paintings include: *Pier Francesco Foschi*, Temple of Hercules, and three stories of Perseus by the *'Master of Serumido'* (beginning of the 16C), formerly attributed to Piero di Cosimo.—The SALA PICCOLA contains a remarkable collection of 'cassone' which were made to contain a bride's dowry of household linen. One of them illustrates the story of Paris (beginning of the 15C), and two reconstructed chests bear four panels of the Triumphs of Petrarch, by *Giovanni de Ser Giovanni (Lo Scheggia)*. The 14C paintings hung here include: *Rossello di Jacopo Franchi*, Madonna del Parto, and *Spinello Aretino*, St Stephen and the Crucifixion.—A corridor leads into the Bedroom known as the CAMERA DELLA CASTELLANA DI VERGI, from the charming painted *Frieze illustrating a medieval French romance.—On the **Third Floor** is the KITCHEN (normally situated on the top floor in medieval houses). Here, the warmest place in the house, the women would spend most of their day, passing their time spinning and weaving, etc. around the big fireplace. Various household utensils are displayed here. There is a view from the window of the dome of San Frediano in Cestello, the tower of Santa Trìnita, and a massive 13C tower ('La Rognosa') rising above a 15C palace nearby. The salone is used for exhibitions, etc.

Next to Palazzo Davanzati is a smaller medieval house (No. 15), and opposite, in the piazza, the old Casa Torre Foresi. Farther along the street can be seen (left) the old *Albergo Porta Rossa* with a projecting upper storey supported on stone 'sporti' and wrought-iron lanterns. The palace was built by the Bartolini-Salimbeni in the early 16C (their heraldic emblems decorate the façade), and the hotel opened here in the mid 19C.—It is now necessary to return along Via Porta Rossa to Via Pellicceria, at the end of which (right) is a little piazza surrounded by an interesting group of old buildings. On the right is *Palazzo Giandonati*, dating from the 14C, with two arches on the ground floor. Next to it is the 15C *Palazzo Canacci* (No. 3) with grisaille decoration and a fine loggia (heavily restored at the beginning of this century). At the end is PALAZZO DI PARTE GUELFA (Pl.16;5; adm. only with special permission from the Ufficio Belle Arti, 21 Via Sant'Egidio), built as the official residence of the Captains of the Guelf party in the 13C.

The 'Parte Guelfa' was a political and military organisation which supported the Pope and virtually controlled the government of the city from c 1267 until 1376. The famous feud between the Guelfs and Ghibellines (on the side of the Emperor) coloured much of the history of the city during the Middle Ages.—The outside stair was modified by Vasari. Beneath the crenellations is a row of 'stemme' and a tall Gothic window. In the 15C the palace was enlarged (see below) by Brunelleschi who built a hall (since restored).

Over: 'Civitas Florentie', the earliest known view of the medieval city, showing the Baptistery and the incomplete Duomo and campanile (detail from the fresco of the Madonna della Misericordia, dated 1342, in the Museo del Bigallo)

FLORENTIE

On the third side of the square is the rough façade of the ex-church of Santa Maria Sovraporta (now a library). Vicolo della Seta leads down by the side of the church to the Mercato Nuovo (see above) and Via di Capaccio (right). Here is *Palazzo dell'Arte della Seta* (No. 3), the headquarters of the Guild of the silk-cloth industry established here at the end of the 14C. It still bears its beautiful 'stemma' encircled by cherubs in the style of Donatello. Next to it, extending to Via delle Terme, is the handsome extension by Brunelleschi to Palazzo di Parte Guelfa (the little loggia on the corner was added by Vasari).

Via delle Terme (Pl.16;5), a pretty medieval street, takes its name from the Roman baths which were in this area. At the beginning (right), by Chiasso Manetti, is the Casa Torre Buondelmonte (Guidi) which faces the back of the medieval portion of Palazzo di Parte Guelfa (cf. above). On the corner of Chiasso di Misure is another interesting palace (No. 9) with a Renaissance courtyard, and (No. 13 red) a medieval tower. Opposite is Palazzo Canacci (cf. above). Beyond Chiasso Cornino is a small house (No. 17), one storey high, above two wide arches. The road skirts the side of the fine Palazzo Bartolini-Salimbeni (see p 157), a 14C building reconstructed in the 16C, with stone benches on the pavement, before emerging in Piazza Santa Trìnita in front of the tall Roman column crowned by a statue of Justice. Here is the grandiose Palazzo Spini-Feroni built in 1289, and the largest of Florentine medieval private palaces, which, together with the other monuments in the piazza, is described in Rte 12.

Borgo Santi Apostoli (Pl.16;5), parallel to Via delle Terme and the Arno, leads back out of the square. This was a Roman road which led from outside the south gate of the city to the Cassia. It had received its present name at least by the beginning of the 13C. On the corner of Via delle Bombarde is *Palazzo Altoviti* with its tower (13C or 14C). In the attractive little Piazza del Limbo is the romanesque stone façade of the church of **Santi Apostoli** (Pl.16;5; usually open only 15.30–18), one of the oldest churches in the city (mentioned as early as 1075). The building is considerably lower than the pavement of the Borgo.

According to legend the church was founded by Charlemagne in 786, but it is now thought to date from the 10C when it was built partly on the remains of a Roman building. It was restored in 1938. The 16C doorway is ascribed to *Benedetto da Rovezzano.*—The Basilican INTERIOR has fine green marble columns and capitals (the first two are from Roman baths). North Aisle. In the 1st chapel is the *Sinopia of the fresco of the Madonna and Child formerly on the façade by *Paolo Schiavo*; in the 4th chapel, *Maso di San Friano*, Nativity (recently restored). At the end of the aisle, *Tomb of Prior Oddo Altoviti, by *Benedetto da Rovezzano* (1507; the sarcophagus is derived from classical models), and a fine *Tabernacle by *Andrea della Robbia* (and assistants), with two sculpted panels below from the tomb of Donato Acciaioli (1333). On the altar is a painting by the school of Orcagna (in restoration). The altarpieces from the S aisle, by *Vasari, Pomerancio*, and others, have been restored after severe damage in 1966 (but have not yet all been returned here).

In the piazza, *Palazzo di Oddo Altoviti* (No. 1) is the work of Benedetto da Rovezzano (c 1512; altered). On the other side of the church is *Palazzo Rosselli del Turco* with various inscriptions and a relief of the Madonna by Benedetto da Maiano. The main façade in the Borgo is by Baccio d'Agnolo (1517). The portone faces its charming little garden created in 1534. Beyond the characteristic Chiasso Cornino are the *Palazzi Acciaioli* (No. 8; 14C) with a tower, bearing the emblem of the Certosa del Galluzzo, which was founded by Niccolò Acciaioli (1340–65). Opposite (No. 27 red) is a building with 13C portions. At No. 19 (red) is the remains of the 13C fabric of the *Palazzo Usimbardi* (*Acciaioli*) whose main 16C façade on the Arno was destroyed in the last War. In the 19C, when it was the Grand Hotel Royal, Ruskin, Dickens, Swinburne, Longfellow, and Henry James all stayed here. The original fabric of the *Buondelmonti* palaces next door has been destroyed except for a 14C rusticated ground floor and a few stone arches; No. 6 is the oldest residence of this Florentine family to have survived. The remainder of the street was badly damaged in the last War; on the corner of Via Por Santa Maria the 13C Baldovinetti tower has been restored.—Across Por Santa Maria (see above) is a secluded little piazza around **Santo Stefano al Ponte** (Pl.16;5; open for concerts), another very old church, first built in 969.

The handsome Romanesque decoration of the façade dates from 1233. The interior was altered by *Ferdinando Tacca* in 1649. It contains altarpieces by *Santi di Tito*, *Matteo Rosselli*, and others, a painting by *Jacopo di Cione*, and a bronze altar frontal of the Stoning of St Stephen by *Ferdinando Tacca*. At the elaborate E end the altar steps (removed from Santa Trìnita) are a remarkable Mannerist work by *Buontalenti* (1574). Beneath is a large crypt. There are long-term plans to open a Diocesan Museum here.

To the right of the church an alley leads past the *Casa dell'Orafo*, a rambling edifice which is honeycombed with the workshops of numerous Florentine goldsmiths. To the left, the dark Volta dei Girolami is spanned by a series of low arches; at the end, Via del Georgofili leads left to Via Lambertesca (with a glimpse right of the Uffizi). In this street several guilds had their headquarters. A short way to the left, Chiasso dei Baroncelli, a narrow medieval lane, with the 14C Palazzo Benini Formichi, continues. It emerges in Piazza della Signoria, dominated by Palazzo Vecchio, begun in 1298 (described in Rte 5). Via Calimaruzza, another road leading into the piazza (left) was the seat from the late 14C of the 'Arte di Calimala' (the wholesale cloth importers). Their 'stemma' (an eagle holding a bale of cloth in its talons) survives at No. 2a.

Via de' Calzaioli leads out of the N side of the Piazza and Via Condotta soon diverges right. On the corner of the characteristic old Vicolo dei Cerchi is the well-preserved *Palazzo Cerchi* (No. 52 red; being restored), dating from the 13C. Beyond, Via delle Farine (right) has a good view of Palazzo Vecchio with its tower. The shop windows in Via Condotta are framed by a series of medieval arches. On the corner of Via dei Cerchi, a local shopping street, with pretty iron lamp brackets, is the medieval *Palazzo Giugni* (reconstructed) with arcading. Via dei Cerchi leads N. On the corner (Canto alla Quarconia) is the *Torre Cerchi* (1292–98), and on Via dei Tavolini stands *Torre Greci* (Galigai) of the 12–13C. Via dei Cimatori (with a view left of Orsanmichele, and right of the towers of the Bargello and the Badia) continues right from Via dei Cerchi. In Via dei Magazzini is the large convent building (with a fine courtyard) of the Badia (cf. Rte 14), now occupied by the law courts, the entrance to which is (left) in the little PIAZZA SAN MARTINO. Here is the splendid 13C *Torre della Castagna*, one of the best-preserved medieval towers in the city. This was the residence of the 'priori' in 1282 before they moved to Palazzo Vecchio. This area is traditionally associated with the great Florentine poet Dante Alighieri. The little chapel of **San Martino del Vescovo** (Pl.16;4; open 10–12, 15–17, except fest.) is on the site of the parish church (986) of the Alighieri and Donati families.

It was rebuilt in 1479 when it became the seat of the Compagnia dei Buonomini, a charitable institution founded in 1442 by St Antoninus, and decorated with charming *Frescoes by the workshop of *Ghirlandaio* (recently attributed to *Francesco d'Antonio del Chierico*). They illustrate the life of St Martin and works of charity, and are of great interest for their portrayal of contemporary Florentine life. Here, too, are two notable *Paintings of the Madonna, one Byzantine and the other attributed to *Perugino* (or *Nicolò Soggi*). On the altar is a bust of St Antoninus attributed to *Verocchio*. Two terracotta angels by the school of Verrocchio have been removed for safety.

On a trattoria (No. 4) in the piazza a terracotta roundel of Mariotto Albertinelli records the Florentine painter who here opened a restaurant. Across Via Dante Alighieri (in which is an entrance to the Badia, see Rte 14), among a group of houses (restored in 13C style in 1911) is the *Casa di Dante*, where the poet is said to have been born (although it is more probable his birthplace was on the present Via Alighieri). It contains a collection of material (little of it original) relating to the poet (adm. see p 60). Via Santa Margherita continues past the little church of SANTA MARGHERITA DE' CERCHI, of 12C foundation, where Dante is supposed to have married Gemma Donati. The 14C porch bears the arms of the Cerchi, Adimari, and Donati who lived in the parish. In the interior, lovely altarpiece of the Madonna enthroned with four female Saints by Neri di Bicci.—An archway leads out onto the **Corso** (Pl.16;4), a Roman road. The church (left) of SANTA MARGHERITA IN SANTA MARIA DE' RICCI (1508) is preceded by a portico by Gherardo Silvani (1611). The interior was reconstructed by Zanobi del Rosso in 1769, and contains paintings by Giovanni Camillo Sagrestani (1707). Nearly opposite is the 13C Torre dei Donati.

Some way along the Corso (left) are several 12C towers on the corner of *Via Sant'Elisabetta*. The ancient round Torre La Pagliazza in Piazza Sant' Elisabetta was used as a prison in the 13–14C. It was over-restored in 1988 for use as a hotel. Via Sant' Elisabetta leads to *Via delle Oche* with the 14C Palazzo Visdomini (restored) and its tower. On the corner of *Via dello Studio* (right) and Via della Canonica is the 13C Palazzo Tedaldini. Via del Canonica, is another pretty old street. Via dello Studio slopes gently downhill to the Duomo (good view of the cupola) and back to the Corso. The ground floor arches betray the medieval origins of the street. A doorway here is surmounted by a pretty Della Robbian lunette. On the corner of the Corso is *Palazzo Salviati* (now the head office of the Banca Toscana), built in 1470–80 by the Portinari family, famous bankers in the 15C. In 1546 the palace was bought and enlarged by Jacopo Salviati, nephew of Maria Salviati, wife of Giovanni delle Bande Nere and mother of Cosimo I. In the banking hall is a 14C fresco of the Madonna and Child. Other parts of the palace may sometimes be seen on special request. The charming little interior courtyard which dates from 1577 is flanked by two barrel-vaulted loggie decorated with mythological subjects including the Story of Ulysses by Alessandro Allori (with the help of Giovanni Maria Butteri and others). Another room here has a vault with grotteschi and small scenes of the Labours of Hercules. The chapel was also decorated by Allori, and a Galleria was added in 1783 with frescoes by Tommaso Gherardini.

The Corso continues E and ends at the Canto de' Pazzi, on the site of the E gate of the Roman city; across Via del Proconsolo (Rte 14) **Borgo degli Albizi** (Pl.6;8) follows the line of the Roman Cassia. The Borgo is named after one of the wealthiest families in Florence in the 14C and 15C who owned numerous palaces in the street. It is one of the most handsome streets in the city. The magnificent palaces at its entrance (Palazzo Pazzi and Palazzo Nonfinito) are described on p 168. Next to Palazzo Pazzi (right) is a palace with 15C rustication on the ground floor. Opposite, *Palazzo Vitali* (No. 28) is a beautiful building attributed to Bartolommeo Ammannati (late 16C), with a handsome coat-of-arms. Next to it, (No. 26) *Palazzo Matteucci Ramirez di Montalvo* is a severe work also by Ammannati (1568). The graffiti decoration is attributed to Bernardino Poccetti. The owner set up the arms of his friend Cosimo I on the façade. On the corner of Via de' Giraldi is a 14C tabernacle with the Madonna enthroned with Saints. Farther on, by Volta dei Ciechi is a house (No. 22) with medieval fragments next to the huge *Palazzo Altoviti* (or 'dei Visacci'; No. 18), which dates from the early 15C. It was enlarged in the late 16C when the amusing marble portraits of celebrated Florentine citizens by Caccini were placed on the façade. Facing a piazzetta is a narrow 14C house (No. 14). Beyond is the grandiose *Palazzo degli Albizi* (No. 12), the principal residence of the Albizi, a famous Florentine family (see above). The 14C fabric survives on the left, and the nine bays on the right were reconstructed by Silvani in the 17C. Opposite, a pretty palace stands next to the larger *Palazzo degli Alessandri* (No. 15), the best-preserved palace on the street. A worn cornice divides the two storeys of its fine 14C façade in pietra forte, rusticated on the lower part. Here Canova had his studio. On the left No. 10 has a bust of Vincenzo Filicaia (1642–1707), who was born here. On the right is a 16C house (No. 11) with a marble bust of Cosimo II, out of the top of which rises a medieval tower, which belonged to the Donati.

The lively little PIAZZA SAN PIER MAGGIORE (Pl.6;8) is the centre of a local shopping area with a few colourful market stalls. The 17C portico by Nigetti is all that survives of the church which gave the square its name. The little *Palazzo Corbizzi* (No. 1) dates from the 13C. Next to a pretty house with a projecting upper storey rises the splendid 13C *Torre Donati* (*Cocchi*). Just out of the piazzetta, beyond the Volta di San Piero, an archway with shops, is the 14–15C *Palazzo Albizi* (enlarged in the 16C and restored).—Via Matteo Palmieri (with a worn terracotta relief of the Madonna and Child on the corner) leads out of the piazza, and crosses Via Pandolfini and Via Ghibellina.

In Via Pandolfini (right) the palace at No. 14 was built for Baccio Valori who led the siege of Florence in 1530 and was hanged in Piazza Signoria in 1537 by order of Cosimo I. In the other direction, at No. 5 (on the corner of Via Verdi) is the *Oratorio di San Niccolò al Ceppo* (usually locked) which was built in 1561 for a confraternity founded in the 14C. In the vestibule are two oval paintings of Saints by Onorio Marinari (1695) and a trompe l'oeil ceiling by Giovanni Domenico Ferretti (c 1735). The statue in stucco of the Madonna and Child is by Camillo Camillani (1572). The Oratory has 17C wood benches and a frescoed ceiling by Ferretti, Pietro Anderlini, and Domenico and Francesco Papi. The altarpiece of the Crucifixion is by Francesco Curradi, and on the walls are two paintings of the Visitation and St Nicholas with two members of the Confraternity by Giovanni Antonio Sogliani (1517–21). On the corner of Via Ghibellina stands the 14C *Palazzo Salviati Quaratesi*. The ground floor provided room for stores and shops. The large tabernacle in Via Ghibellina protects a fresco by Giovanni di San Giovanni (c 1616; not yet returned here since its restoration). Beyond is the entrance to the huge *Teatro Verdi* (restored in 1988). In the other direction, at No. 110, is the grandiose *Palazzo Borghese*, with a neo-classical façade by Gaetano Baccani (1822). It was built in less than a year by Camillo Borghese, husband of Pauline Bonaparte (sister of Napoleon I), for a party to celebrate the marriage of Ferdinando III. The elaborate period rooms (now used by a club; adm. sometimes granted) include the Galleria and Salone degli Specchi heavily decorated with numerous chandeliers, gilded mirrors etc.—At the end of the street can be seen the towers of the Bargello and the Badia.

Via delle Stinche continues across Via Ghibellina past *Palazzo da Cintoia* (*Salviati*), one of the most interesting medieval palaces to survive in the city. It dates from the 14C, and its façade in pietra forte has picturesque 'sporti'. In Via della Vigna Vecchia is the 14C Palazzo Covoni (No. 9). In the little piazza is the church of **San**

Simone (Pl.10;2; open for services only), founded in 1192–93. The fine doorway is in the style of Benedetto da Rovezzano.

The INTERIOR is a good work by *Gherardo Silvani* (1630), with a carved 17C wood ceiling. The fine painting of *St Peter enthroned (1st altar on the right) was painted by the 'Master of Santa Cecilia' in 1307; it was beautifully restored in 1982. Over the last altar on the S side, *Jacopo Vignali*, Christ showing his wounds to St Bernard (1623). At the end of the N side is a charming Gothic tabernacle (1363) with a 15C bust of a lady, surrounded by enamelled terracotta decoration with cherubs by the *Della Robbia*.

Opposite is one of the best-known ice-cream shops in the city. Beyond Via della Burella (right) with another medieval house, the streets follow the shape of the Roman amphitheatre which was built here in the 2–3C AD. It is estimated that it was big enough to hold c 15,000 spectators. Via dei Bentaccordi follows the curve across Via Anguillara (with a view left of the Pazzi Chapel in Santa Croce) and Borgo dei Greci into *Piazza Peruzzi*, named after the famous Florentine family of bankers who reached their greatest prosperity at the end of the 13C. The medieval buildings here include the reconstructed Palazzo Peruzzi (13–14C). An archway leads out into the busy VIA DEI BENCI (Pl.10;2) with its old rusticated houses. The view to the left is closed by the tower of the Duomo of Fiesole; to the right, across the river, the green hills of the Oltrarno provide a background to the medieval buildings in Piazza dei Mozzi. On the corner of Borgo Santa Croce is the polygonal 13C *Torre degli Alberti*, with a 15C loggia below (covered for restoration since 1987). The interesting palaces in the Borgo are described on p 179. On Corso dei Tintori is *Palazzo Alberti* (late 14C or early 15C) with a good courtyard. Opposite the 15C *Palazzo Corsi* (No. 6; described, with the Museo Horne, on p 189) are several handsome palaces. *Palazzo Bardi alle Grazie* (*Serzelli*; No. 5) is an early Renaissance palace attributed to Brunelleschi (c 1430) with a fine courtyard. Here the famous 'Camerata fiorentina di Casa Bardi' introduced operatic melodrama. No. 1, *Palazzo Malenchini*, was reconstructed in the 19C on the site of a 14C palace, the residence of the Alberti, an influential merchant family who were exiled in 1387 for political reasons. The great architect Leon Battista Alberti (who had been born while the family were in exile in Genoa) died here in 1472 (plaque).

VIA DEI NERI (Pl.10;2), named after the confraternity who comforted criminals on their way from the Bargello to execution, leads out of Via dei Benci back towards Palazzo Vecchio (which can be seen at the end of the street). At the beginning on the right Via delle Brache has medieval houses with 'sporti'. On Via de' Rustici *Palazzo Rustici* (*Neri*) dates from the end of the 14C. The road bends at its junction with Via Mosca following the shape of the Roman port of Florence. Here, at No. 23 is the 14C *Palazzo Soldani*. A road (right) with tablets showing the water levels of the Arno in the floods of 1333 and 1966, leads to the church of **San Remigio** (Pl.10;2; open for services only) founded in the 11C, with an exterior in pietra forte.

The INTERIOR (restored), a fine Gothic hall, contains fresco fragments by the school of Giotto and worn roundels of Saints in the vaults (14C). The beautiful panel painting of the *Madonna and Child in the left aisle is by a follower of Cimabue known as the *'Master of San Remigio'*. In the chapel to the left of the high altar is a remarkable painting of the *Immaculate Conception by *Empoli*, which dates from 1591. In a little room below the campanile (adm. on request to the priest) are early monochrome frescoes with hunting scenes, etc.

In Via dei Neri (corner of Via del Guanto) is the 14C Palazzo Fagni (No. 35) next to the *Loggia del Grano* (Pl.16;6), a market erected at the time of Cosimo II by Giulio Parigi and his son Alfonso, and now part of a cinema. In the piazza here work has been underway for years to build a new exit from the Uffizi galleries.—Via della Ninna skirts the side of Palazzo Vecchio to emerge in Piazza della Signoria (Rte 4).

22 The Viali

This route follows the wide avenues (or 'viali') laid out in 1865–69 by Giuseppe Poggi after he had demolished the last circle of walls built around the N part of the city in 1284–1333. The architect left some of the medieval gates as isolated monuments in the course of this ring-road, now busy with traffic. None of the places mentioned are worth visiting on foot; buses are indicated in the text.—At the foot of Ponte della Vittoria begins VIALE FRATELLI ROSSELLI (Pl.4;5,6), named after two brothers, famous leaders of the anti-Fascist movement, murdered in France by order of Mussolini before the last War. The equestrian statue of Vittorio Emanuele II (removed from Piazza della Repubblica) is by Emilio Zocchi (1890), and opposite is a small fountain commemorating the diamond jubilee of Queen Victoria. Here is the entrance to the **Cascine** (Pl.4;5; bus 17c from the Duomo and the Station), a huge public park which skirts the Arno for 3.5km. A big general market is held here on Tuesdays.

The lands of a dairy-farm ('cascina') were acquired by Duke Alessandro de' Medici and the park enlarged by Cosimo I. It was used as a ducal chase in the 17C, and public spectacles and festivals were held here under the grand-duke Pietro Leopoldo in the 18C. The grounds were planned as a huge park by Elisa Baciocchi Bonaparte and first opened regularly to the public c 1811. In these gardens the 'Ode to the West Wind' was 'conceived and chiefly written' by Shelley in 1819, and on the Narcissus fountain here a tablet (1954) commemorates its composition. The long park (only a little more than 100 metres wide), with fine woods, is not as well maintained as it might be. During the day it is used as a recreation ground by numerous Florentines, old and young, and huge public concerts and festivals are held here in summer. It is not enclosed and it is not advisable to visit the park at night. The *Festa del Grillo* is held here on Ascension Day. It contains two racecourses, various sports grounds, tennis courts and a swimming-pool. In the central *Piazzale delle Cascine* is the Institute of Agriculture and Forestry. At the far end is the *Monumento dell'Indiano*, a monument to the Maharajah of Kolhapur who died in Florence in 1870. From here the view is dominated by a modern suspension bridge (1978) over the Arno.

Near Piazza Vittorio Veneto (in Corso Italia) is the *Teatro Comunale* (Pl.4;6), the most important concert hall in the city. The disappointing interior was rebuilt in 1961. Nearby, on Lungarno Vespucci is the American Consulate in a building by Giuseppe Poggi (1860). Nearby is *Villa Favard* (now used by the University School of Economics), surrounded by iron railings and a garden, also built by Poggi (1857). In Via Curtatone is a terrace (now closed in) built in 1820 by Luigi Cambrai Digny from which the grand-dukes watched the 'Corso dei Berberi'.—Viale Fratelli Rosselli continues to *Porta al Prato* (Pl.4;6), an isolated gateway (1284) of the city walls. Here Il Prato leads right to *Palazzo Corsini sul Prato*, begun in 1591–94 by Buontalenti with a fine garden (interesting statuary). It was acquired in 1621 by Filippo di Lorenzo Corsini who employed Gherardo Silvani to complete the palace and garden. Prince Charles Stuart stayed as a guest here in 1774–77. It is still the residence of the Corsini family.

Via della Scala diverges right from the Viale. Near No. 62 is a lunette by Giovanni della Robbia in the façade of a former church. At No. 9 Via Bernardo Rucellai is *St James* (Pl.5;5), the American Episcopal church (open for services, and adm. on request in the morning). It is a neo-Gothic building (1911) with good stained glass by Italian craftsmen. On the right (No. 85) is the 17C *Palazzo degli Orti Oricellari*, formerly Ginori-Venturi, now owned by a bank (Pl.5;5), which contains a fresco by Pietro da Cortona. The *Orti Oricellari* (no adm.), were a famous Renaissance 'selva'. In these gardens Bernardo Rucellai (in Latin, 'Oricellari'), who had married Nannina de' Medici in 1460 (sister of Lorenzo il Magnifico), collected the sculptures stolen after the exile of the Medici in 1494, and refounded the Platonic Academy of Careggi. The villa was sold to Bianca Cappello in 1573, and was transformed in the Romantic era by Cambrai Digny. The colossal 17C statue of Polyphemus is by Antonio Novelli (it can be seen through the trees in winter from Via Bernardo Rucellai).

The Viale continues to an underpass beneath the railway. A handsome subsidiary entrance to the station for pedestrians here was designed in 1990 by Gae Aulenti. The *Railway Station* (Pl.5;5,6) is a pleasant functional building built in 1935 by a group of gifted young Tuscan architects including Giovanni Michelucci and Piero Berardi. Viale Filippo Strozzi continues round the huge pentagonal **Fortezza da Basso** (Pl.5;4; adm. only when exhibitions are in progress), a building which has always been something of a white elephant. A massive fortress on a grand scale designed by Antonio da Sangallo the Younger, it is of the first importance in the history of military architecture. The exterior wall in brick and pietra forte is still intact.

It was erected by order of Alessandro de' Medici in 1534 to strengthen his position in the city as first Duke of Florence, and as a refuge in times of trouble. It became a symbol of Medici tyranny, and Alessandro was assassinated here by his cousin Lorenzino in 1537. It was very soon obsolete as the grand-dukes had little need to defend themselves. In later centuries it was used as a prison, arsenal, and barracks. After years of neglect and discussion about its future, many of the buildings were altered or destroyed when it became an exhibition centre in 1967. The area within the walls was brutally transformed when a huge prefabricated steel building covered with aluminium was built in 1978, and another (circular) one in 1987. Here the 'Mostra dell'Artigianato' and the prestigious 'Pitti' fashion shows are held annually. The entrance on Viale Strozzi is through the 16C keep designed by Sangallo which incorporates the medieval tower of Porta Faenza. A long 19C building is used as a restoration laboratory for paintings by the Opificio delle Pietre Dure. Other buildings are derelict and it is hoped they can be put to good use. Archaeological finds, inlcuding Roman material, have been made here. Public gardens have been laid out on the glacis.

Opposite the Fortezza, across Viale Filippo Strozzi, is *Palazzo dei Congressi*, an international conference centre opened in 1964 on the site of a Contini-Bonacossi villa. It is surrounded by a park created in 1871 by the French poet Alphonse Lamartine. In Via Valfonda is *Palazzo di Valfonda* (No. 9; owned by the Associazione degli Industriali della Provincia di Firenze; sometimes shown on request). The small garden with box hedges here is all that remains of the once famous Gualfonda garden, one of the largest in Florence, created in the early 16C by Giovanni Bartolini, probably on a design by Baccio d'Agnolo. The villa was subsequently bought by the Riccardi who founded their famous library here and gave a celebrated festa in the garden in 1600 for the marriage of Maria de' Medici with Henry IV of France (recorded in the Sala degli Stucchi on the ground floor). In 1638 the palace and garden were enlarged by Gherardo Silvani, but they were greatly altered with the construction of the railway.

A short way to the SE of the Fortezza (reached by Via Ridolfi) is PIAZZA DELL'INDIPENDENZA (Pl.5;4), laid out in 1869 as the first of the 19C squares in Florence. Here are statues of Bettino Ricasoli and Ubaldino Peruzzi, mayor of

Florence in 1870. At the N corner stands the *Villino Trollope*, home of the Trollope family in 1848–66, where the visiting Anthony wrote 'Doctor Thorne' in 1857. Later, when a pensione, it sheltered Thomas Hardy (1887).

From the Fortezza da Basso Bus No. 4 (from the Duomo and Station) runs NE to Via Vittorio Emanuele II for the Museo Stibbert (an uninteresting walk of c 2km). On the *Colle di Montughi*, now a built-up residential area, are many villas. In Via dei Cappuccini (which diverges left from Via Vittorio Emanuele) is the church of the *Convent of the Cappuccini di Montughi*, reconstructed in 1793, with wooden confessionals and altars. It is interesting for its paintings by the late 17C Florentine school, including Lorenzo Lippi (1st chapel on the right) and Empoli (2nd chapel on the left), and, in the Choir above (adm. on request), works by Cigoli and Jacopo Ligozzi. In the sanctuary is a late-15C Crucifix. *Villa Fabbricotti* (No. 48 Via Vittorio Emanuele), now the seat of the Università per gli Stranieri, was where Queen Victoria stayed in 1894. The large park is open to the public. It adjoins the park of the ***Museo Stibbert**, entered from its garden gate at No. 26 Via Federico Stibbert (adm. see p 62; visitors are conducted every hour on the hour; last visit 12.45; on fest. only Rooms 2–7 and 9 are open). This was created by Frederick Stibbert (1838–1906) in his home here. He had an Italian mother, and was born in Florence. Having inherited a great fortune, he became a collector, traveller, artist, and in 1866, a Garibaldian hero. He bequeathed his museum to the British Government which then passed it on to the city of Florence. He built this huge rambling villa (incorporating part of an earlier building) in 1878–1905 with Cesare Fortini as architect, and employed Gaetano Bianchi, Annibale Gatti, and others to decorate the interior. Queen Victoria took pleasure in watching the building works from a balcony. The numerous period rooms were designed for his collections; alterations since Stibbert's death in an attempt to rationalise the arrangement are being slowly eliminated and over the next few years the rooms will be restored, where possible, to their original appearance. One part of the house was designed by Stibbert as a museum, and the other part he used as his residence. There are also long-term plans to move the entrance to the museum to the centre of the building and reopen the N wing to house the collection of costumes, and the 'quadreria'. At present it is difficult to appreciate the exterior of the building covered with a miscellany of escutcheons, plaquettes, and decorative details.—The fine **Park**, also created by Stibbert, contains an Egyptian temple and orangery by Giuseppe Poggi, as well as Venetian Gothic architectural fragments. It is open daily, 9–dusk. The eclectic collection has a remarkably bizarre atmosphere with 57 rooms heavily decorated and crammed with an extraordinary variety of objects. Stibbert's particular interest and field of study was in armour and costume and his collection is famous for its armour (including a remarkable collection of Asiatic armour).

The description given below will be altered as the rooms are rearranged. **Ground Floor**. The present entrance leads into the rooms designed by Stibbert as a museum. The *'Sala della Malachite'* (2), arranged as it was in Stibbert's day, is named after the malachite fireplace and tables, including the splendid table in the centre of the room in the Empire style made by Philippe Thomire for Girolamo Bonaparte. On the mantlepiece are fine gilded candelabra. The tournament and battle armour displayed here was made c 1540–80. The tapestries include one made in Brussels c 1520 with the Resurrection of Lazarus, and one designed by Giulio Romano illustrating the Meeting between Hannibal and Scipio. The two paintings of Susanna and the Elders and the Daughters of Lot are by Luca Giordano. One of the fine cassone frontals was painted by the bottega of Francesco di Giorgio Martini. The paintings, mostly interesting for the costume of their sitters, include a fully armed St Michael by Cosimo Rosselli.—The two small adjoining rooms (3 & 4), both with fine Murano chandeliers, are called the 'Salottino Luigi XV' with period rococo furnishings, and the 'Salottino Olandese' with Flemish and Dutch paintings.—In the 'Sala del Condottiere' (5), decorated by Gaetano Bianchi, is a fully armed 15C condottiere mounted on his steed, and a display of pole arms. There are also cases with Etruscan, Roman, and Lombard armour, and one of the finest collections in existence of spurs.—The 'Salone dell'Armeria' (9, or 'della Cavalcata'; Stibbert's original arrangement is to be restored) is a great neo-Gothic hall built by Cesare Fortini and frescoed by Gaetano Bianchi with a cavalcade of fully armed horses and knights of the 16C, and 16C oriental armour on six soldiers. In front of the fireplace, armour signed by Konrad Treytz the Younger (c 1520), and, nearby, armour by Pompeo della Cesa (c 1585–90). The three large Brussels tapestries with the Labours of Hercules date from c 1535–50. Above the entrance is a life-size equestrian model of St George designed by Stibbert.—The 'Sala del Cavaliere Francese' (11) is named after a mounted French cavalier (1650). The funerary monument from S Germany in polychrome wood dates from 1732. In a cupboard to the left is kept the armour found in the tomb of Giovanni dalle Bande Nere.

Here begin the series of rooms which formed the private residence of Stibbert.—The 'Sala Inglese' (12) was formerly the billiard room. It has interesting Art Nouveau decorations including delightful Copeland tiles and stained glass windows. The entrance door was decorated with pre-Raphaelite paintings by Stibbert himself. Here is displayed English and German armour.—Beyond R 13, the 'Sala della Porcellana' (14) has a fine collection of porcelain, some Oriental.—Room 15 continues the Oriental porcelain display, and also contains gilded bronze objects. The Vecchio Studiolo (16) has interesting furnishings.—Rooms 17 and 18 contain a display of firearms and 19C armour.—The 'Galleria', or corridor (28) outside the ballroom contains 17C cabinets, stained glass, and small bronzes, as well as Stibbert family portraits.—The 'Salone da Ballo' (26), with a frieze painted by Annibale Gatti, has recently been restored to its original appearance, with French empire style furniture and portraits including one of Stibbert as an old man by Edoardo Gelli (on the entrance wall), and of Giulia Stibbert and her daughter by Cesare Mussini (1853).—The charming little Art Nouveau 'Fumoir' (27) was created in 1890 and entirely decorated with ceramics from the Ulisse Cantagalli workshop. The statue of Sleep is by Tito Sarrocchi.—The 'Sala da Pranzo' (29) has also recently been restored to its original appearance as the family dining room.—Beyond the Vecchio Studiolo (see above), the 'Saletta Bianca' (30) has stucco decorations modelled on those at Fontainebleau, and hunting weapons and porcelain are temporarily exhibited here. The four cabinets are made out of ebony and tortoiseshell.—The 'Sala Rossa' (31) has interesting furniture, a Murano mirror and chandelier, and portaits. Beyond the Sala della Porcellana (see above) is the 'Sala delle Bandiere' (32), named after the Sienese flags used at the Palio which decorate the ceiling. Here are displayed the best paintings in the collection, including a Madonna and Child by the school of Botticelli, Saints Catherine and Dominic by Carlo Crivelli, a Madonna and Child and two Saints by the 'Master of Verucchio', and a portrait of a man in profile. Also here are three cassoni with gesso decoration and two painted cassone frontals.—The Hall (33) is situated at the former main entrance to the house. Here is hung a portrait of Ferdinando and Anna Maria Ludovica Medici with their governess, by Justus Sustermans.

A staircase leads up to the **First Floor**. Room 34 has a Madonna enthroned attributed to Jacopo di Cione and a Madonna and Child by Mariotto di Nardo, wood sculptures, as well as church silver and reliquaries.—Room 35, which overlooks the great hall, is normally not open to visitors.—Room 36 was decorated with stucchi in 1880. Here is displayed a Crucifixion by Pietro Lorenzetti and his bottega, and a fine collection of church vestments (late 15–18C).—The pretty 'Salotto Luigi XVI' (37) has furnishings made in 1880 by Tassinari Chatel of Lyons (to be restored by them). Rooms 38–41 display part of the fine collection of costumes, and portraits (particularly interesting for the dress of their sitters). Room 38 has neo-classical frescoes by Luigi Ademollo, which already decorated this part of the house when Stibbert bought it.— Rooms 42–44 (being rearranged) contain Tuscan furniture, and a display of fans.—The gallery (46) overlooking the Salone da Ballo will display ballgowns.—Room 47 is to be rearranged. The 'Camera da Letto' (48),

Stibbert's bedroom has been restored to its original appearance. The paintings, some by Stibbert, include an interesting view of the property before his alterations. There are also family photographs and Stibbert's full dress kilt.— The *'Camera dell'Impero'* (49), Stibbert's mother's bedroom, was also frescoed by Luigi Ademollo. It is furnished in the Empire style. The *'Sala Impero'* (50; the former 'Loggetta') with splendid period decorations, contains Napoleon Bonaparte's costume worn at his coronation as king of Italy in 1805.—The delightful *'Salotto Giallo'* (51) has Venetian furnishings and paintings.— Beyond Room 38 (see above), Room 52 has a notable collection of materials, mostly Italian (15–18C).

The staircase leads back down to the **Ground Floor**. Beyond the Sala della Cavalcata a spiral staircase leads up to three rooms decorated by Gaetano Bianchi in neo-Gothic style, called the *'Sale Japanese'* (55–57). They contain the best *Collection of Japanese armour in Europe (particularly notable for the arms and armour of the Edo period), an interesting collection of swords, saddles, etc.—At the foot of the spiral staircase are the last two rooms (7 & 6) which display the splendid Oriental *Collection of armour, much of it Turkish and used for the first time by Sultan Selim I at the end of the 15C. Also displayed here are Persian and Indian arms and armour and costumes. The stucco decoration of room 6 is modelled on the Alhambra, and the floor tiles were made by the Cantagalli workshop.

Viale Lavagnini continues from the Fortezza (see above) towards Piazza della Libertà. In Via Leone X (left) is the *Russian Church* (Pl.6;1) built with funds raised from the large Russian colony in Florence (including the Demidoff) and consecrated in 1904. Throughout most of the 19C Florence was a fashionable place to spend the winter for many aristocratic Russian families. The architects of the fine building came from Russia, and the pretty majolica decoration on the exterior was carried out by the Ulisse Cantagalli workshop. It is now a national monument owned by the Russian Orthodox community of Florence and open for services (sung mass) on the 3rd Sunday of the month and on major church festivals.— PIAZZA DELLA LIBERTÀ (Pl.7;1) is a handsome arcaded piazza, extremely busy with traffic, where many streets converge. In the centre is the isolated *Porta San Gallo*, another old city gate, and a *Triumphal Arch* hurriedly erected in 1739 to commemorate the solemn entry into the city of the grand-duke Francis of Lorraine, and his wife Maria Teresa, heir to the Imperial throne. The modern sculpture is by Marcello Tommasi.

The *Parterre*, on the N side of the square, was created as a park by the Lorraine grand-dukes on the site of the convent of San Gallo. Here in 1922–39 were erected temporary exhibition halls, which have been partially demolished. Since 1977 the area has been abandoned, although there is a project to restore the area to its original function as a public garden, and to build a car park here.—From the junction just N of the piazza at *Ponte Rosso* (Pl.7;1) is the beginning of **Via Bolognese**, the pretty old road from Florence to Bologna. Here is the *Giardino dell'Orticoltura*, a horticultural Garden created in 1859 (open daily) with a splendid greenhouse (1880; by Giacomo Roster). The gardens are divided by the railway line; from Via Trento the upper gardens with a crescent of pine trees may be visited. Here in 1990 a delightful fountain in the form of a huge snake-dragon was installed. Via Bolognese (Bus No. 25) continues uphill out of the city past a number of villas, including (1.5km) *La Pietra* (No. 120), surrounded by a park. This is the residence of the historian Sir Harold Acton. It contains one of the most interesting private collections of works of art in Florence (formed by Sir Harold's father, Arthur Acton) including a notable group of early Tuscan paintings (admission to scholars sometimes courteously granted by previous appointment). The beautifully cared for Italianate *Garden has topiary laid out in 1904. It is sometimes open for Agriturist group tours; see p 55.

In Piazza Savonarola (Pl.7;3), near Piazza della Libertà, is a handsome studio block (No. 18) on the ground floor of which is the *Galleria Carnielo* (adm. see p 61) with sculptures by Rinaldo Carnielo (1853–1910) left by him to the Comune.

Viale Giacomo Matteotti leads back towards the river. In the centre of PIAZZA DONATELLO (Pl.7;6), on a mound shaded by cypresses, is the disused Protestant cemetery, which has always been known as the 'Cimitero degli Inglesi', or 'English Cemetery'. It was opened in 1828 (adm. 9–13, 15–18, except fest.; ring at the main gate). Here are buried numerous distinguished British, Swiss, North American, Italian, and Russian Protestants. It was closed in 1878 when the new Cimitero degli Allori on the Via Senese was opened. The little house of 1860 is now used as offices. To the left of the central path is buried Elizabeth Barrett Browning (1809–61). The tomb, raised on six little columns, was designed by Robert Browning and sculpted by Lord Leighton (finished by Luigi Giovannozzi). Behind it is the Pre-Raphaelite sarcophagus of Holman Hunt's wife Fanny who died in Fiesole at the age of 33. Also buried here: Isa Blagden (1818–73), Arthur Hugh Clough (1819–61), Walter Savage Landor (1775–1864), Frances Trollope (1780–1863), Theodore Parker of Lexington (1810–60), Robert Davidsohn (1853–1937), the German historian of Florence, and Gian Pietro Vieusseux (1779–1863), the Swiss bibliophile.

Viale Gramsci continues to PIAZZA BECCARIA (Pl.7;8), with another old city gate. Nearby in Via Scipione Ammirato are two Art Nouveau houses, the Villino Caraceni (No. 99) of 1911, and the Villino Ravazzini (No. 101) of 1907–08. They are both by Giovanni Michelazzi with ceramic decoration by Galileo Chini, and the best examples of their period in Florence. On the S side of Piazza Beccaria a huge new building was opened in 1989 to house the *Archivio di Stato*. Founded in 1582, the archives date back to the 8C and provide scholars with a wealth of information on the political and economic history of the city. Via Vincenzo Gioberti, a busy shopping street, leads E from the piazza to Piazza Alberti. Here, on the corner, is *Villa Arrivabene* now owned by the Comune and used for exhibitions. Some of the rooms are decorated with views of the city and grotteschi carried out by pupils of Poccetti in the 17C. The EX-CONVENT OF SAN SALVI, just N of the railway line (c 1.5km from Piazza Beccaria) is reached by Bus No. 6 from the Duomo and Piazza San Marco).

The Vallombrosan abbey of San Salvi has a 14–16C church. The conventual buildings (entrance at No. 16 Via San Salvi; adm. see p 60) were reopened in 1982 after the restoration of the celebrated fresco of the Last Supper by Andrea del Sarto. The long gallery is hung with large 16C altarpieces including works by *Franciabigio* (Adoration of the Shepherds), *Michele di Ridolfo del Ghirlandaio, Vasari, Il Poppi, Carlo Portelli,* and *Giovanni Battista Paggi*.—In the room at the end are beautifully carved *Reliefs by *Benedetto da Rovezzano* from the tomb of St John Gualberto formerly in the church (and damaged during the Imperial siege of 1530).—On the right are two more rooms with good fireplaces and a lavabo by *Benedetto da Rovezzano.* Here have been hung paintings by contemporaries or followers of Andrea del Sarto, including *Giuliano Bugiardini* (*Madonna and Child), *Ridolfo del Ghirlandaio* (*Miracle of St Zenobius and the Translation of his body), *Franciabigio, Pontormo, Giovanni Antonio Sogliani, Maso di San Friano, Raffaellino del Garbo* (Annunciation, and the Madonna enthroned between Saints Francis and Zenobius).—In the Refectory is the *Cenacolo di San Salvi* by *Andrea del Sarto* (1511–27), a masterpiece of Florentine fresco, remarkable for its colouring and dramatic movement. This is perhaps the most famous fresco of the Last Supper in Italy, after that by Leonardo da Vinci in Milan. Here are displayed three more works by *Andrea del Sarto*: a very ruined fresco of the Annunciation detached from the Sdrucciolo di Orsanmichele, a Noli me tangere from the convent of San Gallo, and a Christ in Pietà from Santissima Annunziata. The other works are copies from Andrea del Sarto.—The upper floor, with the convent cells (now a restoration office), may also be opened.—Nearby is the sports ground of Campo di Marte with the *Stadio Comunale*, a remarkable building (1932) by Pier Luigi Nervi, altered and enlarged for the World Cup games in 1990. It was originally capable of holding 66,000 spectators.

Viale Giovine Italia ends at the Arno by another defensive tower near
PONTE SAN NICCOLÒ (Pl.11;4). Across the river begins Viale dei Colli
(described in Rte 20), also laid out by Poggi, which encircles the hills
of the Oltrarno as far as Porta Romana.

*Florence from San Miniato (a photogravure taken soon
after the Viale dei Colli was laid out in 1870)*

ENVIRONS OF FLORENCE

The most attractive and interesting place in the neighbourhood of Florence, and the most frequently visited, is *Fiesole*, which should on no account be missed even on the most hurried visit to the city. Not only is the little town interesting in itself (particularly for its Roman Theatre and Etruscan remains), but also, from its hill, there is a superb bird's-eye view of Florence. Charming walks and drives may be taken in the vicinity. Other places of interest within easy reach of the city (and all within its Province) are described in the routes below. A plan of the immediate environs of Florence is given on Atlas pp 14–15.

Visitors with a little more time at their disposal (and preferably with their own transport), and who wish to see something of the magnificent countryside around Florence, should visit the following districts (all described in 'Blue Guide Northern Italy'). Country bus services from Florence are run by SITA (Via Santa Caterina da Siena 15, Pl.5;5), Lazzi (Piazza Adua; Pl.5;6), CAP (Largo Alinari, Via Nazionale; Pl.5;6), and COPIT (Piazza Santa Maria Novella; Pl.5;8). *Vallombrosa* (SITA bus in 90 minutes), a summer resort on the wooded slopes of the Pratomagno hills, is reached via Pontassieve. In its famous monastery, founded by St John Gualberto in 1040, Milton may have been a guest.—The upper valley of the Arno, beyond Vallombrosa, known as the *Casentino* (SITA bus in c 2 hours) contains several castles, and the little towns of Poppi and Bibbiena, all rich in Florentine history.—The *Chianti* countryside to the S of Florence, where the famous Tuscan wine is grown, is traversed by a beautiful road known as the 'Chiantigiana' (N 222) which runs to Siena via Greve (SITA bus in 1 hour).—The *Mugello*, N of Florence at the foot of the Appenines, an attractive valley, intensely cultivated, with numerous summer resorts on the wooded slopes of the Pratomagno hills, is reached via Borgo San Lorenzo (SITA bus in 1 hour).

The town of greatest importance near Florence is *Prato*, now an industrial town, but with a number of interesting Renaissance monuments in the old centre, including the church of Santa Maria delle Carceri by Giuliano da Sangallo, and the Duomo with a pulpit by Donatello and Michelozzo, and important frescoes in the choir by Filippo Lippi. Described in full in 'Blue Guide Northern Italy', it can be reached by a frequent train service from Florence in c 20 minutes, or by bus, c every 20 minutes, in 30 minutes (via the motorway; services run by Lazzi and CAP).

Other famous Tuscan cities, farther afield, and meriting a prolonged visit (see 'Blue Guide Northern Italy') include *Siena, San Gimignano, Volterra, Pistoia, Lucca, Pisa*, and *Arezzo*. Across the Appenines in Emilia is *Bologna*, also one of the most important and interesting towns in Italy. The best way of reaching these cities is given below.

Siena. Frequent bus services (SITA) terminating in Piazza San Domenico in Siena, in 75 minutes (via the 'superstrada'), or 2 hours (via the old road, N 2). The train service (in 1½–2 hours, with a change sometimes necessary at Empoli), although passing through pretty country on a secondary line, is less convenient since the railway station of Siena is outside the town.

San Gimignano. Frequent bus services (SITA) via Poggibonsi in 1 hour 40 minutes.

Volterra. SITA bus services in 2 hours.

Lucca is on a direct railway line from Florence via Prato and *Pistoia* with frequent (but slow) services (to Lucca in 1½–2 hours; to Pistoia in c 45 minutes). Bus services (Lazzi) to Lucca in 80 minutes; to Pistoia in 50 minutes.

Pisa is reached by rail via Empoli; frequent service in c 1 hour. Bus service run by Lazzi in 1½ hours.

Arezzo is on the main railway line between Florence and Rome; most express trains stop here and there is a frequent service (in c 50 minutes).

Bologna, on the main railway line to the N, can be reached by fast train in 60–75 minutes.

23 Fiesole and San Domenico

BUS No. 7 from the Station, Duomo, and Piazza San Marco. Frequent service (every 10–20 minutes) taking 30 minutes from the station via San Domenico.

There are a number of beautiful narrow old roads up to Fiesole (described below) which provide delightful approaches by foot (the walk takes c 2 hours from Piazza del Duomo). For those with less energy, the bus can be taken up to Fiesole, and then the descent down to Florence made on foot. In any case the beautiful old Via Vecchia Fiesolana between San Domenico and Fiesole should not be missed.

The main road to Fiesole which provides the usual approach for motorists and which is followed by the bus is Viale Alessandro Volta (Pl.7;2; which begins at Piazza delle Cure), and, beyond Piazza Edison, Via di San Domenico which continues to ascend the hillside with a beautiful view of Fiesole and its villas. A double curve precedes San Domenico.

San Domenico may also be approached by one of the beautiful old roads described below. VIA GIOVANNI BOCCACCIO begins just N of Piazza delle Cure and at first runs along the bank of the Mugnone. It then passes (No. 126) *Villa Palmieri*, the garden of which was the scene of one of the episodes in Boccaccio's 'Decameron'. The villa was bought in 1454 by Marco Palmieri. The present garden was laid out after 1697, and is famous for its lemon trees. The road, realigned in 1874 by the Earl of Crawford when he owned the villa, continues up skirting the railings of the grounds of the villa and Fiesole can be seen on the hill ahead. On the left is *Villa Schifanoia* (No. 115–121), used since 1989 by the European University (see below), another fine villa with a delightful garden. Just beyond a little chapel with a rusticated façade (1849) the road narrows and, with a view of the campanile of the Duomo of Fiesole ahead, soon emerges in Piazza San Domenico.—Another pretty approach to San Domenico follows the old walled VIA DELLE FORBICI which is reached from Piazza delle Cure by following Viale Alessandro Volta for c 500m and diverging left past the park (open daily 7.30–sunset except Monday; entrance at No. 12 Via Giovanni Aldini) of *Villa Il Ventaglio* built in 1839–53 by Giuseppe Poggi, now the seat of the Università Internazionale dell'Arte. Farther on, on the left, is *Il Garofano*, identified as the property owned by the Dante and the Portinari (plaque).—VIA DI BARBACANE is another old road, beautifully preserved at its upper end, which climbs the hill from Viale Volta near the beginning of Via di San Domenico. It passes between old walls and case coloniche, and, at a sharp bend emerges beside a little belvedere in front of the *Villa La Meridiana* (No. 10). The delightful view takes in Monte Morello and the Duomo. Beyond is the junction with Via della Piazzola which continues right (with a view of Fiesole) past *Villa l'Ombrellino* with its little gazebo on the garden wall. Beyond the little hospital of Le Camerata, the road descends to San Domenico.

San Domenico and Fiesole can also be approached on foot from the bottom of the hill of Villa Camerata. The narrow Via Lungo l'Affrico follows the picturesque little stream of the Affrico, skirting the garden of Villa Camerata as far as a 'T' junction with Via del Palmerino, by a handsome iron gate. To the right the road leads shortly to Villa Il Palmerino where the writer Vernon Lee (Violet Paget) lived from 1889 until her death in 1935 (plaque on the garden façade). In 1893 Henry James described her as 'by faraway the most able mind in Florence'. In the other direction Via del Palmerino continues left (still skirting the wall of Villa Camerata) to join Via di Camerata (see Atlas 12) which continues up and across the main road (Via di San Domenico).—The pretty Via

del Salviatino up to Maiano and Fiesole from Via Lungo l'Affrico is described
below in the walks in the vicinity of Fiesole.

6.5km **San Domenico di Fiesole** (cf. Atlas p 12) is a little hamlet
within the commune of Fiesole, with several beautiful private villas.
The church of SAN DOMENICO dates from 1406–35; the portico (1635)
and campanile (1611–13) were added by Matteo Nigetti.

INTERIOR (closed 12–15.30). The side chapels have fine Renaissance arches in
pietra serena and some of the altarpieces have handsome Mannerist frames.
The fine chancel was designed in 1603 by *Giovanni Caccini*. SOUTH SIDE, 1st
chapel, wood Crucifix of the mid 14C which formerly belonged to the Compagnia of San Donato, and an interesting painting of the Crucifixion attributed to
the school of Botticelli; 2nd chapel, *Lorenzo di Credi*, Baptism of Christ (a
composition borrowed from the painting by Verrocchio in the Uffizi), and an old
copy of a painting of the Madonna and Child with Saints John the Baptist and
Sebastian by Perugino.—On the high altar is a gilded wood tabernacle of 1613
(*Andrea Balatri*). The two fine carved 16C benches were altered in the 17C and
have recently been restored.—NORTH SIDE, 3rd chapel, *Jacopo da Empoli*,
Annunciation (1615), and a Miracle of St Antoninus by *Francesco Conti* (the
Crucifix by *Antonio da Sangallo* is being restored); 2nd chapel, *Giovanni
Antonio Sogliani* (completed by *Santi di Tito*), Epiphany. 1st chapel, *Fra'
Angelico*, *Madonna with angels and Saints (c 1430; recently restored; light on
right). The architectural background was added by *Lorenzo di Credi* in 1501,
when the frame was redesigned (the paintings of Saints are by a follower of
Lorenzo Monaco). The panels of the predella are copies; the originals are in the
National Gallery, London. While living in the convent Fra' Angelico also
painted an Annunciation (now in the Prado) and a Coronation of the Virgin
(now in the Louvre), photographs of which are displayed here.

In the **Convent of San Domenico** St Antoninus (Antonino Pierozzi, 1389–
1459) and Fra' Angelico (Guidi di Pietro or Fra' Giovanni da Fiesole, 1387–1455)
first assumed the religious habit; they moved down to the convent of San Marco
after 1437. The little CHAPTER HOUSE (ring at No. 4, right of the church) contains
a beautiful fresco of the Crucifixion by *Fra' Angelico* (c 1430) and a detached
fresco (with its sinopia) of the Madonna and Child, also attributed to him. In the
orchard is the little Cappella delle Beatitudine (1588) with frescoes (recently
restored) by *Lodovico Buti*.

The pretty Via delle Fontanelle leads from Piazza San Domenico, passing *La
Torraccia*, a large villa with a loggia, now owned by the Comune of Fiesole and
used by various societies and by the Music School of Fiesole, founded in 1974
(with a high reputation). This was the residence of Walter Savage Landor from
1829 until 1835 when he left his family here. Emerson, Monckton Milnes and
Nathaniel Parker Willis were among his visitors. The 'Valley of Ladies'
described in the 'Decameron' lies within the grounds, which include a fine park
and a charming little Italianate garden.

Via della Badia dei Roccettini, descending to the left from San
Domenico, leads (5 minutes on foot; beware of traffic) to the *Badia
Fiesolana** (see Atlas p 12), the cathedral of Fiesole until 1028. In a
beautiful position, it was probably built on the site of the martyrium
of St Romulus. Bishop Donato of Fiesole (died c 876), thought to have
been an Irishman, was elected to the bishop's see when he stopped
here on his journey back from Rome. It was later a Benedictine and
Lateranensian house. The church was rebuilt in the 15C under the
direction of Cosimo il Vecchio who here founded a library with the
help of Vespasiano da Bisticci.—In the conventual buildings the
European University Institute was established in 1976. The cloister
dates from 1459 and under a pretty loggia of 1461 has been placed a
statue of Plato by Pompilio Ticciati.—The rough stone front of the
church incorporates the charming *FAÇADE of the smaller Romanesque church with inlaid marble decoration.

The simple cruciform *INTERIOR is open only for a service at 11 on Sunday (or
sometimes by request at the European University, from the cloister). The
interesting plan of the small church, begun in 1456, is derived from

The façade of the Badia Fiesolana

Brunelleschi. The side chapels have handsome round arches in pietra serena by *Francesco di Simone Ferrucci*, and five steps precede the E end, also decorated with pietra serena, with an elegant inscription to Piero de' Medici ('Il Gottoso') and the date of 1466. The high altar is a fine work in pietre dure by *Giovanni Battista di Jacopo Cennini* (1612) on a design by *Pietro Tacca*. On the 1st altar on the left is an unusual painting of Christ in pietà with Saints by *Francesco Botticini*. In the left transept, Crucifixion by *Bernardino Campi*. In a room approached from the right transept is a delightful lavabo by *Gregorio di Lorenzo* (1461).

From the charming terrace in front of the church the view extends beyond cypresses and olives to Florence. On a clear day, to the left of the Duomo and campanile, can be seen the towers of Palazzo Vecchio, the Bargello, and the Badia, with Forte di Belvedere beyond, and further left, on the skyline, San Miniato. To the right of the Duomo is the dome of the Cappella dei Principi of San Lorenzo. On the hill opposite the Badia, beyond Via Faentina which follows the floor of the Mugnone valley, is the handsome yellow-coloured *Villa Salviati* with its cypress avenue. It was built in 1490 by Giuliano da Sangallo and contains sculptures by Giovanni Francesco Rustici. Behind the church rises the hill of Fiesole.

From San Domenico the ascent to Fiesole may be made either by the main road or (on foot) by the shorter and prettier old road (Via Vecchia Fiesolana, very narrow and steep; cf. p 232); both are lined with fine villas and beautiful trees and provide splendid views of Florence.

8km **FIESOLE** (295m; pron. 'Fiésole') is a little town (14,100 inhab.) in a magnificent position on a thickly wooded hill overlooking the valleys of the Arno and the Mugnone. It has always been a fashionable residential district, once much favoured by the English, and its beautiful hillside is enhanced by fine villas and gardens, and stately cypress groves. An Etruscan city, its foundation precedes that of Florence by many centuries, and, with its own local government, it is still proudly independent of the larger city. It is crowded with Florentines and visitors in summer when its position makes it one of the coolest places in the neighbourhood of the city. **Plan on Atlas p 12.**

Excavations have proved that the hill was inhabited before the Bronze Age. The site of *Faesulae*, on a hilltop above a river valley, was typical of Etruscan settlements. Probably founded in the 6C or 5C BC from Arezzo, it became one of the chief cities of the Etruscan confederacy. It is first mentioned in 283 BC, when its people, in alliance with other Etruscans, were defeated by the Romans at Lake Vadimone. With the Roman occupation it became the most important town in Etruria, but the barbarian invasions led to the decay of the city. In 854 the county of Fiesole was merged with that of Florence. After a decisive battle in 1125 in which only the Cathedral and the Bishop's Palace escaped destruction, the ascendancy of Florence over the older city was finally assured. The diocese of Fiesole is particularly extensive.

The bus terminates in PIAZZA MINO DA FIESOLE, the spacious main square of the town, called after the Renaissance sculptor (1429–84; born at Poppi in the Casentino) who made Fiesole his home. A market is held here on Saturdays, and there is a Tourist Information office. The **Cathedral** (closed 12–15) was founded in 1028, and enlarged in the 13C and 14C. It was over-restored in 1878–83. The tall bell-tower of 1213 (the crenellations were added later) is visible from Florence and the surrounding hills.

The bare stone INTERIOR, with a raised choir above a hall crypt, is similar in plan to San Miniato al Monte. The massive columns have fine capitals (some of them Roman). Lights in the choir (coin-operated) illuminate the church. Above the W door is a statue of St Romulus, Bishop of Fiesole, in a garlanded niche, by *Giovanni della Robbia* (1521). Stairs lead up to the CHOIR. On the right is the CAPPELLA SALUTATI with frescoes in the vault of the Evangelists by *Cosimo Rosselli* and two of *Mino da Fiesole*'s best works: the *Tomb of Bishop Leonardo Salutati* (1465) with a fine portrait bust, and an *Altar-frontal*. In the next chapel, decorated by Gaetano Bianchi, is a damaged painting with the story of St Romulus by the school of *Domenico Ghirlandaio* (restored in 1986). Opposite is a 19C copy of St Romulus enthroned with four Saints also by the school of Ghirlandaio (the original was on the back of the painting opposite). Over the high altar is a large rich *Altarpiece* by *Bicci di Lorenzo* (c 1440); the apse is frescoed by *Nicodemo Ferrucci* (late 16C). In a nearby chapel is a marble altarpiece by *Andrea Ferrucci* (1493). The SACRISTY contains a precious mitre of 1430 (rarely shown).—The columns in the CRYPT (closed for restoration) have interesting primitive capitals. The granite font is the work of *Francesco del Tadda* (1569). Behind the grille, surrounding the altar of St Romulus, are four marble columns with charming antique Ionic capitals.

The piazza slopes up to the old *Palazzo Pretorio*, now the town hall, with a loggia decorated with the coats-of-arms of many podestà. Next to it stands the church of *Santa Maria Primerana*, rebuilt in the 16–17C, with a quaint porch. The interior contains a 14C painted Crucifix, a bas-relief with the self-portrait in profile of Francesco da Sangallo executed as a thank-offering in 1542, and a Della Robbian Crucifix with the Madonna and Saints. In the sanctuary is a 13C painting of the Madonna in a Gothic tabernacle, and damaged frescoes by *Niccolò di Pietro Gerini*.—The unusual equestrian monument (1906) in the piazza celebrates the meeting between Victor

Emmanuel II and Garibaldi at Teano. The lower end of the square is occupied by the *Seminary* (1697) and the *Bishop's Palace* (1675). Between them Via San Francesco, a very steep paved lane, climbs up the hill, passing (right) a public park (cf. below). Higher up is a terrace, planted with ilexes, with a *View of Florence dominated by the cupola of the Duomo. Here are two war memorials. Above, beside another viewpoint, is the church of SANT' ALESSANDRO, heavily restored in 1814 and again after 1957 (closed 12–15).

Traditionally thought to be on the site of an Etruscan and Roman temple, it is thought to have been founded in the 6C. The Romanesque church was altered in the 16C and 18C. The bare basilican interior is remarkable for its cipollino marble *Columns with Ionic capitals and bases from a Roman building. An oratory off the left aisle (light on right) contains an altarpiece of the Assumption by Gerino da Pistoia (showing the influence of Perugino) and 16C Mannerist frescoes of the Life of the Virgin.

Beyond (left) the church of Santa Cecilia is the top of the hill (345m), the site of the Etruscan and later Roman acropolis. Here are the convent buildings of **San Francesco** (closed 12–15). The church of c 1330 was restored in neo-Gothic style in 1905–07, with an attractive little rose-window. The choir arch is attributed to *Benedetto da Maiano*. On the Right side (1st altar) Marriage of St Catherine by *Cenni di Francesco*, in a frame with paintings of the early 19C, and (2nd altar), *Piero di Cosimo*, Immaculate Conception.—Left side (1st altar), *School of Cosimo Rosselli*, Adoration of the Magi, (2nd altar), *Raffaellino del Garbo*, Annunciation. A Crucifixion and Saints by *Neri di Bicci* has been restored and will probably be returned here.— In the Franciscan friary are several charming little cloisters, some remains of the Etruscan walls, and a missionary MUSEUM (restored in 1990) of Eastern objets d'art (Chinese and Egyptian collections).—A gate admits to a public park with an ilex wood, through which shady paths lead back downhill to the main square.

From Piazza Mino the street beind the apse of the cathedral leads to the entrance to the ***Roman Theatre**, Archaeological Excavations, and Museum (adm. see p 60).

From the terrace there is a good comprehensive view of the excavations in a plantation of olive trees, backed by the Mugnone valley and the dark cypresses of the hill of San Francesco. The excavations were begun in the 19C, and several of the edifices were arbitrarily restored in 1870–92. The ROMAN THEATRE, built at the end of the 1C BC, was enlarged by Claudius and Septimius Severus. The *Cavea*, partly excavated in the hillside (the sides are supported on vaults), is 34 metres across and held 3000 spectators. The seats on the right side are intact; the others have been restored with smaller blocks of stone. Plays and concerts are performed here during a festival held every summer (the 'Estate Fiesolana'; cf. p 58).—On the right of the theatre are the ROMAN BATHS (reconstructed in 1892), probably built in the 1C AD and enlarged by Hadrian. In front are three rectangular swimming baths. The chambers near the three arches (reconstructed) consist of the *hypocausis*, with circular ovens, where the water was heated, the *calidarium* with its hypocaust, and the *tepidarium*. In front of the arches is the *palestra*, and behind them the *frigidarium*.—A small terrace here provides a fine view of a long stretch of ETRUSCAN WALLS (4C–3C BC; reinforced in the Roman and medieval periods), with a gateway, which enclosed the city.—On the other side of the theatre (to the NW) is a ROMAN TEMPLE (1C BC), with its basement intact, and, on a lower level, remains of an ETRUSCAN TEMPLE (4C or early 3C BC), both of them approached by steps. Nearby, are copies of the two original altars from the temples (the larger one is Roman). In this area a Lombard necropolis (6–7C AD) has also been excavated. Near the theatre is a stretch of Roman road.

The MUSEUM was built in 1912–14; the exterior is an idealised reconstruction of the Roman temple. Reopened in 1981, it has been modernised and the collections beautifully rearranged. The material is being re-evaluated in the light of new excavations, etc. Under the portico is a fragment from the frieze of the Roman temple. The first five rooms contain the topographical collection from Fiesole and its territory. ROOM I. Etruscan-Roman finds from Fiesole, including the so-called 'She-wolf' in bronze (in fact the torso of a lioness), found on the probable site of the Capitol of Faesulae. In Case 1 is displayed Bronze Age material recently found on the hill of San Francesco and in the Temple area (the first signs of a prehistoric settlement in Fiesole). Also here, Etruscan stelae, and cases of bronzes.—R. II. Etruscan urns in pietra serena from the necropolis of Bargellino; cylindrical lead cinerary urn decorated with Roman reliefs; inscribed stelae in pietra serena (2C AD); small bronzes; Bucchero ware.—RR. III and IV contain material found in the area of the Roman Theatre and Temples, including terracotta antefixes and other architectural fragments (the finds from the Etruscan Temple were made in excavations since 1955); and a marble frieze from the Theatre (which probably decorated the 'pulpitum'). Also displayed here is a head of Claudius.—Stairs lead up to R. V which contains medieval finds.—The remaining rooms form the Antiquarium. RR. VI and VII contain the well-preserved 'Stele Fiesolana' (5C BC), showing a funerary banquet, and dancing and hunting scenes, and an Etruscan collection including urns from Chiusi, Bucchero vases, bronzes, mirrors, etc.—Among the sculpture displayed in R. VIII is a torso of Dionysius.

The same ticket gives access to the **Antiquarium Costantini** nearby at No. 9 Via Portigiani, opened in 1990. Here is displayed a splendid collection of Greek vases recently donated to Fiesole.On the lower floor excavations made in 1988 can be seen of a sacred edifice (probably dating from the 3C–2C BC) and a well, together with the finds made on the site which include fresco fragments (1C BC–2C AD), and ceramics and glass. There are long-term plans to connect this building by means of a tunnel to the main area of excavations.

In Via Duprè (No. 1), just to the left of the entrance to the Roman Theatre, is the small **Museo Bandini** (adm. see p 61), a collection of Florentine art begun in 1795 by Angelo Maria Bandini, and left by him to the Diocese of Fiesole.

The paintings are arranged chronologically in two rooms on the FIRST FLOOR. They include: 13C Tuscan Crucifix attributed to *Meliore*; *Bernardo Daddi*, St John the Evangelist; *Taddeo Gaddi*, Annunciation; works by *Agnolo Gaddi*, *Jacopo di Cione*, and *Nardo di Cione*.—Works by *Lorenzo di Bicci*, *Bicci di Lorenzo*, *Lorenzo Monaco*, *Giovanni del Ponte* and *Giovanni del Biondo*. *Cosimo Rosselli* and his bottega, Coronation of the Virgin; *late 15C Florentine school*, Three Triumphs; *Neri di Bicci*, Madonna in Adoration; *School of Filippino Lippi*, Madonna and Child with an angel.—On thé GROUND FLOOR a room (not yet reopened) displays sculptural fragments from the Baptistery of Florence, and Della Robbian works.

Lower down the hill a road diverges left from Via Duprè for the Cemetery, where the sculptor Giovanni Duprè (1817–82) is buried (his tomb bears a copy of his Pietà). Against the hill of San Francesco may be seen a large section of the *Etruscan Wall*.—Another stretch of the Wall can be seen by following Via Santa Maria from Piazza Mino. Via Sant' Apollinare or (right) Via Belvedere, with superb views, continue up hill to Via Adriano Mari which skirts the wall along the E limit of the Etruscan city. From here Via Montececeri (also with magnificent views) leads across to the beautiful woods of *Montececeri* (public footpaths), with remarkable disused quarries of pietra serena.—In Via del Bargellino (cf. the Plan) are two Etruscan tombs (4C–3C BC).

Walks in the Vicinity of Fiesole

The walks described below follow many beautiful old roads. Even though most of them are very narrow, they are still used by cars, and those on foot should take great care of the traffic.

A. From Piazza Mino the narrow ***Via Vecchia Fiesolana** descends steeply past the hospital of Fiesole and the convent of *San Girolamo* (15–17C; which includes a pensione), surrounded by a garden and fields. On the left is the *Villa Medici* (no adm.), built by Michelozzo in 1458–61 for Cosimo il Vecchio. Its beautiful garden, one of the earliest of the Renaissance, is built on the steep hillside with a superb view of Florence. It was a favourite retreat of Lorenzo il Magnifico and members of the Platonic Academy. Its present appearance dates from the 17C and 18C. When it was owned in the 19C by William Spence, Holman Hunt and John Everett Millais were guests here. On the other side of the road is the inconspicuous entrance to *Villa Le Balze* (No. 26), now owned by Georgetown University.—The road continues downhill (or a path, Via degli Angeli, may be followed); below Villa Medici, after two sharp bends, there is a breathtaking view of Florence from the road, here lined with venerable cypresses. At the intersection with Via Duprè Via Vecchia Fiesolana continues down to San Domenico (see p 228), passing several beautiful villas. Via Duprè leads right to a fork with Via Fontelucente, an even narrower old road which descends left to the church of *Fontelucente*, built over a spring, in a beautiful isolated spot above the Mugnone valley. It contains (2nd chapel on the right) a triptych by Mariotto di Nardo. Via Duprè continues with a view across the valley towards Via Bolognese, where the hillside was disfigured by modern houses in the 1950s. *Villa Duprè* (No. 19) was the home of the sculptor Giovanni Duprè. The road now climbs uphill to *Villa Le Coste* (No. 18) where the painter Primo Conti (1900–88) lived. In the 16C house in the garden the *Museo di Primo Conti* (adm. 10–13 except Monday and fest.) was opened in 1987, with a representative collection of his works, left to the Comune. The painter is buried here in a chapel of 1702, with the Coronation of St Rosalia and episodes from her life attributed to Francesco Botti (recently restored). The road curves to the right round the hill, and from the hamlet of San Martino, with the campanile of the cathedral of Fiesole prominent ahead, it is a short way back past the Teatro Romano to Piazza Mino.

B. The pretty VIA BENEDETTO DA MAIANO diverges from the main Florence road below Fiesole (cf. the Plan; the bus may be taken downhill from Piazza Mino to the request stop here). It passes the entrance to the *Pensione Bencistà*, a hotel particularly favoured by English visitors. It was formerly Villa Goerike where the painter Arnold Böcklin (1827–1901) lived and died.—At a crossroads (2.5km) is the little group of houses called **Maiano**, the home of the brothers Benedetto and Giuliano da Maiano (1442–92 and 1432–90). In the tabernacle is a modern relief of the Annunciation in terracotta by Antonio Berti. In the church (if closed ring at No. 6), of ancient foundation (restored by Temple Leader), the choir is decorated with pietra serena. Above the W door, in its original frame, is a Madonna and Child with St John and two Saints by Giovanni Battista Naldini. On the right wall the St John the Baptist is in the manner of Carlo Dolci. A farm (produce for sale) now occupies the Benedictine monastery (with a 14C fresco of the Madonna della Misericordia). A road continues uphill for a few hundred metres past two trattorie, and quarries of pietra serena, with fine views of the wooded hills (and the top of the castle of Vincigliata surrounded by cypresses). Via del Salviatino runs from the crossroads down to Florence (Via Lungo l'Affrico, see above). It passes the gate of the *Villa di Maiano* (left) with its tower (restored in 1850 by John Temple Leader) and continues downhill with a view of Fiesole from a hairpin bend. It then skirts the garden wall with cypresses of *Villa il Salviatino* (entrance at No. 21), the 16C home of Alamanno Salviati, surrounded by a thick wood of ilexes. At the bottom of the hill is *Villa Montalto* (No. 6) with a brown and yellow painted façade.—Via Benedetto da Maiano (see above) continues from Maiano past the wall of the Villa di Maiano, and beyond has charming views of the hills of Settignano; just after Villa Sant'Ignazio Via Poggio Gherardo diverges left. It passes the garden gate of Villa Poggio Gherardo (described on p 235). The road continues down to San Martino a Mensola, described, together with Villa I Tatti, and Settignano in Rte 24.

C. From Piazza Mino Via Antonio Gramsci, the main street of Fiesole leads uphill through the town past Piazza Garibaldi where after the demolition of several buildings in 1986 excavations revealed remains of an Imperial Roman edifice and part of a later necropolis. There is a plan to erect here a new building designed by Giovanni Michelucci. The main road joins Via Giacomo Matteotti just above the two Etruscan tombs in Via del Bargellino (cf. above). Beyond the locality of *Borgunto* (where a road leads uphill to Via Adriano Mari and remains of part of the Etruscan walls, see above), Via Francesco Ferrucci (the 'STRADA DEI BOSCONI') continues out of the town with increasingly beautiful views of the wide Mugnone valley. Some way along the main road, a by-road (signposted, Montebeni, Vincigliata, and Settignano) diverges right. This runs along a ridge round the N shoulder of Monte Ceceri through magnificent woods. Just beyond *Villa di Bosco* with a restored tower and Italianate garden, there is a superb view of Florence. The road climbs to a fork;

on the left a road leads to Montebeni and Settignano; and to the right the road continues past *Castel di Poggio* (restored in the 19C; used by a study centre), and then descends, lined with magnificent cypresses, past (5km) the *Castello di Vincigliata*. The castle was built in 1031, and the ruins rebuilt in 1855 by John Temple Leader, who planted the cypresses here. He was visited by Gladstone and Queen Victoria. Further down the hill the road passes Villa I Tatti, before it comes to the main road for Settignano at Ponte a Mensola (see Rte 24).

Longer excursions may be taken to the N of Fiesole. The main street leads uphill out of the town and continues as the 'Strada dei Bosconi' (described above). It runs above the beautiful Mugnone valley with superb views, as far as (9km) *Olmo*. Here it joins VIA FAENZA (N 302) which continues N to Borgo San Lorenzo and the Mugello valley (see the 'Blue Guide Northern Italy').—In the other direction, Via Faenza returns to Florence along the Mugnone through the village of *Le Caldine*, just outside of which (7.5km from Florence) is the little **Convento della Maddalena**, a hospice of the Dominican convent of San Marco, now run by two friars. Here Fra' Bartolommeo lived and painted several frescoes.

From the entrance gate, protected by some ancient cypresses, the drive passes a little chapel in the orchard with a 'Noli me tangere' (seen through the door) by *Fra' Bartolommeo*. Visitors ring at the convent (preferably 10–12, 16–18) and are conducted by a friar. On the site of a 14C hospice, the convent was built c 1470–85 and donated by Andrea di Cresci to the friars of San Marco. The design, similar to San Marco on a reduced scale, is attributed to Michelozzo. The CHURCH has fine pietra serena decoration (including the arms of the founders, the Cresci). Over the high altar is a painting of the *Madonna in Maestà attributed to the 'Master of the Horne triptych' (or a follower of *Taddeo Gaddi*). Over a 17C side altar is a fresco by *Fra' Bartolommeo* of the *Annunciation above a charming presepio with terracotta figures attributed to Andrea della Robbia against a painted background. The beautiful portico outside the W door looks out over the Mugnone valley, with Montesenario in the distance. The little cloister, with a faded lunette by Fra' Bartolommeo of the meeting of St Francis with St Dominic, and the Refectory (with a fresco of the Pietà by Fra Paolino da Pistoia) are also usually shown.—Bus No. 12 from Florence (Via Pacinotti; Pl.7;2) follows Via Faentina as far as La Querciola (request stop at the gate of the convent). The old railway which follows the road is being repaired and may be put back into operation.

From Olmo (see above) a road (5km) leads to *Pratolino* (12.5km from Florence; bus No. 25A from Piazza San Marco; or buses run by SITA) on the Via Bolognese. The huge park of *Villa Demidoff* now belongs to the Province and is open to the public in the summer (1 May–24 September, Friday, Saturday, & fest. 10–20; car park on the left of the main road). Some 17–18 hectares of the splendid well-kept park can be visited (guided tours are also organised). A remarkable garden with numerous fountains was created here in 1569 for Francesco I de' Medici by Buontalenti; only Giambologna's colossal statue of *Appennino (1579–80; restored in 1988) survives from that garden (just behind the large farm buildings). It is one of the most extraordinary sights in Italy. Inside it (no adm.) are grottoes, mosaics and fountains, and behind it Giovanni Battista Foggini added a huge winged dragon in the late 17C. The lake in front of the statue, once planted with lotus flowers, is being restored. In the Medici villa (demolished in 1824) Galileo stayed in 1605–06 as tutor to Cosimo, eldest son of Ferdinando I. The park was transformed in the 19C, and in 1872 was bought by the Demidoff, who built their villa in the pink-coloured Paggeria of the Medici villa. In front of the villa are three magnolia trees and the original feet and hands of the statue of Appennino (substituted in 1877).—8km N, on top of a hill (815m) is the *Convent of Montesenario* set in woods full of grottoes and cells. Here seven Florentine merchants became hermits and established the Servite Order of mendicant friars in 1233.—Via Bolognese returns to Florence via the cemetery of *Trespiano* (near which a by-road leads right to the pretty Romanesque church of Cercina in lovely countryside N of Careggi, described in Rte 29). Via Bolognese enters Florence at Ponte Rosso and Piazza della Libertà (Pl.7;1).

24 Ponte a Mensola and Settignano

BUS No. 10 from Piazza San Marco to Settignano via *Ponte a Mensola* every 10–20 minutes in 30 minutes.

The main road for Settignano diverges left from Lungarno del Tempio near Ponte San Niccolò (Pl.11;4). The long straight Via del Campofiore and its continuation Via Lungo l'Affrico run NE passing close to the ex-convent of San Salvi (see Rte 22). After c 1km Via Gabriele d'Annunzio, signposted for Settignano, diverges right. Beyond Coverciano, the village of **Ponte a Mensola**, at the foot of the hill of Settignano, is reached. Here Via Poggio Gherardo (a beautiful road which leads via Maiano to Fiesole, see p 233) branches left from the main road past the entrance to *Villa di Poggio Gherardo*, traditionally thought to be the setting for the earliest episodes in Boccaccio's 'Decameron'. In 1888 it was purchased by Mr and Mrs H.I. Ross, who here entertained Mark Twain and John Addington Symonds. A small road (right) leads shortly to *SAN MARTINO A MENSOLA (open for services only; at other times ring at the priest's house under the portico on the right), a Benedictine church of the 9C, founded by St Andrew, thought to have been a Scotsman and archdeacon to the bishop of Fiesole, Donato, who was probably from Ireland. In a beautiful position above the village of Ponte a Mensola (from which it is also reached by a path), it is preceded by a 17C loggia. The 15C campanile was damaged by lightning in 1867.

The graceful 15C INTERIOR replaced the Romanesque church (remains of which have been found beneath the nave). It was altered in the 19C and was restored in 1969. Over the altar in the S aisle is a damaged fresco of the Crucifixion, and a painting of the Madonna enthroned with Saints Andrew and Sebastian, dating from the early 16C. At the end of the aisle, is a *Triptych (altered) of the Madonna enthroned with two female Saints, by *Taddeo Gaddi*. The Sanctuary is preceded by a beautifully carved arch in pietra serena with two pretty little tabernacles. On the high altar is a triptych of the Madonna and Child with the donor, Amerigo Zati, and Saints, by a follower of Orcagna (1391), known, from this painting, as the 'Master of San Martino a Mensola'. At the end of the N aisle, *Annunciation, by a follower of Fra' Angelico. In the pavement a stone marks the burial place of St Andrew. Over the other altar in this aisle is a worn fresco lunette of St Francis receiving the stigmata, and an altarpiece of the *Madonna and four Saints by *Neri di Bicci*.—A tiny room off the sanctuary (left) contains a MUSEUM. Here is a wooden *Casket, decorated with good paintings by the school of Agnolo Gaddi, which formerly contained the body of St Andrew, first abbot of the priory. The reliquary bust in wood of St Andrew dates from the end of the 14C. The intarsia cupboard in the little sacristy (opposite) is attributed to *Benedetto da Maiano*.

The little by-road leads from the church to a group of houses by the garden entrance to **Villa I Tatti** (the main entrance is on Via Vincigliata which begins at Ponte a Mensola, and skirts the garden up to the house). The unusual name is probably derived from the Zati family who lived here. It was the home of Bernard Berenson (1865–1959), the art historian who was a pioneer scholar of the Italian Renaissance as author of 'The Italian Painters of the Renaissance'. The house was left by him with his library and art collection to Harvard University as a Centre of Italian Renaissance Studies. The son of Lithuanian parents who emigrated to Boston when he was nine years old, Berenson won a scholarship to Harvard. He first came to I Tatti in 1900, and purchased it in 1905. He had acquired most of his collection by 1918 and it remains here more or less as he arranged it in the rooms he lived in: 'my house, I trust, expresses my needs, my tastes, and aspirations'. A beautiful Italianate garden laid out by Cecil Pinsent in 1908–15 surrounds the villa which contains Berenson's library (open to post-doctorate scholars), photograph library, and *Collection of Italian paintings, including works by Domenico Veneziano, Sassetta, Michele Giambono, Cima da Conegliano, Luca Signorelli, Bergognone, and Lorenzo Lotto, as well as his small Oriental collection. The house is not open to the public, but is shown to scholars with a letter of presentation, by previous appointment. Berenson and his wife Mary are buried in the 18C chapel in the garden.

A pretty by-road continues from I Tatti up the hill through woods past the castles of Vincigliata and Poggio to (6km) Fiesole (see p 234). Another beautiful by-road follows Via Poggio Gherardo from Ponte a Mensola to Maiano and Fiesole (see p 233).

In Via Vincigliata at the bottom of the hill are two plaques recording the writers and artists who lived and worked in the neighbourhood. Via di Corbignano leads to *Villa Boccaccio* (rebuilt), once owned by the father of Giovanni Boccaccio who here probably spent his youth. This pretty, narrow road continues as Via Desiderio da Settignano and, at a little group of cypresses, skirts the *Oratorio della Vannella* (1719–21) recently restored (but kept locked). The venerated fresco of the Madonna and Child attributed to Botticelli has been restored. The road ends at the cemetery of Settignano (see below).

From Ponte a Mensola the road continues up to Settignano, winding across the old road; both have fine views of the magnificent trees on the skyline of the surrounding hills. The main road passes the conspicuous neo-Gothic Mezzaratta by Alfonso Coppedè (1920) and (right) *Villa Viviani* where Mark Twain wrote 'Pudd'nhead Wilson'.— 7.5km **Settignano** (178m), a peaceful village on a pleasant hill, little visited by tourists. It has very narrow picturesque lanes and numerous fine villas surrounded by luxurious gardens. Delightful country walks can be taken in the vicinity. It is known for its school of sculptors, most famous of whom were Desiderio (1428–64) and the brothers Rossellino (Antonio Gamberelli, 1427–79, and Bernardo Gamberelli, 1409–64). The bus terminates in the piazza with the church of *Santa Maria*, built in 1518, reconstructed at the end of the 18C, and restored in 1976. It contains a charming group of the *Madonna and Child and two angels in white enamelled terracotta attributed to the workshop of Andrea della Robbia (in the sanctuary). The 16C organ was reconstructed in 1908 and has been restored. The pulpit was designed by Bernardo Buontalenti. In the dome above the high altar, Assumption of the Virgin by Pier Dandini. North side. On the 2nd altar, painted terracotta statuette of St Lucy attributed to Michelozzo, surrounded by frescoes of 1593; on the 1st altar is a Resurrection traditionally attributed to Maso di San Friano.—In the piazza is a statue by Leopoldo Costoli of Niccolò Tommaseo, the patriotic writer, who died here in 1874.—In the lower Piazza Desiderio, with a monument to the sculptor, there is a superb view of Florence, including the Duomo.

The numerous narrow lanes in and around Settignano, mostly with splendid views over unspoilt countryside, are well worth exploring on foot. From the right of the church Via Capponcina leads past some pretty houses. Beyond Via del Pianerottolo, near No. 57, there is a splendid view over a low wall of the Villa Gamberaia with its garden (see below). Via Capponcina continues downhill and, at the junction with Via dei Buonarroti-Simoni is the 18C garden gate of *Villa Michelangelo* (No. 65; no adm.), with wisteria climbing over its double loggia (plaque). Here Michelangelo passed his youth (a charcoal drawing attributed to him of a triton or satyr, found on the kitchen wall, was detached and restored in 1979). Farther downhill, surrounded by a garden with cypresses and pine trees, is *Villa La Capponcina* (No. 32) where Gabriele d'Annunzio lived in 1898–1910 and wrote most of his best works. He was here visited by Claude Debussy. The narrow road continues down to join Via Madonna delle Grazie. This can be followed on foot right past the fine 16C *Villa Strozzi Querceto*, with a clock of 1812 in the centre of its façade. It is approached by a beautiful avenue of pine trees and has a lovely garden (no adm.). The road continues (with an unusual view of the Duomo) past several case coloniche and then traverses fields to emerge on Via Gabriele d'Annunzio through an open gate (No. 212) just above Ponte a Mensola (see above).

The narrow main road (Via San Romano) of the village of Settignano continues from the piazza and Via Rossellino soon diverges right. It passes a little hamlet and then ascends (left) to the **Villa Gamberaia** (No. 72), which was once owned by the Gambarelli family of stone-masons, architects and sculptors. It has a famous *Garden (open weekdays 8–17; entrance fee; ring), remarkable for its topiary. Olive groves and an ilex wood surround the garden which includes two elaborate grottoes, a fine collection of azaleas, and ancient cypresses and pine trees. From the terrace there is a view of Settignano on its ridge and the Duomo beyond. The beautiful old narrow road passes through a tunnel beneath the garden and continues towards Montebeni.

Another road (signposted) from the main street of Settignano leads to the Cemetery where the novelist Aldo Palazzeschi is buried. Just beyond it, on the right of an old avenue of cypresses is a casa colonica (farmhouse; at the beginning of Via del Fossataccio) where a plaque records the birthplace of Desiderio da Settignano. The road beyond the cemetery which curves to the left leads to the Oratorio della Vannella, Corbignano, and Ponte a Mensola (see above).

The main street continues and at a fork (Via della Pastorella and Via Ciolli), beside a war memorial surrounded by cypresses, is the Oratorio di San Romano (key at No. 10 Via Ciolli), with early-16C frescoes of five Saints and two donors and relics from the War. Via Ciolli continues steeply uphill towards Montebeni and joins a pretty road to Fiesole (cf. above) at Vincigliata. Fiesole may also be reached across the hills from Settignano via Maiano.

25 Poggio Imperiale and Pian de' Giullari

BUS No. 11 from Piazza San Marco and the Duomo for Poggio Imperiale. Also BUS No. 38 (infrequent service) from Porta Romana for Poggio Imperiale (Largo Fermi) and for Pian de' Giullari.

Outside Porta Romana (Pl.8; 6) Viale del Poggio Imperiale (Pl.9; 7), laid out in the 17C, a long straight cypress avenue lined with handsome villas and their gardens leads up to the huge Villa of **Poggio Imperiale** (adm. readily granted by previous appointment), with a neo-classical façade by Pasquale Poccianti and Giuseppe Cacialli (1814–23). At the entrance are a number of restored Antique statues.

After its confiscation by Cosimo I in 1565 from the Salviati family, the villa remained the property of the grand-dukes of Florence and takes its name from the grand-duchess Maria Maddalena. Mozart gave a concert here in 1770. Since 1865 it has been used as a girls' boarding school run by the Educandato della Santissima Annunziata which became extremely fashionable in this century after Princess Marie José of Belgium (later Queen of Italy) was a pupil here during the First World War. It is now also the seat of a state school, and an international Liceo was founded here in 1989.

The number of rooms shown depends on the staff available, but usually most of those mentioned below are included in the visit. The central Courtyard (now closed in) was designed by Giovanni Battista Foggini c 1690; it is decorated with busts, some Antique and some dating from the 16C. The first four rooms called the 'Parlatori' have the earliest decorations by Matteo Rosselli and others (1623). On the left is the Sala delle Regine Imperatrici with a vault decorated by Matteo Rosselli, and on the walls three neo-classical views of Medici villas. The next two rooms were built by Giuseppe Cacialli for Ferdinando III in 1821–23: the Sala di Achille has neo-classical frescoes by Domenico Nani (l'Udine), and, beyond a little Empire-style bathroom, is the Sala Verde overlooking the garden, with charming landscapes beneath a painted sky by Giorgio Angiolini. The little room known as the 'Volticina' or 'Sala di Cosimo II' has frescoes by Ottavio Vannini (1623). The next series of rooms in the garden wing were built by Gaspare Maria Paoletti and decorated by Giuseppe Maria Terreni in 1773. The delightful Sala di Diana, with hunting dogs and game, was probably painted by Giuseppe del Moro. Beyond the neo-classical Segreteria di Pietro Leopoldo is the last room, the Sala dei Putti, with frescoes by Tommaso Gherardini.—The Sala di Vittoria della Rovere, now used as the school refectory, has trompe l'oeil frescoes of 1686.

Upstairs is the *Salone degli Stucchi* built by Paoletti in 1779 and decorated with white stucchi by Grato and Giocondo Albertolli. The Galleria is above the central courtyard and the Loggia, called the '*Peristilo*' over the front entrance was built by Giuseppe Cacialli and decorated with stucchi and paintings. The remarkable 16C table here in pietre dure, with classical monuments, was probably made in Rome.

To the left of the villa, in Largo Fermi, is the entrance to the *Observatory of Arcetri*, part of the Institute of Astronomics of the University. Several narrow roads meet here, and there is a bus terminus (No. 38). On the left is the windy *Via di San Leonardo* (one-way to Viale Galileo), the continuation of which (Pl.10;7,5) to Forte di Belvedere is described in Rte 20. To the right Via del Pian de' Giullari (now called Via Guglielmo Righini) winds up past *Villa Capponi* (No. 3), with a beautiful 16C *Garden, to the junction with Via del Giramontino (from Viale Galileo, see Rte 20). Here is the garden of *Torre del Gallo*, part of it recently acquired by the State. It was reconstructed in medieval style by Stefano Bardini in 1904–06, and is a conspicuous feature of the wooded skyline of the hills S of the Arno. The adjacent *Villa Gallina*, also now partly owned by the State, contains interesting frescoes of dancing figures by Antonio del Pollaiolo. In Via della Torre del Gallo is the 17C *Villa Arrighetti*, heavily restored in this century, with an extensive garden. The road continues (with a view back of the Observatory) to the pretty little village of **Pian de' Giullari**. *Villa di Gioiello* (No. 42) was the house where the aged Galileo lived, practically as a prisoner, from 1631 until his death in 1642. Here he wrote some of his most important tracts and was visited by Evangelista Torricelli, Vincenzo Viviani, Thomas Hobbes, and possibly also Milton. The 16C house and farm, with lovely gardens, are owned by the State and they have been restored and are used by the University (for adm. ask at the Observatory). Here is the terminus for Bus No. 38.

There are several pretty roads which can be explored on foot from the bus terminus, including Via del Pian de' Giullari which continues along the ridge to the church of *Santa Margherita a Montici* (open for a service at 11am on fest. only) with a crenellated campanile in a panoramic position. It contains two paintings by the Master of Santa Cecilia, one of which, with St Margaret and scenes from her life is thought to date from before 1300. In the apse is a ciborium by Andrea Sansovino.

26 Monteoliveto and Bellosguardo

BUS No. 13 (red) from the Station to Viale Raffaello Sanzio (for *Monteoliveto*) and Piazza Torquato Tasso (for *Bellosguardo*). BUS No. 42 (infrequent service) for Bellosguardo (going on to Marignolle) from Porta Romana.

On the S bank of the Arno, near Ponte della Vittoria (Pl.4;7) is the thickly wooded hill of **Monteoliveto**, with some beautiful private villas and a military hospital. It is reached via Viale Raffaello Sanzio and (right) Via di Monteoliveto (Pl.8;1). The hospital occupies the convent of the church of *San Bartolomeo* (for adm. ring at No. 72A), with a worn Renaissance portal. It was founded in the 14C and rebuilt in 1472.

INTERIOR. At the entrance are two unusual stoups in the form of Vestal Virgins, the one on the right is attributed to *Giovanni Caccini* (1547), and the other dates from the 17C. The W wall and triumphal arch bear good frescoes by *Bernardino Poccetti*. On the 2nd altar on the S side, Assumption of the Virgin signed and dated 1592 by Domenico Passignano. On the high altar, Entry of Christ into Jerusalem by *Santi di Tito*. On the left wall has been placed an interesting fresco fragment (with its sinopia opposite) of the Last Supper by *Sodoma* (very damaged), detached from the convent refectory. The altarpieces on the North Side are by *Simone Pignone* and *Fabrizio Boschi*. A series of early-18C scaqliola altar-frontals also belong to the church.

The road ends in front of an entrance to the **Villa Strozzi** (open daily 9–dusk), a beautiful wooded park, with fine views owned by the Comune of Florence since 1974. The buildings are being restored. There are two other entrances, one on Via Pisana (Pl.4;7), and one on Via Soffiano.

The adjoining hill to the S is aptly called **Bellosguardo**. It can be reached by foot from Monteoliveto by the pretty Via di Monteoliveto (see Pl.8;1,3), or by car from Piazza San Francesco di Paola (Pl.8;4). In the piazza is the church of *San Francesco di Paola* (1589; open for services only), with early-18C decorations, and a detached fresco of the Madonna del Parto by Taddeo Gaddi. The ex-Convent (No. 3) was bought by the sculptor Adolf Hildebrand in 1874. He added a top floor flat for his friend the painter Hans von Marées. It is surrounded by a beautiful Romantic park. To the right is the fantastic *Villa Pagani* with an eccentric tower built by Coppedè in 1896. Via di Bellosguardo climbs uphill past an ancient little farmhouse (left). On the right a narrow road leads past a little public garden to Via di Monteoliveto (see above) with the ancient little church of *San Vito* (Pl.8;3; open for a service on fest. mornings), preceded by a pretty porch. The interior was remodelled in 1662. Nearby can be seen the *Villa dello Strozzino*, a fine Renaissance villa with a pretty loggia at one corner. Via di Bellosguardo continues uphill with a superb view back of Florence, and, on the right beside a group of pine trees is *Villa Brichieri-Colombi* (No. 20), owned by Miss Isa Blagden in 1849–73 who was often visited here by the Brownings. Elizabeth Barrett describes the view from the villa in the seventh book of 'Aurora Leigh'. Here in 1887 Henry James wrote 'The Aspern Papers'. The old road narrows and a sharp turn left (Via Roti Michelozzi) ends at *Torre di Bellosguardo*, recently well restored as a hotel with a delightful garden with magnificent views of Florence. Above the door is an unusual marble group of Charity, attributed to Francavilla. Adjoining it (entrance from Piazza di Bellosguardo) is the *Villa dell'Ombrellino*, ostentatiously restored in 1988 as a 'trade centre' and used for congresses, etc. The villa was rented by Galileo in 1617–31. Violet Trefusis lived here until her death in 1973. In La Torricella nearby (demolished) Ugo Foscolo lay sick in 1812. On the wall of the villa is a plaque with the names of foreigners who have lived on the hill. In *Piazza di Bellosguardo*, at No. 6 is *Villa Belvedere di Saraceni* by Baccio d'Agnolo with a courtyard. Via San Carlo leads out of the piazza towards the conspicuous tower of *Villa di Montauto* where Nathaniel Hawthorne stayed in 1859. It provided the setting for the castle of Monte Beni in 'The Marble Faun'. There is a view from the road of the side of Villa Belvedere di Saraceni, and the wooded hill of Villa Strozzi and the new buildings of Scandicci beyond.

From Piazza di Bellosguardo Via Piana (Pl.8;5) continues past more luxurious villas. It ends at Via di Santa Maria a Marignolle. To the left (no entry to cars) this leads to *Villa La Colombaia* (Pl.8;7; No. 2), with a closed-in loggia, now a convent school. Here Florence Nightingale was born (plaque on the garden façade). From here the narrow old Via della Campora (or Via Ugo Foscolo) can be followed back downhill to Porta Romana (Pl.8;6), both with pretty views of Florence.

27 The Certosa del Galluzzo and Impruneta

BUSES 37 and 36 from Piazza Stazione to the *Certosa del Galluzzo*; No. 37 continues to Tavarnuzze. CAP bus from 13–14 Via Nazionale c every hour to *Impruneta* in 40 minutes.

At Porta Romana (Pl.8;6) is the beginning of the Via Senese which climbs and then descends through Gelsomino, passing (right) the thick cypresses of the *Cimitero Evangelico degli Allori*, formerly a cemetery only for Orthodox Greeks, and the Protestant cemetery of Florence since 1878. A turn of the road reveals the picturesque hill of the Certosa.—5km *Galluzzo*, beside the Ema. A road just before the piazza diverges right and ascends behind the Certosa to *Villa I Colazzi* (9km), a beautiful Mannerist villa with fine trees.—Just past the village of Galluzzo, immediately to the right of the road on the *Colle di Montaguto* (110m), stands the *Certosa del Galluzzo (or di Val d'Ema*; adm. see p 60). There is a view of the monks' cells, the church, and the Gothic Palazzo degli Studi on the edge of the hill.

A road ascends to the car park. Visitors are conducted by a monk. The monastery was founded in 1342 by the Florentine Niccolò Acciaioli, High Steward of the Kingdom of Naples. In 1958 the Carthusians were replaced by Cistercians, their first reappearance to the area since their expulsion by the Grand Duke of Tuscany 176 years earlier. There are now 12 monks here. The spacious *Courtyard dates from 1545. The CHURCH is divided into two parts: the *Monk's Choir* has fine vaulting (covered in the 17C with frescoes by *Orazio Fidani*) and good 16C stalls. On the W wall is a fresco by *Bernardino Poccetti* (1591–92). Beyond a corridor with side chapels, brightly decorated in 1794–1801, is the church of *Santa Maria* built in 1404–07 (stained glass window by *Niccolò di Pietro Gerini*), but remodelled in 1841. Beneath the *Lay Brethren's Choir* is a chapel with the magnificent *Tomb-slab of Cardinal Agnolo II Acciaioli*, formerly attributed to Donatello and now thought to be the work of Francesco da Sangallo. Also here are three other beautiful pavement tombs of the Acciaioli family, and the Gothic monument to the founder, Niccolò Acciaioli (died 1365).—The extensive conventual buildings include two fine cloisters, the *'Colloquio'*, with interesting 16C stained glass, and the *Chapter House*, with another expressive tomb-slab by Francesco da Sangallo (of Leonardo Buonafede; 1550) and a good fresco of the Crucifixion by Mariotto Albertinelli (1506). The secluded *GREAT CLOISTER is decorated with 66 majolica tondi of Saints and Prophets, by Andrea and Giovanni della Robbia. In the centre is a well of 1521 and the monks' cemetery. One of the monks' cells may be visited; they each have three rooms, a loggia, and a little garden. The *Foresteria*, off the entrance courtyard, where Pius VI and Pius VII both stayed is also shown.

The PALAZZO DEGLI STUDI was begun by Niccolò Acciaioli as a meeting place for young Florentines to study the liberal arts (and completed after his death). The splendid Gothic hall designed by Fra' Jacopo Passavanti on the ground floor is to be reopened to the public as a museum. The upper floor at present houses a PICTURE GALLERY, dominated by five frescoed *Lunettes of the Passion cycle, by *Pontormo* (1522–25), detached from the Great Cloister. These were painted when he came to live in the monastery in order to escape the plague in Florence in 1522. Also exhibited in the main hall: *School of Orcagna*, Tondo of the Madonna and Child; *Raffaellino del Garbo*, Saints Peter Martyr and George; *Ridolfo del Ghirlandaio*, Madonna enthroned with Saints; *Mariotto di Nardo*, Coronation of the Madonna with Saints. The Crucifix dates from 1350–60. Other paintings by Florentine masters of the 14C and 15C, including a Madonna by *Jacopo del Casentino*, and a Madonna and Child with St John by *Lucas Cranach* (stolen in 1973) are not at present on display. An adjoining room displays 16–17C works, including a series of paintings of the Apostles by *Orazio Fidani* (1653), and a detached fresco by *Empoli*.

From (7.5km) *Le Rose* a long but pleasant walk follows a narrow road through beautiful countryside, up to Impruneta (it emerges on the Pozzolatico road which should then be followed right to

Impruneta).—The main road continues beneath the motorway to a road junction at the entrance to the motorway and the 'superstrada' for Siena. Here a secondary road (N 2) for Siena (signposted for Impruneta) continues to (9km) *Tavarnuzze*.

From the Siena road beyond Tavarnuzze, a by-road soon diverges right for (3km) *Sant'Andrea in Percussina*. Here in the 'Albergaccio' (plaque) Niccolò Machiavelli lived and worked on 'The Prince'. The 'Osteria' in front of the villa is the successor to one frequented by the great statesman and historian.

A by-road ascends from Tavarnuzze to (14km) **Impruneta** (correctly, *L'Impruneta*; 275m), a large village (13,600 inhab.), on a plateau, where the great cattle fair of St Luke is still celebrated (mid-October), although it has now become a general fair. The clay in the soil has been used for centuries to produce terracotta for which the locality is famous. The kilns here still sell beautiful pottery (flower pots, floor tiles, etc.). In the large central piazza (where the fair is held) is the COLLEGIATA (*Santa Maria dell'Impruneta*), with a high 13C tower, and an elegant portico by Gherardo Silvani (1634).

The INTERIOR was restored, after severe bomb damage in 1944, to its Renaissance aspect which it acquired in the mid 15C under the Piovano Antonio degli Agli. South side, 1st altar, *Cristofano Allori*, Martyrdom of St Laurence; 2nd altar, *Passignano*, Birth of the Virgin. In the nave chapel, bronze Crucifix attributed to *Giambologna*.—At the entrance to the presbytery are two CHAPELS (c 1452) by *Michelozzo*, with beautiful *Decoration in enamelled terracotta by *Luca della Robbia*. They were reconstructed and restored after bomb damage. The Chapel on the right was built to protect a piece of the True Cross given to the church by Pippo Spano in 1426. It contains an enamelled terracotta ceiling, and an exquisite relief of the Crucifixion with the Virgin and St John in a tabernacle, flanked by the figures of St John the Baptist and a Bishop Saint. Beneath is a charming predella of adoring angels.—The Chapel on the left protects a miraculous painting of the Virgin traditionally attributed to St Luke which was ploughed up by a team of oxen in a field near Impruneta. For centuries it was taken to Florence to help the city in times of trouble. It had to be 'restored' in the 18C by the English painter Ignazio Hugford. The beautiful ceiling is similar to the one in the other chapel. The frieze of fruit on the exterior incorporates two reliefs of the Madonna and Child. The figures of Saints Luke and Paul flank a tabernacle which contains the image of the Madonna and Child (usually covered; exposed only on religious festivals). The silver altar frontal designed by Giovanni Battista Foggini replaces a 15C relief now exhibited in the Treasury (see below).—The large high altarpiece (1375) was partially recomposed after it was shattered in the War. It is the work of *Tommaso del Mazza* and *Pietro Nelli*.—On the N side of the nave are 16C inlaid stalls and a 15C cantoria. In the Baptistery a painting by the school of Orcagna has been removed for years for restoration.—A door beneath the portico on the right leads into two CLOISTERS; off the second (left) is the little CRYPT (11C), with sculptural fragments.

Above the portico of the church (entrance on the left of the church door) the TREASURY was well arranged in 1987 (adm. see p 61). Here are displayed a gilded silver *Cross attributed to Lorenzo Ghiberti (c 1420–25); two paxes attributed to *Antonio di Salvi*, a Cross of the 13C and 14C; 15 silver votive vases of 1633; and 17C and 18C church silver. Also here is the marble schiacciato relief attributed to a follower of Donatello showing the discovery of the miraculous painting of the Madonna of Impruneta (cf. above), formerly in the chapel inside the church. Vestments and illuminated choirbooks (13–16C) are also exhibited here.

From Impruneta the return by car to Florence may be made by continuing through the town to join (4km) the 'Chiantigiana' (N 222), just N of Strada. This beautiful road (described in 'Blue Guide Northern Italy') runs from Florence to Siena through the countryside where the famous Chianti wine is made. On the way back to Florence it passes the golf course of *Ugolino* (18 holes), laid out in the 1930s and beautifully landscaped with pine trees, olives, and cypresses. The club house was designed by Gherardo Bosio. The road continues through the large village of *Grassina* which is noted for its Good Friday Passion play. An alternative route from Impruneta to Florence (12km) follows the road to

Pozzolatico; a hilly and narrow by-road (signposted Grassina and San Gersolè) diverges right, with spectacular views, and continues through beautiful countryside to Grassina.—The road continues beneath the motorway, and a by-road diverges right for *Ponte a Ema*. The first turning on the right in the village (signposted Bagno a Ripoli) continues (1km; signposted; keep right) to **Santa Caterina dell'Antella**, in pretty countryside, beside kennels. This little chapel was built by the Alberti family in 1387 and frescoed by Spinello Aretino with the *Story of St Catherine (now owned by the Comune of Bagno a Ripoli and closed for restoration).—The main road continues into Florence through *Badia a Ripoli*. Here, beyond the ancient church of San Pietro, is the Abbazia in the piazza, founded in 790 with a church (16C portico) and convent (frescoes by Bernardino Poccetti).

28 Badia a Settimo and Lastra a Signa

BUS (Lazzi) from the Station via San Giuliano a Settimo to Lastra a Signa and San Martino Gangalandi in c 30 minutes.

Beyond Monteoliveto (see Rte 26) the Pisa road leads out of Florence past suburbs on the plain where many factories have been built in the last few years.—5km *San Quirico* has a pretty Renaissance church, served by Fra' Filippo Lippi in 1442. At *Scandicci* much new building has taken place since the War. To the S, about 2km beyond Vingone, is San Paolo a Mosciano, where in the Villa Mirenda (next to the little cemetery and church), D.H. Lawrence stayed in 1926–27 while completing 'Lady Chatterley's Lover' (first published in Florence in 1928). In 1927 he wrote from the villa: 'rather hot and Florence one of the most irritable towns on earth.... I feel better when it's fresco. The garden is full of peas and beans and carciofi, which is all to the good: really a happy vegetarian moment'.—8km *Casellina*. Just beyond a power station, a by-road (signposted) leads to the church of *San Martino alla Palma* (c 4km SW; open only for services; at other times ring at the green door under the portico), in a magnificent position in low rolling hills (seen from the main road). It was founded in the 10C, and contains a charming Madonna by a follower of Bernardo Daddi, known as the 'Master of San Martino alle Palme' (1325–30).—About 1km beyond (9km) *Piscetto*, and 5 minutes to the right of the road, is the church of *Santi Giuliano e Settimo*, an 8C building, altered in subsequent centuries.—About 2km NW of (11km) *Fornaci* is the **Badia di San Salvatore a Settimo**, a 10C abbey, rebuilt for Cistercians in 1236–37, walled and fortified in 1371, and restored since 1944.

The church has a rebuilt campanile and a Romanesque façade with a round 15C window. Open only for services; at other times ring the (inconspicuous) bell by the gate to the left of the façade. Over the 2nd altar on the south side, *Lodovico Buti*, Martyrdom of St Lawrence (1574). Behind the high altar in pietre dure is the Choir with a Della Robbian enamelled terracotta frieze of cherubims and the Agnus Dei, and two frescoed tondi of the Annunciation by the school of Ghirlandaio. On the left of the high altar is a little marble *Tabernacle, beautifully carved and attributed to Giuliano da Sangallo. The chapel on the left of the high altar has good *Frescoes (in poor condition) by *Giovanni di San Giovanni* (1629). The wall-tomb on the N side dates from 1096. In the Sacristy are kept two paintings formerly in the church, one of the Adoration of the Magi and one an unusual scene of Christ at the sepulchre, both attributed to *Ghirlandaio* or his school.—The interesting remains (carefully restored) of the MONASTERY (now privately owned, but sometimes courteously shown; ring at the Cloister) include much of the old fortifications, and the Chapter house and remarkable vaulted Lay Brothers Hall.

13km **Lastra a Signa**, a large village near the confluence of the Vingone and the Arno, has long been famous for the production of straw hats. The old centre (right of the main road) is remarkable for its walls of 1380, with three gates. Here is the *Loggia di Sant'Antonio* (it has been undergoing restoration for many years, now almost completed), formerly a Hospital erected at the expense of the Arte della Seta in 1411. The portico of six arches (the seventh is walled up) has traditionally been attributed as an early work to Brunelleschi. Nearby is the ex-*Palazzo Pretorio*, a little building (in need of restoration), with the escutcheons of many podestà. Just out of the main square is the church of *Santa Maria* (for adm. ask at the Misericordia) with a Madonna and Child by the school of Cimabue (removed for restoration).

Just beyond the town, off the main road (signposted), is the church of *San Martino a Gangalandi*, at the end of an attractive row of houses. Founded in the 12C or earlier, it has a restored campanile and a 15C loggia at the side. The Baptistery at the W end is decorated on the exterior and in the vault with frescoes by Bicci di Lorenzo and his school (1432; restored in 1982). The font was sculpted by a follower of Ghiberti. Here is hung a painting of St John the Baptist attributed to Bernardo Daddi (1346; in very poor condition). Over the first S altar is an unusual painting of five female Saints attributed to Piero Salvestrini da Castello, a pupil of Poccetti; over the 3rd S altar, Immaculate Conception by Matteo Rosselli (1615). The fine semicircular apse was decorated in pietra serena by Leon Battista Alberti, who was rector here from 1432–72. The high altar bears the date 1366. On the N wall is a large detached fresco of St Christopher, and fragments of 14C frescoes over the 2nd altar. Above a little room with fine capitals, now used as the Sacristy, off the left side of the church, a small *Museum* has recently been arranged (adm. on request, preferably by appointment). It contains 18C church silver and paintings including a Madonna of Humility by Lorenzo Monaco (from San Romolo a Settimo), two panels of the Annunciation of the early 15C Florentine school, and a Madonna and Child attributed to Jacopo del Sellaio.

In the hills to the SW is the castle of *Malmantile* (1424), an outpost of Castracani against the Florentines, celebrated in a poem by Lorenzo Lippi.

29 The Medici Villas of Careggi, La Petraia, and Castello. Sesto Fiorentino

BUS No. 14C from the Station or Duomo to *Careggi* (the penultimate request stop before the terminus).—BUS No. 28 from the Station for *La Petraia, Castello,* and *Sesto*. A bus is recommended to traverse the uninteresting N suburbs of Florence, but pretty country walks may be taken in the hills behind Careggi and La Petraia.

From the Fortezza de Basso Via del Romito (Pl.5;1) and its continuation, Via Corridoni, lead N, followed (as far as the one-way stystems allow) by bus 28 and 14 as far as (3km) Piazza Dalmazia, in the suburbs of *Rifredi*. Here on part of the site of the ex-'Galileo' factory a Museum of Contemporary Art is being built. In Via delle Panche, is the 10–11C church of *Santo Stefano in Pane*, with Della Robbian works. In an oratory here interesting 17C Florentine frescoes have recently been restored. A statue by Antonio Berti in the forecourt recalls Don Facibeni, founder of the charitable institution known as the Madonnina del Grappa. Bus 14C diverges right along the broad Viale Morgagni for *Careggi*, which has given its name to the main hospital of Florence. At the top of the hill, beyond the buildings of the hospital (request-stop), in a well-wooded park, is the **Villa Medicea**

di Careggi, now used as offices by the hospital (adm. only with special permission).

The 14C castellated farmhouse was acquired by the Medici in 1417. Cosimo il Vecchio returned here after his exile in Venice in 1434, and engaged Michelozzo to enlarge the villa and add a loggia. It became the literary and artistic centre of the Medicean court, and is traditionally taken as the meeting place of the famous Platonic Academy which saw the birth of the humanist movement of the Renaissance. Among its members, who met in the gardens here, were Marsilio Ficino, Angelo Poliziano, Pico della Mirandola, and Greek scholars, including Gemisthos Plethon and Argyropoulos, who came to Florence after the fall of Constantinople. In the villa Cosimo il Vecchio, Piero di Cosimo, and Lorenzo il Magnifico all died. It was burnt after the expulsion of the Medici at the end of the 15C, but renovated by Cosimo I. In 1848 it was restored by Francis Sloane.

The bus (No. 14C) terminates in the little circular Piazza di Careggi. Here is the *Convento delle Oblate* (adm. as for the Villa Medicea di Careggi) in an old Vecchietti castle. The interesting art collection includes a painting attributed to Giottino. In Via di Careggi is the bright red *Villa Le Fontanelle*, purchased by Cosimo il Vecchio for Marsilio Ficino. It was restored in the 19C by Francis Sloane. Nearby in Via Cosimo il Vecchio is the church of San Pietro with a 17C portico.

Several pretty walks may be taken in the hills behind Careggi at the foot of Monte Morello. A road follows the Terzolle stream past the little oratory of the *Loggia dei Bianchi*, with a miniature cupola, through the hamlet of Serpiolle towards CERCINA (which can also be reached in c 1hr on foot) where the fine Romanesque church (*Sant'Andrea*) has an ancient campanile and Renaissance porch. It contains a polychrome wood statue of the Madonna enthroned (13C) and early frescoes attributed to Domenico Ghirlandaio. The 15C cloister has frescoes with charming country scenes. An unusual festival is held here on the feast of St Anthony Abbot, with a mounted procession and the blessing of animals.

Another walk (30 minutes) follows the road (left) beyond the villa which leads down across the Terzolle towards *Villa La Quiete*, owned since 1650 by the sisters of the Convent of Le Montalve, who here run a school (adm. by appointment when the school timetable allows). Its collection of paintings includes a Coronation of the Virgin with Saints, by the workshop of Botticelli, Four Saints by Ridolfo del Ghirlandaio, and a painted Crucifix of the 13C. The gallery is painted by Giovanni da San Giovanni, and in the church is a monument (1698) to Vittoria della Rovere attributed to Giovanni Battista Foggini. Via di Boldrone continues past a tabernacle on the corner of Via dell'Osservatorio (which contained a fresco by Pontormo, removed to the Accademia del Disegno; see p 209) to the Villa della Petraia (see below).

From Piazza Dalmazia Bus 28 continues along the busy Via Reginaldo Giuliano. Just beyond (5km) the locality of Il Sodo (request-stop), a narrow road on the right leads up to **Villa della Petraia** (adm. see p 63).

Originally a castle of the Brunelleschi, the villa was rebuilt in 1575 for the grand-duke Ferdinando I de' Medici by *Buontalenti*. In 1864–70 it was a favourite residence of Victor Emmanuel II, and in 1919 it was presented to the State by Victor Emmanuel III.—A pretty GARDEN and moat precede the villa, which still preserves a tower of the old castle. On the upper terrace of the garden (view) with orange and lemon trees, is the base of a fountain by *Tribolo* and *Pierino da Vinci*. The bronze statue by Giambologna has been removed to the inside of the villa since its restoration (see below), and may be replaced here by a copy. The huge ilex (400 years old) was a favourite tree of Victor Emmanuel II (who built the tree house). A magnificent Park, with ancient cypresses, extends behind the villa to the E. The park and gardens are beautifully maintained.

The VILLA is shown on request (ring bell; cf. p 63). The Courtyard was covered with a glass roof and used as a ball-room by Victor Emmanuel II. The decorative *Frescoes beneath the two side loggias, illustrating the history of the Medici family, are by *Volterrano* (1636–46); those on the other two walls are by *Cosimo Daddi*. The ground floor rooms were furnished as state apartments in the 19C; they are hung with 17C tapestries, and contain a number of interesting clocks. In the Chapel (1682–95), with frescoes attributed to *Pier Dandini* or *Del Moro*, is a painting of the Madonna and Child by *Pier Francesco Fiorentino*, and an altarpiece of the Holy Family by the school of *Andrea del Sarto*.—On the first floor the private apartments, decorated in neo-classical style, contain: a long Chinese painting of the Port of Canton; the original bronze statue of *Venus (or 'Florence wringing the water of the Arno and Mugnone from her hair') by *Giambologna*, removed since its restoration in 1980 from the fountain in the garden (to which it was transferred from the Villa di Castello in 1785); copies of pastels by *Rosalba Carriera*; and paintings by the school of *Mattia Rosselli*. The gaming room is a remarkable 'period piece', hung with 17C paintings by *Francesco Curradi, Passignano*, and *Mattia Rosselli*.

In Via della Petraia is *Villa Corsini*, rebuilt for Filippo Corsini in 1698–99 by Antonio Ferri, with an interesting Baroque façade. A plaque records the death here in 1649 of Sir Robert Dudley. The villa has been restored since its acquisition by the State, and is at present used as a store for works of art awaiting restoration. The villa and garden are sometimes open for exhibitions and concerts, etc. (often in May). In front of the villa Via di Castello leads shortly to **Villa di Castello** (adm. to the gardens only, as for La Petraia). It is now the seat of the Accademia della Crusca, founded in 1582 for the study of the Italian language. The first edition of the institute's dictionary dates from 1612.

The gardens of Villa di Castello

The villa was acquired by Giovanni and Lorenzo di Pierfrancesco de' Medici, Lorenzo il Magnifico's younger cousins, around 1477. Here they hung Botticelli's famous 'Birth of Venus'. Botticelli's 'Primavera' and 'Pallas and the Centaur' were also later brought here (and all the pictures remained in the house until 1761). The villa, inherited by Giovanni delle Bande Nere, was sacked during the siege of 1530, but restored under Giovanni's son, Cosimo I, by Bronzino and Pontormo. Like La Petraia it was presented to the State in 1919.

The typical Tuscan GARDEN, described by numerous travellers in the 16C and 17C, including Montaigne in 1580, was laid out by *Tribolo* for Cosimo I in 1541. The *Fountain by *Tribolo* (with the help of *Pierino da Vinci*) was crowned by bronze figures of *Hercules and Antaeus by *Ammannati* (1559–60; removed and restored in 1982). Beneath the terrace is an elaborate *Grotto (c 1570; covered for restoration) full of weird animals and encrusted with shell mosaics and stalactites. Giambologna's bronze birds, now in the Bargello, were removed from here. In the floor are water spouts so that visitors could be surprised by a thorough drenching from their hosts. From the upper terrace, backed by woods, there is a good view. Here, surrounded by ilxes, is a colossus representing Appennino rising out of a pool and feeling the cold, by *Ammannati*. The huge Orangery should not be missed.

To the left of the villa the narrow Via Giovanni da San Giovanni leads shortly up to the *Villa il Pozzino*, now used as an orphanage by the Isitituto Antoniano Femminile (sometimes shown on request). It was reconstructed in 1586; the tower has a pretty loggia. The interior courtyard, with the well from which the villa takes its name, has a double loggia with well preserved grotteschi, attributed to Giovanni da San Giovanni, in the vaults. A hall off the courtyard has another delightful vault decorated with shells and paintings and a pebble floor. In the garden is a limonaia and a grotto. Lovely country walks may be taken on the hillside above.

A narrow rural road (Via di Castello; parallel to the main road lower down the hill) continues beyond Villa di Castello towards Sesto (see below). It passes the neo-classical *Villa Paolina*, built by Camillo Borghese in 1831 and named after his wife Paolina Bonaparte. It is connected to its garden across the road by an iron flying-bridge. In the hamlet of *Quinto*, is the church of Santa Maria (to the right, above the road). The paintings by the 'Master of the Madonna Straus' and Spinello Aretino have been removed for safety. Here, in Via Fratelli Rosselli is the *Villa Torrigiani*, with a 19C park, where Alfred Lord Tennyson stayed, and an ETRUSCAN *TOMB known as 'La Montagnola' (ring at No. 95 on Saturday or Sunday 10–13), a tumulus containing a remarkable domed tholos burial chamber (discovered in 1959).

The bus route ends at (9km) **Sesto Fiorentino**, a small town (41,900 inhab.). At the entrance on the left is *Villa Corsi Salviati*, where exhibitions are held, with an 18C garden. The 15C Palazzo Pretorio survives, and the church has slight Romanesque remains (and a painted Crucifix by Agnolo Gaddi). Next to the Ginori porcelain factory, the MUSEO DELLA PORCELLANE DI DOCCIA (adm. see p 62; entrance at 31 Viale Pratese), in a fine modern building (by Piero Berardi, 1965), contains a large well-displayed *Collection of porcelain made in the famous Doccia factory founded by Marchese Carlo Ginori in 1735. It includes some of the earliest porcelain painted by Carlo Wendelin Anreiter von Zirnfeld of Vienna, and the first models by Gaspero Bruschi and Massimiliano Soldani. The monumental fireplace was also designed by Gaspero Bruschi in 1754. The firm, known as Richard-Ginori since 1896, continues to flourish. Across the road, in an inconspicuous one-storey warehouse, Ginori seconds can be purchased.—At the foot of the hills is the *Villa Ginori* at Doccia, with a huge park and cypress avenues created by Leopoldo Carlo Ginori in 1816. Here exceptionally interesting remains of the old Ginori factory survive.—Pietro Bernini, father of the famous sculptor Gian Lorenzo, was born in Sesto in 1562.

From Sesto a road leads inland via Colonnata to the 'Strada panoramica dei Colli Alti' which skirts the wooded slopes of *Monte Morello* (934m), with magnificent views, as far as Via Bolognese (see p 223).

30 Poggio a Caiano and Artimino

BUS (COPIT) from Piazza Stazione every 30 minutes in c 30 minutes to *Poggio a Caiano*. From Poggio a Caiano CAP bus via Comeana to Artimino in 20 minutes, and via Seano to Carmignano (in 20 minutes).—Bus No. 29/30 from the Station to *Perétola*.

Near Porta al Prato Via delle Porte Nuove (Pl.4;4) is signposted for Pistoia.—6km **Peretola** (pron. Perétola), was the home of the Vespucci family before they moved to Florence. The church of *Santa Maria* contains a *Tabernacle by Luca della Robbia (1441; moved here from Sant'Egidio in Florence). The beautiful marble sculptures of two classical angels and the Pietà are framed by decoration in colourful enamelled terracotta, Luca's first documented work in this medium. The font is by Francesco di Simone Ferrucci. On the left wall is a fresco of Saints by Giusto d'Andrea (1466).—At the small airport of Peretola (used by light aircraft and some domestic and European flights), the motorway from Florence to the coast diverges to the right. At the 'Firenze-Nord' exit on the motorway, a few kilometres N, is the church of San Giovanni Battista, built in 1960–64 by the Tuscan architect Giovanni Michelucci.—9km *Brozzi*, a suburb of Florence severely damaged in the flood of 1966. The pieve of San Martino contains an interesting font and ciborium. The church of *Sant'Andrea a Brozzi* (15C), farther on, contains frescoes by Domenico Ghirlandaio and pupils, and a Crucifix by Giovanni di Francesco.—18km **Poggio a Caiano**, at the foot of Monte Albano, is famous for its royal *VILLA reopened in 1986 (adm. see p 63). It was acquired from the Strozzi in 1480 by Lorenzo il Magnifico who commissioned Giuliano da Sangallo to rebuild it. It became Lorenzo's favourite country villa, and is surrounded by a fine park and garden.

It was used by the Medici dynasty, including Francesco I and Bianca Cappello, and subsequently by the Austrians and French. It was given by Victor Emmanuel III to the State in 1919. Distinguished guests were received at the villa before they entered the city, among them Montaigne in 1581.

The villa is a fine rectangular building on a broad terrace surrounded by a colonnade. A classical Ionic portico on the first floor with the Medici arms in the tympanum bears a beautiful frieze (a copy of the original now displayed inside the villa). Pasquale Poccianti replaced the original straight outside stairs by the semicircular steps in 1802–07.

On the **Ground Floor** is the little *Theatre* built in the 17C by Marguerite-Louise of Orléans, wife of Cosimo III, and redecorated after 1860. Here is displayed the polychrome enamelled terracotta *Frieze, removed from the façade, a classical representation of a Platonic myth. Restored in 1986, it is now thought to be the work of Andrea del Sansovino (c 1490–94). The *Billiard Room* has charming 19C painted decorations. Another room, with a 16C fireplace and staircase forms part of the apartment used by Bianca Cappello: she died in the Villa in 1587 on the same day as Francesco I.—On the **First Floor** the decoration of the *Salone, with a barrel vault, was begun by Lorenzo's son Leo X in 1513–21. The two frescoes by Franciabigio and Andrea del Sarto illustrate incidents in Roman history paralleled in the history of Cosimo il Vecchio and Lorenzo. They were completed by Alessandro Allori in 1578–82 when he added the other frescoes and a lunette. The remarkable *Lunette of Vertumnus and Pomona is a very fine work by Pontormo (c 1520). Other decorated rooms here include an Empire bathroom added by Elisa Baciocchi, sister of Napoleon, and the bedrooms of Victor Emmanuel II and his wife. Beneath the Loggia on the façade (with a fine barrel vault) are remains of a fresco by Filippino Lippi, part of Lorenzo's original decoration. In 1987 a large wooden merry-go-round which dates from 1799 was found in the villa.—The delightful **Garden** and **Park**, which descends behind the villa to the Ombrone, contain numerous fine trees. The huge Orangery was built by Poccianti in 1825.

From the main street of Poggio a Caiano a road (signposted for Carmignano, Comeana, and Artimino) leads SW. The road for (3km) *Comeana* soon diverges left. Just before the village, beside the cemetery, the road passes (right; signposted) the Etruscan tomb of Boschetti (7C BC), once in a tumulus and now covered for protection. Just beyond, at a road fork, a sharp turn left continues in 100 metres to the *Tumulus of **Montefortini**, now covered with oak trees, beside the road (entrance gate on left; adm. 9–13 except Monday; ring). Here an Etruscan chamber tomb was found in 1962, with an entrance corridor (or 'dromos') open to the sky. The antechamber and rectangular funerary chamber both have interesting 'false vaults'. The huge monolith which sealed the entrance survives. The stone shelf which runs round the walls of the inner chamber probably served for the illustrious defunct's possessions. The tomb dates from c 620 BC. Next to it excavations have been in progress since 1980 of a second tomb in the same tumulus, with a longer dromos, and a circular inner chamber. This seems to have been the more important tomb, built some 30 years earlier. The vault may have collapsed in an earthquake.

The main road winds up steeply through pretty woods to emerge beside (7km) the beautiful *Villa of Artimino** (also known as 'La Ferdinanda'), designed by Bernardo Buontalenti (1594) for Ferdinando I. In a delightful position surrounded by superb Tuscan countryside, this is one of the finest Medici villas. Its numerous different chimneys are a characteristic feature. Galileo was a guest here in 1608. The villa is now used for conferences, and in the basement is a small Etruscan Museum (open Saturday, Sunday, Monday), with local finds. The 'Paggeria' or service wing, also by Buontalenti, is now a hotel. Etruscan and Roman finds are being excavated in the district. On the little hill in front is the charming borgo of *Artimino*, and the fine Romanesque church of San Leonardo.

From Poggio a Caiano another pretty by-road (signposted; see above) leads to (5km) *Carmignano* where the church of San Michele contains a remarkable altarpiece of the *Visitation by *Pontormo* (c 1530) on the 2nd S altar. At the E end are two detached frescoes by *Andrea di Giusto*. At *Seano* a sculpture park was opened in 1988 with works by the native sculptor Quinto Martini.—The road continues with a view on the skyline of the Villa of Artimino (see above) across Monte Albano past the Romanesque church of San Giusto (unlocked by the custodian who lives next door), and then descends to (20km) *Vinci* (described in 'Blue Guide Northern Italy'), where Leonardo was born. In the 11C castle a small museum contains models of machines and apparatus invented by Leonardo.

INDEX OF THE PRINCIPAL ITALIAN ARTISTS

whose works are referred to in the text, with their birthplaces or the schools to which they belonged.—Abbreviations: A. = architect, engr. = engraver, G. = goldsmith, illum. = illuminator, min. = miniaturist, mos. = mosaicist, P. = painter, S. = sculptor, stuc. = stuccoist, W. = woodworker, Flor. = Florence.

INDEX

Topographical names are printed in **bold** type, names of eminent persons in *italics*, other entries in roman type.

#11 – Passagio to lovely oval court on rear of san spirito campanile.

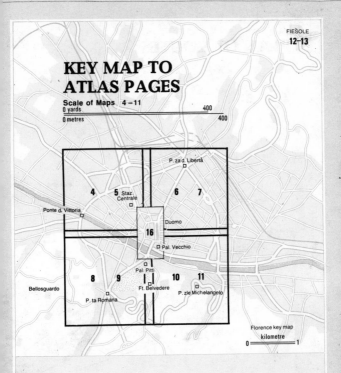

KEY MAP TO ATLAS PAGES

Scale of Maps 4–11

0 yards   400

0 metres   400

P.za d. Libertà

4   5 Staz Centrale   6   7

Ponte d. Vittoria

Duomo

16

□ Pal. Vecchio

Pal. Pitti

8   9   10   11

Bellosguardo

Ft. Belvedere

P. ta Romana   P. zle Michelangelo

Florence key map

kilometre

0   1

ATLAS CONTENTS

PLAN OF ROUTES

2

Fortezza da Basso

Porta al Prato

PIAZZALE VITTORIO VENETO

Stazione

Ponte d. Vittoria

S. Maria Novella

Ognissanti

Ponte Amerigo Vespucci

Porta S. Frediano

Ponte alla Carraia

S. Trinita

Ponte S. Trinita

S.M. del Carmine

S. Spirito

Palazzo Pitti

Giardino di Boboli

Porta Romano

Key

1. Baptistery & Duomo
2. Piazza del Duomo
3. P.za del Duomo to P.za Signoria
4. P.za della Signoria
5. Pal. Vecchio
6. Uffizi
7. Uffizi to Pitti
8. Pitti and Boboli Gdns
9. Accademia & SS. Annunziata
10. S. Marco, Pal. Medici & S. Lorenzo
11. SM. Novella & Ognissanti
12. S. Trinita, Pal. Strozzi & Pal. Rucellai
13. Bargello
14. Badia to SM. Nuova
15. S. Croce & Casa Buonarroti
16. S. Ambrogio & SM. Madd. dei Pazzi
17. The Arno
18. S. Spirito & SM. del Carmine
19. The Oltrarno
20. S. Miniato & Forte di Belvedere
21. Medieval Florence
22. The Viali

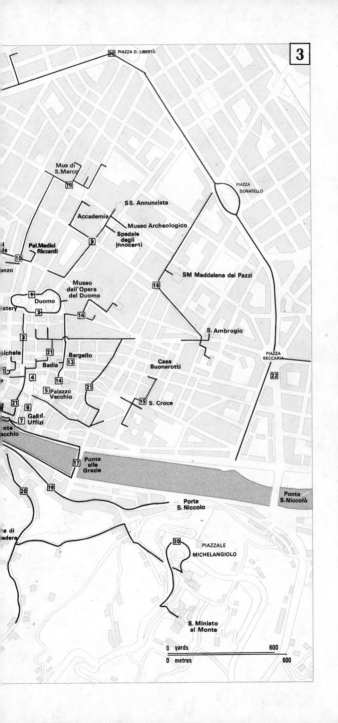

3

PIAZZA D. LIBERTÀ

Mus di
S.Marco

PIAZZA
DONATELLO

SS. Annunziata

Accademia

Museo Archeologico

Spedale
degli
Innocenti

Pal.Medici
Riccardi

SM Maddalena dei Pazzi

Museo
dell'Opera
del Duomo

Duomo

S. Ambrogio

PIAZZA
BECCARIA

Bargello

Casa
Buonarotti

Badia

Palazzo
Vecchio

S. Croce

Gall.d.
Uffizi

nte
cchio

Ponte
alle
Grazie

Ponte
S.Niccolò

Porta
S. Niccolo

e di
edere

PIAZZALE
MICHELANGIOLO

S. Miniato
al Monte

0   yards   600

0   metres   600

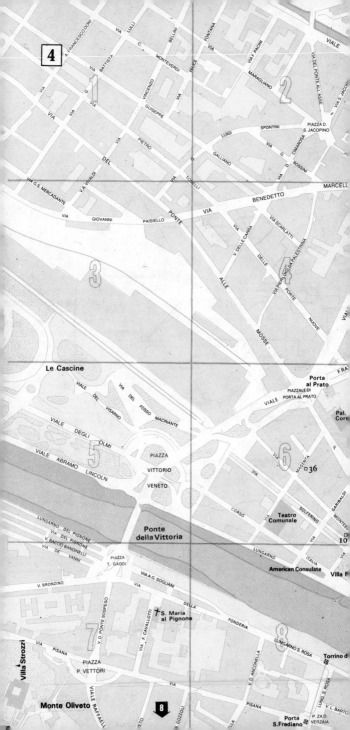

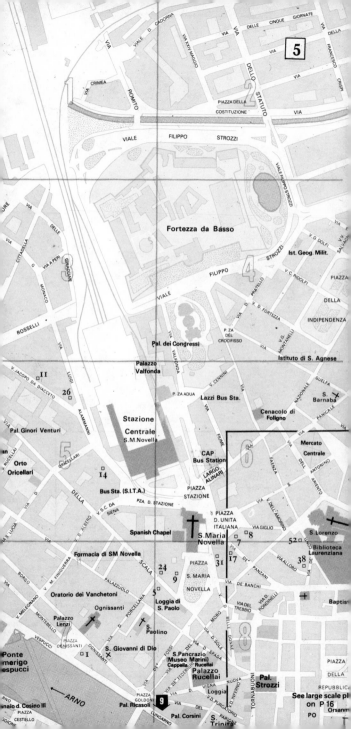

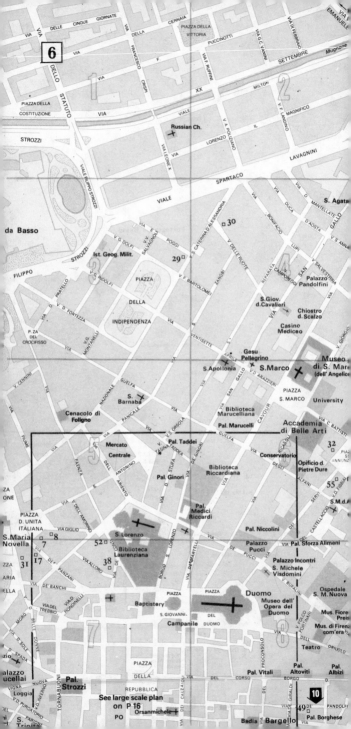

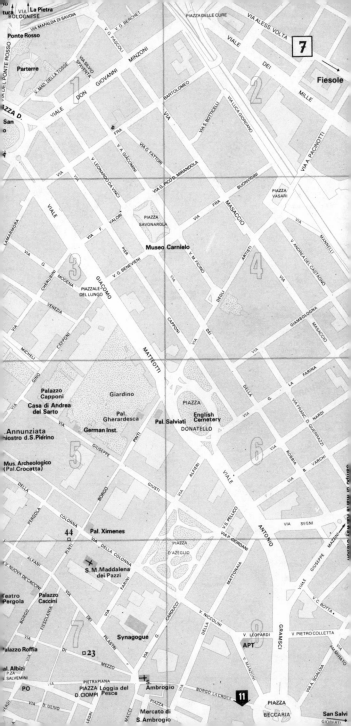

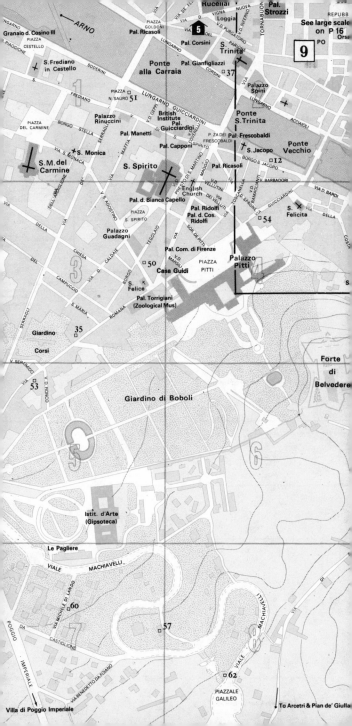

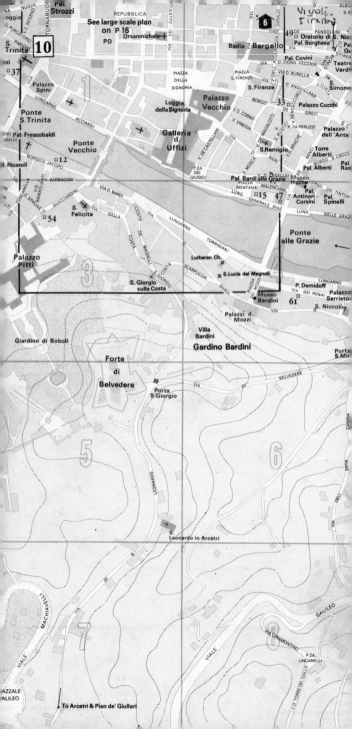

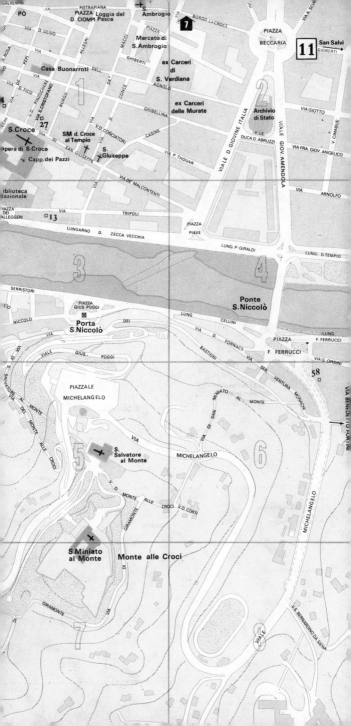

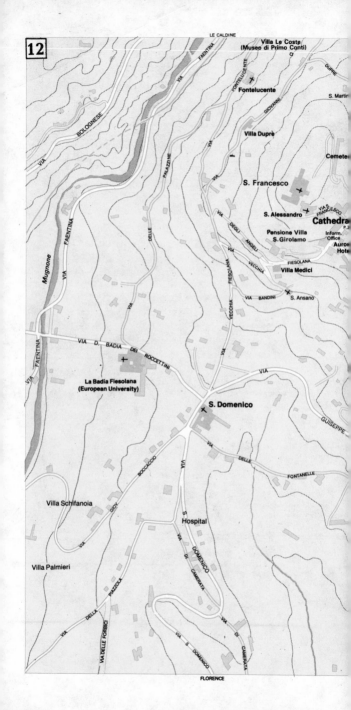

LE CALDINE

Villa Le Coste
(Museo di Primo Conti)

Fontelucente

Villa Duprè

S. Francesco

S. Alessandro

Cathedral
P. 2

Pensione Villa
S. Girolamo

Inform.
Office

Aurora
Hotel

Villa Medici

S. Ansano

Cemetery

S. Martini

S. VIA FRANCESCO

FIESOLANA

VIA BANDINI

VIA D BADIA DEI ROCCETTINI

La Badia Fiesolana
(European University)

S. Domenico

DELLE

FONTANELLE

GUISEPPE

Villa Schifanoia

Hospital

Villa Palmieri

VIA DELLE FORBICI

FLORENCE

Mugnone

VIA FAENTINA

VIA BOLOGNESE

VIA FAENTINA

VIA PALAZZINE

VIA DELLE

VIA FIESOLANA

VIA VECCHIA

VIA FONTELUCENTE

VIA GIOVANNI

VIA DEGLI ANGELI

DUPRÉ

VIA S. DOMENICO

VIA DI CAMERATA

VIA DI CAMERATA

VIA DELLA PIAZZOLA

VIA GIOV BOCCACCIO

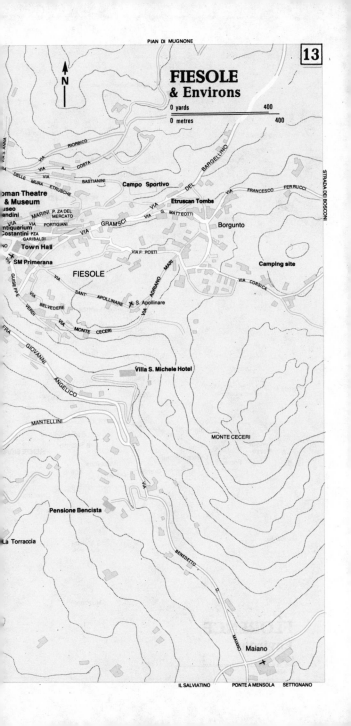

FIESOLE
& Environs

0 yards   400

0 metres   400

N

STRADA DEI BOSCONI

VIA S. ANNA

VIA RIORBICO

VIA A. COSTA

VIA DELLE MURA ETRUSCHE

VIA BASTIANINI

Campo Sportivo

DEL BARGELLINO

VIA FRANCESCO FERRUCCI

Roman Theatre & Museum

Museo Bandini

MARINI

P. ZA DEL MERCATO

VIA PORTIGIANI

VIA GRAMSCI

VIA G. MATTEOTTI

Etruscan Tombs

Antiquarium Costantini

PZA GARIBALDI

NO

Town Hall

SM Primerana

VIA GUISEPPE

VIA F. POETI

Borgunto

Camping site

VIA CORSICA

FIESOLE

SANT APOLLINARE

S. Apollinare

VIA ADRIANO MARI

VIA BELVEDERE

VIA VERDI

VIA MONTE CECERI

FRA

GIOVANNI

ANGELICO

Villa S. Michele Hotel

MANTELLINI

MONTE CECERI

VIA

Pensione Bencista

La Torraccia

BENEDETTO

D.

MAIANO

Maiano

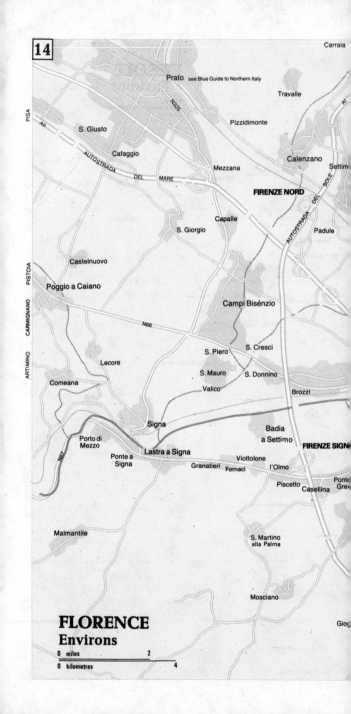

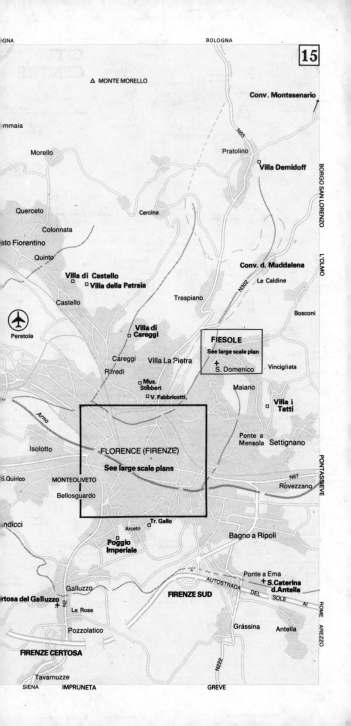

GNA

BOLOGNA

△ MONTE MORELLO

Conv. Montesenario

mmaia

Morello

Pratolino

Villa Demidoff

Querceto

Cercina

Colonnata

sto Fiorentino

Quinto

Conv. d. Maddalena

Villa di Castello

Le Caldine

Villa della Petraia

Trespiano

Castello

Bosconi

Villa di Careggi

Peretola

Careggi

Villa La Pietra

FIESOLE

See large scale plan

Rifredi

S. Domenico

Vincigliata

Mus. Stibbert

Maiano

V. Fabbricotti

Villa i Tatti

Arno

FLORENCE (FIRENZE)

Isolotto

See large scale plans

Ponte a Mensola

Settignano

S.Quirico

MONTEOLIVETO

N67

Bellosguardo

Róvezzano

Tr. Gallo

ndicci

Arcetri

Bagno a Ripoli

Poggio Imperiale

Ponte a Ema

AUTOSTRADA

S.Caterina d.Antella

Galluzzo

DEL

SOLE

rtosa del Galluzzo

Le Rose

FIRENZE SUD

A1

Pozzolatico

FIRENZE CERTOSA

Grássina

Antella

Tavarnuzze

SIENA

IMPRUNETA

GREVE

BORGO SAN LORENZO

L'OLMO

PONTASSIEVE

ROME

AREZZO

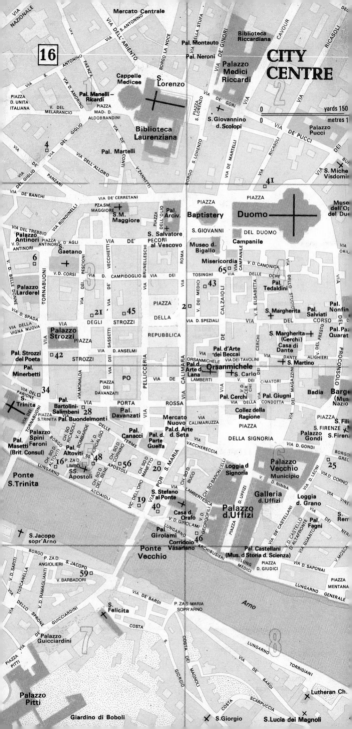